Communications
in Computer and Information Science 277

Reiner Wichert   Kristof Van Laerhoven
Jean Gelissen (Eds.)

Constructing Ambient Intelligence

AmI 2011 Workshops
Amsterdam, The Netherlands, November 16-18, 2011
Revised Selected Papers

 Springer

Volume Editors

Reiner Wichert
Fraunhofer IGD
Fraunhoferstr. 5
64283 Darmstadt, Germany
E-mail: reiner.wichert@igd.fraunhofer.de

Kristof Van Laerhoven
Technical University Darmstadt
Hochschulstr. 10
64289 Darmstadt, Germany
E-mail: kristof@ess.tu-darmstadt.de

Jean Gelissen
Philips Research
High Tech Campus 34 (5.058)
5656 AE Eindhoven, The Netherlands
E-mail: jean.gelissen@philips.com

ISSN 1865-0929   e-ISSN 1865-0937
ISBN 978-3-642-31478-0   e-ISBN 978-3-642-31479-7
DOI 10.1007/978-3-642-31479-7
Springer Heidelberg Dordrecht London New York

Library of Congress Control Number: Applied for

CR Subject Classification (1998): H.4, H.5, H.3, C.2, I.2, J.4

Typesetting: Camera-ready by author, data conversion by Scientific Publishing Services, Chennai, India

Printed on acid-free paper

Springer is part of Springer Science+Business Media (www.springer.com)

Preface

This volume contains the refereed papers selected for the Workshop Proceedings of the International Joint Conference on Ambient Intelligence (AmI-11) held in Amsterdam in November 2011. The workshops provided a forum for scientists, researchers and engineers from both industry and academia to engage in discussion on newly emerging or rapidly evolving topics in the field of ambient intelligence (AmI). Ambient intelligence is the vision of our future environment where we will be surrounded by various kinds of interfaces supported by computing and networking technology, which will provide intelligent, seamless, and non-obtrusive assistance to humans. In this way, the environment is able to recognize the persons in it, to identify their individual needs, to learn from their behavior, and to act and react in their interest. This broad vision addresses all areas of human life, such as home, work, health care, travel and leisure activities. A great amount of interdisciplinary research will be required in order to achieve this vision.

Since this vision is influenced by many different concepts in information processing and combines multi-disciplinary fields in electrical engineering, computer science, industrial design, user interfaces, and cognitive sciences, considerable research is needed to provide new models of technological innovation within a multi-dimensional society. Thus the AmI vision relies on the large-scale integration of electronics into the environment, enabling the actors, i.e., people and objects, to interact with their surrounding in a seamless, trustworthy, and natural manner.

The Workshop Chairs reflected these unique characteristics of the AmI conference series in the call for workshop proposals using two corresponding measures: (1) by particularly soliciting workshops on in-depth topics to the above-mentioned ambient intelligence flavor of post-PC research and (2) by offering workshop threads for advanced topics. We established a careful review process in which we involved other members of the AmI-11 Organizing Committee and tried to resolve conflicts of overlapping. The large number of very positive responses as well as the large number of attendees (the combined workshops had almost the same number of attendees as the conference) reflect the great success of the event.

The nine accepted workshops turned out to be well distributed over the two threads. The first, WS1 "Aesthetic Intelligence: Designing Smart and Beautiful Architectural Spaces," discussed the visual and perceptual possibilities that arise from the use of ambient intelligence technology. The focus of the workshop was on the relevance of beauty and aesthetic values for AmI.

Workshop WS2 entitled "Role of Ambient Intelligence in Future Lighting Systems" focused on LED-based artificial lighting. This workshop explored how the vision and principles of the AmI paradigm can be applied to future lighting controls, where lighting is no longer only a functional on/off system, but a flexible system capable of creating a large range of functional/decoration and ambient light effects.

The workshop on "Interactive Human Behavior Analysis in Open or Public Spaces", WS3, looked into open spaces where humans exhibit a much larger and interesting range of behaviors, from their interaction with the environment to the way they communicate with each other.

A further workshop theme was dedicated to "User Interaction Methods for Elderly, People with Dementia" in WS 4. It drew on existing developments in this field, ranging from end-user research to interaction development and evaluations.

WS5 "Empowering and Integrating Senior Citizens with Virtual Coaching" focused on the effects of virtual coaches on elderly users and how they can be used to improve the quality of life by aiding in planning daily life activities and mediating meaningful relationships to maintain and expand the social network of the elderly persons.

WS6 "Integration of AMI and AAL Platforms in the Future Internet (FI) Platform Initiative" discussed a new generation of the Internet of the Future, the Future Internet Privacy Public Partnership (FI-PPP), which has been established with help of the European Commission. This workshop focused on the challenges of integrating AMI and AAL platforms with this kind of platform.

"Ambient Gaming" was the focus of WS7 with the aim to create novel player experiences in games by taking inspiration from aspects of AmI and translating these into a gaming context. Various issues were discussed from different perspectives like game design, games research and technology.

WS8 "Human Behavior Understanding: Inducing Behavioral Change" dealt with the problem of modeling human behavior under its multiple facets, for example, expression of emotions, display of complex social and relational behaviors, performance of individual or joint actions.

"Privacy, Trust and Interaction in the Internet of Things" was addressed in workshop WS9. Special attention was given to whether and how experiences with privacy and trust from related areas can be applied to the IoT, where existing conceptualizations need to be extended or modified and where radically new concepts are required.

In conclusion, the valuable contributions compiled in this volume manifest the success and high scientific quality of the workshops within the AmI conference series. With the present proceedings we are all privileged to harvest the fruits of hard work in the preparation, realization and compilation of the workshops. We hope that they are considered by the readers as worthwhile and valuable to be used as a basis for future work.

December 2011   Reiner Wichert
                                                        Kristof Van Laerhoven
                                                              Jean Gelissen

Table of Contents

Aesthetic Intelligence: Designing Smart and Beautiful Architectural Spaces

Aesthetic Intelligence – Concepts, Technologies and Applications 1
Kai Kasugai, Carsten Röcker, Daniela Plewe,
Takashi Kiriyama, and Virpi Oksman

Aesthetic Design of Interactive Museum Exhibits 5
Takashi Kiriyama and Masahiko Sato

Interactive Architecture in Domestic Spaces 12
Carsten Röcker and Kai Kasugai

Towards Strategic Media 19
Daniela Alina Plewe

Ambient Intelligence in Future Lighting Systems

The Role of Ambient Intelligence in Future Lighting
Systems – Summary of the Workshop 25
Bernt Meerbeek, Dzmitry Aliakseyeu, Jon Mason,
Harm van Essen, and Serge Offermans

Results of the 'User Interaction Techniques for Future Lighting
Systems' Workshop at INTERACT 2011 29
Dzmitry Aliakseyeu, Jon Mason, Bernt Meerbeek, Harm van Essen,
Serge Offermans, Andrea Alessandrini, Valentina Sanesi,
Paulo Carreira, and Chad Eby

Illumination of Calendar Events in the Household of Older Persons 35
Wilko Heuten and Susanne Boll

Dynamic Lighting as a Design Tool to Achieve Amenity in Open
Space 41
Aimilia Karamouzi, Dimitris Papalexopoulos, and Tasos Varoudis

On the Use of Mixed Reality Environments to Evaluate Interaction
with Light 45
Vassilis-Javed Khan, Martin Walker, Dzmitry Aliakseyeu, and
Jon Mason

Improving the Mood of Elderly with Coloured Lighting 49
Andre Kuijsters, Judith Redi, Boris de Ruyter, and
Ingrid Heynderickx

Interacting with Light Apps and Platforms 57
    Serge Offermans, Harm van Essen, and Berry Eggen

Interacting with Light 63
    Alexander Wiethoff and Sven Gehring

Interactive Human Behavior Analysis in Open or Public Spaces

International Workshop on Interactive Human Behavior Analysis in
Open or Public Spaces 68
    Hayley Hung, Jean-Marc Odobez, and Dariu Gavrila

Look at Who's Talking: Voice Activity Detection by Automated
Gesture Analysis 72
    *Marco Cristani, Anna Pesarin, Alessandro Vinciarelli,
    Marco Crocco, and Vittorio Murino*

User Behaviour Captured by Mobile Phones 81
    Wouter B. Teeuw, Johan Koolwaaij, and Arjan Peddemors

Kinect Sensing of Shopping Related Actions 91
    *Mirela Popa, Alper Kemal Koc, Leon J.M. Rothkrantz,
    Caifeng Shan, and Pascal Wiggers*

A Feature Set Evaluation for Activity Recognition with Body-Worn
Inertial Sensors 101
    *Syed Agha Muhammad, Bernd Niklas Klein,
    Kristof Van Laerhoven, and Klaus David*

Person Detection for Indoor Videosurveillance Using Spatio-temporal
Integral Features 110
    Adrien Descamps, Cyril Carincotte, and Bernard Gosselin

Person Authentication and Activities Analysis in an Office Environment
Using a Sensor Network 119
    Shuai Tao, Mineichi Kudo, Hidetoshi Nonaka, and Jun Toyama

Using Human Motion Intensity as Input for Urban Design 128
    *Esben S. Poulsen, Hans J. Andersen, Rikke Gade,
    Ole B. Jensen, and Thomas B. Moeslund*

User Interaction Methods for Elderly, People With Dementia

Sensor Based Monitoring for People with Dementia: Searching for
Movement Markers in Alzheimer's Disease for a Early Diagnostic 137
    *Andre Hoffmeyer, Kristina Yordanova, Stefan Teipel, and
    Thomas Kirste*

Functional Requirements for Assistive Technology for People with
Cognitive Impairments and Dementia............................... 146
    F.J.M. Meiland, M.E. de Boer, J. van Hoof, J. van der Leeuw,
    L. de Witte, M. Blom, I. Karkowski, M.D. Mulvenna, and
    R.M. Dröes

Concept and Realization of an Individual Reminder Service for People
Suffering from Dementia 152
    Holger Storf, Mario Schmitt, Taslim Arif, Wolfgang Putz,
    Michael Eisenbarth, and Özgür Ünalan

Graphical User Interface for an Elderly Person with Dementia 157
    Christian Tamanini, Martin Majewski, Andreas Wieland,
    Christian Schlehuber, and Felix Kamieth

Empowering and Integrating Senior Citizens with Virtual Coaching

Empowering and Integrating Senior Citizens with Virtual Coaching
(Workshop Summary) 162
    Andreas Braun, Peter H.M.P. Roelofsma, Dieter Ferring, and
    Milla Immonen

Technology and Aging: Inhibiting and Facilitating Factors in ICT
Use 166
    Anja Leist and Dieter Ferring

How Older Adults Experience Wellness Monitoring? 170
    Salla Muuraiskangas, Jaana Kokko, and Marja Harjumaa

How Avatar Based Communication Can Improve Decision Making
Quality 175
    Peter H.M.P. Roelofsma

Preference for Combining or Separating Events in Human and Avatar
Decisions 181
    Peter H.M.P. Roelofsma and Leo Versteeg

Dynamic User Representation in Video Phone Applications 184
    Andreas Braun and Reiner Wichert

Sex Differences in User Acceptance of Avatars 189
    Leo Versteeg and Peter H.M.P. Roelofsma

User-Centered Design for and with Elderly Users in V2me............. 192
    Kerstin Klauß and Peter Klein

Development of a Socio-technical System for an Age-Appropriate
Domestic Environment   196
    Daniel Tantinger, Sven Feilner, Matthias Struck, and
    Christian Weigand

Using Technology for Improving the Social and Physical Activity-Level
of the Older Adults   201
    Milla Immonen, Anna Sachinopoulou, Jouni Kaartinen, and
    Antti Konttila

Integration of AMI and AAL Platforms in the Future Internet (FI) Platform Initiative

Workshop: Integration of AMI and AAL Platforms in the Future
Internet (FI) Platform Initiative   206
    Antonio Kung, Francesco Furfari, Mohammad-Reza Tazari,
    Atta Badii, and Petra Turkama

Ambient Gaming

Ambient Gaming and Play: Opportunities and Challenges   213
    Janienke Sturm and Ben Schouten

Around Play and Interaction Design Research   218
    Vanessa De Luca, Maresa Bertolo, and Michele Zannoni

Gaming for Therapy in a Healthcare Smart Ambient   224
    Rui Neves Madeira, Octavian Postolache, and Nuno Correia

Evocative Experiences in the Design of Objects to Encourage
Free-Play   229
    Andrea Rosales, Ernesto Arroyo, and Josep Blat

Playful Moments of Activity   233
    Rob Tieben, Janienke Sturm, Tilde Bekker, and Ben Schouten

i-PE: A Decentralized Approach for Designing Adaptive and Persuasive
Intelligent Play Environments   238
    Pepijn Rijnbout, Linda de Valk, Mark de Graaf, Tilde Bekker,
    Ben Schouten, and Berry Eggen

An Investigation of Extrinsic-Oriented Ambient Exploration for
Gaming Applications   245
    Radu-Daniel Vatavu and Ionuţ-Alexandru Zaiţi

Human Behavior Understanding: Inducing Behavioral Change

Challenges of Human Behavior Understanding for Inducing Behavioral
Change   249
    Albert Ali Salah and Bruno Lepri

Human Behavior Understanding for Inducing Behavioral Change:
Social and Theoretical Aspects   252
    Bruno Lepri, Albert Ali Salah, Fabio Pianesi, and
    Alex Sandy Pentland

Privacy, Trust and Interaction in the Internet of Things

Privacy, Trust and Interaction in the Internet of Things   264
    Johann Schrammel, Christina Hochleitner, and Manfred Tscheligi

On the Internet of Things, Trust is Relative   267
    Lothar Fritsch, Arne-Kristian Groven, and Trenton Schulz

How Will Software Engineers of the Internet of Things Reason about
Trust?   274
    Andrew J.B. Fugard, Elke Beck, and Magdalena Gärtner

Privacy Implications of the Internet of Things   280
    Ivan Gudymenko, Katrin Borcea-Pfitzmann, and Katja Tietze

In Things We Trust? Towards Trustability in the Internet of Things
(Extended Abstract)   287
    Jaap-Henk Hoepman

Privacy in Pervasive Social Networks   296
    Olfa Mabrouki, Abdelghani Chibani, and Yacine Amirat

Doctoral Colloquium

Self-adaptive Architectures of Building Management Systems:
Approaches, Methods, Algorithms   302
    Aliaksei Andrushevich, Ralf Salomon, and Alexander Klapproth

A Pattern Language of Firefighting Frontline Practice to Inform the
Design of Ubiquitous Computing   308
    Sebastian Denef

Understanding Total Hip Replacement Recovery towards the Design of
a Context-Aware System   313
    Juan Jimenez Garcia

Model-Based Evaluation of Adaptive User Interfaces.................... 318
  Michael Quade

Supporting Behavior Change in Cooperative Driving 323
  Qonita Shahab

Author Index.. 329

Aesthetic Intelligence – Concepts, Technologies and Applications

Kai Kasugai[1], Carsten Röcker[1], Daniela Plewe[2],
Takashi Kiriyama[3], and Virpi Oksman[4]

[1] RWTH Aachen University, Germany
{kasugai,roecker}@humtec.rwth-aachen.de
[2] National University of Singapore
danielaplewe@nus.edu.sg
[3] Tokyo University of the Arts, Japan
kiriyama@gsfnm.jp
[4] VTT Tech. Res. Centre of Finland
virpi.oksman@vtt.fi

Abstract. This paper reports on the ideas and results of the First International Workshop on Aesthetic Intelligence (AxI'11) held as a satellite workshop during the International Joint Conference on Ambient Intelligence (AmI'11).

Keywords: Ambient Intelligence, Aesthetics, Design, Architecture.

1 Introduction

The *First International Workshop on Aesthetic Intelligence* (AxI'11) was jointly organized by the RWTH Aachen University (Germany), the National University of Singapore, the University of Tokyo (Japan), and the Technical University of Sydney (Australia). On previous visits at the AmI conference, we noticed that, while the concept and idea of ambient intelligence was already well established, one question that was often left open was how 'ambient' technology should actually look like, how it should appear, and whether it should appear at all. Thus, we asked participants to report on aesthetic qualities of ambient intelligence and the meaning of aesthetics in ambient intelligence projects. For a start, we referred to this topic as 'aesthetic intelligence'. In this first workshop, we had contributions from various domains and jointly explored the relevance of aesthetics for these fields.

In the following section, we will present selected workshop talks focusing on concepts, technologies and applications of aesthetic intelligence.

2 Concepts, Technologies and Applications of Aesthetic Intelligence

Addressing conceptual aspects of Aesthetic Intelligence, Plewe [2] introduced the idea of *strategic media* referring to media applications, which support activities

R. Wichert, K. Van Laerhoven, J. Gelissen (Eds.): AmI 2011 Workshops, CCIS 277, pp. 1–4, 2012.

related to the design and implementation of strategies in business or personal contexts. Under strategic activities the author subsumes the sequence of actions from defining goals/intentions, the collection of relevant information, a planning phase, leading to decision making and the implantation of the strategy followed by some sort of a feedback channel to ensure long term effects. Inspired by so called strategic dash boards and trading platforms for the business context it is asked, what could be useful design heuristics supporting such strategic media applications in general. Three conceptual prototypes developed by the author illustrated the concepts.

User-centered design approaches are an important step towards the wider acceptance of Ambient Intelligence applications. Oksman presented their key findings from two user studies exploring the perception of an ambient home design application concept, which combined features of social media, augmented reality and 3D modeling. The talk summarized the results from a scenario-based survey with N=241 respondents on ambient home design applications and two co-design focus groups, which were composed of bloggers in the field of interior design.

Fig. 1. Arithmetik Garden, Pool of Fingerprints and The Nominal Divide

Focusing more on the application side, Kiriyama and Sato [1] presented three museum exhibits they created in the last five years (see Figure 1). In the first exhibit, *Arithmetik Garden*, the visitor tries to make an initial number equal to 73 by going through arithmetic gates. The visitor is tracked using RFID sensors in the gates. By analyzing data of over 71,000 visitors, they found some patterns of human behavior. In the second exhibit, *Pool of Fingerprints*, a number of fingerprints are swimming in a large horizontal display. When the visitor scans his/her fingerprint, it starts to swim in the display. When the visitor scans the same finger for the second time, the fingerprint released earlier comes back. People feel emotional attachment to their fingerprints for the first time when they see their fingerprints swim back to them. Animating separation and reunion with fingerprint causes this emotion. The third exhibit, *The Nominal Divide*, uses face recognition system to divide the visitor between male and female, under 29 and over 30, and smiling and blank. People feel as if being accepted by someone when the gate in front of them opens. Space is carefully designed in all three exhibits, because the existence of other visitors around the exhibit is essential to extend the visitor's experience.

Further application examples illustrating the potential of Aesthetic Intelligence in domestic spaces were presented by Kasugai and Röcker [3]. The talk included different prototypes of interactive architecture for increased quality of life in home environments: *MyGreenSpace*, *MeetingMyEating* and *UbiGUI* (see Figure 2).

MyGreenSpace is an interactive three-dimensional wallpaper, which virtually extends physical spaces by using large-scale displays to render nature scenes that automatically adjust their perspective to the position of the viewer. In the presented example, a forest scene is shown on an entire wall of the living room and, by tracking the head position of the user, the perspective of the forest adjusts according to the view of the user. Linking head position and displayed image content creates an immediate, yet indirect way of interaction between a user and the ambient display. *MeetingMeEating* allows two persons at separate locations to dine together. The presented system combines video conferencing technology and the concept of a virtual room extension illustrated in the previous example. This time, two users at different locations sit on tables that are placed in front of large-scale display units, which show the video streams of the remote dining partner and a part of the partner's table. In the final part of the talk, the authors presented *UbiGUI*, a graphical user interface, specifically designed for large, interactive displays. *UbiGUI* is an ongoing research project that introduces new functionalities to rooms by connecting users and system using the wall as the interface. Currently, the system is used to control and visualize different healthcare devices. However, *UbiGUI* can also serve as an interface for other applications like smart home controls, presentations and games.

Fig. 2. myGreenSpace, MeetingMeEating and the UbiGui Interface

3   Conclusion

The talks held at the workshop included reports on an electronic healthcare environment, fashionable skins for mobile phones, business strategies and negotiation visualizations, e-commerce and design applications for furniture, as well as interactive art installations illustrating abstract concepts like mathematical operations. We found the examples very inspiring and see high potential in understanding aesthetic principles of ambient intelligence technology in relation to the functionality, usability and acceptance of these systems.

References

1. Kiriyama, T., Sato, M.: Design and Analysis of Interactions with Museum Exhibits. In: Keyson, D.V., Maher, M.L., Streitz, N., Cheok, A., Augusto, J.C., Wichert, R., Englebienne, G., Aghajan, H., Kröse, B.J.A. (eds.) AmI 2011. LNCS, vol. 7040, pp. 182–189. Springer, Heidelberg (2011)
2. Plewe, D.: Transactional Arts - Art as the Exchange of Values and the Conversion of Capital. Cases of Transactional Arts, Characteristics and Conclusion. Submitted 2010 at the Sorbonne Paris I, ch. III (2010)
3. Kasugai, K., Röcker, C., Bongers, B., Plewe, D., Dimmer, C.: Aesthetic Intelligence: Designing Smart and Beautiful Architectural Spaces. In: Keyson, D.V., Maher, M.L., Streitz, N., Cheok, A., Augusto, J.C., Wichert, R., Englebienne, G., Aghajan, H., Kröse, B.J.A. (eds.) AmI 2011. LNCS, vol. 7040, pp. 360–361. Springer, Heidelberg (2011)

Aesthetic Design of Interactive Museum Exhibits

Takashi Kiriyama and Masahiko Sato

Tokyo University of the Arts, Yokohama 231-0001, Japan

Abstract. Over the last five years, we have worked on creating museum exhibits by utilizing sensing technologies including RFID, fingerprint recognition, and face recognition. Unlike the complexity of underlying technologies, the installations were kept as simple as possible, so the visitor could concentrate on interactions. Space played a key role in the interactive behaviors in these exhibits. In this paper, we discuss three museum exhibits; Arithmetik Garden, Pool of Fingerprints, and the Nominal Divide.

1 Arithmetik Garden

Arithmetik Garden is an interactive art installation, consisting of eight gates of arithmetic transformations $+5$, $+8$, $\times 3$, $\times 7$, 4, and $\div 2$, as well as the entrance and the exit marked with $=73$. As shown in Figure 1, the visitor picks up a card at the entrance gate and hangs it around the neck. An initial number -8, -1, 2, 4, 5, 7, 8, 36, 87, or 91 is printed on the surface of each card, as depicted in Figure 2.

Starting from the initial number, the visitor tries to make the number equal to 73 by going through the gates. For instance, if the visitor starts with 2 and goes through the $\times 7$ gate, the current number will be $2 \times 7 = 14$. The visitor can successfully leave the exit gate if the current number becomes 73. After the exit gate, the visitor receives a piece of paper showing the path taken such as $(2 \times 7 + 8) \div 2 \times 7 - 4 = 73$.

The gates read RFID tags embedded in the cards. The visitor does not need to touch sensors, so they can concentrate on mathematical operations while they walk among the gates. When the visitor leaves the exit gate, he or she receives a piece of paper showing the path they walked. There is a large panel on the wall showing all possible paths to the gate. The visitor may reflect on his/her path and find other possibilities.

The installation of Arithmetik Garden is built on a floor of $10m \times 10m$. The area is surrounded by a low brick fence, making inside a dedicated space. The visitor can also stand outside the fence to watch people inside walking from gate to gate.

During the exhibition of Arithmetik Garden, we gathered data of paths taken by visitors. People started to run near the end of the path when they became confident about how to make the goal [3,4]. The data indicated that the intervals from a gate to the next became shorter near the end of path. We located such decreasing intervals and reviewed the video of that moment. The video showed that people were indeed excited at finding how to reach the goal.

R. Wichert, K. Van Laerhoven, J. Gelissen (Eds.): AmI 2011 Workshops, CCIS 277, pp. 5–11, 2012.
© Springer-Verlag Berlin Heidelberg 2012

Fig. 1. Arithmetik Garden

Fig. 2. Cards embedded with RFID tags

Fig. 3. Monitor

2   Pool of Fingerprints

Pool of Fingerprints is intended to provide a new way of looking at fingerprints. As shown in Figure 4, the installation consists of a large horizontal display and a fingerprint scanner. Nine of 46-inch flat panel monitors are put together in a 3 by 3 matrix. In the display, a group of fingerprints are swimming like a school of fish (Figure 5). When the visitor places his/her finger on the scanner, a scanned image of the fingerprint appears on the display. A moment later, the fingerprint starts to swim away to join the group of other fingerprints. Later on, when the visitor comes back and scans the same finger, the one released earlier will come back to the owner. The fingerprint then gradually diminishes in front of the visitor, as if it is absorbed into the fingertip (Figure 6).

Inside the exhibit, a fingerprint matching system is working to store and retrieve scanned fingerprint [2]. Such a system usually extract features from fingerprints and discard scanned images. In this exhibit, however, we used scanned images to animate group behaviors of fingerprints.

We usually do not care of fingerprints, nor feel any emotion to it. At the pool of fingerprint, some visitors told us that they found emotional attachment to their fingerprints for the first time. In fact, most visitors tried to scan twice to make sure that their fingerprints can recognize the owners. Animating separation and reunion with fingerprints reinforce the emotional attachment to them.

The display surface of the Pool of Fingerprints measures $3.1m \times 1.8m$. We reserved a floor space of $10m \times 6m$ for this installation, so that visitors could watch fingerprints around the display. They could also see other visitors pointing at their fingerprints. Since behaviors and conversations of other visitors are part of the interaction, the margin space around the installation plays an essential role for the experience.

Fig. 4. Pool of Fingerprints

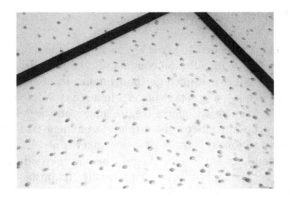

Fig. 5. Swimming Fingerprints

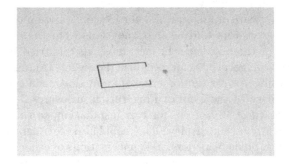

Fig. 6. A fingerprint returning to the owner

Fig. 7. Installation space

3   The Nominal Divide

The Nominal Divide is an installation to present how ones̀ face is recognized by computer vision in Figure 8. Its installation consists of six gates arranged in three rows. The gates are marked with Male/Female, Under 29/Over 30, and Smile/Blank as shown in Figure 9.

In the first row, the visitor is asked to stand in front of the male or the female gate, depending on their belief. The system decides gender of the visitor and opens the corresponding gate. The visitor must go through the one opened, even if it is different from the actual gender. In the second row, the visitor stands in front of the under 29 or the over 30 gate, and the system opens that one. In the third row, the visitor stands in front of Smile or Blank gate. If a smile of 20% is sustained for two seconds, the Smile gate opens. If five seconds has passed before the smile gate opens, the Blank gate opens instead.

The nominal divide was located in a long, narrow space. We built walls in both sides of the space. The row of gates in a narrow space was visually challenging the visitor. People waiting for their turn saw previous visitors and virtually experience the feeling of other visitors.

We collected data of which gates visitors chose in The Nominal Divide. The data still need detailed analysis, but an initial look indicates that the visitor is emotionally influenced by the system positively or negatively, depending on whether the system agrees with the choice of visitor. For instance, if a visitor chooses the under 29 gate and the system opens it, the visitor feels as if he or she is approved by the system. It seems to cause a faster movement to the next

Fig. 8. The Nominal Divide

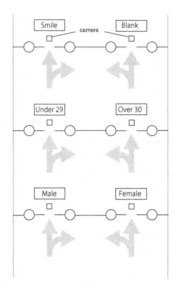

Fig. 9. Layout of The Nominal Divide

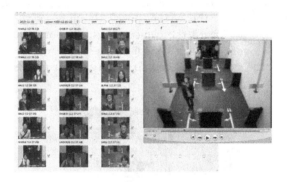

Fig. 10. Analysis of The Nominal Divide

gate. We are statistically verifying correlation between agreement and positive emotions. Figure 10 depicts a screenshot of the analysis tool. For each visitor and each row of gate, the tool visualizes the one chosen by the visitor and the one the system opened, along with a time stamp of opening. We can also see the movement of visitor in a video that synchronizes with the analysis tool.

4   Conclusions

The use of the surrounding space is critical for the experience of visitors. In Pool of Fingerprints, space was reserved around the display for viewing. People surrounding the exhibit are part of the process of interaction with the system. The nominal divide was built in a long, narrow space. People waiting for their turns see other visitors go through gates.

By observing visitors, we believe that Pool of Fingerprints made visitors feel emotional attachment to their fingerprints. Animation of fingerprints help develop this emotion. In The Nominal Divide, the visitor feels approved when their choice of gate agrees with the result of face recognition. The change of emotion influences the movement of visitor from a gate to the next one. We will confirm the influence in data collected during the exhibition. By designing interactions with museum exhibits, we can explore new relationship with the environment and thus accumulate knowledge for deploying ambient intelligence.

Acknowledgments. The authors are thankful to NEC Corporation, Samsung Japan, Omron Corporation, Toshiba Corporation, and Security Gate Japan for supporting the exhibits presented in this paper. The authors are also thankful to Miyuki Tanaka, curator of The Definition of Self.

References

1. 21_21 DESIGN SIGHT, Exhibition "The Definition of Self" (2010),
   http://www.2121designsight.jp/en/program/id/
2. Mizoguchi, M., Hara, M.: Fingerprint/Palmprint Matching Identification Technology. NEC Technical Journal 5(3), 18–22 (2010)
3. Kiriyama, T., Sato, M.: Observing Human Behaviors in an Interactive Art Installation. In: Desmet, P.M.A., Tzvetanova, S.A., Hekkert, P., Justice, L. (eds.) Proceedings from the 6th Conference on Design & Emotion (2008)
4. Kiriyama, T., Sato, M.: Analyzing Human Behaviors in an Interactive Art Installation. In: Jacko, J.A. (ed.) HCI International 2009. LNCS, vol. 5613, pp. 345–352. Springer, Heidelberg (2009)

Interactive Architecture in Domestic Spaces

Carsten Röcker and Kai Kasugai

Human Technology Centre, RWTH Aachen University, Germany
{Roecker,Kasugai}@humtec.rwth-aachen.de

Abstract. Research in the field of smart home environments is still very much technology driven. While technical aspects like system reliability, performance or data security are undeniable important design factors, potential end users desire more than pure technical functionality favoring systems with high social and hedonic value. So far, the integration of digital information layers into the architectural environment and their consequences for human perception are still largely unexplored. In this paper we present three examples of interactive architecture for increased quality of life in domestic spaces: *myGreenSpace*, *meetingMyEating* and *ubiGUI*.

Keywords: Ambient Intelligence, Large Domestic Screens, Smart Spaces, Aesthetics, Design, Architecture.

1 Introduction

Large displays are a common sight in most urban landscapes. With the rapid advances in display technology in terms of size and cost, large displays are gaining increased presence in all areas of our everyday life. Less than ten years ago, for example, any public viewing of a sport event would have taken place inside pubs on standard television sets. Today, we gather in public spaces and watch such happenings live on display walls [10]. Information screens in airports or train stations are not located exclusively in the waiting hall anymore, but large, medium, and small sized displays are distributed across those places to provide helpful information for travelers.

However, it is not only visible information that alters the way we see space and move through it. Who hasn't ever changed his location within a room for no other motive than seeking better wireless network reception? Like people looking for metal on the beach with metal detectors, we are holding our wireless devices into all corners of the room in search for the best or any signal. By doing this, we get aware of the spatial boundaries of the signal. Wireless network coverage (whether GSM, UMTS or IEEE 802.11) forms one part of what we call Ambient Intelligence and is one invisible information layer whose limits and layout many of us are conscious of [1].

Thus, it may be the lack of information that stands out. What is a hotel lobby or a lounge at a conference if it doesn't provide wireless network access? In some cities, the same holds true for cafés. In architecture or in an urban context, one might think about using such an invisible yet ever-present phenomenon for implicit zoning. Technology can add to traditional architectonical parameters and can help to form places where people gather and feel at ease.

R. Wichert, K. Van Laerhoven, J. Gelissen (Eds.): AmI 2011 Workshops, CCIS 277, pp. 12–18, 2012.

The idea of wireless network coverage as a three-dimensional form that overlays our physical space brings the concept of ambient technology close to concrete boundaries. On the other hand, an example that does quite the opposite are navigation systems. Integrated into the car and, more recently, omnipresent in our smart phones, they can be considered as ambient information. Using a navigation system detaches the user from physical space, especially when driving in a car. Even if the point of destination is clearly visible as a landmark on one side, the system might suggest turning to the other side. The digital map and the point that shows the car's current location potentially receive more attention than the physical environment surrounding the user. These are just some examples illustrating how digital technology changes physical spaces. In the remainder of this paper we will focus on interactive architecture and in particular large interactive screens in domestic settings.

2   The Importance of Aesthetics in System Development

Research in the field of smart home environments is still very much technology driven and potential users are rarely integrated in the design process of future systems [3][6][17]. While technical aspects like system reliability, performance or data security are undeniable important design factors, potential end users desire more than pure functionality. A variety of authors, including Hassenzahl [1] or Heidrich et al. [8] showed that users wish for more than the pure technical functionality and prefer devices with a high social and hedonic value. And as future ICT devices will be increasingly used within home environments, these aspects are likely to gain additional importance in the future.

Today, large-scale visual displays usually provide explicit information, which require a comparably high cognitive effort to decode and process. What is often overlooked by system designers is the fact that many users consider a permanent confrontation with audiovisual impressions as unpleasant and distracting [15]. A variety of studies (see, e.g., [2]) showed that users often wish to avoid needless distractions by dynamic information displays, favoring quiet and elegant peripheral interfaces. Some authors, like Fogarty et al. [4] even come to the conclusion that peripheral displays are primarily chosen and installed because of their aesthetic properties. Consequently, designing calm and unobtrusive interfaces is especially important in living spaces, which are traditionally used for recreational purposes and personal well-being.

A variety of authors addressed this challenge by developing so-called ambient displays, which combine the paradigms of ubiquitous computing and calm technology in an aesthetically pleasing way. Ambient displays present information within the user's environment through subtle changes in light, sound and movement, which can be processed in the background of awareness [16]. The term 'display' in this context means any construction, which makes information visible. Hence, an ambient display must not necessarily be a traditional display like a computer monitor, but it may also be a dynamic light installation, a water fountain or any other artefact, which is able to display information [12]. In most cases, information is not visualized directly. Instead, different degrees of abstraction are used to display data, which requires less attention and makes the interpretation of the information content easier [11]. Prominent examples of ambient displays using large-sized screens or projections include *Kandinsky System* [4], *Weather Composition* [9] or *InfoRiver* [14]. These systems successfully demonstrate the potential of peripheral information presentation in technology-enhanced environments. Through their abstract, aesthetic and non-disruptive nature, most existing prototypes effectively reside in the user's periphery of attention. Nevertheless, they are still distinct objects in the physical surrounding instead of being seamlessly integrated into the user's existing environment. So far, the integration of digital information layers into the architectural environment and their consequences for human perception are still largely unexplored. In the following section, we show some examples of interactive architecture for domestic spaces.

3   Interactive Walls for Increased Quality of Life in Domestic Spaces

Rather than following the concept of most existing ubiquitous computing applications, in which devices are spatially scattered or are worn on ones body, we aimed to integrate computational intelligence into the environment. By doing this, we are leaving the desktop metaphor and are using architectural elements like walls as interfaces to computers. To illustrate our approach, we developed the following three sample applications, which will be further elaborated in the remainder of this section:

- *myGreenSpace* extends a space virtually by using a display wall to render a forest scene that adjusts the perspective to the position of the viewer.
- *meetingMeEating* enables two persons, both sitting alone in front of a large screen, to dine together - over a distance.
- *ubiGUI* is an interface for medical health care applications that allows multiple input methods and is optimized for large screens.

3.1   myGreenSpace

MyGreenSpace can be described as a virtual three-dimensional wallpaper. A forest scene is shown on an entire wall of the living room and, by tracking the head position of the user, the perspective of the forest adjusts according to the view of the user. Linking head position and displayed image content creates an immediate, yet indirect way of interaction between a user and the ambient display. When a user is sitting or standing in the room, the perspective will only show minor changes, similar to the view out of a window. However, when the person is moving within the room, the perspective will reveal new views, again following the window metaphor. Thereby, the display only draws attention to it when the user is walking, but does not distract when he is still.

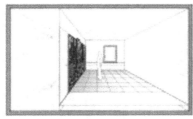

Fig. 1. Section through the system setup (left), screenshot of myGreenSpace (center), and person sitting in front of the display wall showing myGreenSpace (right)

The system is following the concept of a spatial extension [1] and creates the perception of a larger room. Metaphorically, the display becomes a transparent pane that separates the physical room from virtual space. With current technology, the illusion works only for a single user. The image on the screen is two-dimensional, spatiality is created by movement of the user's head, as described by Overbeeke et al. [17]. But future technology could enable multiple users to view *myGreenSpace* without using 3D-glasses. Exhibited during *CEATEC 2011*, *NICT* and *JVC* Kenwood presented a 200 inch display that supports multiple viewing angles.

Additional to displaying calm and relaxing scenery, *myGreenSpace* transports ambient information by showing distinct objects in the forest. In our demo setup, forest ghosts appearing in the scene can notify the user about events or can represent information. The user can select what they stand for - they can be a reminder to take medication, but they could also represent the number of friends online in a social network. In cases like the medicine notification, the user might wish not to be stigmatized by medical technology and the abstraction of information can provide privacy.

3.2   meetingMeEating

MeetingMeEating allows two persons at separate locations to dine together. Here, we combined a video conferencing system and the concept of the spatial extension. Two users at different locations sit on tables that are placed in front of display walls. The display walls show the video streams of the dining partner and a part of the partner's table.

Similar to *myGreenSpace*, the display wall becomes a part of the room, again extending the users space. But rather than showing a purely virtual space, the representation of a real space is shown, partly connecting two distant physical spaces into one visual contiguity. *MeetingMeEating* is using head tracking to adjust the perspective and uses background segmentation to overlay the video content with virtual three-dimensional content.

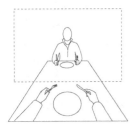

Fig. 2. System concept (left), person sitting in front of display wall, which is showing the video stream of the dining partner (center), and integration into virtual scene (right)

Students at our lab have conducted several user studies to prototype a social network around this application. The studies proposed a website where user profiles can be stored in order to find possible matches for a pleasant dinner. While today, social networking is mostly text and photo based, we envision that in the future, social networking could include real social interaction and that it could integrate into our domestic space instead of being only available on desktop computers and mobile devices.

3.3   ubiGUI

UbiGUI is a graphical user interface, specifically designed for large, wall-sized displays. It is an ongoing research project that introduces new functionalities to rooms by connecting users and system using the wall as the interface. We developed and used it to control and visualize different healthcare devices. However, *ubiGUI* also serves as an interface for other applications like smart home controls, presentations and games.

Large screens present a variety of specific issues, which we want to address by creating a user interface that is optimized for this type of scale. Input modalities are one central issue. Users need to be able to interact with the screen from different locations: sitting on a sofa, walking freely in the room or standing right next to the wall. While on the sofa, a mouse or track pad might still be an adequate input method, gestures might be more suitable when standing. When the wall is within reach for the user, touching the wall could be the best way to interact. There cannot be a sole input method for a large screen, which is why *ubiGUI* combines different input methods such as mouse input, gestures (pointing, using marker-less motion tracking) and multi-touch input.

Variable scale can also be important when dealing with larger screen sizes. From a distance, the entire screen is visible to the user. However, when approaching it, the level of perceivable content decreases with the narrowing field of view. At the same time, the user will be able to see finer detail. Displayed content will have to have different scales and levels of abstraction, depending on the user's location.

Another issue that we addressed is privacy. A large screen is an exposed element within a room and attracts attention. The size and also the fixed position and spatial orientation make it less suited to display private content. In a domestic environment, and especially in rooms that are usually shielded from the outside, the system should adjust private content, depending on whether or not other users are present.

4   Conclusion

As illustrated above, research in the field of smart home environments is still very much technology driven. While technical aspects like system reliability, performance or data security are undeniable important design factors, potential end users desire more than pure technical functionality favoring systems with high social and hedonic value. So far, the integration of digital information layers into the architectural environment and their consequences for human perception are still largely unexplored. In this paper we presented three examples of interactive architecture for increased quality of life in domestic spaces: *myGreenSpace*, *meetingMyEating* and *ubiGUI*.

References

1. Arnall, T., Knutsen, J., Martinussen, E.S.: Immaterials: Light painting WiFi (2011) Video available at,
   http://yourban.no/2011/02/22/
   immaterials-light-painting-wifi/
2. Cadiz, J.J., Czerwinski, M., McCrickard, S., Stasko, J.: Providing Elegant Peripheral Awareness. In: Extended Abstracts of the Conference on Human Factors in Computing Systems (CHI 2003), pp. 1066–1067 (2003)
3. Coughlin, J.F.: Invention vs. Innovation: Technology and the Future of Aging. Aging Today: The Bimonthly Newspaper of the American Society on Aging 27(2), 3–4 (2006)
4. Fogarty, J., Forlizzi, J., Hudson, S.E.: Aesthetic Information Collages: Generating Decorative Displays that Contain Information. In: Proceedings of the 14th Annual ACM Symposium on User Interface Software and Technology, pp. 141–150 (2001)
5. Fogarty, J., Forlizzi, J., Hudson, S.E.: Aesthetic Information Collages: Generating Decorative Displays that Contain Information. In: Proceedings of the 14th Annual ACM Symposium on User Interface Software and Technology, pp. 141–150 (2001)
6. Haines, V., Mitchell, V., Cooper, C., Maguire, M.: Probing User Values in the Home Environment Within a Technology Driven Smart Home Project. Personal and Ubiquitous Computing 11(5), 349–359 (2007)
7. Hassenzahl, M.: Experience Design – Technology for All the Right Reasons. Morgan & Claypool, San Rafael (2010)
8. Heidrich, F., Ziefle, M., Röcker, C., Borchers, J.: Interacting with Smart Walls: A Multi-Dimensional Analysis of Input Technologies for Augmented Environments. In: Proceedings of the ACM Augmented Human Conference (AH 2011). ACM Press (2011)
9. Holmquist, L.E., Skog, T.: Informative Art: Information Visualization in Everyday Environments. In: Proceedings of the International Conference on Computer Graphics and Interactive Techniques in Australasia and South East Asia (GRAPHITE 2003), pp. 229–236 (2003)

10. Kasugai, K., Ziefle, M., Röcker, C., Russell, P.: Creating Spatio-Temporal Contiguities Between Real and Virtual Rooms in an Assistive Living Environment. In: Bonner, J., Smyth, M., O'Neill, S., Mival, O. (eds.) Proceedings of Create 2010 - Innovative Interactions, Elms Court, Loughborough, UK, pp. 62–67 (2010)
11. Laakso, M.: Ambient Displays and Changing Information. Paper presented at the Seminar on User Interfaces and Usability, Helsinki University of Technology, Finland (2004)
12. Mankoff, J., Dey, A.K.: From Conception to Design: A Practical Guide to Designing Ambient Displays. In: O'Hara, K., Perry, M., Churchill, E., Russell, D. (eds.) Public and Situated Displays: Social and Interactional Aspects of Shared Display Technologies, pp. 210–230. Kluwer Academic Publishers (2003)
13. Overbeeke, C.J., Stratmann, M.H.: Space Through Movement. A Method for Three Dimensional Image Presentation. Dissertation at TU Delft, Netherlands (1988)
14. Prante, T., Stenzel, R., Röcker, C., Streitz, N.A., Magerkurth, C.: Ambient Agoras – InfoRiver, SIAM, Hello.Wall. In: Dykstra-Erickson, E., Tscheligi, M. (eds.) Extended Abstracts and Video Proceedings of the ACM Conference on Human Factors in Computing Systems (CHI 2004), pp. 763–764. ACM Press (2004)
15. Röcker, C.: Universal Access to Awareness Information: Using Smart Artefacts to Mediate Awareness in Distributed Teams. To appear in: International Journal on Universal Access in the Information Society (2011)
16. Wisneski, C., Ishii, H., Dahley, A., Gorbet, M., Brave, S., Ullmer, B., Yarin, P.: Ambient Displays: Turning Architectural Space into an Interface between People and Digital Information. In: Yuan, F., Konomi, S., Burkhardt, H.-J. (eds.) CoBuild 1998. LNCS, vol. 1370, pp. 22–32. Springer, Heidelberg (1998)
17. Ziefle, M., Röcker, C., Holzinger, A.: Medical Technology in Smart Homes: Exploring the User's Perspective on Privacy, Intimacy and Trust. In: Proceedings of the IEEE 35th Annual Computer Software and Applications Conference Workshops, pp. 410–415. IEEE Press (2011)

Towards Strategic Media

Daniela Alina Plewe

National University of Singapore, University Scholars Program,
18, College Avenue East, Singapore 138593
danielaplewe@nus.edu.sg

Abstract. We assume that visualizations will increasingly not only display data, but allow for actions and the execution of strategies *within* visualized environments. With the term strategic media we refer to media applications supporting the activities related to the design and implementation of strategies in business or personal contexts. Inspired by so called strategic dash boards for the business context we ask, what could be useful design heuristics supporting such strategic media applications in general. As a starting point we propose, that strategic media integrate *aspirational, executional/transactional* and *epic* aspects representing intentions, functionalities critical to implementation and long term monitoring and feedback. Three conceptual prototypes developed by the author illustrate the concepts.

Keywords: Visualization, visual interfaces, strategic, epic, aspirational and transactional interfaces, business software interfaces, dashboards.

1 Introduction

Under strategic activities we subsume the sequence of actions from defining goals/intentions, the collection of relevant information, a planning phase leading to decision making and the implantation of the strategy followed by some sort of a feedback channel to ensure long term effects. While there are whole industries occupied with the middle processes in this sequence of actions, the very beginning and the end of this sequence, i.e. representing strategic goals and long term interactions seem less explored and commercialized. When we propose the concept of "strategic media" thereby referring to applications supporting all steps of strategizing, we would need to integrate and support exactly these activities. We believe that ambient intelligent media in the wider sense with visualized interfaces may be a promising approach for such strategic applications.

Visual interfaces may still not be as widely accepted as one would expect them to be. Business analytics and data visualization become increasingly intertwined and open up new opportunities for all sorts of visual interfaces also within ambient media. Various tools help to visually identify trends, patterns and anomalies thereby supporting decision making. Inspired by these dashboards and business performance management systems we would like to enquire general design principles supporting various strategic activities.

R. Wichert, K. Van Laerhoven, J. Gelissen (Eds.): AmI 2011 Workshops, CCIS 277, pp. 19–24, 2012.

2   Strategic Media with Aspirational, Executional/Transactional and Epic Aspects

When exploring heuristics for the support of strategic activities we will use the notion of *strategic media*. All activities including the execution of the strategy are meant to be supported within *one system* connecting strategic and tactical activities on every level. Every strategy starts with ideas, intentions, preferences, goals, objectives which then become subject to planning activities. We subsume these aspects under the notion of *aspirations* in the widest sense. Strategic media somehow should allow for the representation of aspirations as counterfactual form of information as opposed to factual data. We are aware, that the nature of goal-oriented behavior is discussed and questioned within various disciplines, but for the time being we do find it a valuable approach to facilitate interactions in relation to their underlying aspirations.

Aspirational information is by its nature highly sensitive and unlikely to be communicated freely, it is therefore realistic to offer it optionally and or let profiling systems generate it according to predefined privacy settings. Users may not be able or willing to explicate this information and represent it in even well protected systems. This kind of *aspirational* media could also represent opportunities for search engines and match making software.

The idea of *actionable interfaces* [2] has been discussed in the literature around strategic dashboards[3]. Applied to ambient and visualized media, we find it desirable link visualization, the execution of strategies its related interaction as close as possible. Many visualizations allow the display of information, but do not facilitate other functionalities. They may offer form, but actually little function. How could media look like, where the actual visualizations facilitate not only the display, but also strategic interactions and execution of strategies? The advantage would be a direct contextualization of information and the related actions/reactions, therefore highly intuitive decision support systems facilitating action. In the context of financial trading platforms e.g. the dominant activities become transactions. For example, Bloomberg's [4] proprietary "Launchpad" is a case of a highly visual system displaying information of financial data, mostly in charts. It could easily be envisioned with different and more complex visualizations than charts and market maps combined with the trading interfaces. In the corporate environment we have seen various approaches to dash-boards displaying information to the management, e.g. often in the metaphor of a tachometer. All these examples merely display visualizations, but they do not usually facilitate the interactions related to them. Often the type of visualization may be altered and also the values change, but there are usually not contextual interactions offered. Acting on the information requires usually a switch into another menu or window. The proprietary trading platform of Saxo Bank [5] allows opening the trading window from within a chart, which is a step towards the integration of information display and interfaces. But like most of today's complex systems it still requires different cognitive models for the understanding of decision relevant information and the execution of actions. It does not support the representation and planning of actions, i.e. the process of strategizing.

Any strategy relies on feedback and needs to monitor its outcomes. Representing long periods of time therefore seems in any strategic view important. Therefore we argue, an epic kind of representation is for most applications desirable. A chronologically, as the "life streams" envisioned by D. Gelernter [1] seems plausible for most applications, but other organizing principles may also be possible. Instead of accumulating unstructured disconnected interactions (actually a form of micromanagement), it seems advisable to capture long-term information in some sort of "big picture" approach. A challenge for epic media is how to aggregate meaningful abstractions over qualitative data. Generally speaking an epic view on data helps to form a coherent system offering various levels of abstraction. In the age of social media and services like Facebook or Apple's iTunes which may accompany us through a life time this aspect may become a relevant factor for the construction of our identities.

2.1   Selected Projects

We would like to introduce three conceptual sketches developed by the author and derive from them ideas for strategic media. All three could be envisioned as ambient solutions based on sensory input, speech recognition, gesture recognition and other in and output channels. They also may be more or less displayed on ambient and/or mobile devices.

Strategizing and developing goals in the context of large organizations is subject of the *Big Picture*.[1] Project. In this visual editing system, all business management activities including the communication for the strategic management of large organizations are supported. *Big Picture* is based on the strategic management approach "Balanced Scorecard" by R.S. Kaplan D. P. Norton [6] from the Harvard Business School. This methodology allows capturing organizational strategies in the form of "strategy maps" displaying all activities within an organization and aligning them to the organization's overall strategic goals. The traditionally 2D chart-like strategy maps are here embedded in a 3D landscape, for at all processural levels of an organization with all their initiatives and key performance indicators etc.

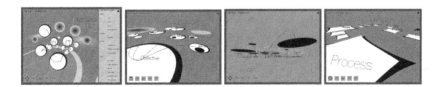

Fig. 1. Big Picture 3 D Editing Tool, Screenshots from Strategic Level with Main Menu and the Process Level

---

[1] The first software prototype was developed by the author during a grant of the European Union hosted at the V2 Lab in Rotterdam 2005 and programmed by Daniel Stucht.

As an alternative to conventional dashboards we install a dynamic visual pattern conveying the overall state of the organization. This display serves as executive information system showing selected customizable aggregated data for the senior management. The semantics of these patterns are to be understood intuitively allow drilling down into the underlying business analytics and strategic initiatives, yet providing an intuitive ambient display.

Fig. 2. Animated "Big Picture" Level

Presenter is a sketch of a visual approach to the biographies of individuals and illustrates an example of epic representation. This system could be applied be relevant support for social networks, visualizing the past and future aspirations of individuals via a visual interface. The user's past, present and future but also their intentions and aspirations are represented on a vertical time axis similar to the life streams by Gelernter. On 2D surface users may interact and learn about their commonalities including individuals, themes and topics, institutions etc. The 3D view displays the past along a vertical time axis; continuities of activities and relationships are mapped as the length of the cylinders, the intensity of the relationship as their width. Naturally, the visibility of this representation will be fully defined by the user. The data may be accumulated and aggregated via automatic profiling methodologies.

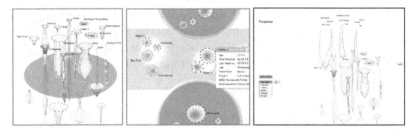

Fig. 3. Presenter: representation of "me"and my past interests in people, topics and projects along the vertical time-axis; in the contact mode, and a visualisation of strategic alignment with personal goals

This system aims to display long periods of time perhaps even a full life span, i.e. an *epic* time dimension. In this sense it is an attempt to connect and structure the mass of single apparently disconnected interactions. The users may also represent privately ambitions and aspirations without sharing them. In this sense the system may be considered an individualized version of a strategy map in the sense of Kaplan and Norton.

Ossò.com is an online market place with a visual interface facilitating any kind of deal-making in the internet. Through the interface users can negotiate, conclude contracts and execute transactions online. In a so called pre-negotiation phase users may define goals and projects to be achieved or post specific bids and offers. Users may interact with known or anonymous partners on the platform. Through the visual negotiation platform the parties can then start to negotiate through drag and drop interactions visual elements representing terms, conditions and clauses. If an agreement is reached, it is captured as a visualized contract. Again, having the option to represent aspirations and goals allows representing long term strategies. The outcome of negotiations may be improved according findings in the field of interest based negotiation agents by sharing goals in certain cases. Thereby alternative ways to attain the goals of all involved parties may be discovered and improve the quality of the agreements.

Fig. 4. Osso.com, with Interface for personal preferences, the strategizing zones on both sides of a market field, the visualized contract

The innovative combination of functionalities and the visual interface support all steps from interaction to transaction within *one* system. The commercial potential lies in supporting the various business communities emerging around the subjects they negotiate. We consider all three sketches strategic media, with Presenter the least executional but most epic, Osso the most transactional and perhaps least epic and Big Picture the most genuinely strategic and least epic.

2.2   Outlook and Further Research

The here discussed aspects were inspired from the experimental works introduced above. For a more systematic elaboration of strategic media one could refer to the different approaches to strategizing in the various disciplines ranging from business management, military studies and psychology etc. These theoretical approaches could then inform further heuristics for the design of strategic media in a broader sense. Especially the fields of ambient intelligent systems and transactional systems seem promising domains for the development of strategic media in general.

References

1. Gelernter, D.: The cyber-road not taken. The Washington Post (April 1994)
2. Few, S.: Information Dashboard Design: the Effective Visual Communication of Data. O'Reilly Media, Inc. (2006)

3. Eckerson, W.: Performance Dashboards: Measuring, Monitoring, and Managing Your Business. Wiley Publishing (2005)
4. Bloomberg Terminal, proprietary software by Bloomberg LP, http://www.bloomberg.com
5. Saxo Trader, proprietary trading software by Saxo Bank, http://www.saxobank.com
6. Kaplan, R.S., Norton, D.P.: Strategy Maps: Converting Intangible Assets into Tangible Outcomes. Harvard Business School Press (2004)
7. Jacquemin, C., Gagneré, G.: Image de synthèse temps réel pour la performance augmentée dans le spectacle vivant. In: Saleh, I., Regottaz, D. (eds.) Interfaces Numériques. Hermes - Lavoisier, Paris (2007)
8. Jacquemin, C., Gagneré, G.: Image de synthèse temps réel pour la performance augmentée dans le spectacle vivant. In: Saleh, I., Regottaz, D. (eds.) Interfaces Numériques. Hermes - Lavoisier, Paris (2007)
9. Kwastek, K.: Interactivity - A Word in Process in the Art and Science of Interface and Interaction Design. SCI, vol. 141 (2008)
10. Laudon, K.C., Laudon, J., Price, J.: Management Information Systems: New Approaches to Organization & Technology. Prentice Hall International (1998)
11. Plewe, D.A., et al.: Ultima Ratio – A Framework for Argumentation. In: Proc. of International Conference on Autonomous Agents, Minneapolis. Springer (1998)
12. Plewe, D.A.: Homepage, http://www.danielaplewe.com
13. Prante, T., Röcker, C., Streitz, N.A., Stenzel, C., Magerkurth, van Alphen, D., Plewe, D.A.: Hello.Wall – Beyond Ambient Displays. In: Ljungstrand, P., Jason, B. (eds.) UbiComp 2003 (2003)
14. Schroeder, M., Plewe, D.A., Raab, A.: Ultima Ratio - A Visual Language for Argumentation. In: Proceedings of International Conference on Information Visualization, London, UK. IEEE Press (July 1999)
15. Tufte, E.R.: Envisioning Information. Graphics Press (1990)
16. Tufte, E.R.: The Visual Display of Quantitative Information, 2nd edn. Graphics Press (2001)
17. Tufte, E.R.: Visual Explanations: Images and Quantities, Evidence and Narrative. Graphics Press (1997)
18. Visualizeme. Proprietary Software, http://vizualize.me/nmdlb

The Role of Ambient Intelligence in Future Lighting Systems – Summary of the Workshop

Bernt Meerbeek[1], Dzmitry Aliakseyeu[1], Jon Mason[1], Harm van Essen[2], and Serge Offermans[2]

[1] Philips Research Europe, 5656 Eindhoven, The Netherlands
[2] TU Eindhoven, Industrial Design department, Eindhoven, The Netherlands
{bernt.meerbeek,dzmitry.aliakseyeu,jon.mason}@philips.com,
{h.a.v.essen,s.a.m.offermans}@tue.nl

Abstract. LED-based lighting systems have introduced radically new possibilities in the area of artificial lighting. Being physically small the LED can be positioned or embedded into luminaires, materials and even the very fabric of a building or environment. Hundreds of LEDs can be used in a single luminaire or space, of which could also have different light output properties. The light switch therefore in many situations will need to be enhanced or fully replaced by intelligent controls and smart environments that are sensitive to the context and responsive to the people in the environment. Future lighting systems will become a part of the Ambient Intelligence (AmI). In this workshop, we explored how the vision and principles of the AmI paradigm can be applied to future lighting systems that are capable of creating a large range of functional, decorative, and ambient light effects. This paper summarizes the workshop paper contributions and the outcome of our discussion on the key design and research challenges for the field of Interactive Ambient Lighting systems.

Keywords: Ambient Intelligence, Lighting, User Interaction, LED.

1 Introduction

The Light Emitting Diode (LED) has caused a profound change within the lighting industry. This is due in part to the LED's key properties of being physically small, highly efficient, digitally controlled and soon, very cheap to manufacture. Being physically small the LED can be positioned or embedded into luminaires, materials and even the very fabric of a building or environment [1]. In other words, our future lighting systems will be *ambient*.

In the past, the single light bulb was controlled using a single switch; on and off. LED-based lighting systems can easily consist of hundreds of separate light sources, with each source having many individually controllable parameters including colour, intensity, and saturation. The price to pay for all this functionality and flexibility is complexity. It is unreasonable and unrealistic to assume that end-users of such lighting systems will be able or willing to manage this complexity. The ratio of the

R. Wichert, K. Van Laerhoven, J. Gelissen (Eds.): AmI 2011 Workshops, CCIS 277, pp. 25–28, 2012.
© Springer-Verlag Berlin Heidelberg 2012

effort required to obtain the reward of beautiful and advanced LED lighting needs to be carefully managed. One direction that is being explored is to enrich lighting systems with sensor networks that will enable automatic lighting control based on contextual information [2]. However, other directions will need to be defined and explored also. But in sum, future lighting systems will need to be *intelligent*.

In many situations, such as setting up atmospheric lighting, an explicit user interaction may still be required. Moreover, as functionality and complexity of light systems grow, the mapping between the sensors data and the desired light outcome will become fuzzy and may require an explicit user interaction for fine tuning the outcome or for adjusting the mapping between the sensors' inputs and the light output. Thirdly, explicit interaction can be desired to allow users to feel in control while interacting with intelligent lighting systems. The light switch therefore in many situations, will need to be replaced by novel forms of interactions that offer richer interaction possibilities such as tangible, multi-touch, or gesture-based user interfaces. As the proliferation of LEDs continue, it becomes more important to go beyond scattered design efforts [2, 3] and systematically study user interaction with emerging lighting systems.

For the reasons mentioned above, we decided to organize a full-day workshop on the 'The Role of Ambient Intelligence in Future Lighting Systems' at the International Joint Conference on Ambient Intelligence 2011 in Amsterdam. In the remainder of this paper, we elaborate on the goal and the results of this workshop.

2   Goal and Setup of the Workshop

The goal of this workshop was to explore how the vision and principles of the Ambient Intelligence [4] (i.e. embedded, context-aware, personalized, adaptive, and anticipatory) can be applied to the interaction with future lighting systems. This exploration should help to identify and formulate the key research and design challenges for Interactive Ambient Lighting Systems.

In the morning session of the workshop, a video presentation on the topic by Prof. Emile Aarts ('Liberation of Light') was shown to and discussed among the workshop participants [5]. Thereafter, all accepted papers were shortly presented by the authors and discussed with the audience. During the presentations, participants wrote keywords on cards to capture topics that were considered relevant for the afternoon discussion on the domain of Interactive Ambient Lighting systems. In the afternoon, the cards with keywords were put on a large table, discussed and clustered by the participants (see Figure 1). In this affinity diagramming exercise, also the relations between clusters were identified. In a second round, each cluster was discussed in more detail. Are these topics in the right cluster? Are there any topics missing? Do we consider this cluster of topics in the core of the emerging research field?

Fig. 1. Affinity diagramming: discussing and clustering cards with keywords on a big table

3   Workshop Results

Seven papers were accepted and are included in the Ambient Intelligence 2011 workshop proceedings. The first paper describes the main results of a similar workshop that was held in conjunction with INTERACT 2011 in Lisbon, Portugal [6]. The paper of Heuten and Boll addresses the topic of light as an information carrier. They investigate the use of light to remind older people of calendar events. Kuijsters and colleagues also focus on lighting applications for the elderly. More specifically, they present their plans to investigate the effect of coloured lighting on the mood of elderly. Two other papers focus on lighting in the public domain. Karamouzi et al. describe their idea to use dynamic lighting as a design tool to achieve amenity and sustainability in public open spaces. Wiethoff and Gehring present two examples of novel interaction methods with light, through explicit and implicit control mechanisms. Kahn and colleagues propose a new evaluation method of user interaction with lighting that uses mixed reality environments. Finally, Offermans, Van Essen en Eggen describe their vision on using an apps and platform approach to interact with future lighting systems, and illustrate this vision with a few concepts implemented in a living lab environment.

A wide variety of topics and domains have been addressed in the workshop papers, all with domain-specific and general challenges when it comes to the design of the user-system interaction. During the paper presentation session, we had lively discussions and interactions about the subject. These discussion and interaction continued during and after the lunch.

In the afternoon, we collected all cards (±150) with the keywords that participants wrote. An extensive and in-depth discussion followed to cluster the cards and create a common view on the research field. The physical cards proved to be very useful tools. These helped to keep focus, to centralize the discussion, and to create a visual group mind map. The cards could easily be moved around which facilitates clustering and making connections between words. Furthermore, participants could easily take turn in the discussion by grabbing a card.

Figure 2 visualizes the results of our afternoon exercise. The words in the circle represent the key topics of the field of Interactive Ambient Lighting. Words outside of the circle represent adjacent research communities, such as Human-Computer Interaction, Ambient Intelligence, Embedded Lighting technology, etc.

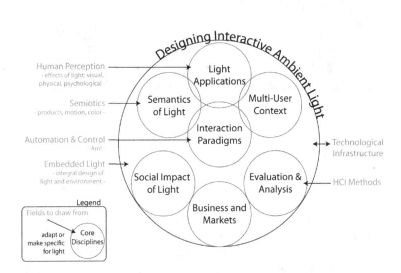

Fig. 2. Our view on the Interactive Ambient Light field

4   Future Work

During the workshop we have only outlined the field of Interactive Ambient Lighting. As a follow up, we plan to organize workshops that will focus on a specific topics identified during the workshop. We would like to thank all participants of the workshop for their enthusiasm and valuable input.

References

1. Price, C.: Light Fantastic. Digital Home Magazine (November 2003)
2. Bhardwaj, S., Ozcelebi, T., Lukkien, J.: Smart lighting using LED luminaries. In: Proc. of PERCOM Workshops, pp. 654–659. IEEE (2010)
3. Lucero, A., Lashina, T., Terken, J.: Reducing Complexity of Interaction with Advanced Bathroom Lighting at Home. I-COM, Oldenbourg 5(1), 34–40 (2006)
4. Aarts, E., Marzano, S.: The new everyday: views on ambient intelligence. 010 Publishers, Rotterdam (2003)
5. http://www.lightingami.id.tue.nl/
6. http://interactingwithlight.id.tue.nl/

Results of the 'User Interaction Techniques for Future Lighting Systems' Workshop at INTERACT 2011

Dzmitry Aliakseyeu[1], Jon Mason[1], Bernt Meerbeek[1],
Harm van Essen[2], Serge Offermans[2], Andrea Alessandrini[3],
Valentina Sanesi[3], Paulo Carreira[4], and Chad Eby[5]

[1] Philips Research Europe, 5656 Eindhoven, The Netherlands
{bernt.meerbeek,dzmitry.aliakseyeu,jon.mason}@philips.com
[2] TU Eindhoven, Industrial Design department., Eindhoven, The Netherlands
{h.a.v.essen,s.a.m.offermans}@tue.nl
[3] Communication Science Department., University of Siena, Italy
alessandrini@media.unisi.it, v.sanesi@gmail.com
[4] INESC-ID, Lisbon, Portugal
pjc@inesc-id.pt
[5] Florida State University, Tallahassee, Florida, U.S.A.
ceby@fsu.edu

Abstract. Technological advances in lighting lead towards the development of intelligent LED systems and require reconsidering the way we interact with lighting systems. In this paper, we report on the workshop 'User Interaction Techniques for Future Lighting System' that was held in conjunction with INTERACT 2011 in Lisbon, Portugal. It was organized to initiate a dialogue between HCI researchers in the lighting domain and establish a research community around this emerging topic, as few researchers systematically study this matter. The goal of the workshop was to formulate the key research challenges for user interaction with future lighting systems. This paper summarizes the workshop paper contributions and the results of a creative session held during the workshop. Moreover, we present an initial list of research challenges for this emerging field.

Keywords: User Interaction, Lighting, LED, Smart lighting, Ambient Intelligence.

1 Introduction

The Light Emitting Diode (LED) is causing a profound change within the lighting industry. This is mostly due to the LED's key properties of being physically small, highly efficient, digitally controlled and soon, very cheap to manufacture [1].

In the past, the single light bulb was controlled using a single switch: on and off. In contrast, LED-based lighting systems can easily consist of hundreds of separate light sources, with each source having many individually controllable parameters including color, intensity, and saturation. It is unreasonable and unrealistic to assume that end

R. Wichert, K. Van Laerhoven, J. Gelissen (Eds.): AmI 2011 Workshops, CCIS 277, pp. 29–34, 2012.
© Springer-Verlag Berlin Heidelberg 2012

users of such lighting systems will be able or willing to manage this complexity. One way to address it is to enrich lighting systems with sensor networks that will enable automatic lighting control that is based on contextual information [2]. However, as functionality and complexity of light systems grow, the mapping between the sensor data and the desired light outcome will become fuzzy; the users therefore, may wish to control this mapping rather than the light directly, or they may require an explicit user interaction for simply fine tuning the light outcome generated by an autonomous system. Explicit interaction may be more desirable for end-users, since they want to feel in control while interacting with intelligent lighting systems. The light switch therefore in many situations will need to be replaced by novel forms of interactions that offer richer interaction possibilities such as tangible, multi-touch, or gesture-based user interfaces.

From literature, there are only a few examples of how such emerging user interfaces (UIs) can be applied to lighting. Lucero et al. present a light control for controlling atmospheric lighting in a bathroom that uses the weather as a metaphor for describing light effects. They use a device with a small touch screen that can replace a conventional light switch [3]. Ross introduced a tangible object to set atmosphere in a living room [4]. In another publication, Mason and Engelen have described a tangible user interface for controlling light in a hotel room [5]. As proliferation of LED light continues, it becomes more important to go beyond scattered design efforts and systematically study user interaction with emerging lighting systems.

This change in how we illuminate our environments needs to be understood from a number of perspectives. How will people appreciate the greater functionality offered by the LED? How will they use LED systems and interact with it? What aspects do they want to control?

For the reasons mentioned above, we decided to organize a full-day workshop on user interaction techniques for future lighting systems at the 13th IFIP TC13 Conference on Human-Computer Interaction [6]. In the remainder of this paper, we elaborate on the goals and the results of this workshop.

2   Workshop Setup

The focus of this workshop was on formulating key research challenges for user interaction with future lighting systems, creating initial design guidelines, and proposing novel interaction techniques for these systems. The main goals of the workshop were:

1. *Take a first step toward expanding the scope of interactive technologies to include new forms of decorative, ambient, and task lighting;*
2. *Identify key challenges of UI for controlling new forms of lighting systems;*
3. *Establish a link with existing interaction paradigms that can be (re-)used for control of future lighting systems.*

In the morning session of the workshop, a video presentation on the topic by Prof. Emile Aarts ('Liberation of Light') was shown to and discussed among the workshop participants [7]. Thereafter, all accepted papers were presented by the participating authors. At the end of the morning session, we extracted the main research challenges from the presented material. In the afternoon, the topic was explored in a playful way through a creative session involving brainstorming, mood board creation, and ideation with physical props.

3   Results of the Workshop

In this section, we summarize the results of the three main activities of the workshop: the paper contributions, the discussion on the key research challenges for this new domain, and the creative session.

3.1   Paper Contributions

Six papers were accepted and included in the INTERACT 2011 workshop proceedings [7]. Segall and others introduce the concept of Semantic Light and the Semantic Light research program at KTH in Stockholm, which deals with creating smarter lighting solutions that have awareness of humans, context, and semantic information [8]. Offermans and colleagues propose the concept of lighting platforms and apps [9]. Other than developing interesting lighting concepts and a service infrastructure, the authors aim to investigate new paradigms for interaction with these new environments. The third paper reports on an exploratory study into the perception of dynamic lighting and how this type of research contributes to an understanding of the potential of LED systems and new UI concepts [10]. The authors of the fourth paper explore the use of LED-based lighting in the office environment [11]. They developed and evaluated two user interfaces: one with individual control of light parameters and the other preset-based. Alessandrini and others present the MeShirt concept; an interactive t-shirt that allows text and simple graphics to be visualized, using the fabric and LED based displays [12]. It allows users in real-time to express their opinions and comments on the world around them, in a citizen journalism spirit. The final paper addresses the problem of energy efficiency in underground parking garages and the authors propose new illumination control strategies that leverage the unique features of LEDs and take into account the specificity of parking garages and their usage patterns [13].

A wide variety of topics and domains have been addressed in the workshop papers, all with domain-specific and general challenges when it comes to the design of the user-system interaction. Several key challenges were extracted from the paper presentations, as well as from the video presentation 'Liberation of Light', and served as a starting point for the formulation and discussion of the main research themes in user interaction techniques for future lighting systems.

3.2   Formulating Research Themes

During the workshop, a list of research topics related to LED illumination was structured and discussed. The main research themes that emerged from the presentations and follow-up discussions were:

- Human perception of light
  - Perception of dynamic lighting
  - Visual comfort of LEDs
  - Understanding perception of light and colours
  - Intercultural differences
- Impact of light on people
  - Psychological effects of light
  - Physiological effects of light
- Light as medium
  - Light as information carrier
  - Ambient displays
- Lighting UI solutions
  - Natural interaction solutions
  - Multiple users support
  - Mental models for light and colours
  - Control for large area illumination
  - Allocation of control (system vs. user)
- Illumination of environments
  - Balance between functional lighting and fun / decorative lighting
  - Integration of natural light and artificial light
  - Balance between energy saving and optimal user comfort
- Lighting applications
  - Lighting services and platforms
  - Quantifying the added value of UI solutions in lighting systems

Please note that this is just an initial list of interesting research topics that we hope will grow and become more concrete in the future. While discussing the above challenges, the multi-disciplinary nature of this emerging research field became apparent. It was suggested by several participants to re-use knowledge, methods, and models. from other disciplines including computer science, human factors, human-computer interaction, environmental psychology, physics, human perception, biology, and design.

3.3   Creative Session

In the afternoon part of the workshop, we held a creative session with the goal to generate innovative user interaction ideas for future lighting systems. First, the participants brainstormed about the potential *who* ('Who is controlling the lighting system?'), *what* ('What elements of the lighting system are being controlled?'), *where* ('In which context is the lighting system used'), and *why* ('Why is the user controlling the light') of a future lighting system. Subsequently, three arbitrary combinations of *who, what, where,* and *when* were made. These combinations were the starting point for a group to create a mood board reflecting the envisioned future lighting system. Figure 1 shows an example of a mood board that was created during the workshop.

When assessing the constructed mood boards it became patently clear that there was a great variety of lighting ambiences that were possible and most were of a complex nature such as dappled sunlight through trees. These would be complex to design and a number of control issues were envisioned based on the specific context or user, which supports our plea to rethink how people interact with future lighting systems.

At the end of the workshop, one mood board was selected and each participant had one minute to come up with an innovative user interaction solution, while making use of a physical prop that he or she got from the moderator. Video recordings were made while participants acted out the new interaction solutions.

Fig. 1. Impression of the creative session (left) and an example of a mood board (right). More pictures can be found on the workshop website [7]

As the mood board session, the physical prop session demonstrated how many different methods there could be to control light in these different contexts. Many ideas from the participants seemed to be novel, which may also be an indication that there is opportunity in expanding the scope of interaction technology to include lighting as a 'material' or service to be controlled.

4   Discussion and Future Work

The aim for this workshop was to explore three aspects of lighting and its control. The first aspect was to expand the scope of interaction technology to include lighting control. From the discussion and output of this workshop it appears that this is indeed possible and necessary should we want to ensure a future with light that we can control and enjoy. The second aim was to determine the challenges for future UI. With the aid of mood board generation, it became clear that light is complex and varied enough to require further investigation into how it should be controlled. A long list of potential research topics was also generated that provides a starting point from which to explore this topic area. The third aspect was to identify interaction paradigms that could be utilized for the purpose of lighting control and at this early stage, the prop session resulted in inspiring ideas for tangible interaction.

It became clear that putting the new forms lighting at the service of humans is a highly relevant research topic that will have to be pursued in multidisciplinary fashion drawing contributions from experts in areas such as illumination, computer science, communication sciences, among other.

Using the research topics identified during the workshop the follow up workshop that is focusing on combining intelligent control systems with explicit user control is being organized.

Acknowledgments. We would like to thank all authors of the workshop for their contributions. Special thank to all participants of the workshop for their enthusiasm and fruitful discussions. We also like to thank the INTERACT 2011 organization and student volunteers for hosting our workshop.

References

1. Price, C.: Light Fantastic, Digital Home Magazine (November 2003)
2. Bhardwaj, S., Ozcelebi, T., Lukkien, J.: Smart lighting using LED luminaries. In: Proc. of PERCOM Workshops, pp. 654–659. IEEE (2010)
3. Lucero, A., Lashina, T., Terken, J.: Reducing Complexity of Interaction with Advanced Bathroom Lighting at Home. I-COM, Oldenbourg 5(1), 34–40 (2006)
4. Ross, P., Keyson, D.V.: The case of sculpting atmospheres: towards design principles for expressive tangible interaction in control of ambient systems. Personal and Ubiquitous Computing 11, 69–79 (2007)
5. Mason, J., Engelen, D.: Beyond the Switch: can lighting control provide more than illumination? In: Proc. of Design & Emotion (2010)
6. http://www.interact2011.org (last retrieved October 6, 2011)
7. http://interactingwithlight.id.tue.nl (last retrieved October 6, 2011)
8. Segall, Z., Eby, C., Lungaro, P.: Semantic Light. In: Proceedings of the Workshop on User Interaction Techniques for Future Lighting Systems, Interact 2011 (2011)
9. Offermans, S., van Essen, H., Eggen, B.: Interacting with Light Apps and Platforms. In: Proceedings of the Workshop on User Interaction Techniques for Future Lighting Systems, Interact 2011 (2011)
10. Hoonhout, J., Jumpertz, L., Mason, J.: The future of interaction with light and lighting dynamics. In: Proceedings of the Workshop on User Interaction Techniques for Future Lighting Systems, Interact 2011 (2011)
11. van Boerdonk, K., Mason, J., Aliakseyeu, D.: User Interface for Task Lighting in Open Office. In: Proceedings of the Workshop on User Interaction Techniques for Future Lighting Systems, Interact (2011)
12. Alessandrini, A., Grönvall, E., Manuli, P., Sanesi, V., Melaragni, S., Oliviero, M.T.: MeShirt: concepts for provocation and promotion. In: Proceedings of the Workshop on User Interaction Techniques for Future Lighting Systems, Interact 2011 (2011)
13. Carreira, P., Nunes, R.: Towards Efficient Illumination Control for Underground Parking. In: Proceedings of the Workshop on User Interaction Techniques for Future Lighting Systems, Interact 2011 (2011)

Illumination of Calendar Events
in the Household of Older Persons

Wilko Heuten[1] and Susanne Boll[2]

[1] OFFIS - Institute for Information Technolgy,
Escherweg 2, 26121 Oldenburg, Germany
wilko.heuten@offis.de
http://www.offis.de/en
[2] University of Oldenburg, Media Informatics and Multimedia Systems
Escherweg 2, 26121 Oldenburg, Germany
susanne.boll@uni-oldenburg.de
http://medien.informatik.uni-oldenburg.de/

Abstract. Living a self-determined life at home is typically very important for older persons. For this the individual needs to still be able to follow the daily and weekly routines, maintain social contacts, and comply to certain treatment plans. As the mental skills are slightly decreasing over the years an intelligent reminder system might compensate for this. In our research, we are exploring ambient light as a modality to present calendar information to older persons in their household. This modality promises high acceptance, easy integration and unobtrusive presentation of the different relevant events for the person in the household. Our user studies show that under a careful design of the information presentation upcoming events can be indicated and are perceived by the person in the household – and in consequence support the individual's daily course.

Keywords: hci, light, reminder, older persons, household.

1 Introduction

Current assistance systems in the household of older persons use existing screens such as the TV or wearable devices such as wristbands to provide information, alarm signals and speech guidance. We can observe from studies of our projects with older persons that with respect to usability and acceptance users would either not use the system in their daily life, or they tend to miss the relevant information. Some reasons for these issues are that many assistance systems are too obtrusive, current tasks have to be interrupted or the presented personal information is undesirably made public to other residents or visitors. Other reasons are that the resident is currently not in front of the screen or the assistance device is not worn.

The residential homes offer a high potential for different interaction techniques, which can seamlessly integrated into the physical environment. In the

R. Wichert, K. Van Laerhoven, J. Gelissen (Eds.): AmI 2011 Workshops, CCIS 277, pp. 35–40, 2012.
© Springer-Verlag Berlin Heidelberg 2012

Lower Saxony Research Network Design of Environments for Ageing (GAL)[1] we investigate the residential home as a design space for an interactive reminder system for older persons. We designed multimodal presentation techniques to provide emergent and pervasive interaction between system and human. Several prototypes were evaluated with end-users in labs and in an exemplary senior apartment. In this paper, we focus on light as one suggested mean to present calendar events in the household and discuss challenges and potentials of ambient light for this domain.

2   Illumination of Calendar Events

The specific design space in households differs from traditional stationary or mobile applications. Important factors for the design in households are: *privacy* – it may happen that visitors are present; the information to be presented might be private or public, *location of the resident* – the user is not always sitting in front of a device, but may walk between rooms, changing his perception focus to different elements in the household, and *obtrusiveness* – system integrated into the household are usually "always on" and should therefore present information with care in respect to the need of paying attention explicitly. Additionally, the requirements derived in our project GAL show that the information design is crucial not only with regard to the acceptance of the system. The system must avoid a complete takeover of the full responsibility of reminding to prevent a (further) degradation of the mental skills of the user.

2.1   Presentation Design for Reminders

We developed a two stage presentation design (see Figure 1) [2] for an illumination of calendar events. According to Shneiderman's *Visual Information Seeking Mantra* [4] the presentation is separated into an overview and a detailed view. The overview stage provides a continuous awareness about upcoming events and delivers abstract information about the reminder's content. That allows the elderly user to remember actively details before he or she requests them on demand based in the second stage. This presentation design enables the presentation of information in an unobtrusive way but offers also a detailed view of the concrete information. Both reminder stages employ different interaction modalities to deliver information to the user. The overview stage concentrates on unobtrusive presentation methods like non-speech sounds, ambient light or tactile feedback. To request details on demand, the user can also use different methods, such as traditional desktop based systems with mouse and keyboard or tablet PCs. We also developed speech dialogues for interacting with the system, such as adding new events, requesting more details or confirming events. In addition, requested details can be presented on the TV or digital picture frames.

---

[1] Lower Saxony Research Network Design of Environments for Ageing (GAL): http://www.altersgerechte-lebenswelten.de/

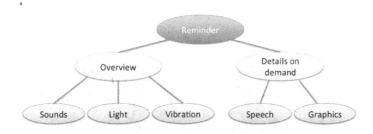

Fig. 1. Presentation concept for multimodal reminders

2.2 Lumicons for Presenting Calendar Events

We developed several low-fidelity and hi-fidelity prototypes [3] with the objective to design and test concrete solutions for the presentation of calendar events. We chose the modality of ambient light for information presentation in households, as it can address many of the requirements for the first stage in the reminding process: it is suitable in noisy environments, less obtrusive than auditory presentations, and offers the possibility for a continuous presentation. Ambient light can be perceived by the peripheral vision, i.e., the user needs not to switch the visual focus to the presentation, which would require the interruption of a current task. Modern home lighting devices are capable of being controlled in similar ways to event lighting systems. We can use different colors (color, saturation and intensity) or different rhythms for presenting information. Rhythmic presentation includes the use of specific color values but also multiple types of transitions between given values like cutting, fading or different kinds of pulsation. In that way, we form visual patterns, which we call *Lumicons* [1]. Beside presentations using single lighting devices also combinations of more lamps or similar lighting units are possible. Ambient light output may be perceived by other people, but the degree of privacy is high and most likely a lamp emitting colored light would be assumed to be just a part of the furniture. The light can be emitted in a direct way, e.g., using lamps or also in an indirect way by, e.g., illuminating walls or furniture.

The first low-fidelity prototype was developed using a projector emitting different colors projected through a translucent glass (see Figure 2). This prototype was created in order to find out how different colors can be matched with different types of calendar events, such as health related events (taking medicine, doing sports), leisure related events (appointments with friends) and tasks (e.g. housework, filling out tax return forms). In a second prototype, we used the Philips Living Colour[2], and its remote control in our showroom IDEAAL[3], in order to investigate the use of different saturation and intensity levels for

---

[2] Philips Living Colour:
http://www.philips.co.uk/c/choose-your-luminaire/
livingcolors-frosted-white-6914387pu/prd/, last accessed Oct, 11th 2011
[3] IDEAAL Apartment: http://www.ideaal.de/, German only.

indicating an upcoming event. We also wanted to find out, where the lamp should be placed in the apartment. Some potential locations are presented in Figure 2.

Fig. 2. (1) Low-fidelity prototype; (2+3) example locations for potential light presentations on the floor besides the sofa and on a board in the kitchen

Based on these first studies we conceptually designed Lumicons for calendar events. The presentation of an calendar event is divided into an *approach-phase* and an *overdue-phase* (see Figure 3). The approach-phase should prepare the resident for an upcoming event and provide a clue about what type of event is upcoming as well as when approximately the event will take place. The overdue-phase is designed as escalation, i.e. this phase should inform the resident that the event is already taking place.

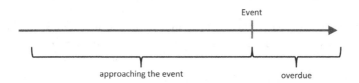

Fig. 3. Presentation concept for reminders with light

Afterwards, we have designed four different mappings of light parameters (Lumicons) exemplarily to encode the type of event, priority, time left to the event, and overdue as follows, in order to qualitatively measure the preferences of potential users.:

1. Lumicon 1: (type of event, color), (priority of the event, intensity), (time left to event, saturation), (overdue, duration)
2. Lumicon 2: (type of event, color), (priority of the event, intensity), (time left to event, duration), (overdue, saturation)
3. Lumicon 3: (type of event, color), (priority of the event, saturation), (time left to event, intensity), (overdue, duration)
4. Lumicon 4: (type of event, color), (priority of the event, saturation), (time left to event, duration); (overdue, intensity)

3   Results from Our User Studies

We performed different end-user studies in the context of our research project. A very initial study suggested that older persons rather like portable lamps, instead of integrated lights into cupboards, floor or ceiling. The two-stage process of reminding was very welcome. A low-fidelity prototype including the modalities auditory output, vibration, and light was tested with 32 typified participants (50% female). The results show that light output is mainly accepted in combination with acoustic stimuli. In another study with 6 participants (50% female) we tested the four above-mentioned Lumicons for calendar events and asked the participants to rate the different mappings on scale from 1 to 10 with regard to visibility, intuitively, ambience and acceptance. The results show that the participants favor Lumicon 1 (mean 7,75), followed by Lumicon 3 (mean 6,67), followed by Lumicon 2 (mean 5,17), followed by Lumicon 4 (mean 4,67). A further study in the IDEAAL room with 6 participants (50% female) aimed to investigate the effectivity of perception when changing Lumicons over time – changing light parameters dynamically – while performing a task (e.g. reading, solving crosswords). The study showed that the perception or non-perception mainly depends on the light color and rhythm. Some of the events have been missed by the participants, which might be an indication that for important situations different modalities should be used in addition to light or the way (location, projection size etc.) should be improved. The time left to the calendar event, was not perceived accordingly by all participants. This also needs further investigation in the future.

4   Conclusion and Outlook

In summary, light has a high potential to serve as presentation technique in households, in particular for unobtrusive and private information presentation. As a portable consumer device, it is not stigmatizing: a light device can be moved wherever the user needs it and does not require any expensive installations. However, the use of light for information presentation is just in the beginning of research. Many further investigations have to be performed for evaluating the specific design of Lumicons and their long-term acceptance. In the upcoming two years of our project, we will conduct further long term studies in the households of older persons.

Acknowledgments. The Lower Saxony research network Design of Environments for Ageing acknowledges the support of the Lower Saxony Ministry of Science and Culture through the Niederschsisches Vorab grant programme (grant ZN 2701). We further thank Sören Samadi, Eike-Michael Meyer and Markus Meis for their help conducting the presented studies.

References

1. Boll, S., Heuten, W., Meis, M., Meyer, E.M.: Development of a multimodal reminder system for older persons in their residential home. Informatics for Health and Social Care, Special Issue Ageing & Technology 35(3-4), 104–124 (2010)
2. Meyer, E.M., Heuten, W., Meis, M., Boll, S.: Multimodal presentation of ambient reminders for older adults. In: AAL Kongress 2010. VDE (2010)
3. Rogers, Y., Sharp, H., Preece, J.: Interaction Design: Beyond Human-Computer Interaction, 2nd edn. Wiley (2007)
4. Shneiderman, B.: The eyes have it: A task by data type taxonomy for information visualizations. In: IEEE Visual Languages, pp. 336–343 (1996)

Dynamic Lighting as a Design Tool to Achieve Amenity in Open Space

Aimilia Karamouzi[1], Dimitris Papalexopoulos[2], and Tasos Varoudis[3]

Abstract. This paper presents our research objectives about dynamic lighting as a tool to achieve amenity in open space. We are currently reviewing theory and technology and we outline our main research methodology. We aim to study how dynamic lighting patterns can impact on amenity and people's engagement in public space, oriented towards a sustainable development, and then to create a parametric tool that demonstrates these dynamic lighting patterns as visual salient objects in public space.

Keywords: Architecture, urban lighting design, dynamic, engagement, sustainability, parametric tool.

1   Introduction

There is a positive aspect of implementing dynamic lighting in open space. Dynamic lighting is present in urban relighting projects that have reported a generally psychologically more inviting environment, in essence providing sustainability.

Our motivation is that currently, more than ever, dynamic lighting has been perceived to promote this engagement. Criticism has already become powerful that warns against sensory overload and an overflow of information that expend themselves ever more quickly and demand ever stronger stimuli to wrest attention. In the meantime very precise decisions are made between the temporary and the permanent light installations. The problem however is that the struggle for attention demands rules. And what temporarily surprises, gives pleasure and stimulates the senses could quickly become annoying as everyday life [1]. One area of considerable debate with regard to exterior lighting design is the use of colour and more recently the dynamic aspects of colour change [2].

2   The Methodology

This research aims to overcome the lack of a formalized way to analyse architecture, dynamic lighting technology and digital technology. By reviewing bibliography, a new set of rules and ideas will form the base for developing the second part of this research. In addition to the literature review a preliminary study of reviewing technology about digital recording equipment and software implementation will be carried out.

R. Wichert, K. Van Laerhoven, J. Gelissen (Eds.): AmI 2011 Workshops, CCIS 277, pp. 41–44, 2012.

Then we will try to find key design parameters of light and space that transform the patterns of light into dynamic salient objects in the city. Important issues are the tools and the case studies selection. There will be a coupling between theories about architecture, space, morphology and the most interesting technological tools that are likely to be used in order to document and analyse the case studies.

At last we aim to design a parametric tool that demonstrates dynamic lighting patterns as visual salient objects and produces amenity and sustainability in public space, with increased interest in open areas in the city. The result will be demonstrated on an open area in the city of Athens. This open area will probably be the Kotzia Square as far as the selection of each case study is also subject to the later analysis and any additional forthcoming criteria. This methodology aims to create a theory and a tool as the final products of this study.

3   A New Set of Rules and Ideas about Dynamic Lighting and the City

This section refers to the background theory of urban lighting as dynamic components in the city and the lighting and digital technology that is currently used to create dynamic lighting effects. We aim to introduce a formalized methodology about the dynamisation and the digitisation of light.

There is a broad literature concerning architecture, light and information that should be combined to create a basis for a concrete theory about dynamic lighting and architecture. Theories about dynamic and public lighting, parametric and hybrid architecture, time and space will be combined to the underlying lighting and digital technology and their potential to create amenity lighting and engagement in public space.

This research sets out to the theme of the dynamisation of light and the digitisation of light sources and poses the question of how the architectural space is defined when units of light are digitally addressed, constituting a luminous dynamic spatial grid of pixels. It is an architectural-philosophical approach, noting the origins and effects of today's urban light technology as applied to architectural surfaces.

The dynamisation of light has been an underlying trend in recent years. Dynamic lighting is lighting that changes   that is not always static. It is a thing of the past that light could only be turned on or off [1].

Our notion is that light is enriched by information; light becomes informed. Materiality is increasingly being enriched with digital characteristics, which substantially affects architecture's physicality [3]. Artificial lighting works as a structural and a building material under the scope of the visual perception and the interaction with the architectural surface.

The underling idea is that of digital controlling the lighting characteristics of architectural spaces. Further study needs to be carried out in order to find key design parameters in the context of light and information that define the luminous surface of architecture.

4   Lighting Parameters and Space

This study aims to review theories about the spatial and formal configuration in relation to lighting properties and a scientific approach observing regularities or unordered space time phenomena through the analysis of the case studies which integrate dynamic lighting. A hypothesis of the main characteristics of dynamic light patterns, that influence the way public space is used, can be tested by observing the outcome of the case studies.

The case studies have been selected according to their spatial characteristics and the effect of dynamic lighting in the environment and will be analysed according to the patterns of light in space and time, that they create, as well as their potential to attract attention. The case studies will represent basic types of dynamic lighting installation, which has an effect on public space and they work as a different, additional level of public lighting.

A detailed documentation will be carried out in order of being able to recover the state of the effects and make further analysis of the phenomena. According to the preliminary study of technology about digital recording equipment and software implementation, mobile equipment will be needed to carry out the onsite documentation. We speculate that the main light parameters are the luminance and the colour contrast and the main space parameters is the viewing distance and the geometry of the luminance pattern in relationship to how people move and engage the space.

Parameters of light that transform the patterns of light into dynamic salient objects in the city should be examined under the scope of existing theories concerning the human factors (safe movement, visual orientation, visual comfort, facial recognition, a general feeling of safety). Visual perception is a complex phenomenon and many studies have been carried out to examine different aspects of perception. This research will be mainly survey theories about selective attention as salience maps, color constancy, engagement, image based lighting and theory.

Concerning space, Bill Hillier in his book "Space is the machine", refers to the social logic of space. A key outcome is the concept of "spatial configuration" meaning relations which take account of other relations in a complex. He says that architecture begins when the configurational aspects of form and space, through which buildings become cultural and social objects, are treated not as unconscious rules to be followed, but are raised to level of conscious, comparative thought, and in this way made part of the object or creative attention [4].

5   Parametric Analysis and Demonstration

This part will focus on the development of a stand-alone software implementation that will demonstrate a set of dynamic lighting patterns as visual salient objects. Before the main development phase, there will be a lengthy procedure of translating the theoretical and analytical findings of the previous working packages to better reflect the software development approach.

The result will be demonstrated on site at an open area in the city of Athens. The public space and the social attitude, engagement and aesthetics, amenity and city iconography are some of the underlying theories that will be combined to a human factor analysis in order to create a realistic tool.

Key points in the software tool will include: a) Selection of the best reviewed technologies for each field from the previous working packages and b) Translation of the lighting parameters and architectural understanding towards an easy to use interface.

A key point of the demonstration is to create dynamic effects related to the recreational requirements of different social and lifestyle groups wanting access to the square. This includes design that adds new user contexts and publicly accessible activities that manage to be socially inclusive and promote social encounters and cultural exchange.

6   Conclusion

The objective of this paper is to highlight the key issues and provide some form of framework for detailed discussions of the various topics involved. We aim to design a tool for dynamic lighting design that shall respect and interact with the diversity of existing building typologies and with the distinctive spatial aspects of the public space. This may include allowing to incorporate new lighting installation and to promote an aesthetic reinterpretation in the context of the city. An artistic and eventful dimension will interact with the existing identity of the open space. The tool demonstration should result in new urban spaces. A human scale will promote opportunities to spend time and engage in activities in the square's public areas.

References

1. Bien, H.M., Helle, M.: International Lighting Design Index 2010, Germany (2009)
2. Raynham, P.J.: Urban Scene and Luminance Patterns,
   http://mpe.arkitektur.lth.se/fileadmin/miljopsykologi/
   images/pdf_filer/light_and_colour._litteratur_Raynham.pdf
3. Gramazio, F., Kohler, M.: Digital Materiality in Architecture, Germany (2008)
4. Hillier, B.: Space is the machine, A configurational theory of architecture, Space Syntax, UCL (2007),
   http://www.spacesyntax.com/en/downloads/library/books.html

On the Use of Mixed Reality Environments to Evaluate Interaction with Light

Vassilis-Javed Khan[1], Martin Walker[1], Dzmitry Aliakseyeu[2], and Jon Mason[2]

[1] NHTV Breda University of Applied Sciences, Academy of Digital Entertainment,
Mgr. Hopmansstraat 1, 4817 JT Breda, The Netherlands
{khan.j,walker.m}@nhtv.nl
[2] Philips Research Europe, Human Interaction & Experiences group,
High Tech Campus 34, room 5.029 5656 AE Eindhoven, The Netherlands
{dzmitry.aliakseyeu,jon.mason}@philips.com

Abstract. This position paper presents a proposal for evaluating interaction with light in a mixed reality setup. Current processes of designing and testing new forms of user interaction (UI) for controlling lighting are long and end up being restricted in actually testing a small number of possible interactions. Apart from the apparent advantage of overcoming testing a small number of potential interactions, the advantages of a simulated environment lie in the fact that such an environment is fully controllable and adaptable to the researchers' needs. Finally, we sketch potential challenges of using a mixed reality setup for evaluating interaction with light.

Keywords: Lighting, User Interaction, Mixed Reality.

1 Introduction

Over the last few years, there has been a gradual transition towards computer-generated imagery being utilized to replace conventional photography. This has been accelerated in part by financial / budget restrictions forcing marketing departments to adopt more frugal approaches to their sales strategies, coupled with the increase in overall quality and affordability of advanced 3D rendering software and hardware

Typical industries that have long since used computer image visualization such as architecture and automotive design are now broadening into sectors such as furniture design and interior decor/design, as well as lighting design. This is largely due to the affordability and accessibility to high quality photo-realistic imagery. Once the reserve of larger organizations that had the budget for high-end hardware and software, not to mention access to skilled staff to operate such software, 3D software is now becoming a household product. Applications such as Google SketchUp, and various game engine level editors allow for free tools and information to the masses, and as the software evolves, it becomes ever more user friendly and "high level".

R. Wichert, K. Van Laerhoven, J. Gelissen (Eds.): AmI 2011 Workshops, CCIS 277, pp. 45–48, 2012.
© Springer-Verlag Berlin Heidelberg 2012

The cost and logistics of creating a photographic "set" of a kitchen, bathroom, office etc. are drastically higher than that of commissioning 3D images. Coupled with the benefit that 3D scenes are easily interchangeable and editable. The photorealistic quality offered by the latest software makes it difficult to visually discern the real from the virtual.

Moreover, the current process of designing and testing new forms of user interaction (UI) for controlling lighting is a long procedure of 6 to 12 months. The final manageable number of ideas can vary from 3 to 15 but inherently such filtration will inevitably mean the dismissal of many other ideas. The few short-listed solutions will then be built and tested with end users in a controlled and realistic environment. The main flaw of this approach is that after a number of months there is user feedback on only one or two different UI concepts. Moreover this approach limits what can be tested since some concepts, for example, include new forms of luminaries that would be simply impossible to evaluate in real settings.

In the few research studies that focused on evaluating user interaction with light, the setup of the study included lab studies in which participants interacted with light through a PDA [2], as well as lab studies which used a projector to imitate different light parameters and settings with a touch UI and a physical handle [4]. Another type of setup was reflecting upon a video of different light designs [3].

This position paper presents a proposal for evaluating interaction with light in a mixed reality setup.

2   Proposed Method

We propose an alternative approach for testing UI for lighting. This approach is via virtual prototyping, where the test environment is not physical but a virtual (pre-rendered) environment in form of a picture, animation or interactive 3D space. When assessing a new UI, the tested interface itself is as important as the output that this interface is driving or influencing. Users must not only understand the input device but also recognize the output and feedback from this interaction.

The advantages of a simulated environment lie in the fact that such an environment is fully controllable and adaptable to the researchers' needs. It is perfectly suited for experimental research where researchers need to control the environment while at the same time be able to observe and meticulously record observations and participant responses [1].

Our initial plan is to design and undertake a comparative user study between at least two different environments (real environment, virtual replica of the real environment). For this purpose we are currently busy implementing a virtual environment with a number of different light settings. An initial 3D rendering of the environment can be seen in Figure 1. This virtual environment is based on an existing physical one, which would enable us to conduct validation studies.

Fig. 1. Virtual representation of the existing lab. Participants will be asked to evaluate interacting with light in both the virtual and the actual lab.

2.1 Existing Setup

In our lab at NHTV Breda University of Applied Sciences we have developed a CAVE (Cave Automated Virtual Environment). A simulated 3D model of the living room of Philips Research's Experience Lab has been modelled in Maya and rendered in OGRE. This 3D model is projected in 4 rear- projection screens (each 3.6 meters wide by 2.6 meters high.

Our lab in equipped with a Microsoft Kinect that tracks the participants' head and limbs. In that way participants can move within the real space while the perspective of the 3D model is corrected, in real-time, according to the actual angle of viewing. In essence, the participant acts as a "human joystick", whereby the virtual camera will move in the direction the user is stepping, relative to the CAVE's center. In contrast with head-mounted displays, the CAVE does not block out the physical world, which offers the opportunity to use physical objects and the representation of the participant's own physical body. In this particular case it gives us the possibility to use gestures, an actual smartphone, or tablet device to actually control interaction with the virtual light sources.

2.2 Challenges

The virtual environments NHTV has been developing offers an immersive experience based on panoramic computer generated imagery. There are however immediate and obvious drawbacks.

To obtain photo-realistic results, we have adopted to create pre-rendered "still" images. The use of real-time graphics is an option, but at the cost of visual quality, which is paramount for a highly realistic lighting scenario. Such effects as high quality global illumination, caustic reflections, high quality shadowing is still much more realistic in pre-rendered images. Nevertheless, this will change in the near future as the advances in real-time engines and hardware advances.

Other restrictions we perceive are those of the physical environment of the CAVE. In reality a large contributor to the global illumination of any given room is light that is reflected from the ceiling. The CAVE requires an "open top" to allow for placement of the projection equipment.

Acknowledgments. NHTV authors would like to express their gratitude to the financial sponsor: the Dutch Ministry of Education, Culture and Science (OCW), RAAK scheme (project RAAK Pro). NHTV authors would also like to extend their gratitude to research director Dr. Hans Bouwknegt and to colleagues Dr. Koos Nuijten and Nils Deslé as well as to IGAD & IMEM colleagues and students for their work in creating the existing laboratory setup.

References

1. Dubois, E., Gray, P., Nigay, L. (eds.): The Engineering of Mixed Reality Systems. Human-Computer Interaction (2010), doi:10.1007/978-1- 84882-733-2_1
2. Lucero, A., Lashina, T., Terken, J.: Reducing Complexity of Interaction with Advanced Bathroom Lighting at Home. I-COM, Oldenbourg 5(1), 34–40 (2006)
3. Ross, P.R., Overbeeke, C.J., Wensveen, S.A.G., Hummels, C.C.M.: A transformational approach to interactive lighting system design. In: de Kort, Y., IJsselsteijn, W., Smolders, K., Vogels, I., Aarts, M., Tenner, A. (eds.) Proceedings Experiencing Light 2009 International Conference on the Effects of Light on Wellbeing, Eindhoven, The Netherlands, October 26-27, pp. 129–136. Eindhoven University of Technology, Eindhoven (2010)
4. van Boerdonk, K., Mason, J., Aliakseyeu, D.: User Interface for Task Lighting in Open Office. In: Proceedings of the Workshop on User Interaction Techniques for Future Lighting Systems (in conjunction with Interact), pp. 23–27 (2011)

Improving the Mood of Elderly with Coloured Lighting

Andre Kuijsters[1], Judith Redi[1], Boris de Ruyter[2], and Ingrid Heynderickx[1,2]

[1] Delft University of Technology, Delft, The Netherlands
[2] Philips Research, Eindhoven, The Netherlands

Abstract. The ACE project aims at developing an adaptive ambience creation platform which can improve the well-being of elderly people in care centers. The system will contain a sensing platform, which measures and analyses the context in a room and an ambience creation platform, which creates ambiences with proven effectiveness for improving the mood of the elderly. It has been shown in literature that lighting can influence people's mood; however, consistent effects have scarcely been documented. The effects of lighting characteristics on atmosphere perception, on the other hand, are better documented. It has been proved that ambiences with a positive affective meaning (e.g. cosy, activating) can be created with the combination of functional and atmospheric LED lighting. We expect that these ambiences can improve the mood of elderly towards its affective meaning. The experiments we intend to perform in order to achieve that goal are discussed in the paper.

Keywords: Mood, Ambience, Atmosphere perception, LED lighting, Elderly.

1   Introduction

The advent of LED technology radically increased the possibilities for generating light of various colours and intensities at any place and time. As a consequence, the variety of new opportunities for designing lighting in a room has grown tremendously. These new opportunities do not only concern functional lighting effects, but enable also a richness of decorative and ambient lighting effects. A combination of these effects can be used to more easily take into account the needs of occupants in a room, and possibly to improve his/her well-being. It has been shown that the combination of functional and decorative ambient lighting can be used to create ambiences with a clear affective meaning [1]. How people experience the affective meaning of these ambiences is referred to as atmosphere perception. In addition, it is known that colour can affect people's mood [2]. Hence, we believe that also (coloured) lighting ambiences have the potential to improve the mood and emotional state of the people occupying a room.

Our idea is based on biological and psychological processes that, triggered by light and colour, impact on mood. The biological effects of bright light on melatonin levels are well documented [3,4]. Night time melatonin release can be phase advanced or delayed with the right exposure to bright light [4], thereby influencing the circadian rhythm of humans. Disruptions to circadian rhythms (e.g. due to jetlag or shift work)

R. Wichert, K. Van Laerhoven, J. Gelissen (Eds.): AmI 2011 Workshops, CCIS 277, pp. 49–56, 2012.
© Springer-Verlag Berlin Heidelberg 2012

can cause mood disorders [5]. Seasonal affective disorders (characterized by depression symptoms in the winter) are also considered to be the result of a disturbance of the circadian rhythm, caused by the failure to adapt to the shift in day length as a result of seasonal change. Bright light therapy, existing of 1500lx or more at eye level, significantly reduce depression symptoms for people with seasonal mood disorders [6].

The psychological effects of white light on mood have been studied extensively, revealing mixed results. Some studies reveal no significant effects of white lighting on mood [7]. Other studies reported only small interaction effects between gender, illumination and colour temperature [8-11]. For instance, Knez and colleagues [11] reported that females' negative mood decreased while working under warm light conditions (3000K) and increased under cool light conditions (4000K), while an opposite effect was found for males. However, in a later study Knez and Enmarker [10] found an opposite result; men's negative mood increased more under cool white light conditions (4000K), while females' negative mood increased more in warm white light conditions (3000K).

Studies on the psychological effects of colour (e.g. coloured walls) on mood suggest that the right amount of ambient colour can improve the mood of people. Küller and colleagues [2] found that office workers which judged their offices as colourful experienced a better mood throughout the year than office workers that judged their offices as neutral or colourless.

This short summary of the existing literature clearly shows that lighting ambiences and colour can indeed impact people's mood. So far, the effects of these two elements on mood have been studied disjoint. The advent of LED-based systems drastically increased the possibilities of combining functional and coloured lighting, e.g. creating different colours on walls. Therefore, new opportunities in influencing affective states with colour and light are now open. Based on the literature, we hypothesize that such a combination of functional and coloured lighting is beneficial to mood improvement, and we aim at extending the existing research in order to better understand the direction and extent of such improvement.

A successful design of mood-improving ambiences based on lighting is expected to be of high relevance for different applications, such as in classrooms, hospital rooms, and day care facilities. Our research focuses on care centres for elderly people, where negative mood states are often experienced, especially at the moment of relocation. The goal of our project is therefore to design an adaptive ambience creation system with proven effectiveness in improving negative moods of elderly, e.g. relaxing those elderly that feel disoriented and anxious, or activating those who feel sad and depressed.

2   ACE Project

The Adaptive Ambience Creation in Care Centres for Elderly project (ACE) aims at designing a system that can automatically adapt the ambience in a care centre room to the needs of the elderly occupying it. A number of factors have to be considered to create the appropriate ambience, among which are the context in the room, the intended ambience in the room, the activities and mood of the inhabitants and their personal preferences. Thus, a sensing platform that measures and analyses the context in the room and the activities and mood of its inhabitants is needed to enable the ambience creation platform to generate the appropriate ambience. The sensing platform will be designed using off-the-shelf low-cost sensors and intelligent algorithms. The affective state of the room's occupant will be determined by analysing e.g. posture, type and level of activity, speech characteristics and facial expressions. The output of the sensing platform should be the indication for a desired ambience change and its desired affective direction.

The ambience creation platform will be based on a combination of functional and atmospheric light, to which sound (i.e. music) and fragrance could be added in a second stage. As mentioned before, the platform will at first focus on two ambiences, with an associate relaxing and activating atmospheres respectively. How to create these ambiences for elderly needs more research. For younger people there is already more insight on how to combine atmospheric light with functional light in order to convey specific atmospheres [12, 13] (see also chapter 3). It is also known that there is a considerable degree of freedom in the actual lighting settings before a given atmosphere is lost. Hopefully, this degree of freedom also exists for elderly people, and may then be used to personalize the system towards optimal or preferred performance for individual elderly. In that case, the elderly is expected to tune some of the light characteristics that determine a given atmosphere once, and the resulting settings are then stored in the ambience creation system.

Near the end of the project, the sensing and ambience creation platforms will be integrated, using a control unit, into a complete intelligent ambience creation system. The system should be able to automatically detect the atmosphere and context in a room and the emotional state of its inhabitant. Based on the outcome of the sensing platform in combination with information on the intended ambience and personal preferences of the elderly, the appropriate ambience will be created. The control of the platform and the ability to include personal preferences are expected to be crucial for the acceptance of the platform.

3   Mood and Atmosphere Perception

At the core of the implementation of the ambience creation platform is the investigation of the added value of LED technology in improving the mood of elderly. We base our approach on the notion of atmosphere [14]. Atmosphere differs from mood; it does not represent the affective state of a person, but rather the affective state of an environment. As such, an atmosphere may have the *potency* to changing a person's mood. Independent of a person's emotional state when entering a room with a specific atmosphere, the affective state of the environment may be immediately recognized. On the longer term the atmosphere is expected to change the emotional state of the person towards that same affective state. The latter is supported by the underlying aspects of mood and atmosphere perception, which suggest a relation between the two concepts. Mood can be quantified in a two-dimensional affective space, with the bipolar axes pleasantness and arousal [15]. Atmosphere can be quantified in a four-dimensional affective space, of which the first three dimensions, i.e. coziness, liveliness and tenseness, are most important [14]. Clearly the dimensions of coziness and tenseness in atmosphere perception have a link with the pleasantness dimension of mood. The same holds for the dimension of liveliness in atmosphere perception and the dimension arousal in mood. For instance, being excited is a high arousing, pleasant mood state, while an activating ambience is a high arousing (i.e. lively), pleasant atmosphere (see Figure 1). Hence, because of this underlying relationship we believe that ambiences with a recognized, positive atmosphere could to some extent drive the occupant's mood towards the same affective direction.

Recent research revealed consistent effects of lighting characteristics on atmosphere perception. Warm white light (2800K) was perceived as more cozy and less tense as compared to cold white light (6000K) [14]. Increasing the illuminance (from 40 to 400lx) resulted in a less tense, and more lively perception of the ambience [14]. Spot light was considered livelier and less tense than more diffuse light. Finally, yellow and red colours at low saturation were found to contribute to coziness perception, while highly saturated red light was considered as tense [16].

Thus, the knowledge on atmosphere perception of a younger population is substantial, but so far there is no information on how elderly people perceive these light effects. Hence, by first investigating the atmosphere perception of elderly, we expect to be more effective in indentifying the lighting components that impact the mood of elderly people.

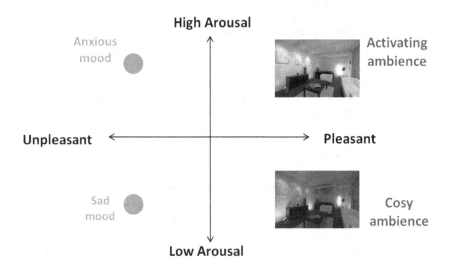

Fig. 1. Two-dimensional affective space [15]. Containing two unpleasant mood states, low arousing (Sadness) and high arousing (Anxiousness) and two pleasant affective ambiences, low arousing (Cosy) and high arousing (Activating).

4   Plan of Research

The first question is whether elderly people perceive atmosphere in a way comparable to that of younger people. A positive answer in this sense would make previous knowledge on the affective meaning of ambiences [1, 8] exploitable for the purposes of our research. It is known that younger people can recognize and distinguish between ambiences created with lighting [1]. We will investigate whether age related deterioration of the visual system and possible different attitudes towards coloured lighting influence the atmosphere perception. The goal of the experiment is to identify a high arousing, positive ambience (i.e. activating) and a low arousing, positive ambience (i.e. cosy).

A second and core question is whether the identified ambiences can really induce a mood change in accordance with their affective meaning. In other words, an activating ambience should be more effective in activating sad elderly (i.e. increasing both their arousal level and pleasure) than a neutral ambience (see Figure 2). On the other hand, a cosy ambience should be more effective in relaxing anxious elderly (i.e. decreasing their arousal level and increasing their pleasure) than a neutral ambience (see Figure 3).

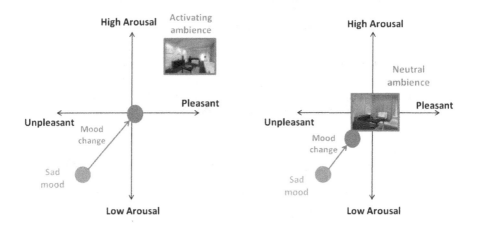

Fig. 2. Expected influence of an activating ambience (left) and a neutral ambience (right) on an anxious mood state; depicted in the two-dimensional affective space [15]

We address the core question in a two step approach. In the first step, the effect of the ambiences on the mood of the elderly will be investigated under controlled laboratory conditions. In this way we can control all other possible influences (e.g. temperature, sunlight) on the mood of the elderly. However, the experienced mood states of the elderly participating in the experiment are most likely different from the mood states (i.e. sadness and anxiousness) we aim to improve. Therefore we will induce negative mood states. Different mood induction procedures exits for inducing mood states in the laboratory (see [17] for a review), and include listening to music, viewing movies and viewing affective slides. The induction should be effective in inducing the targeted mood and the mood state should last after the induction procedure. Changes in the mood of elderly will be measured both subjectively and objectively. The elderly will assess their current mood state on several times during the experiment on the pictorial Self Assessment Manikin (SAM). The heart rate, skin conductance and skin temperature of the elderly will be monitored throughout the whole experiment. In a later stage, the effect of the affective ambiences will be investigated under more realistic circumstances. In collaboration with the Vitalis WoonZorg Groep Eindhoven, the system will be tested with elderly experiencing actual negative mood states.

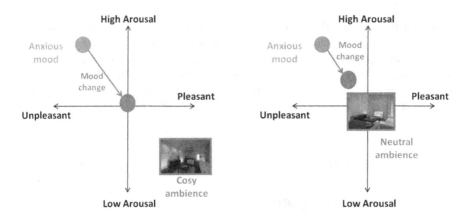

Fig. 3. Expected influence of a cosy ambience (left) and a neutral ambience (right) on an anxious mood state; depicted in the two-dimensional affective space [15]

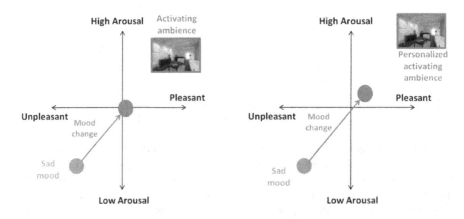

Fig. 4. Expected influence of an activating ambience (left) and a personalized activating ambience (right) on a sad mood state; depicted in the two-dimensional affective space [15]

The third question is test the effect of personalization of the ambiences. It is known that quite some variation in lighting settings is allowed within an ambience, without losing its affective meaning [13]. This variation may be used by people to personalize their ambiences; i.e. to make the cosy ambience cosier and the activating ambience more activating according to their own perception. The elderly participants will be able to adjust several lighting setting (e.g. colour in the ambience, illumination, colour temperature of the white light), starting from the original ambiances (e.g. cosy or activating). The resulting variation in settings will illustrate how important personalization is for the elderly. Subsequently, the impact of a personalized ambience will be compared to the impact of an averaged ambience (as illustrated in Figure 4). In a final stage other adaptive senses (e.g. music and fragrance) might be added to enhance the affective experience of the ambience.

The ACE project is expected to improve the well-being of elderly people in care centres, which is, despite the tendency of a longer independence for elderly, still a growing group of people in the future. Improving the well-being of these elderly is expected to reduce their demand on the nursing personnel. In addition, the basic ideas resulting from this project can be reused in different contexts, such as hospital rooms and schools.

Acknowledgments. The ACE project is a collaboration between Philips and TUD funded by PointOne of Agentschap NL. We are grateful to Vitalis WoonZorg Groep for supporting us in our research.

References

1. Vogels, I.M.L.C., de Vries, M., van Erp, T.A.M.: Effect of Coloured Light on Atmosphere Perception. In: Association Internationale de la Couleur, AIC (2008)
2. Küller, R., Ballal, S., Laike, T., Mikellides, B., Tonello, G.: The impact of light and colour on psychological mood: a cross-cultural study of indoor work environments. Ergonomics 49, 1496–1507 (2006)
3. McIntyre, I.M., Norman, T.R., Burrows, G.D., Armstrong, S.M.: Human melatonin suppression by light is intensity dependent. Journal of Pineal. Research 6, 149–156 (1989)
4. Lewy, A., Wehr, T., Goodwin, F., Newsome, D., Markey, S.: Light suppresses melatonin secretion in humans. Science 210, 1267–1269 (1980)
5. Boyce, P., Barriball, E.: Circadian rhythms and depression. Aust. Fam. Physician 39, 307–310 (2010)
6. Golden, R.N., Gaynes, B.N., Ekstrom, R.D., Hamer, R.M., Jacobsen, F.M., Suppes, T., Wisner, K.L., Nemeroff, C.B.: The Efficacy of Light Therapy in the Treatment of Mood Disorders: A Review and Meta-Analysis of the Evidence. Am. J. Psychiatry 162, 656–662 (2005)
7. Baron, R.A., Rea, M.S., Daniels, S.G.: Effects of indoor lighting (illuminance and spectral distribution) on the performance of cognitive tasks and interpersonal behaviors: The potential mediating role of positive affect. Motivation and Emotion 16, 1–33 (1992)
8. McCloughan, C.L.B., Aspinall, P.A., Webb, R.S.: The impact of lighting on mood. Lighting Research and Technology 31, 81–88 (1999)

9. Knez, I., Niedenthal, S.: Lighting in Digital Game Worlds: Effects on Affect and Play Performance. CyberPsychology & Behavior 11, 129–137 (2008)
10. Knez, I., Enmarker, I.: Effects of Office Lighting on Mood and Cognitive Performance And A Gender Effect in Work-xRelated Judgment. Environment and Behavior 30, 553–567 (1998)
11. Knez, I.: Effect of indoor lighting on mood and cognition. Environmental Psychology, 39–51 (1995)
12. Seuntiëns, P.J.H., Vogels, I.M.L.C.: Atmosphere creation: Atmosphere and light characteristics. Philips Research (2008)
13. Choy, K.: Atmosphere creation in the living room: The freedom of light characteristics in atmosphere perception for the living room. Media and Knowledge Engineering. Delft University of Technology, Delft (2009)
14. Vogels, I.M.L.C.: Atmoshere metrics. In: Westerink, J.H.D.M., Ouwerkerk, M., Overbeek, T.J.M., Pasveer, W.F., de Ruyter, B. (eds.) Probing Experiece: From Assessment of User Emotions and Behaviour to Development of Products. Philips Research Book. Springer, The Netherlands (2008)
15. Russell, J.A., Pratt, G.: A description of the affective quality attributed to environments. Journal of Personality and Social Psychology 38, 311–322 (1980)
16. Vogels, I.M.L.C.: How to make life more colorful: From image quality to atmosphere experience. In: 17th Color Imaging Conference, pp. 123–128 (2009)
17. Martin, M.: On the induction of mood. Clinical Psychology Review 10, 669–697 (1990)

Interacting with Light Apps and Platforms

Serge Offermans, Harm van Essen, and Berry Eggen

Eindhoven University of Technology, Department of Industrial Design
Postbus 513, 5600MB, Eindhoven, The Netherlands
{s.a.m.offermans,h.a.v.essen,j.h.eggen}@tue.nl

Abstract. In the near future, highly dynamic light sources will be embedded in the areas in which we live and work, as well as in the objects within these areas. All these light elements will be connected, and digitally controlled. This development will turn our environments into lighting platforms that will not only allow us to observe our surroundings and perform our tasks, but can also support many other functions and activities. Furthermore, through sensor networks, such platforms will have knowledge about their environment, and will be able to autonomously respond to users. This vision requires us to rethink the way we interact with light as well as the way light interacts with us.

Keywords: Light, Apps, Platforms, Interaction, Office, Breakout.

1   Introduction

The developments in artificial lighting are very rapid. Modern LED light sources are small, energy efficient, and durable. They are highly dynamic and properties such as brightness, color (temperature), direction, and focus can be can be easily controlled and adapted to our desires. The nature of this new type of lighting will allow many light sources to be embedded in the environments in which we live and work. All these sources are connected to each other as well as to sensors and other equipment. These environments can be seen as platforms that can provide various services, supporting people in performing the activities they intend to do.

In contrast to the technological developments, the way we interact with the modern light sources has hardly changed since the invention of electric light. We still use switches (although sometimes in modern disguise such as capacitive touch) to turn on a single lamp or a pre-defined group of lamps. In some cases we are able to gradually dim our lights, or to choose a preferred color. However, dynamically controlling settings like intensity and color of more complex sets of light sources is almost exclusively done via complicated systems that are supposed to be used by trained professionals (e.g. for use in theatres and clubs).

Also practices towards application of lighting in smart environments according to the Ambient Intelligence vision are rather conservative. Most autonomous behavior of lights concerns simply switching on or off, triggered by either a timer or a passive infra red (PIR) motion sensor. Some systems use the level of (natural) light to determine how much extra light is required from an artificial light source to meet the desired light levels.

R. Wichert, K. Van Laerhoven, J. Gelissen (Eds.): AmI 2011 Workshops, CCIS 277, pp. 57–62, 2012.

We envision a future in which light systems are part of an intelligent platform. The system supports or even stimulates the users in their activities and enhances their experience. Lighting will be controlled in collaboration with the environment. The user will no longer control individual light sources, but rather interact with the environment as a whole. In the remainder of this paper we formulate important directions of research to develop this vision. We also introduce a case in which we will explore our research questions in a research-through-design approach [1].

2   Directions for Research

Our research will be explored in three important areas: first new opportunities for the use of intelligent lighting, second the development of light platforms and services, and third the development of new interaction styles for user-system interaction.

Opportunities for Lighting. Providing adequate visibility to be able to perform a task is a primary function of lighting. Even in this area many opportunities arise to better support tasks by more flexible lighting, able to adaptively respond to changing needs and circumstances (eg. tasks, number of persons, multi-purpose environments, social relationships, daylight conditions etc.).

Moreover, many services on the envisioned light platforms can go beyond adequate or appropriate task lighting. Exploring the (latent) needs of users in a particular domain, combined with existing knowledge on the effects of light can provide useful starting points to find innovative concepts. Knoop [2] discusses the visual (e.g. perception and cognition), emotional (e.g. mood and atmosphere) and biological (e.g. circadian rhythms, alertness) effects of lights. Applying the knowledge about these effects of light can for instance lead to more productive or comfortable working environments. Another interesting effect of lighting is the social dimension [3]. Light has an effect on the social relations and social interaction between people. Using this knowledge, we can for instance create ambient lighting that can be used to encourage cooperation. Lighting can also be used to influence behavior using principles of persuasive technology [4], [5].

Besides the effects on people and their behavior, we recognize opportunities in the use of light as an information medium. We do already get a lot of information from the light in our environment. Natural light subtly tells us something about the time of the day, and lights in your neighbors' house lets you know they are home. The notion 'information decoration' [6] describes a class of ambient displays [7] in which unobtrusively and aesthetically presented information informs the user in the periphery of his attention. Light could very well function as a medium in this concept. Lighting could for instance be used to display presence and availability information. But if light is used as an information medium, then how will this information be understood? And how is informative light distinguished from illuminative light?

Light Apps and Platforms. Modern electronic products often serve multiple purposes. These are systems that provide various services to the user. Services offer functionality and information that is tailored toward the user with respect to context (eg time, location, activity, company) and user preference. This trend is most obvious in modern smart-phones platforms. An added value for such platforms is especially created by the 'user generated content', which means that new services can emerge and be build on other services. Lighting solutions could benefit from a similar structure: the applications will determine the actual function and value of the system at a given moment. Lighting solutions will shift from single-function luminaires towards light 'apps' and 'platforms'. These platforms can provide us with suitable atmospheres, information about our environment, support our social connections, and support our activities in many other ways. Applications can be provided by experts, but also by the end-users themselves. Exploring the potential of end-user programming of light apps is an area of interest.

There are several prerequisites to make the platforms and apps a success: not only technical issues in terms of connectivity, repositories and so on, but also business model and user experience issues are relevant. Who will be app developers; professional experts or end-users? Where will people download or buy their apps? What critical mass of apps has to be developed for a community to take off? What standards and protocols need to be established? What business model will underlie this concept? How will we integrate sensor networks and third party lighting equipment? How do applications rely on the platform elements in different locations? In other words, will an app work if you take it to another location? Who will adapt or fine-tune apps for specific locations or platforms.

User-System Interaction. In contrast to the relation between a switch and a light bulb, the relation between a person and a light platform is not straight forward, as the platform has many light sources that each has various properties. Controlling dynamic lighting that comes from many different sources creates the need for new forms of interaction. Furthermore, the amount of different functions that such a lighting system will perform in a dynamic context, creates additional challenges for the interaction. A comprehensive interaction paradigm is required that allows various users to select, control, and configure applications in a meaningful way.

It is tempting to develop a smart-phone app to allow people to control the light platform. However, there are alternative ways of controlling these light apps, which may be more attractive or appropriate depending on various parameters such as the context and frequency of use. For instance the field of Tangible Interaction [8] offers advantages such as direct manipulation and physical affordances to create meaningful interaction.

As we also envision the platform and the environment to be an active participant in the interaction with the user, an important part of the interaction research concerns the behavior of the system. Within the field of Ambient Intelligence a central question regards the balance between user control and system automation. We believe that this balance can be achieved by considering user and system as two agents in a collaborative decision making process that can be initiated by any of the two agents. The system may provide a suggestion, and the user may suggest a change. Over time, user and system will be able to learn from one another resulting in more fluent interaction. Analogy with concepts in human-human interaction, such as social translucency and common ground [9] may provide useful starting points and brings up other interesting directions such as the matter of intention and surprise. In some occasions, a specifically intended effect is desirable, while in other cases there is room for variation and new suggestions.

3   Case: The Modern Office

Offices are becoming more open and dynamic. People work on flexible desks in open spaces, and the office provides new types of spaces for activities focused on for instance social interaction, (informal) meetings and relaxation. The needs of the 'new' office workers could be addressed and supported by dynamic lighting solutions. Time management, space appropriation, presence awareness and knowledge sharing are some of the relevant topics. An interesting type of space in the modern office is the 'breakout area'. This is an area where people can have informal meetings, sit down to read, have a brainstorm or just have a coffee. The dynamic use of this space makes it particularly interesting as the initial context to explore the opportunities of light apps and the interaction with the platform. Lighting solutions could support the different activities in the breakout area by providing a suitable atmosphere or stimulate for instance concentration, creativity, or relaxation. Light could also be used to create separate zones in the breakout area to support the use of the area for multiple activities that go on simultaneously. Finally, light could be used as an information source, providing information about the use of the area, the people in it, or about other things that are relevant to the different activities.

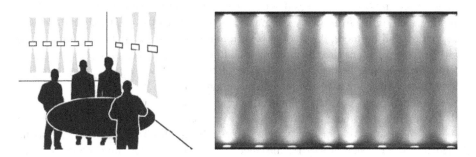

Fig. 1. Prototype by Occhialini et al.; Light indicating the progress in a meeting

An example of such a system was developed by Occhialini et al. [10] see figure 1. Their system supported timekeeping in meetings or a series of presentations using an unobtrusive lighting pattern on the wall that constantly informs the people about the progress of their meeting. We have taken this concept and implemented it in an initial light app on a new light platform element. This same platform element was also used for another app that provides atmospheric lighting, and could again be used for numerous other applications, see figure 2.

Fig. 2. Initial element of a lighting platform running the 'meeting timer' app (left) and the 'atmospheric lighting' app (right)

Development of a Testbed. To further explore the potential of light apps in the case of the breakout area, we are developing a testbed, see figure 3. The testbed is situated in our department and is used on a daily basis by staff and students of the department for the intended purposes. The area contains basic light infrastructure with wall washing, down-lighting, and dedicated lamps. All lights are electronically controlled and the functions described above are available to the users.

Fig. 3. Initial arrangement of the Breakout area testbed, featuring an individual area (right) and small group facilities (left) with dynamic lighting equipment and sensors

In the breakout area testbed, we will explore and develop new applications, various light platform elements and novel interaction styles, see figure 4. Formative evaluations using qualitative methods (both longitudinal in situ studies, as well as controlled studies) of these systems will allow us to identify the common or valuable elements. The main questions are: 1) How can we support the activities that take place in the breakout area using light? 2) How will the user experience the light concepts? (*how do users actually "use" the system, what is the perceived usefulness of different apps, is there any stress or distraction? etc.*) 3) How will the users communicate with the system and how will the system behave? (*do people understand how to interact with the service, accurately perceive the displayed information, what is the cognitive load of interaction? etc.*) Follow-up design iterations will allow us to work towards a new paradigm for the interaction with light.

Fig. 4. Selection of initial interaction opportunities (left-to-right): Information decoration display, smart phone lighting control, meeting timer hourglass, atmosphere selection cube

4   Conclusion

In the future, our environments will contain many embedded light sources that will together form light platforms on which various applications will run depending on the current usage of an area. Besides interesting light concepts and a service infrastructure, a new paradigm for interaction with these environments is required in order to benefit from its full potential. Our current research frames these questions.

We employ a design-research approach in the context of a breakout area to develop and explore new interaction styles with various applications and a light platform. Successive iterations of evaluation and design will allow us to work towards a new paradigm for the interaction with light apps.

References

1. Edelson, D.C.: Design Research: What We Learn When We Engage in Design. Journal of the Learning Sciences 11, 105 (2002)
2. Knoop, M.: Dynamic lighting for well-being in work places: Addressing the visual, emotional and biological aspects of lighting design. In: Proc. of the 15th Symposium Lighting Engineering, pp. 63–74. Lighting Engineering Society of Slovenia (2006)
3. Magielse, R., Ross, P.: A Design Approach to Socially Adaptive Lighting Environments. Presented at the CHItaly, Alghero, September 13 (2011)
4. Fogg, B.J.: Persuasive Technology: Using Computers to Change What We Think and Do. Morgan Kaufmann (2002)
5. Petty, R.E., Cacioppo, J.T.: Communication and Persuasion: Central and Peripheral Routes to Attitude Change. Springer, New York (1986)
6. Eggen, B., Mensvoort, K.: Making Sense of What Is Going on "Around": Designing Environmental Awareness Information Displays. In: Markopoulos, P., De Ruyter, B., Mackay, W. (eds.) Awareness Systems, pp. 99–124. Springer, London (2009)
7. Pousman, Z., Stasko, J.: A taxonomy of ambient information systems. In: Proceedings of the Working Conference on Advanced Visual Interfaces, AVI, Italy, p. 67 (2006)
8. Ullmer, B., Ishii, H.: Emerging frameworks for tangible user interfaces. IBM Syst. J. 39, 915–931 (2000)
9. Clark, H.: Using Language. Cambridge University Press, New York (1996)
10. Occhialini, V., van Essen, H., Eggen, B.: Design and Evaluation of an Ambient Display to Support Time Management during Meetings. In: Campos, P., Graham, N., Jorge, J., Nunes, N., Palanque, P., Winckler, M. (eds.) INTERACT 2011, Part II. LNCS, vol. 6947, pp. 263–280. Springer, Heidelberg (2011)

Interacting with Light

Alexander Wiethoff[1] and Sven Gehring[2]

[1] LMU University of Munich, 80333, Munich Germany
alexander.wiethoff@ifi.lmu.de
[2] German Research Center for Artificial Intelligence (DFKI), Saarbrücken, Germany
sven.gehring@dfki.de

Abstract. Embedding lighting systems into architectural structures offers new interaction possibilities. They can be exposed to a large number of users, thus there is a demand for such interface solutions that fit the context of use. Using two examples of experimental, novel interaction methods with light, we propose that there are various potential approaches to using implicit and explicit control mechanisms. We share our implementations in hopes that they will inspire possible future projects and have applications in other contexts.

Keywords: Interactive Lighting Design, Interface.

1 Introduction

Lighting systems embedded in architectural structures are an emerging field of research because they offer new, ubiquitous interaction possibilities, as described by Seitiger et al. [3]. When designing these systems, one challenge is how to present the control mechanism to the user and how to determine what degree of participation is required. Verplank et al. [5] classified control mechanisms that affect the environment in terms of their degree of participation: (1) *Discrete controls* trigger pre-defined (semi-automated) actions, and (2) *continuous controls* leave the user in permanent (manual) command over the environment.

The use of lighting systems in the context of urban environments is strongly reflected in the choice of the interface technology. In our research, we want to raise the question of how we might design and implement new interaction types, ones that control lighting systems in ways that are beneficial to users, including having such systems be quickly learned through playfully discoverable interfaces

In the following work, we present two examples from recent implementations of novel interaction techniques that use lighting systems embedded in the interiors and exteriors of buildings. From these examples, we propose potential extensions of their input methods, allowing for (a) implicit interaction through an embodied approach, which is a form of discrete-control mechanism, and (b) explicit interaction through an augmented approach, an extension of a continuous-control mechanism.

R. Wichert, K. Van Laerhoven, J. Gelissen (Eds.): AmI 2011 Workshops, CCIS 277, pp. 63–67, 2012.

1.1   Example: Implicit Interaction

Concept

ColourVision, by Wiethoff et al. [6], is an interactive installation that allows users to engage in an intensive dialogue with colors. Seating postures, such as active, relaxed, or reflective positions, are captured and translated, triggering a rapid change of the room's color. In an article that analyzed the psychological effects of environmental colors on the human body, Stone et al. [4] claimed that "red and yellow are naturally experienced as stimulating and disagreeable," and that "these colors focus people on the outward environment," and that "they produce forceful, expansive behavior, whereas green and blue are experienced as quieting and agreeable, focusing people inward, and produce reserved, stable behavior. The embodied interface that is used in this installation corresponds to these circumstances and controls the room and the resulting colors. Red, for example, is activated as a response to an open, active seating position. Green is the color for introverted reflection and is generated if a person employs a thoughtful, closed position. A person sitting on the chair in a stretched, relaxed position plunges the room into a cool blue, the color for calm (figure 1). The environment incorporates a very subtle interaction mechanism that is controlled through implicit interaction. The explorative nature of this interaction invites users to learn, in a very playful manner, how the environment reacts. It is an example of a novel discrete-control mechanism, displaying predefined sequences (colors) in the system that are triggered by body postures.

Fig. 1. Different colors generated in response to various seating positions

Advantages and Limitations

The main advantage of using an interface solution with a tracking system is that no additional hardware is required for users to carry. Furthermore, there is no graphical interface or other tangible hardware visible in the environment. There is also no need for the user to focus on the system and actively interact with it. However, the invisible nature of the interface also leads to clear limitations: an accidental interaction can be triggered when, for example, users want to perform a completely different task that does not include interacting with the lighting system. A second limitation is that the type of trigger required for interaction with the system (such as signage, etc.) has to be viewable, which breaks with the simplicity of the invisibility.

1.2   Example: Explicit Interaction

Concept

iRiS, by Boring et al. [2], is a remote, direct-manipulation system that is meant to allow for ubiquitous interaction with media facades at a distance. An experimental setup was installed at the ARS Electronica building in Linz, Austria. Its 1087 windows contain about 40,000 LEDs that can be manipulated through digital multiplexing (DMX) signals. The size of the building allows for a viewing distance of up to 300 meters, with an optimal interaction distance being around 50 meters. To allow for interaction with and manipulation of the facade with *iRiS*, we adopted *Touch Projector*, a system introduced by Boring et al. [1], and combined it with the concept of interaction through live video *at-a-distance*. The system runs on a camera-equipped mobile device, turning the device into an interactive, see-through panel (see Figure 2).

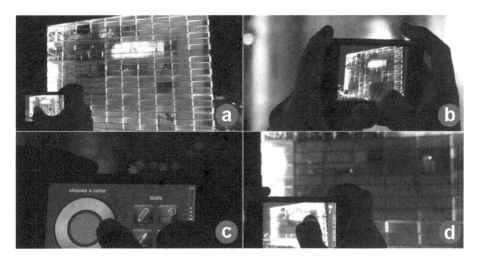

Fig. 2. The building's facade (a) is directly manipulated using a video image on a mobile device (b). A tool palette (c) allows users to paint the building in different colors at a distance (d)

Advantages and Limitations

The concept of *iRiS* relies on a device-based interaction in which the user is able to interact with the building directly using the display of his or her mobile device. The user points the camera of the mobile device at the building so that the building is displayed in the live video stream. By touching the mobile device's display, the user can interact with the building. In contrast to *ColourVision*, *iRiS* requires the user to interact explicitly by providing efficient continuous control. From the client side and from a usability perspective, one major appeal of this concept is the high availability and acceptance of smartphones and their corresponding usability concepts. Applications can easily be developed based on an existing infrastructure. As well, taking into account users' familiarity with apps and the usability aspects of smartphones, the application of a concept based on *iRiS* can be directed more focused on a specific area. The main disadvantage of such a concept is the requirement that users be equipped with devices. In the case of *iRiS*, a facade controller (such as a smartphone) needs to be available to allow the application to interact with the facade.

2   Discussion

An important aspect that must be dealt with when designing a novel control mechanism for lighting systems embedded in architectural structures is the mechanism's context of use. We described two exemplary projects that are both implemented in artistic contexts and therefore do not seek to provide task-oriented practical solutions. However, the novel interaction mechanisms proposed in this work have potential applications for industrial systems (e.g. controlling brightness levels on a façade), if modified effectively. We envision a combination of both approaches so that basic interactions are carried out though implicit mechanisms, and changes in the environment that are more detailed are applied through additional, explicit-control elements. After observing participants interacting with our prototypes, we have concluded that there is a great potential for multimodal input techniques that offer (a) interfaces based on familiar interaction paradigms and (b) extensions of the forms suggested in this work.

3   Conclusion and Future Work

In this work, we examined the use of an implicit and embodied interface as a mechanism for the discrete control of lighting as well as the use of a mobile device for continuous, explicit control. Both approaches provide new ways of interacting with light. In a follow-up project, we will again explore interaction forms such as those proposed in this work. However, we will employ them in a task-oriented context in order to investigate their transferability to everyday situations.

References

1. Boring, S., Baur, D., Butz, A., Gustafson, S., Baudisch, P.: Touch Projector: Mobile Interaction Through Video. In: Proc. CHI 2010 (2010)
2. Boring, S., Gehring, S., Wiethoff, A., Bloeckner, M., Schoening, J., Butz, A.: Multi-User Interaction on Media Facades through Live Video on Mobile Devices. In: Proc. CHI 2011 (2011)

3. Seitinger, S., Perry, D., Mitchell, W.: Urban pixels: painting the city with light. In: Proc. CHI 2009 (2009)
4. Stone, N.J., English, A.J.: Task type, posters, and workspace color on mood, satisfaction, and performance. Journal of Environmental Psychology 18 (1998)
5. Verplank, B., Sapp, C., Mathews, M.: A course on controllers. In Proc. NIME 2001 (2001)
6. Wiethoff, A., Butz, A.: ColourVision—Controlling Light Patterns through Postures. In: Taylor, R., Boulanger, P., Krüger, A., Olivier, P. (eds.) Smart Graphics. LNCS, vol. 6133, pp. 281–284. Springer, Heidelberg (2010)

International Workshop on Interactive Human Behavior Analysis in Open or Public Spaces

Hayley Hung[1], Jean-Marc Odobez[2], and Dariu Gavrila[1,3]

[1] University of Amsterdam, The Netherlands
[2] Idiap Research Institute, Switzerland
[3] Daimler Research and Development, Germany

Abstract. Human behaviour, and in particular interactive or social behaviour in public spaces is rich and highly varying. It is a great source of information about people's attitudes towards strangers, friends and family, and how they chose to navigate through and familiarise themselves with the urban environment. This paper provides a summary of our workshop on interactive human behaviour analysis in open or public spaces, and in particular, highlighting the future applications, challenges, and goals that such an area of research should have. We discuss the outcomes of the discussions, talks and presentations of the day.

Keywords: Human Behaviour, Interaction, Multimodal Sensing, Computer Vision, Surveillance, Sensor Fusion.

1 Introduction

Public spaces contains a rich source of interactive or social human behaviour. It is the space that is accessible to everyone, making it a potential for a highly diverse cross-section of the local community. These are the places that the community shares, with the potential to provide a sense of identity and belonging. One aspect of the future of ambient intelligent environments lies in understanding people's interactive behaviours in these spaces to improve our sense of well-being, safety and quality of life.

2 Structure of the Workshop

To address the future of this research, we gathered together researchers and practitioners from computer science, urban studies, human geography, anthropology and industry to exchange ideas and find potential links that could move towards our goal of ambient intelligent public spaces. The day contained 4 invited talks, 2 oral presentations and 5 poster presentations. The oral presentations were selected from submitted papers that were closest to the the goals of the workshop.

R. Wichert, K. Van Laerhoven, J. Gelissen (Eds.): AmI 2011 Workshops, CCIS 277, pp. 68–71, 2012.
© Springer-Verlag Berlin Heidelberg 2012

3   Invited Talks

The first invited talk was from computer vision scientist David Forsyth (University of Illinois at Urbana-Champaign, USA), who motivated the importance of designing automated human behaviour analysis systems to help predict what might happen next within the context of who it could affect. He advocated automated methods that could detect attributes to visual content to reason about half hidden objects, activities or behaviour that may or may not have been seen before. Finally, he showed an example of automatically tracking humans in a public space. They found that a particular part of the tarmac above a wide set of stairs was worn more that anywhere else, which correlated with higher occupancy but their tracking method could not explain the higher occupancy in this region. This example provides an excellent motivation for systems that can analyse human behaviour in more detail than just trajectories.

The second talk was from geoscientist Eric Laurier (Edinburgh University, UK), who first motivated the importance of understanding social behaviour, in particular, in public spaces by describing the early studies of Whyte [8] who was one of the early pioneers of video analysis in urban geography. He then described a study of human interactive behaviour in the semi-public space of a café. The study highlighted significant differences in the order of service as well as the behaviour of regular and unfamiliar customers. For café regulars, the staff try to create an ongoing relationship with them by keeping track of their activities outside of the caf, and even asking them where they have been during long periods of absence. This study provided an excellent example of how to collect data of natural social behaviour in a semi-public environment.

The third talk was made by computer vision scientist Nico van der Aa, from Noldus Information Technology with contributions from Lucas Noldus. The company makes software for scientists who want to carry our behaviour experiments. They provide both software to make annotations but also some tools for automated analysis. Particular emphasis was made of the research work carried out in the restaurant of the future, which is a video-monitored self-service restaurant in Wageningen university. They use it to carry out experiments such as understanding consumer food choices and analysing the role of parents in children's eating behaviours. Not much work is carried out on the social aspects of food choice and dining, though this would be an interesting next step.

The final invited talk was from ethologist Elisabeth Oberzaucher (Vienna University) who is interested in observing behaviours that are out of our cognitive control and studies whether their analysis can be used to understand more complex behaviours such as attraction. She showed a few experiments that could predict the physical attraction between subjects using just video frame subtraction to capture body motion. Classification tasks were carried out using a time-delayed neural network. Her talk highlighted the potential for analysing human behaviour automatically by extracting features from unconscious behaviours.

4   Submitted Papers of the Workshop

Submissions for this workshop[1] covered a number of different techniques that could be used for automated interactive behaviour analysis. A wide range of sensor types were used including inertial sensors [3], mobile phones [7], thermal cameras [5], infrared sensors [6], video cameras [2,1], microphones, as well as depth sensors [4]. Some of the papers presented methods to address the general problem of behaviour analysis, like the detection of people in video images [2], individual motion activity from body sensors [3], or office activities [6]. Teeuw et al. studied behaviour on a larger scale, by collecting urban mobility patterns and proposing ways to influence the travelling behaviour of individuals [7]. Popa et al. proposed a method for an automated shopping assistant to recognize when a shopper needed assistance [4].

Work that addressed interactive behaviour more directly was the work of Cristani et al. [1], who proposed a method to detect speakers in a conversation by automatically extracted motion activity. This could have great potential in public spaces where recording people's conversations would be ethically questionable. Skouboe et al. [5] carried out a study to see how automated analysis of activities in a public space could be used to help design interventions in the space. They proposed that such an analysis would help to guide design enhancements such as smart lighting.

5   Outcomes of the Workshop

A panel discussion at the end of the day highlighted many significant issues to be addressed, particularly with the collection of natural data for carrying out further experiments. There was also a general consensus that understanding human social interaction in particular, was very important. Many applications for automated interactive behaviour understanding in public spaces was discussed in public spaces such as for health and well-being, the entertainment industry, or enhancing working and leisure environments, showing the rich potential for this research domain.

Acknowledgements. The organization of this workshop was partially supported by the European Community through FP7/2007-2013 under grant agreement nr. 218197 (ADABTS), nr. 248907 (VANAHEIM), and a Marie Curie Research Training fellowship in the project "AnaSID" (PIEF-GA-2009-255609).

References

1. Cristani, M., Pesarin, A., Vinciarelli, A., Crocco, M., Murino, V.: Look at who's talking. In: Workshop on Interactive Human Behaviour in Open and Public Spaces, InterHuB (2011)

---

[1] http://www.idiap.ch/workshop/interhub2011/

2. Descamps, A., Carincotte, C., Gosselin, B.: Person detection for indoor videosurveillance using spatio-temporal integral features. In: Workshop on Interactive Human Behaviour in Open and Public Spaces, InterHuB (2011)
3. Muhammad, S.A., Klein, N., Laerhoven, K.V., David, K.: A feature set evalution for activity recognition with body-worn inertial sensors. In: Workshop on Interactive Human Behaviour in Open and Public Spaces, InterHuB (2011)
4. Popa, M., Rothkrantz, L., Shan, C., Wiggers, P., Kemal-Koc, A.: Kinect sensing of shopping related actions. In: Workshop on Interactive Human Behaviour in Open and Public Spaces, InterHuB (2011)
5. Skouboe, E., Andersen, H.J., Jensen, O.B.: Using human motion intensity as input for urban design. In: Workshop on Interactive Human Behaviour in Open and Public Spaces, InterHuB (2011)
6. Tao, S., Kudo, M., Nonaka, H., Toyama, J.: Authentication and activities analysis in an office environment using a sensor network. In: Workshop on Interactive Human Behaviour in Open and Public Spaces, InterHuB (2011)
7. Teeuw, W., Koolwaaij, J., Peddemors, A.: User behaviour captured by mobile phones. In: Workshop on Interactive Human Behaviour in Open and Public Spaces, InterHuB (2011)
8. Whyte, W.H.: The Social Life Of Small Urban Spaces. Project for Public Spaces Inc. (January 1980)

Look at Who's Talking: Voice Activity Detection by Automated Gesture Analysis

Marco Cristani[1,2], Anna Pesarin[1], Alessandro Vinciarelli[3,4],
Marco Crocco[2], and Vittorio Murino[1,2]

[1] Dipartimento di Informatica, University of Verona, Italy
[2] Istituto Italiano di Tecnologia, Italy
[3] University of Glasgow, UK
[4] Idiap Research Institute, Switzerland
{marco.cristani,anna.pesarin}@univr.it,
Alessandro.Vinciarelli@glasgow.ac.uk,
{marco.crocco,vittorio.murino}@iit.it

Abstract. This paper proposes an approach for Voice Activity Detection (VAD) based on the automatic measurement of gesturing. The main motivation of the work is that gestures have been shown to be tightly correlated with speech, hence they can be considered a reliable evidence that a person is talking. The use of gestures rather than speech for performing VAD can be helpful in many situation (e.g., surveillance and monitoring in public spaces) where speech cannot be obtained for technical, legal or ethical issues. The results show that the gesturing measurement approach proposed in this work achieves, on a frame-by-frame basis, an accuracy of 71 percent in distinguishing between speech and non-speech.

1 Introduction

It is common experience to observe that people accompany speech with *gestures*, the "[...] *range of visible bodily actions that are, more or less, generally regarded as part of a person's willing expression* [...]" [10]. Far from being independent phenomena, speech and gestures are so tightly intertwined that every important investigation of language has taken gestures into account, from *De Oratore* by Cicero (1st Century BC) to the latest studies in cognitive sciences [9, 11, 14] showing that the two modalities are "[...] *components of a single overall plan* [...]" [10].

Hence, this paper proposes the detection of gesturing as a means to perform Voice Activity Detection (VAD), i.e. to automatically recognize whether a person is speaking or not. The main rationale is that audio, the most natural and reliable channel when it comes to VAD, might be unavailable for technical, legal, or privacy related issues; this is a condition that applies in particular to surveillance scenarios, where people are monitored in public spaces and are not necessarily aware of being recorded.

Several approaches have exploited the relationship between speech and other cues to accomplish different technological tasks. The synchronization between pitch and gestures has been used to make artificial agents more realistic [13].

R. Wichert, K. Van Laerhoven, J. Gelissen (Eds.): AmI 2011 Workshops, CCIS 277, pp. 72–80, 2012.
© Springer-Verlag Berlin Heidelberg 2012

Multimodal speaker diarization techniques (detection of *who speaks when*) based on the joint modeling of speech, facial and bodily cues (e.g., mouth movement, fidgeting, body pose, etc.) have been proposed in [1, 6, 8, 15–18]. To the best of our knowledge, the only work where diarization has been tried with solely visual cues is in [7], where the experiments showed that the performance decrease when the audio is absent.

This paper aims at performing VAD with solely visual cues, but it considers a scenario more challenging than the one proposed in [7] for diarization. While the experiments of the latter work are performed in a smart meeting room setting (multiple cameras capturing each person individually at close distance), the results of this paper have been obtained in a surveillance scenario where there is only one camera positioned 7 meters above the scene (see Figure 2 for an example). In particular, the experiments focus on people involved in standing conversations, with a tracker that follows each individual. (see in [5] how groups of interacting people are detected). The VAD approach is based on a local video descriptor that extracts the body optical flow, encoding its energy and "complexity" using an entropy-like measure. This allows one to discriminate between body oscillations or noise introduced by the tracker, where the optical flow is low and homogeneous, and genuine gestures, where the movement of head, arms and trunk produces a local flow field which is diverse in both intensity and direction. The descriptor extracted for each participant produces a signal that can be used for VAD.

The proposed approach is interesting under three main respects. The first is that the relationship between speech and gestures has been widely documented and studied, but relatively few quantitative investigations of the phenomenon have been made. The second is that approaches like the one proposed here might help to infer information about privacy protected data (speech in this case) from publicly accessible data (gestures in this case). This is important to establish whether the simple absence of a certain channel is sufficient to protect the privacy of people and how much. The third is that inferring missing data from available ones can make techniques dealing with challenging scenarios more effective and reliable.

The rest of the paper is organised as follows. In Sect. 2, the VAD methods is described, detailing the entropy-like measure utilised. Section 3 illustrates the experimental trial on a publicly available video dataset and, finally, conclusive remarks and future activities are summarised in Section 4.

2 Gesturing Activity Measurement

This section describes the technique adopted to measure the gesturing activity in videos like those shown in Figure 2. Once a group of interacting individuals has been detected (see [5] for the technique applied), each person is tracked individually and a square *Region of Interest* (ROI) is defined around her. The size of the ROI is set automatically to include all gestures of the individual. Areas where multiple ROIs overlap have been ignored to avoid possible confusions between neighboring people.

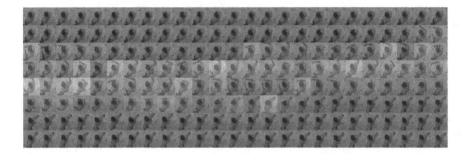

Fig. 1. Qualitative analysis of our descriptor: in the sequence above, an high tonality of red means great gesture activity

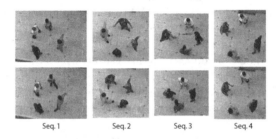

Seq. 1   Seq. 2   Seq. 3   Seq. 4

Fig. 2. Some frames of the video sequences used

The measurement technique is applied to each ROI individually and it is expected to accomplish two goals: the first is to discriminate between gestures and postural oscillations typically observed when people stand. The second is to normalize the tracking errors that cause abrupt and spurious shifts of the ROI. The body parts most commonly involved in gesturing are hands, arms, head, and trunk. Their individual movements tend to be very different during gesturing and the measurement values associated to a given ROI try to capture such an aspect:

$$v(t) = \max_{\text{int}}(\{f(t)\}) \times S_{\text{int}}(\{f(t)\}) \times S_{\text{ori}}(\{f(t)\}) \tag{1}$$

where $\{f(t)\}$ is the set of motion flow vectors associated to each pixel of the ROI at time t, $S_{\text{int}}(\{f(t)\})$ is the entropy of the motion flow intensities, and $S_{\text{ori}}(\{f(t)\})$ is the entropy of the orientation values, both calculated over $\{f(t)\}$[1]. The maximum over the flow intensities values $\max_{\text{int}}(\{f(t)\})$ encodes the "energy" associated to the movement, while the two entropic terms serve to highlight those motion flow values which exhibit higher variability in intensity and orientation. In this way, postural oscillations and shifts due to unprecise tracking

---

[1] The optical flow has been obtained with the package available at the following URL: http://server.cs.ucf.edu/~vision/source.html.

receive a low score because they cause a global, homogeneous set of intensities and orientations, corresponding to low entropy values. Alternative expressions of $v(t)$ have been considered that use mean and median rather than maximum, or do not include one of the entropy terms. In all cases, the resulting performance is lower than the one obtained with the expression above. A graphical idea of the measurement is given in Figure 1, where colours shift towards red when gesturing activity is higher.

3 Experiments

The goal of the experiments is twofold: first, to provide a quantitative measure of the correlation between gestures and speech; second, to measure the effectiveness of the function $v(t)$ (see Section 2) in a VAD task. Both tasks have been accomplished over *TalkingHeads*, a new dataset publicly available upon request[2] (see some frames in Figure 2).

The dataset contains four conversations lasting, on average, 6 minutes. The data was recorded in a 3.5×2.5 meters wide outdoor area, during a cloudy day in summer. The total number of subjects is 15 (1 female and 14 males), with 4 different participants per conversation (only one subject participated in two conversations). The subjects include 4 academics, 5 undergraduate students, 2 MSc students, 3 postdoctoral researchers, and 1 PhD student. The ages range between 20 and 40 years and the subjects were unaware of the actual goals of the experiments.

Data were captured at 25 frames per second with a camera positioned 7 meters above the floor and facing downward. The subjects were asked to wear differently colored shirts, in order to make the tracking/localization easier. Tracking has been performed by simple template association. The motion flow has been computed by considering one frame every 4, reducing the video sampling period to 160 ms. The audio was recorded at 44100 Hz with 4 wireless headset microphones, each transmitting to its own receiver.

Each audio recording has been segmented into speech and non-speech segments using a robust VAD algorithm based on pitch [12]. This latter was extracted at regular time steps of 10 ms with Praat [3], a package including the pitch extraction technique described in [2]. The motivation behind this choice is not only that silence segments are characterized by frequencies higher than those observed in speech, but also that the pitch tends to be correlated with the "beat" gesture, typically accompanying syllables where the intonation is stressed [4, 20]. Then, in order to synchronize audio and video data, audio was resampled according to the video frame rate, averaging the pitch values occurring in each time period. The averaged pitch values constituted the samples of the audio signal that will be analyzed in the following.

---

[2] http://profs.sci.univr.it/~cristanm/datasets/TalkingHeads/

3.1 Pitch-Gesturing Correlation Analysis

This section shows how the correlation between the pitch (as extracted with Praat), and the gesturing activity (as measured with the approach proposed in Section 2) has been measured.

After the application of the techniques described in the previous sections, each sequence results into two signals per person, showing the value of pitch and $v(t)$ at regular time steps of 160 ms. Plots (a) and (b) of Figure 3 provide an example of such signals. The simple visual inspection shows that the two signals tend to change according to one another. However, $v(t)$ appears to be more noisy of the pitch because of the sensibility of the optical flow. Hence, both signals have been smoothed with an average filter applied to 8 s long windows. Figure 3 (c) shows the smoothed version of $v(t)$, while the smoothed audio and video signals of a complete conversation, normalized with respect to their maximum value, are compared in Fig. 4.

Table 1. Quantitative measures: correlation coefficients matrix for Seq. 1. The matrix rows and columns corresponds respectively to the four subsampled video signals (Vsub) and the four subsampled audio signals (Asub) (the non-significant coefficients (p-value$\geq$ 0.05) are underlined in red.

	A sub.1	A sub.2	A sub.3	A sub.4
V sub.1	**0.7310**	0.1338	0.2490	0.0670
V sub.2	0.1900	**0.6454**	0.4460	0.0254
V sub.3	0.1867	0.1966	**0.4838**	-0.0356
V sub.4	-0.2592	0.0472	0.0389	**0.4204**

Table 1 reports the Pearson correlation coefficients between $v(t)$ and pitch. Off-diagonal values account for correlations between signals extracted from different individuals. In this way, it is possible to better assess how strong is the correlation between speech and gestures for a given individual.

We performed a similar analysis on the other conversations, with the same parameters, obtaining in total four correlation matrices. Mediating over all the entries in the main diagonal (they were all statistically significant), we obtained a mean correlation score of 0.53, while considering the statistically significant off-diagonals entries we get 0.19. This suggests that $v(t)$ might be a reliable indicator of voice activity. Hence, in the following section, we show how the video signal can be employed to perform VAD.

3.2 Voice Activity Detection

The VAD task proposed in this section consists of labeling each frame as *speech* or *non − speech*. As an approximation, each person is treated independently of the others even though the exchange of turns (the opportunity of speaking) tends to follow regularities that might be helpful in improving the performance.

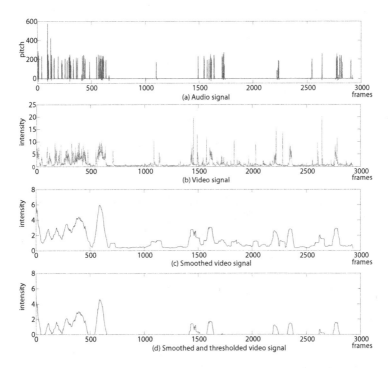

Fig. 3. Examples of signals employed in the analysis. (a) Audio input signal. (b) Video signal produced by our descriptor of a subject involved in the Seq.1. (c) The video signal was smoothed for evaluating the crossmodal correlation (Sec. 3.1). (d) The video signal was thresholded for the audio classification (Sec. 3.2).

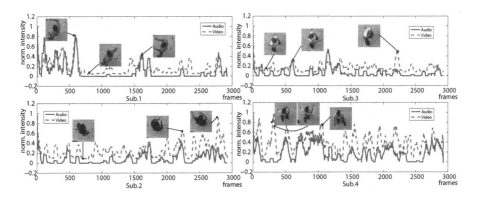

Fig. 4. Visual analysis of the audio and video smoothed data: each plot depicts the smoothed audio (solid blue) and the smoothed video (dashed red) signals for each participant to the dialog. The thumbnails give the feeling of the gesturing activity carried out in a particular instant.

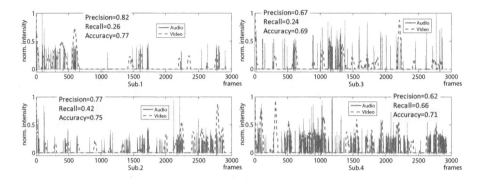

Fig. 5. Audio classification by video analysis. Each plot portrays the audio (solid blue) and the video (dashed red) signals for each participant to the dialog. For the sake of clarity, we report the (normalized) continuous signals, and not their binary versions (that we used). Precision, recall and accuracy scores related to each individual are also indicated.

The original pitch signal, which has non-zero entries only when the subjects talk, is used as groundtruth.

As a video signal to be used to infer speech, we considered the smoothed signal described above for the correlation analysis. In this way, high frequency components of the original signal have been filtered. The discrimination between speech and non-speech samples has been performed with a thresholding technique. Essentially, as suggested by Fig. 3 and Fig. 4, the video signal has a continuous component caused by small values of optical flow that are always present in the analysis. For this reason, we subtracted the mean to the signal, and we keep the intensities above zero, setting them at 1's. Smoothing and subtraction of the mean represent a thresholding operation that does not need the tuning of any parameter.

At this point, we can compare the two signals, and the detailed analysis of Seq. 1 is shown in Fig. 5.

For the sake of clarity, we report in the figure the (normalized) continuous signals, and not their binary versions which were actually used. As visible, many of the speech samples are correctly captured by the video signal. The figure also reports the precision, recall and accuracy values. In this sequence, the classifier tends to have low recall and high precision (assuming the speech as positive values). Considering all the subjects employed, we reach an average accuracy of 71%, average precision of 67%, and average recall of 40%.

4   Conclusions

This work has proposed a gesturing-based approach for performing VAD, the automatic detection of people that speak. The reason for using gestures in VAD, typically performed using speech recordings, is that the use of microphones is difficult or illegal in many scenarios of potential interest, including surveillance of public spaces, monitoring of potentially dangerous plants, etc. The core idea behind the approach is that cognitive sciences have demonstrated that speech and gestures, far from being independent expression modalities, are two faces of the same phenomenon. Therefore, gestures can be considered a reliable evidence of speech taking place at the same time.

The preliminary results presented in this paper provide a quantitative confirmation of the finding above and, most importantly, show that the detection of gesturing activity helps to predict whether a person is speaking or not with an accuracy of 71 percent (on a frame-by-frame basis). While not being conclusive about the possibility of reconstructing the actual turns and of performing diarization, the results are certainly promising in the direction of reconstructing conversational dynamics in absence of audio. This appears particularly important as turn-organization has been widely shown to be fundamental in inferring socially important information such as roles, dominance, personality, etc [19].

Besides, this work shows that it is possible to infer information about missing data (speech in this case) from available evidence (videos in this case). In a surveillance setup like the one of the experiments, this opens two conflicting perspectives: on one hand, surveillance approaches can be significantly improved by predicting phenomena considered so far non-accessible with the sensors at disposition. On the other hand, privacy protection measures applied so far (i.e., legal limitation on the use of microphones in public spaces) might become obsolete and uneffective. In this respect, experiments of the type presented in this work might change the notion of privacy and of its protection.

Future work can take two major directions: the first is to move from VAD to full diarization. This requires the application of probabilistic sequential models taking into account temporal constraints between neighboring frames and a larger amount of data. The second is to try automatic conversation analysis based on gestures and to verify whether (and to what extent) it is possible to perform tasks like role recognition, conflict detection, etc., typically performed using turn-organization and other conversational cues.

References

1. Anguera, X., Bozonnet, S., Evans, N., Fredouille, C., Friedland, G., Vinyals, O.: Speaker diarization: A review of recent research. IEEE Transactions on Audio, Speech, and Language Processing 20(2), 356–370 (2011)
2. Boersma, P.: Accurate short term analysis of the fundamental frequency and the harmonics to noise ratio of a sampled sound. IEEE Transactions on Image Processing 17, 97–110 (1993)
3. Boersma, P.: Praat, a system for doing phonetics by computer. Glot International 5(9/10), 341–345 (2001)
4. Cassell, J., Steedman, M., Badler, N., Pelachaud, C., Stone, M., Douville, B., Prevost, S., Achorn, B.: Modeling the interaction between speech and gesture. In: Proceedings of the Sixteenth Annual Conference of the Cognitive Science Society, pp. 153–158 (1994)

5. Cristani, M., Bazzani, L., Paggetti, G., Fossati, A., Bue, A.D., Menegaz, G., Murino, V.: Social interaction discovery by statistical analysis of f-formations. In: Proceedings of the British Machine Vision Conference (2011)
6. Fisher, J.W., Freeman, W.T., Darrell, T., Viola, P.: Learning joint statistical models for audio-visual fusion and segregation. In: Advanced in Neural Inf. Process. Syst., vol. 13, pp. 772–778 (2001)
7. Hung, H., Ba, S.O.: Speech/non-speech detection in meetings from automatically extracted low resolution visual features. In: ICASSP, pp. 830–833 (2010)
8. Hung, H., Huang, Y., Yeo, C., Gatica-Perez, D.: Associating audio-visual activity cues in a dominance estimation framework. In: First IEEE Workshop on CVPR for Human Communicative Behavior Analysis (2008)
9. Kendon, A.: Gesticulation and speech: Two aspects of the process of utterance. In: The Relationship of Verbal and Nonverbal Communication, pp. 207–227 (1980)
10. Kendon, A.: Language and gesture: unity or duality?, pp. 47–63. Cambridge University Press (2000)
11. Kendon, A.: Gesture: Visible Action as Utterance. Cambridge University Press, Cambridge (2004)
12. Khondaker, A., Ghulam, M.: Improved noise reduction with pitch enabled voice activity detection. In: ISIVC 2008 (2008)
13. Kopp, S., Wachsmuth, I.: Synthesizing multimodal utterances for conversational agents. Computer Animation and Virtual Worlds 15(1), 39–52 (2004)
14. McNeill, D.: Hand and mind: What gestures reveal about thought. Chicago University Press, Chicago (1992)
15. Noulas, A., Englebienne, G., Krose, B.J.A.: Multimodal speaker diarization. IEEE Transactions on Pattesrnss Analysis and Machine Intelligence 99 (2011)
16. Rao, R., Chen, T.: Cross-modal prediction in audio-visual communication. In: IEEE International Conference on Acoustics, Speech, and Signal Processing, ICASSP-1996, vol. 4, pp. 2056–2059 (1996)
17. Siracusa, M.R., John, W.F.: Dynamic dependency tests: Analysis and applications to multi-modal data association (2007)
18. Vajaria, H., Islam, T., Sarkar, S., Sankar, R., Kasturi, R.: Audio segmentation and speaker localization in meeting videos. In: 18th International Conference on Pattern Recognition, ICPR 2006, vol. 2, pp. 1150–1153 (2006)
19. Vinciarelli, A., Pantic, M., Heylen, D., Pelachaud, C., Poggi, I., D'Errico, F., Schröder, M.: Bridging the gap between social animal and unsocial machine: A survey of social signal processing. IEEE Transactions on Affective Computing (2011) (to appear)
20. Wells, G., Petty, R.: The e_ects of over head movements on persuasion. Basic and Applied Social Psychology 1(3), 219–230 (1980)

User Behaviour Captured by Mobile Phones

Wouter B. Teeuw, Johan Koolwaaij, and Arjan Peddemors

Novay, Capitool 15, 7521 PL Enschede, The Netherlands
{wouter.teeuw,johan.koolwaaij,arjan.peddemors}@novay.nl

Abstract. The i-Zone initiative proposes a new approach to urban mobility management by using the latest mobile ICT technologies. It is about mobile phones that measure and analyse user behaviour in order to influence travel behaviour. By providing feedback to the traveller (self monitoring), by information sharing, or by providing positive incentives to travellers by road authorities and other stakeholders, improved mobility in a city may be achieved. The information is targeted on individual travel behaviour, and thus allows a personalized approach to influence travel behaviour. This enables a shift from a focus on intelligent transport systems, with the emphasis on infrastructure and car-to-car systems, to a more human-centric approach based on ambient intelligence.

Keywords: mobile persuasion, mobility management, tracking and tracing, automatic behaviour analysis, influencing behaviour.

1 Introduction

The most common sensor used for observing the public domain is video surveillance, often applied for reasons of public safety. However, video is just one sensor like there are many sensors for many applications. The Sensor City initiative, e.g., implements a large-scale urban measuring network that will enable various applications for complex sensor systems to be developed for practical use like noise, pollution, or travel time prediction in public spaces [1]. Also, the combination of different sensors enhances results. With respect to face recognition, for example, Hulsebosch and Ebben show that the difficult problem of identification in (semi)public spaces can be reduced to a verification problem –with much more reliability– by taking other sensors, in particular mobile phones, into account [2]. An entirely new development is participatory or urban sensing, in the sense of people like you and me who are, equipped with today's mobile and web technology, observing the public space and share the results with everyone using social media.

This paper is about using mobile phones to measure, analyse, and eventually influence behaviour in public spaces. We use urban mobility as a (first) case. In our opinion, mobile phones are core components for future appliances anyhow, and for urban mobility management in particular. This paper is organised as follows. Section 2 explains the challenges in the domain of urban mobility and how mobile phones can be used to measure traffic flows. Section 3 describes the state of the art

R. Wichert, K. Van Laerhoven, J. Gelissen (Eds.): AmI 2011 Workshops, CCIS 277, pp. 81–90, 2012.
© Springer-Verlag Berlin Heidelberg 2012

with respect to influencing travel behaviour, with again a focus on the role of mobile phones. Section 4 describes the i-Zone project in which we implemented a pilot platform to measure and analyse travel behaviour, in order to influence it positively. In section 5 we present some preliminary results of analysing travel behaviour. Section 6 ends with our conclusions and further research issues.

2   Using Mobile Phones to Measure Urban Mobility

Managing urban mobility means dealing with conflicting interests: Visitors and employees want to enhance mobility while at the same time municipalities or road authorities want to reduce traffic to enhance accessibility and reduce pollution. This is a common challenge to all major cities in Europe. How to deal with these conflicting system and personal objectives? The challenge is to achieve system goals like reduced congestion, reduced air pollution or improved safety by influencing personal goals in terms of stimulating people to change their individual travelling behaviour. Changing urban mobility patterns basically means changing the behaviour of people, i.e., replacing the one habit by another (preferably more optimal) habit or motivating people to change. Therefore, a human-centred approach is needed to encourage different travel behaviour. This is exactly where personal, mobile devices and Ambient Intelligence fit in perfectly.

We observe that much research and development in 'intelligent transport systems (ITS)' focuses on efforts to add information and communications technology to transport infrastructure and vehicles. What Ambient Intelligence adds to this developments is the focus on people and their personal mobile devices rather than vehicles and in-car systems. The technology becomes invisible, which shifts the focus on the traveller. We claim Ambient Intelligence technology may help to achieve system goals like reduced congestion, reduced air pollution or improved safety by influencing personal goals in terms of stimulating people to change their individual travelling behaviour.

For other reasons, transportation is mentioned among the promising application domains for Ambient Intelligence technology as well, together with domains as smart homes or smart offices (workplaces) and healthcare [3]. These domains coincide the application domains of the 'Internet of Things', which refers to the pervasive presence of a variety of objects (or 'things') that are able to interact with each other and to cooperate to reach common goals [4]. For example, the domain of transportation is characterized by the emergence of advanced cars, trains and buses that become more and more instrumented with sensors and actuators. The same holds for the roads and/or rails themselves that send information to traffic control sites, which in turn monitor and influence transportation vehicles. Apart from the logistics and monitoring issues, applications focus on assisted driving (like collision avoidance), mobile ticketing and augmented maps.

Besides, in-car navigation systems as well as mobile phones of users are used to track vehicles. Measuring and recognizing behavior using mobile devices is an emerging research field. In general, dedicated monitoring infrastructures systems are used to acquire traffic flow information. They mainly use inductive loop detectors or video cameras. Herrera et al. [5] propose to use in-vehicle GPS-enabled mobile phones to get the same information: Their experiments include 100 vehicles driving around with GPS-enabled mobile phones for 8 h on a freeways. Results show that 2-3% penetration of cell phones in the driver population provides accurate information on the velocity of the traffic flow. Personal travel statistics for households are currently mainly gathered by diary surveys (writing down all trips). Compared with those self-report surveys, mobile phones might be more accurate. Experiments of Stopher et al. [6] show, e.g., that the average number of trips per person per day is significantly higher from GPS respondents than from dairy respondents. Yang et al. [7] present how accelerometer and GPS features may be used to recognize physical activity, in particular to classify a stationary, walking, running, cycling or in-vehicle mode. Reddy et al. [8] show that in this way accuracy levels up to 94% are reached (Nokia n95 phone). It is not possible, however, to distinguish between different types of motorized transport (bus, car, train). Reddy et al. propose to use in-situ experience sampling for these purposes. Also, they note the need for energy efficient classification methods. Nonetheless, mobile phones seem very suited to gather information on personal travel statistics.

3   A Personal Approach to Influence Travel Behaviour

Current measures to influence and manage urban mobility may range from parking bans or speed ramps to discourage car usage, to blocking off access roads entirely, e.g. during rush hours. Some measures depend on ICT, with the electronic toll collection and zones with congestion pricing as well-known examples. A disadvantage of restrictive measures is that they are basically involuntarily and inflexible. Therefore, they are not a sustainable solution. As soon as someone is given the opportunity to get round the banning order, one will certainly do. These measures may even force people to make a detour, only moving problems. Therefore, one should make use of rewards rather than restrictions.

An example are 'monetized' inducements for adopting particular travel practices like discounted tickets for using public transport at certain times, public transport price reductions due to bulk or annual purchase, or discounted rates for entrance to certain tourist and visitor attractions for those who arrive by train or bus. The clearest evidence of the impact of financial reward on travel behaviour is that of the initiative *Spitsmijden* in the Netherlands [9] where financial inducements have shown to reduce car travel at peak times.

These forms of incentives are not particularly new and have been in widespread use throughout Europe for some time. The evidence suggests that they can influence particular journeys for particular purposes, but it is less clear that they can be used to influence people away from routine car travel, such as commuter traffic. Forms of incentives that reward longer term behaviour such as loyalty bonuses are widespread in the retail sector but less widely applied in transport. Ambient Intelligence (AmI) technology and mobile devices might be used to learn long-term behaviour and change habits in an ambient way. Current AmI technology enables a personal advice to be based on the actual data of the transport systems. The ITRAVEL project [10], for example, offers a service platform for the connected traveller to assist in context-aware, personalized travel planning prior to and during an actual journey. Or the social mobile application Waze [11] provides free GPS navigation based on the live conditions on the road, measured by other Waze users.

Ambient Intelligence enables a personal travel advice, anticipating on what the system has learnt from the historical traffic situation and the personal travel behaviour and preferences. In recent years, there has been much interest using direct personalized techniques to provide individuals or households with information enabling them to reduce car use and/or increasing the use of more sustainable transport modes. Salim [12] introduces the concept of adaptive mobile mashup, which is a learning system that uses context-aware filtering to selectively present or visualize integrated information in order to reach a targeted behaviour. Froehlich et al. [13] researched the use of displays on mobile phones to give users feedback about sensed and self-reported transportation behaviour. Both examples use mobile devices that, according to Fogg [14], are the most important platform for changing human behavior. To change the behaviour of people, personal mobile devices are key.

4   Incentive Zone Case

We apply the above mentioned principles of personalized advice, incentives and communities to a specific geographical area in Enschede, The Netherlands, which we called an Incentive Zone (in short: i-Zone). The objective of i-Zone is 5% less traffic (measured in car kilometres in a specific area) during the rush hours. We want to achieve this system goal by influencing personal goals in terms of stimulating people to change their individual travelling behaviour.

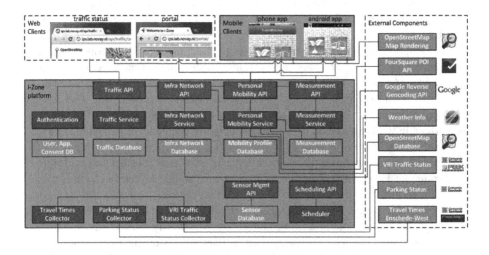

Fig. 1. Architecture of the i-Zone platform

Fig. 1 shows the architecture of the i-Zone platform. The idea of a platform approach means that there is a platform that gathers data about the status of the traffic network in the city as well as data on a personal level, aggregates and analyses this data and provides meaning full information toward applications that run on top of the platform. Currently, there is only one application called TravelWatcher (implemented as iPhone and Android app). We currently collect infrastructure data from in-pavement detectors about the number of cars that pass the (main) traffic lights (VRI Traffic), the available number of free parking lots in the urban parking garages, and travel times collected by an Automatic Number Plate Recognition system (ANPR). Besides, we use data from external sources, in particular map related data from Google and Open Street Map, places from Foursquare, and weather info from Buienradar.nl.

Most relevant for behaviour analysis, however, we collect data on the personal level. To collect individual information, as well as to distribute incentives that are triggered by the context and the individual behaviour of citizens, i-Zone uses IYOUIT concepts [15]. IYOUIT is mobile service to share personal experiences or context data with others while on the go [16]. An application (measure tool) has been implemented that reads the location (GPS), acceleration, and electronic compass sensors on the mobile phones of i-Zone participants, and automatically detects the trips people make. More detailed analysis of mobility data is performed on the i-Zone platform server. The measurement tool has currently been implemented for iPhone and Android smart phones.

In the i-Zone web portal, users can register themselves, and are presented with a wealth of personal mobility statistics, as described in the next section. Also, using a simple and transparent interface, users can decide which personal information they want to make available for which application. On a website, the current or expected traffic status is shown as well.

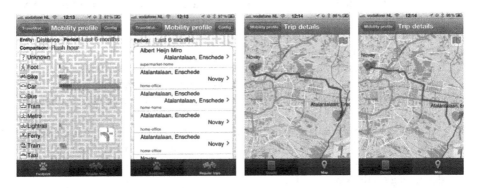

Fig. 2. Screenshots of the TravelWatcher mobile sensing application

Fig. 2 shows four screenshots of the mobile measurement application that has been developed. The application has been named TravelWatcher and records trips on a 24/7 basis, automatically recognizes modality choices, visited places, frequent routes and mobility footprint. It will show neat statistics on the personal balance between human powered transport (walking, cycling), fuel powered personal transport (car, motor) and public transport (bus, train, plane). Finally, situational dependencies are charted for their personal modality choices, and show the impact of rush hour, rain or fog, and events on the choices they make.

TravelWatcher provides a means for self-monitoring, one of the seven strategies that are commonly used in persuasive technology [17], which is already an incentive to change behaviour. Self-monitoring allows people to monitor their own mobility patterns and to inform them how they could modify their travel behaviour. A next step is to provide commercial incentives, like an employer offering an e-bike or a restaurant with a food offering to stimulate new ways of working an travelling; and to evaluate the effect on travel behaviour. For this reason, the European SUNSET project [18] has been developed, which will use i-Zone as a living lab. The community aspect is taken care of by creating groups of users (e.g. users belonging to an employer) and by introducing a gaming element (earning points by travel behaviour). These issues are currently under development.

5   Analysing Travel Behaviour

The data collected by mobile phones is combined with external (sensor) sources and analysed to provide enriched user data. We are currently able to automatically analyse the following travel behaviour:

- The detection of single-modality trips, and an end-to-end journey by concatenating consecutive single-modality trips. Trips are detected on the client (mobile phone) using location sensors (GPS, GSM, WiFi). Being present for at least five minutes at a certain location marks the end of a trip. Errors may occur due to, e.g., long waiting for a traffic light or in a traffic queue, inaccurate location information from the sensors, or switch back and forth between GSM masts. This is periodically corrected at the server side, e.g., concatenating trips into end-to-end journeys or removing 'ghost trips'.
- Automatic detection of personal places, those places frequently visited by the user (on an address level and name level, e.g., the name of a shop). Places are the start and end points of trips and automatically named by either the address (from map information) or a name (Foursquare places). It is possible to manually overwrite the names.
- Automatic classification of personal places: what is the user's home, office, school, etc. The time of day is used for these purposes: where you regularly sleeps is your home, where you are at office times is your work or school, depending on the kind of place, etc.
- Automatic detection of the modality used: is the user travelling by car, bike, train, etc. The algorithms mainly use speed and map information to automatically detect this information. As opposed to approaches using accelerometers, we can distinguish between types of motorized transport (car, bus, train) by using location dependent models (map information).

- Automatic analysis of regular trips: Identifying the frequent trips the user makes. Trips are identified by the start and end place and the mode of transport used.
- Accompany detection: automatic analysing whether people travel or stay together, as an indication of people carpooling, travelling together on a business trip, or people who could potentially do car sharing on specific days.

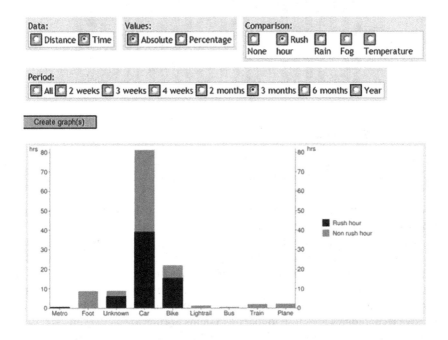

Fig. 3. Example of a personal mobility pattern

The pilot system is currently in a test phase with, at the moment, 40 users, who made more than 5000 trips with over 800 cities involved. The about 30.000 hours of location data gathered allows behaviour analysis on both an individual and an anonymous group level. For example, on a personal level one may analyse the modalities used in relationship to, e.g., the weather or rush hours (see Fig. 3). Identically, group modality statistic are possible. Other group analyses include, e.g., an analysis of all participants going to a specific place during a specific period.

Our system is a reference-implementation that is currently in a test phase, searching for its potential. The quality of the system is continuously improving. Users are able to manually correct erroneously recognized modalities or improve place classifications. Automatic modality detection is done in a batch process at night. Based on trips that are manually tagged before they are automatically labelled, we have an indication of the quality of our system. From the over 1000 manually tagged trips, 75.1% appears to be correctly classified. For the users in our pilot area Enschede 76.7% is correct (see Fig. 4). Currently, all trips are automatically classified. They can be manually corrected by users in case the modality is not correct. An experiment to compare automatic classification with a dairy survey is still to be planned.

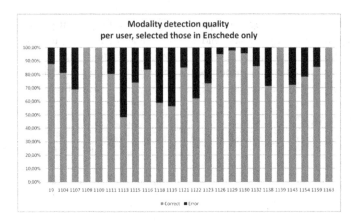

Fig. 4. Quality of modality detection for the Enschede users

6 Outlook and Conclusions

To our opinion, the research agenda for mobility should shift from intelligent transport systems, with a lot of emphasis on infrastructure and car-to-car systems, to a more human-centric approach. This fits the research agenda of ambient intelligence, in particular the ambient technology focusing on learning systems for personalization, adaptation and anticipation on behaviour. Mobile phones are important sensors and actuators for these purposes. Using mobile phones one may measure behaviour on both an individual, and a group level; as well as one may influence behaviour. For, persuasive technologies are close to mobile systems [14].

From our current experiences, we observe four main areas for further research. First, advances in the analysis of human behaviour by, e.g., the integration of many real-time sensors from personal devices and (road) infrastructures, detect modality transitions even better, and to estimate mobility consequences in terms of time, costs and emissions. Second, research on the role of mobiles in ambient environments. In our current system, the users are in control. Ambient Intelligence means the environments is aware of the presence of people and reacts on it. The environment may trace mobiles as well, e.g., based on Bluetooth, for which the technology exists (and is applied in traffic as well [19]). This allows additional behaviour analysis for users that do not want to install monitoring software. Third, power management for mobile devices needs research. For, using GPS to trace mobiles uses too much battery power. As long this issue is not solved by better batteries or energy harvesting itself, smart algorithms must 'solve' the problem by only track and trace if necessary, and using personal historic information to decide if detailed location measurements are really necessary for a regular commuter trip. And fourth, privacy is a research issue. We need to find the balance between empowering a user with all kind of information on the one hand, and the protection of personal data and the (implicit) influencing of behaviour on the other hand [20].

References

1. Sensor City project (in Dutch), http://www.sensorcity.nl/
2. Hulsebosch, R.J., Ebben, P.W.G.: Enhancing Face Recognition with Location Information. In: Proceedings of the Third International Conference on Availability, Reliability and Security ("ARES 2008 – The International Dependability Conference"), Barcelona, Spain, March 4-7 (2008)
3. Cook, D.J., Augusto, J.C., Jakkula, V.R.: Ambient intelligence: Technologies, applications, and opportunities. Pervasive and Mobile Computing 5, 277–298 (2009)
4. Atzori, L., Iera, A., Morabito, G.: The Internet of Things: A survey. Computer Networks 54(15), 2787–2805 (2010)
5. Herrera, J.C., Work, D.B., Herring, R., Ban, X., Jacobson, Q., Bayen, A.M.: Evaluation of traffic data obtained via GPS-enabled mobile phones: The Mobile Century field experiment. Transportation Research Part C: Emerging Technologies 18(4), 568–583 (2010)
6. Stopher, P., Clifford, E., Swann, N., Zhang, Y.: Evaluating voluntary travel behaviour change: Suggested guidelines and case studies. Transport Policy 16, 315–324 (2009)
7. Yang, J., Lu, H., Liu, Z., Boda, P.P.: Physical Activity Recognition with Mobile Phones: Challenges, Methods and Applications. In: Shao, L., et al. (eds.) Multimedia Interaction and Intelligent User Interfaces: Principles, Methods and Applications, pp. 185–213. Springer, London (2010)
8. Reddy, S., Mun, M., Burke, J., Estrin, D., Hansen, M., Srivastava, M.: Using mobile phones to determine transportation modes. ACM Transactions on Sensor Networks 6(2), Article 13 (2010)
9. Spitsmijden project. The effects of rewards in Spitsmijden 2: how can drivers be persuaded to avoid peak periods? Spitsmijden Group, The Hague (October 2009)
10. ITRAVEL project, http://www.i-travelproject.com/
11. WAZE, http://world.waze.com
12. Salim, F.D.: Towards Adaptive Mobile Mashups: Opportunities for Designing Effective Persuasive Technology on the Road. In: Proc. IEEE 24th International Conference on Advanced Information Networking and Applications Workshops, Perth, Australia, April 20-23, pp. 7–11 (2010)
13. Froehlich, J., Dillahunt, T., Klasnja, P., Mankoff, J., Consolvo, S., Harrison, B., Landay, J.A.: UbiGreen: Investigating a Mobile Tool for Tracking and Supporting Green Transportation Habits. In: Proc. of the 27th International Conference on Human Factors in Computing Systems (CHI 2009), Boston, MA, April 04-09, pp. 1043–1052 (2009)
14. Fogg, B.J.: The future of persuasion is mobile. In: Fogg, B.J., Eckles, D. (eds.) Mobile Persuasion: 20 Perspectives on the Future of Behaviour Change. Persuasive Technology Lab, Stanford University, Stanford, CA (2007)
15. Koolwaaij, J., Wibbels, M., Böhm, S., Luther, M.: Living Virtual History: A mobile Game around the World. The Visual Computer (Special Issue on Serious Games and Virtual Worlds) 25(12) (2009)
16. Boehm, S., Koolwaaij, J., Luther, M., Souville, B., Wagner, M., Wibbels, M.: Introducing IYOUIT. In: Sheth, A., Staab, S., Dean, M., Paolucci, M., Maynard, D., Finin, T., Thirunarayan, K. (eds.) ISWC 2008. LNCS, vol. 5318, pp. 804–817. Springer, Heidelberg (2008)

17. Fogg, B.J.: Persuasive technology: Using computers to change what we think and do. Morgan Kaufmans Publishers, San Francisco (2003)
18. SUNSET project, http://www.sunset-project.eu/
19. http://www.dutchdailynews.com/bluetooth-to-measure-dutch-traffic-jams/
20. van 't Hof, C., van Est, R., Daemen, F.: Check in/check out: The public space as an Internet of Things. Rathenau Institute/NAi Publishers, Rotterdam (2011)

Kinect Sensing of Shopping Related Actions

Mirela Popa[1,2], Alper Kemal Koc[1,2], Leon J.M. Rothkrantz[1,3],
Caifeng Shan[2], and Pascal Wiggers[1]

[1] Man-Machine Interaction group, Department of Mediamatics,
Delft University of Technology, Mekelweg 4, 2628 CD, Delft, The Netherlands
[2] Video and Image Processing Department, Philips Research, HTC 36,
5656 AE, Eindhoven, The Netherlands
[3] Sensor Technology, SEWACO Department, Netherlands Defence Academy,
Nieuwe Diep 8, 1781 AC, Den Helder, The Netherlands
{m.c.popa,l.j.m.rothkrantz,p.wiggers}@tudelft.nl,
{caifeng.shan}@philips.com

Abstract. Surveillance systems in shopping malls or supermarkets are usually used for detecting abnormal behavior. We used the distributed video cameras system to design digital shopping assistants which assess the behavior of customers while shopping, detect when they need assistance, and offer their support in case there is a selling opportunity. In this paper we propose a system for analyzing human behavior patterns related to products interaction, such as browse through a set of products, examine, pick products, try on, interact with the shopping cart, and look for support by waiving one hand. We used the Kinect sensor to detect the silhouettes of people and extracted discriminative features for basic action detection. Next we analyzed different classification methods, statistical and also spatio-temporal ones, which capture relations between frames, features, and basic actions. By employing feature level fusion of appearance and movement information we obtained an accuracy of 80% for the mentioned six basic actions.

Keywords: Shopping Behavior, Action Recognition, Surveillance, Kinect.

1 Introduction

In the last decade a lot of effort has been devoted to developing methods for automatic human behavior recognition, having a great potential in enhancing human-computer interaction, affective computing, and social signal processing. Especially in the context of ambient intelligence, multimodal analysis of behavior opens up new venues of applications such as behavioral biometrics, automated care for the elderly or improved customer assistance in the marketing domain.

For assisting customers, usually human shop assistants are available, but given peak hours they are too expensive to meet the whole demand. A supporting alternative can be provided by developing digital shop assistants. By using the available surveillance systems of video cameras in shops [1], we aim at assessing customers shopping behavior and detecting when there is a need for support or a

R. Wichert, K. Van Laerhoven, J. Gelissen (Eds.): AmI 2011 Workshops, CCIS 277, pp. 91–100, 2012.
© Springer-Verlag Berlin Heidelberg 2012

selling opportunity. The semantic interpretation of the shopping behavior is based on the way of walking (trajectory analysis) and the recognition of customer-product interaction related actions. Furthermore given a representation of the shopping area into Regions of Interest (ROI) such as products, passing, pay desk, or resting areas, detecting basic actions in a specific ROI contributes to the semantic modeling of uncertainty. Interaction of customers with the environment or between each other is recorded using different sensors (video cameras, Kinect sensor). Next, data analysis is performed by extracting different types of information, trajectory and also actions related features. Automatic recognition of basic actions represents the first step towards developing a complex system designated at shopping behavior understanding, given that every behavior is composed of basic actions. In this work we considered the following actions: pick a product, examine it, browse through a set of products, try a product to see how it fits, wave for assistance and interact with the shopping basket/cart. The complexity of the analyzed problem resides in modeling human shopping behavior, due to its diversity among different individuals. But we observed that in a specific ROI, only a limited number of basic actions are being displayed. We designed an automatic system for the assessment of shopping behavior in a hierarchical manner, by employing different levels of abstraction, from low sensory level up to the reasoning level about customers' behavior. The architecture of the proposed system is presented in Fig. 1.

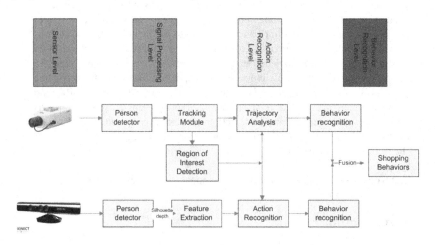

Fig. 1. System Architecture

Assessment of shopping behavior based on trajectory analysis is presented in details in [1], the discrimination between customers' buying and non-buying events is discussed in [2], while the scope of this paper consists in researching the most suitable methods towards basic actions detection. We used the Kinect Sensor developed by Microsoft [3], for recordings, due to its advantages. Regarding characteristic features for action recognition we investigated both appearance and movement features and we proposed fusing them in order to benefit of the most complete information. Different classification methods are tested for finding the most suitable one for our problem. By considering a segmentation of action data into constant size segments and using a sliding-window approach, we investigated the suitability of using our system in real-time conditions. The outline of the paper is as follows. In the next section related work is reported, then the action recognition module is presented in details, followed by the description of the data acquisition process. Next, the discussion of the experimental results is provided and finally we formulate our conclusions and give directions for future work.

2   Related Work

Action recognition based on body pose estimation can be applied in many fields such as: "surveillance, medical studies and rehabilitation, robotics, video indexing, and animation for film and games" [4]. There are two main approaches used for analyzing human motions and actions: model-based and appearance-based.

Model-based approaches employ a kinematics model for representing body parts relations with respect to each body action. In [5] Akita et al. decomposed the human body into six parts: head, torso, arms, and legs, and built a cone model with the six segments corresponding to counterparts in stick images. This type of approaches are very dependent on the reliability of body parts detection and tracking. A method with a remarkable computational performance for human body pose estimation was proposed in [6] by Shotton et al., by employing the Kinect Sensor.

Appearance-based methods build a mapping from a set of image features to an action class, without explicitly representing the kinematics of human body. A good example is template matching, which is widely used as an appearance-based action recognition algorithm. Bobick et al. introduced in [7] temporal templates constructed from Motion-Energy Images (MEI) and Motion-History Images (MHI), for the recognition of human movements. Silhouette-based features were successfully applied for action recognition, by considering either distances to the local maxima points of the silhouette contour [8], or edge features extracted from the contour of the silhouette image [9]. In [10] another method based on silhouettes is introduced for detecting the interaction of people with an object. They can detect if someone has something in his/her hand, or just left it somewhere.

It is also important which method is used for the classification task. Classification methods can be divided into two categories, one is based on the stochastic model such as Hidden Markov Models (HMMs) [11], [12], and [13] while the other one is based on a statistical model such as Support Vector Machines [14] and [15], Nearest Neighbor Classifier (NNC) [16], or Linear Discriminant Analysis [17]. Those examples show that there could be different choices for the classification method and they are all proved to be successful with a good feature set.

In [14], Schindler et al. address the problem of finding the number of frames required to perform an action or to represent an action. The proposed sequences of actions contain a number of frames from 1 to 10 and it is proven that they lead to the same performance as processing the whole video sequence.

Analyzing the presented works on action recognition provided us with an overview of the problems existing in this field and also with potential solutions. We present next our approach towards basic action detection in the shopping context.

3   Action Recognition Module

An important problem for action recognition is to find the appropriate image representation in order to extract meaningful features for action recognition. The role of image segmentation is to get such an image representation in which the salient object or person is given prominence. In video with static background, the silhouette is a good image representation, which can be obtained by background subtraction; still in many cases this option is not feasible or is not optimum due to varying lighting conditions. Therefore by employing the Kinect sensor developed by Microsoft, we are able to obtain silhouette data of each person in the scene, independent of the background or the ambient light conditions, given that the senor has been placed at a distance of at least 1 meter away from the person(s). Kinect sensor has an RGB camera and two IR cameras which enable extracting the depth map of the scene and contribute to improving the detection rate.

Next, given silhouette information, we aim at investigating the most appropriate feature descriptors for action recognition. Moment invariants seem a good approach as they are compact in description, are capable of selecting different levels of detail [18], and represent a global shape descriptor. We start from first order geometric moments, m_{10} and m_{01}, or x and y axis projections (1), computed for the image intensity function f(x, y), which in our case is a binary function, having values of 1 for the pixels belonging to the person.

$$m_{pq} = \sum_I \sum x^p y^q f(x, y), \; m_{10} = \sum_I \sum x f(x, y), \; m_{01} = \sum_I \sum y f(x, y) \qquad (1)$$

An example of a silhouette image and the corresponding projections is presented in Fig. 2.

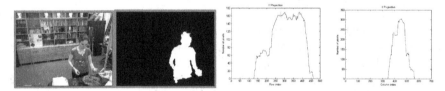

Fig. 2. (a) Original image. (b) Silhouette image. (c) Y projection. (d) X projection.

Given that the position of the person in the image frame can be changing over time, we obtain invariant features under translation, by computing central moments (2) with respect to the silhouette image centroid $(\overline{x}, \overline{y})$.

$$\overline{x} = \frac{m_{10}}{m_{00}}, \quad \overline{y} = \frac{m_{01}}{m_{00}}, \quad \mu_{pq} = \sum_{I}\sum(x-\overline{x})^p(y-\overline{y})^q f(x,y) \tag{2}$$

Next we investigated different feature sets, by considering several orders of central moments. The optimum feature set for our problem, given in (3), contains statistical measures such as the mean, the variance, the standard deviation, the skewness, and the index for peak values computed for both x and y projections. The third order central moment (μ_{30}, μ_{03}), or the skewness, characterizing the degree of asymmetry of a distribution around its mean, can be interpreted in our case as an indicator of a body limb being apart from the rest of the body.

$$featV = [mean_x, var_x, \sqrt{\frac{1}{n-1}\mu_{20}}, skew_x, \max_{i=1}^{N}(x_i-\overline{x}), mean_y, var_y, \sqrt{\frac{1}{m-1}\mu_{02}}, skew_y, \max_{j=1}^{M}(y_j-\overline{y})]$$

$$skew_x = \frac{\frac{1}{n}\sum_{i=1}^{n}(x_i-\overline{x})^3}{\left(\sqrt{\frac{1}{n}\sum_{i=1}^{n}(x_i-\overline{x})^2}\right)^3}, skew_y = \frac{\frac{1}{m}\sum_{j=1}^{m}(y_j-\overline{y})^3}{\left(\sqrt{\frac{1}{m}\sum_{j=1}^{m}(y_j-\overline{y})^2}\right)^3} \tag{3}$$

Besides spatial patterns described by the featV feature set and computed on a frame basis, we also compute motion related features by employing frame differencing between two consecutive silhouette images (see an example in Fig. 3), using the intensity difference function: $m_i(x,y) = f_i(x,y)-f_{i-1}(x,y)$, i=2,n. The resulting motion image matrix has values in the (-1, 0, 1) set. Pixels with value 0 represent the constant human area, without movement, the -1 valued pixels represent the area from where the movement originated, while the pixels with value 1 are depicting the regions to which the person moved to. The extracted motion feature vector featV' is obtained by applying eq. (1), (2), and (3) to the motion image.

Fig. 3. (a) Silhouette frame image i (b) Silhouette frame image i+1. (c) Frame differencing

Besides silhouettes, depth information is also valuable as it contains information about the distances between the body and the limbs and the distance relative to the sensor. New feature sets are extracted from depth data in the same manner as for silhouettes, with the distinction that in the previous equations (1),(2), and (3) the binary function f(x, y) is replaced by a distance function d(x, y) representing the distance of each pixel from the Kinect sensor (see Fig. 4).

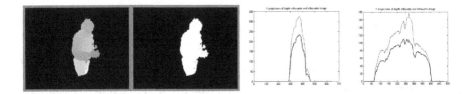

Fig. 4. (a) Silhouette frame image i. (b) Silhouette frame image i+1. (c) Depth based frame differencing on x axis. (d) Depth based frame differencing on y axis.

Finally, as appearance and movement features are complimentary, we obtain new feature sets by fusing the information coming from the two sources, both for silhouettes and depth information.

The next step, after extracting relevant feature characteristics, consists of applying different pattern recognition methods in order to discriminate between the different action classes. For the classification task we used some of the most commonly employed classifiers in literature, both statistical ones: SVM, K-NN, LDC and also stochastic ones as, namely HMMs. Due to their properties, such as incorporating dynamics of motion features during time and ability to capture temporal correlations, we use HMMs both at the action recognition level as well as for detecting sequences of actions. In the following section we present our data collection process, the performed experiments and the analysis of results.

4   Experiments

4.1   Data Acquisition

In order to define shopping behavioral models, we made observations of people during shopping in supermarkets, retail and clothes shops. From our observations we noticed the most common shopping scenarios which can be furthermore decomposed into basic shopping actions. We asked five students and researchers to play these scenarios in a controlled environment; still we gave them the freedom to show individual behavior. Each considered scenario (looking for a favorite item, examine the differences between similar products, get the attention of the shop assistant, and finally purchase the desired products) is composed of basic actions. In the definition and validation process of the proposed set of basic actions, not only the researchers but also experts in the field have been involved. In the table below an explanation and an example for each considered basic action is provided. It needs to be mentioned that we considered different view angles and also single and duo-shopper cases.

Table 1. Basic shopping actions description

Actions	Description	Key Pose(s) – single shopper	Key Pose(s) – duo shopper
Browsing	The person goes through the products on the table using the hands.		
Examining	The person holds one or more products in her/his hand, looking at them more closely.		
Trying on	The person is putting on a product, like a jacket, scarf, vest, or sun glasses etc.		
Picking	The person leans to the table, picks a product, and takes the hand back.		
Looking for help (waving one hand)	Having one or two arms in the air, the person waves at some direction, trying to get the attention of an assistant.		
Shopping Cart Interaction	The person is holding the shopping cart, drives it in shop (pushes or pulls it) and interacts with it.		

4.2   Experimental Results

For testing the proposed approach towards basic actions recognition, we used a 5-fold cross validation method and the error rates of the employed classifiers for each considered feature set are presented in Table 2. As introduced in Section 4.1 we considered 6 basic shopping actions, and the total number of samples was 94.

Appearance features extracted from silhouette data (1) seem to be performing quite good achieving an accuracy of 77,50%, better than the movement related features (2). By employing feature level fusion of both types of information, appearance and movement, we obtain an improvement in accuracy of 2,5% using the Linear Bayes Normal classifier.

Table 2. Error rates of different classifiers using the proposed feature sets

feature set	SVC	LDC	K-NN
Silhouette projections(1)	24,26	22,39	23,71
Silhouette projection differencing (2)	33,33	33,83	34,33
Fusion of (1) and (2)	23,48	**20,04**	22,56
Depth projections (3)	28,63	27,96	29,63
Depth frame differencing (4)	27,63	26,88	28,71
Fusion of (3) and (4)	26,83	24,33	25,60

Regarding depth related feature sets, the fusion of appearance and movement information proved to be beneficial, leading to the best result of 75% accuracy, still they were not performing better than the silhouette features, showing that the pose information was more discriminative than the distance to the sensor.

For a better understanding of the results, not only in terms of performance but also regarding the discriminative power of the proposed features for each particular action, we also include the confusion matrix for the best performing classifier (see Table 3).

Table 3. Confusion matrix of LDC classifier for the silhouete fusion feature set

%	Browse	Examine	Pick	Try-on	Wave	Shopp. cart
Brow.	**84,31**	7,84	5,88	0	0	1,96
Exam.	4,65	**75,58**	8,13	8,13	1,16	2,32
Pick	6,25	6,25	**75**	12,50	0	0
Try on	0	8,82	0	**82,35**	8,82	0
Wave	0	0	12,50	12,50	**75**	0
Shopp. cart	0	0	0	0	0	**100,00**

From the table above we can notice that some actions are more difficult to be classified, being easily confused with other ones, for example 'browsing' with 'examining' and 'picking', as they contain similar hand movements, or 'waving' which is also similar with 'try on' and 'picking' actions.

Next we investigated the real-time recognition of basic actions, when no indication is provided regarding the starting or ending time of one action. Using a sliding window of 0.5s (10 frames) and an overlap of 0.25s we trained prototypes for each action class. The features extracted for each segment were similar to the ones presented in Section 3, with the difference that instead of considering the total number of frames of one action, we computed them for each 10 consecutive frames. Using the best performing classifier (LDC), we tested each segment against all trained action prototypes and the one with the highest probability was selected as the segment label. Finally the accuracy was computed by dividing the ratio of correctly classified action segments over the total number of segments and we obtained an average of 75%. This experiment proved that by applying a sliding window approach, the accuracy remains high, while the continuous recognition of actions is achieved.

5   Conclusions and Future Work

In this paper we proposed an automatic system for assessing customers' shopping behavior based on action recognition. We made recordings, using the Kinect sensor, which enabled extraction of people silhouettes under different lighting conditions. Feature level fusion of appearance and movement information proved to be beneficial, achieving an average accuracy of 80% on six basic actions. By applying a sliding window of 0.5s and training prototypes for each considered action, we were able to recognize basic actions in continuous scenarios.

There are still many ways in which the proposed system can be improved. Currently we only tested our system on pre-defined scenarios in a controlled environment on a limited number of samples. Next, we plan to use interest-points models and to assess the performance of our system on real-life recordings of customers in a supermarket.

Acknowledgments. This work was supported by the Netherlands Organization for Scientific Research (NWO) under Grant 018.003.017 and the Visual Context Modeling (ViCoMo) project.

References

1. Popa, M.C., Rothkrantz, L.J.M., Yang, Z., Wiggers, P., Braspenning, R., Shan, C.: Analysis of Shopping Behavior based on Surveillance System. In: 2010 IEEE Int. Conf. on Systems, Man, and Cybernetics (SMC 2010), Istanbul, Turkey (2010)
2. Popa, M.C., Gritti, T., Rothkrantz, L.J.M., Shan, C., Wiggers, P.: Detecting Customers' Buying Events on a Real-Life Database. In: Real, P., Diaz-Pernil, D., Molina-Abril, H., Berciano, A., Kropatsch, W. (eds.) CAIP 2011, Part I. LNCS, vol. 6854, pp. 17–25. Springer, Heidelberg (2011)
3. Microsoft Corp. Redmond WA. Kinect for Xbox 360
4. Moeslund, T.B., Hilton, A., Kruger, V.: A Survey of Advances in Vision-based Human Motion Capture and Analysis. Computer Vision and Image Understanding (2006)
5. Akita, K.: Image sequence analysis of real world human motion. Pattern Recognition 17(1), 73–83 (1984)
6. Shotton, J., Fitzgibbon, A., Cook, M., Sharp, T., Finocchio, M., Moore, R., Kipman, A., Blake, A.: Real-Time Human Pose Recognition in Parts from Single Depth Images. In: CVPR (2011)
7. Bobick, A.F., Davis, J.W.: The recognition of human movement using temporal templates. IEEE Trans. PAMI (2001)
8. Ekinci, M., Gedikli, E.: Silhouette Based Human Motion Detection and Analysis for Real-Time Automated Video Surveillance. Turkish Journal of Electrical Engineering and Computer Sciences 13(2), 199–230 (2005)
9. Jiang, H., Drew, M.S., Li, Z.-N.: Action Detection in Cluttered Video with Successive Convex Matching. IEEE Transactions on Circuits and Systems for Video Technology 20(1) (2010)
10. Haritaoglu, I., Cutler, R., Harwood, D., Davis, L.S.: Detection of People Carrying Objects Using Silhouettes. In: International Conference on Computer Vision, Corfu, Greece (1999)

11. Moore, D.J., Essa, I.A., Hayes, M.H.: Exploiting Human Actions and Object Context for Recognition Tasks. In: IEEE International Conference on Computer Vision, Corfu, Greece (1999)
12. Brand, M., Oliver, N., Pentland, A.: Coupled Hidden Markov Models for Complex Action Recognition. In: Proceedings of IEEE Computer Vision and Pattern Recognition (1996)
13. Yamato, J., Ohya, J., Ishii, K.: Recognizing Human Action in Time-Sequential Images using Hidden Markov Model. In: Proceedings of IEEE Conference on Computer Vision and Pattern Recognition, pp. 379–385 (1992)
14. Schindler, K., Van Gool, L.: Action Snippets: How Many Frames Does Human Action Recognition Require? In: IEEE Computer Society Conference on Computer Vision (2007)
15. Shüldt, C., Laptev, I., Caputo, B.: Recognizing Human Actions: A Local SVM Approach. In: Proceedings of the 17th International Conference on Pattern Recognition (2004)
16. Gorelick, L., Blank, M., Shechtman, E., Irani, M., Basri, R.: Actions as Space-Time Shapes. IEEE Transactions on Pattern Analysis and Machine Intelligence 29(12) (2007)
17. Weinland, D., Ronfard, R., Boyer, E.: Free Viewpoint Action Recognition using Motion History Volumes. Computer Vision Image Understanding 104(2), 249–257 (2006)
18. Prismall, S.P.: Object reconstruction by moments extended to moving sequences, PhD thesis, Department Electronic and Computer Science, University of Southampton (2005)

A Feature Set Evaluation for Activity Recognition with Body-Worn Inertial Sensors

Syed Agha Muhammad[1], Bernd Niklas Klein[2],
Kristof Van Laerhoven[1], and Klaus David[2]

[1] TU Darmstadt, Darmstadt, Germany
{muhammad,kristof}@ess.tu-darmstadt.de
[2] University of Kassel, Kassel, Germany
{niklas.klein,klaus.david}@comtec.eecs.uni-kassel.de

Abstract. The automatic and unobtrusive identification of user activities is a challenging goal in human behavior analysis. The physical activity that a user exhibits can be used as contextual data, which can inform applications that reside in public spaces. In this paper, we focus on wearable inertial sensors to recognize physical activities. Feature set evaluation for 5 typical activities is performed by measuring accuracy for combinations of 6 often-used features on a set of 11 well-known classifiers. To verify significance of this analysis, a t-test evaluation was performed for every combination of these feature subsets. We identify an easy-to-compute feature set, which has given us significant results and at the same time utilizes a minimum of resources.

1 Introduction

Physical activity can be defined as "any bodily moment produced by skeletal muscles that result in energy expenditure" [1]. For decades, activity recognition has been a topic of fundamental interest for practitioners and scientists. The need to know how humans behave and act in different situations and contexts has been suggested to be of use for doctors, psychologists and good health professionals [12]. Activity recognition systems could play an important role in ubiquitous computing scenarios. Providing services to the users based on their location or activity is an active research area. A well-designed system in a public space benefits from an understanding of its users' states and their environment.

In addition to the context aware systems, activity recognition systems found their relevance in the field of health-care related applications [14]. In principle, activity recognition can be used for social benefit, especially in human-centric applications such as elderlycare and health-care. Activity recognition systems also can assist people to stay physically fit and maintain their health by designing assessment tools [13].

In this paper, we focus on the feature set evaluation on inertial data for such activity recognition. Different feature sets are created of the time domain

R. Wichert, K. Van Laerhoven, J. Gelissen (Eds.): AmI 2011 Workshops, CCIS 277, pp. 101–109, 2012.
© Springer-Verlag Berlin Heidelberg 2012

features. In a first evaluation, they are used with popular machine learning algorithms to find their impact on accuracy. Normally, the importance of features depends upon the activity to be detected. For activities such as running, walking, climbing, descending and related gait, frequency information from 3-axis accelerometer is important. Different feature subsets are evaluated to find their accuracy and significance. We focus on easy-to-compute feature sets, which utilise minimal resources and produce results which are acceptable in terms of accuracy. At the end, we evaluate the results with a two-tailed t-test to find the significance of the feature subsets.

The remaining part of the paper is organised as follows: In Section 2, we discus the related work. In Section 3, we discus the experimental setup and methodology, which includes hardware devices, number of users, number of tests, extracted features, and classification classifiers used. In Section 4, evaluation results and the accuracies of the feature sets are discussed. We introduce a new feature "Meantilt", which was included into the feature sets, and focus on finding suitable features for activity recognition, which would provide us the highest accuracy results. We investigate also whether some features have a prominent role or certain features are negligible for activity recognition. In Section 5, two-tailed t-test is discussed to find out whether the differences between the recognition results using all the features and with certain features removed are significant. In Section 6, the main conclusions of this paper are summed up.

2   Related Work

Human activity recognition is an important field and this fact has been acknowledged by the rich content of literature available in this area [2],[3],[4],[5],[6],[9],[7], [11]. Activities such as walking, standing, sitting, climbing stairs and descending stairs naturally impart themselves to recognition using acceleration sensors, since these activities are clearly defined by the motion and relative positions of the body parts. Small and cheap sensors can be easily integrated into accessories such in garments or mobile phones to recognize these activities as described in [2], [3], and [4].

In the past, some research has focused on feature selection in the field of activity recognition. The authors of [15] have a combination of discriminative and generative classifiers. With eight different sensors, 651 different features were extracted. The authors have used AdaBoost to automatically select the best features and to learn an ensemble of static classifiers to recognize different activities. Second, the classification margins from the static classifiers were used to compute the posterior probabilities, which are then used as inputs into HMM models to capture the temporal regularities and smoothness of activities.

Forward-Backward sequential search methods for feature selection has been suggested by [16], [17]. In [16] features such as mean, standard deviation, correlation (x, y axes), mean crossing, as well as heart rate mean were tested with forward-backward search, which is a well-known feature selection algorithm. With this procedure, a subset of best (giving the best classification result) features can be determined for the final analysis. Later, a multilayer perception model and KNN were applied to classify the activity.

The authors of [9] propose to use a simple measure of cluster precision to evaluate the best features for discriminative activities. It shows, how the selection of different features can improve the recognition rates. Fast Fourier Transform (FFT) features had the highest cluster precision, with different components and window lengths required for different activities. The authors also conclude that variance has consistently high precision values acceleration data with most of the activities.

3   Experimental Setup and Methodology

This section presents the experimental setup, the feature extraction methods and the classifiers chain used in this paper.

3.1   Experimental Setup

Sun SPOT wireless sensor nodes [10] were used to perform the experiments discussed in this paper. After several experiments, we found that the position which suits our set of activities the best was the thigh. We performed ten experiments on six test subjects. Four out of six subjects participated twice in the test. The test data was taken for 350 minutes with each test covering an interval of 35 minutes. Each subject was requested to carry the Sun SPOT in the trousers' pocket and to perform the movements, which are sitting, standing, walking, climbing stairs, and descending stairs. Subjects were told to perform the sequence of activities but not specifically how to do them. The movements were annotated using the Nokia N800 tablet. This provided the annotation of the movements, which will be used as class information for the training and testing the classifiers. The recorded data and annotations were synchronized afterwords.

3.2   Feature Extraction

In order to detect activity information using classification algorithms, the raw data must be pre-processed to extract the more useful information. This process is called feature extraction. Popular computed time-domain features used in activity recognition include mean [5][6][7], variance or standard deviation [5][6], energy [5][6][7], entropy [5], and correlation between axes. In most of the cases, energy and entropy are calculated using the frequency domain [6] [7] [13].

In frequency domain features, first we have to transform the window of signal data into the frequency domain using the fourier transform. Normally, the output of FFT gives us the set of coefficients [6] which represents the distribution of the signal energy and amplitude of the frequency component of the signal. However, FFT requires multiple components to discriminate different activities. Hence it will increase computation and is not suitable for real time applications. As the time domain features can be easily extracted in real time, they are more popular in many practical acceleration activity recognition systems [15].

The used features include mean, variance and standard deviation of the acceleration data. We have also included energy and entropy of the FFT. All combinations of possible feature subsets were used for evaluation. Apart from the above mentioned features, we have introduced another feature to our feature set, called Meantilt [1] along axes. It was calculated as shown in equation 1.

$$Meantilt_j = \sqrt{\left(\sum_{i=j}^{j+W} x_i\right)^2 + \left(\sum_{i=j}^{j+W} y_i\right)^2 + \left(\sum_{i=j}^{j+W} z_i\right)^2 /W} \qquad (1)$$

Where x, y and z represents the tilt along the respective axis, W stands for window length. Similarly, j indicates the window overlapping percentage, which is 50% for the window length of 32. Experiments have shown that our introduced features has produced better results, and at the same time it is easy to calculate.

Features were extracted from inertial data using a sliding window approach with a window size of 32 with 16 overlapping between the consecutive windows. Window overlapping with 50% have shown success in previous works [6][7][11]. At the sampling rate of 32Hz, each window represents data for 1 second. After labeled data was acquired, the features were extracted, to which the classification algorithms were applied.

3.3   Classification Chain

We have used the wide range of classification algorithms available in the Weka Toolkit[2]. The base-level classifiers are decision tree (DT), support vector machine (SVM) or sequential minimal optimization (SMO) in weka toolkit, K-nearest neighbours (KNN), and naive bayes (NB). So-called meta-level classifiers use bagging, boosting, and voting on the top of these classifiers. The classification was carried out using 10 fold cross validation. Figure 1 shows the data flow cycle of the complete process, with all features and classifiers.

4   Evaluation of the Feature Sets

Table 1 shows the accuracy results when certain features were removed from the full set of feature (S10), for all classifiers and feature sets [3]. Meta-level classifiers have the better overall accuracy compared to base-level classifiers, but they tend to be slower.

---

[1] for the detailed discussion of tilt calculation from accelerometers please visit, http://www.sunspotworld.com/docs/AppNotes/AccelerometerAppNote.pdf, last visited at 28 July 2011.

[2] http://www.cs.waikato.ac.nz/ml/weka/, last visited at 27th July 2011.

[3] S1= all features; S2= mean, standard deviation, energy, and entropy; S3= mean, standard deviation, variance, and entropy; S4= mean, energy, and entropy; S5= mean, standard deviation, variance; S6= mean, standard deviation, and entropy; S7= mean, and variance; S8= mean, and energy; S9= mean, standard deviation, variance and Meantilt; S10= all features and Meantilt.

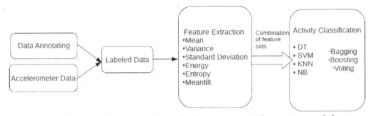

Fig. 1. Overview of how data was classified using a wide variety of feature sets and classifiers

Table 1. Comparison between the different feature sets, denoted by S1,..., S10

Algorithm	S1	S2	S3	S4	**S5**	S6	S7	S8	**S9**	**S10**
J48(DT)	83.28	84.27	84.75	82.5	**82.05**	82.73	81.71	81.01	**84.59**	**84.94**
Naive Bayes(NB)	80.62	80.44	78.80	81.22	**77.42**	79.48	78.42	79.67	**82.95**	**83.28**
SVM	81.90	84.46	67.06	77.26	**69.76**	83.45	64.54	63.46	**83.28**	**84.03**
Bagging(DT)	85.54	84.83	85.31	83.22	**82.76**	83.45	81.54	80.95	**85.42**	**85.98**
Bagging(KNN)	80.06	79.35	80.58	77.50	**78.05**	77.09	75.64	73.48	**80.06**	**83.77**
Bagging(SVM)	78.61	77.42	69.98	77.26	**69.77**	75.09	64.91	63.50	**78.61**	**84.06**
Boosting(DT)	84.18	82.98	83.40	81.74	**80.38**	80.58	78.55	77.74	**84.18**	**85.33**
Boosting(KNN)	80.0	79.29	80.45	77.44	**77.96**	77.02	74.57	74.36	**80.0**	**83.65**
Boosting(SVM)	78.61	77.75	69.61	77.26	**65.44**	75.95	66.5	63.70	**78.61**	**84.03**
Voting(KNN&SVM)	80.0	79.29	80.45	77.44	**77.96**	77.02	75.51	73.47	**80.0**	**83.65**
Voting(DT&KNN)	80.71	80.05	80.64	78.09	**78.1**	77.56	67.56	73.84	**80.71**	**83.35**

For base-level classifiers, DT has the best recognition accuracy between 81.01 % and 84.94%. For meta-level classifiers, bagging with DT has achieved the best recognition accuracy, between 80.95% and 85.98%. Boosting with DT has achieved accuracies between 77.74% and 85.33%.

The results acquired using **S10, S1, S2, S3** and **S9** have the best overall results. The elimination of one and two feature **(S1, S2, and S3)** does not affect the overall results. The elimination of three features (S4, S5 and S6) results in overall decline of the algorithm accuracy. Entropy and energy are derived from the FFT domain, in cases where they are eliminated simultaneously, the performances of certain algorithms have declined. They are typically useful features for certain activities. For instance if the user is climbing stairs, the mean and standard deviation will lie in the same region as descending stairs, but energy will change which will help to recognize the activity. Similarly, eliminating variance and standard deviation has also produced weaker overall results. These features help to differentiate between daily activities. With the elimination of two features, there is a decline of overall 2% in the performance of every algorithm. The results overall are still acceptable, but the performance of some algorithms such as SVM has drastically gone down. When we eliminated four features S7, and S8, the performances of the algorithms have degraded further. It results in the lowest accuracies, but consumes minimum resources, resulting from the fact that all the accuracies are calculated using two features.

S10 has the best accuracy results, but if we compare the results produced using **S9**, they do not have a large difference. The differences between the two are hardly more than 1%, which might be insignificant. The amount of resources used for **S10** will be higher. By including Meantilt as a feature, the accuracy reaches the same range as **S10**, but it is easy to calculate and consumes minimal resources. It has improved the accuracy of classifiers. In terms of easy-to-compute features, **S9** and **S5** have acceptable results and at the same time consume minimum resources. By skimming the results acquired using these subsets, one will analyze that **S9** has an accuracy improvement of at least 2% for every classifier and in some cases even more. For bagging with SVM, there is an accuracy improvement of more than 8%. Similarly for NB, there is the accuracy improvement of more than 5% between the two sets, but the biggest difference was observed for SVM as a base-level classifier and boosting with SVM, which have the improvement of 13%.

We thus prefer **S9** over the other feature sets at this point because it has the second highest results in terms of accuracy after **S10**, and at the same time consumes significantly less resources. The inclusion of entropy and energy results in a slightly improved accuracy, but they have higher computation cost and consume memory [6][7], which makes them less suitable for real time applications. For example, if we have a data logged over a longitudinal period of time and one uses FFT to compute the coefficients, it will take a huge time and consume a lot of memory, compared with the time domain features, which are easy to calculate and consumes less memory.

From the above discussion, we have observed that, after adding extra features, the processing time will increase, but it will also help to increase accuracy. Certain feature sets will help to recogniz certain activities or classes of activities, but a full feature set could be useful in detecting a wide range of activities. A classifier or model could then automatically select the feature subset that is most suited for a given task. There is a tradeoff between accuracy, and processing and memory consumption. But if we can achieve satisfactory results using easy-to-compute features, then there is no point in using complex features.

With every feature set, bagging and boosting with DT and DT as a base-level classifiers have the best accuracy results, followed by NB with 79.48 % accuracies. In Figure 2, the black line shows the average accuracy for each of the classifiers and accuracy results for the feature sets. The bars in Figure 2 show the results for selected feature sets.

5   Significance t-test Evaluation

The evaluations were repeated by performing a two-tailed t-test to find out if the differences between the recognition results using all the features and with certain features removed are significant, and to investigate whether some features are negligible.

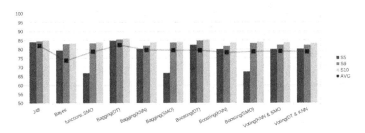

Fig. 2. Accuracy results for different feature sets and average results for all classifiers

5.1 Hypothesis

Our null hypothesis is stated as, "There is no significant difference between the accuracy of the machine learning algorithms, when certain features were removed". Our alternative hypothesis is stated as, "There is a significant difference between the accuracy of the machine learning algorithms, when certain features were removed." We have performed a two-tailed t-test with $alpha$=0.1, which mean hat, $alpha$ for each side will be 0.05. The significance value is t=±1.73. To reject our null hypothesis, the value of t must be either significantly higher or lower than the significance value.

Tables 2, and 3 show the results, for which there was a significant difference in the result. The dash (-) sign represents that there was no significant difference between the two data sets. We have compared the data sets values of the feature sets with each other. Initially we have compared the data sets values from S1 with the remaining sets till S8. After that we compared S2 with the remaining sets and so on. It can be observed that SVM is effected most by the variations in feature subsets, DT as a base-level classifier did not show any significant differences with the change of feature sets.

When we compared S1 with remaining sets till S8, highest significant values were observed for S7 and S8. Similarly there was not significant differences between S1 and S2. For data sets S4, S5 and S6 the differences are moderate. Similarly for S2 maximum significance was observed with S7 and S8, while for S4 significance was minimum. By comparing S7 and S8 with the other sets, the highest significance was observed, proving the fact that the accuracy differences between these sets and other are significant.

In few feature sets, there were only one or two classifiers, which were effected by the variation of feature sets. For example in Table 1, the accuracy differences between S9 and S10 are almost 1% or in some cases even more than 1% for every algorithm, which seems like a differences, but after performing the significance test, we found that there is no significant difference between them. Similarly there are no significant differences between between S1 and S2, S2 and S6 etc.

Table 2. Evaluation results of activity recognition with certain features removed

	Algorithm	S3	S4	S5	S6	S7	S8		S3	S4	S5	S7	S8		S4	S6	S7	S8
	SVM	7.47	7.68	6.35	-	7.008	-		3.78	3.10	3.93	3.84	7.12		3.70	3.80	-	3.71
	Bagging(DT)	-	-	-	-	3.27	2.43		-	-	-	-	1.83		-	-	-	2.16
	Bagging(KNN)	-	-	-	-	3.46	3.13		-	-	-	-	2.57		1.84	-	1.78	3.16
S1	**Bagging(SVM)**	4.61	-	4.73	-	4.57	3.81	S2	3.77	-	3.92	3.84	-	S3	-	3.71	3.71	-
	Boosting(DT)	-	-	1.81	2.16	3.43	4.16		-	-	-	2.08	2.81		-	-	2.48	3.20
	Boosting(KNN)	-	-	-	-	-	2.95		-	-	-	-	2.30		-	-	-	2.91
	Boosting(SVM)	4.29	-	4.34	4.07	4.70	-		3.77	-	3.69	4.02	-		3.45	3.55	-	3.3
	Voting(KNN&SVM)	-	-	-	-	-	3.11		-	-	-	-	2.56		-	-	1.78	3.10
	Voting(DT& KNN)	-	-	-	1.95	2.17	3.61		-	-	-	7.53	3.05		-	-	1.97	3.27

Table 3. Results achieved using S2 and S5 compared with the other feature sets

	Algorithm	S5	S6	S7	S8		S6	S7	S8		S7	S8		S10
	SVM	2.93	3.24	3.74	3.85		3.92	3.89	4.12		3.83	4.18		-
	Bagging(KNN)	-	-	-	-		-	-	3.02		-	2.17		-
	Bagging(SVM)	3.91	-	3.75	-		-	3.81	3.02		3.84	3.84		-
S4	Boosting(DT)	-	-	-	1.96	S5	2.80	-	2.17	S6	-	-	S9	-
	Boosting(KNN)	-	-	-	-		-	-	2.62		-	-		-
	Boosting(SVM)	3.50	-	3.82	-		3.60	3.56	3.35		3.93	3.97		-
	Voting(KNN&SVM)	-	-	-	-		-	-	2.85		-	2.15		-
	Voting(DT& KNN)	-	-	-	-		-	-	2.76		2.49	2.29		-

6   Conclusions

This paper's contributions are twofold: A new feature for activity recognition on inertial data, 'Meantilt', is presented. Our experimental results have shown that the introduced feature has improved the accuracies of classifiers by slightly more than 2%. Our second contribution lies in the evaluation and significance testing of all combinations of feature sets. We have evaluated our feature sets with different base-level and meta-level classifiers to find out how the accuracy and significance of these feature sets are affected.

Within this evaluation and significance test, we have focused and selected sets of easy-to-compute features, which consume minimal resources while providing acceptable results. The most promising set of features was found to contain mean, standard deviation, variance and Meantilt. We have concluded that meta-level classifiers provide the best accuracy results compared to base-level classifiers. Bagging or boosting with a decision tree, and decision tree as a base level classifier have the best accuracy results for almost all the feature sets. Adding other features increased the accuracy results slightly with 1%, but comes at a considerably higher processing cost.

References

1. Caspersen, C.J., Powell, K.E., Christensen: Physical Activity, Exercise, and Physical Fitness: Definitions and Distinctions for Health-Related Research. Public Health Rep. 100, 126–131 (1985)

2. Makikawa, A., Asajima, S., Shibuya, K., Tokue, R., Shinohara, H.: Portable Physical Activity Monitoring System for the Evaluation of Activity of the Aged in Daily Life. In: Conference and the Annual Fall Meeting of the Biomedical Engineering Society EMBS/BMES Conference. IEEE, Housto (2002)

3. Maurer, U., Smailagic, A., Siewiorek, D.P., Deisher, M.: Activity Recognition and Monitoring Using Multiple Sensors on Different Body Positions. In: Proceedings of the International Workshop on Wearable and Implantable Body Sensor Networks. IEEE, Washington (2006)

4. Chun, Z., Weihua, S.: Human Daily Activity Recognition in Robot-assisted Living Using Multi-sensor Fusion. In: 2009 IEEE International Conference on Robotics and Automation Kobe International Conference Center, Kobe, Japan, May 12-17 (2009)

5. Wang, S., Yang, J., Chen, N., Chen, X., Zhang, Q.: Human Activity Recognition with User-Free Accelerometers in the Sensor Networks. In: IEEE Int. Conf. Neural Networks and Brain, vol. 2, pp. 1212–1217 (2005)

6. Bao, L., Intille, S.S.: Activity Recognition from User-Annotated Acceleration Data. In: Ferscha, A., Mattern, F. (eds.) PERVASIVE 2004. LNCS, vol. 3001, pp. 1–17. Springer, Heidelberg (2004)

7. Ravi, N., Dandekar, N., Mysore, P., Littman, M.L.: Activity Recognition from Accelerometer Data. In: Proceedings of the Seventeenth Innovative Applications of Artificial Intelligence Conference, pp. 1541–1546 (2005)

8. Sa-kwang, S., Jaewon, J., Soojun, P.: A Phone for Human Activity Recognition Using Triaxial Acceleration Sensor. In: International Conference on Consumer Electronics, Las Vegas, USA (2008)

9. Huynh, D.: Human Activity Recognition with Wearable Sensors, PHD Thesis (2008)

10. Sun Microsystems,
http://www.sunspotworld.com/docs/Red/Tutorial/Tutorial.html
(last visited May 1, 2011)

11. Lau, S.L., Knig, I., David, K., Parandian, B., Carius-Dssel, C., Schultz, M.: Supporting Patient Monitoring using Activity Recognition with a Smartphone. In: The Seventh International Symposium on Wireless Communication Systems, ISWCS 2010 (2010)

12. Pltz, T.: How To Do Good Researc In Activity Recognition, Position paper, Newcastle, UK (2010)

13. Tapia, et al.: Real-Time Recognition of Physical Activities and Their Intensities Using Wireless Accelerometers and a Heart Rate Monitor. In: Wearable Computers 11th IEEE International (2007)

14. Preece, et al.: Activity Identification using Body-Mounted Sensors- a Review of Classification Techniques. Physiological Measurement 30(4), R1–R33 (2009)

15. Danny, W., Matthai, P., Tanzeem, C.: Unsupervised Activity Recognition using Automatically Mined Common Sense. In: The Proceedings of the Twentieth National Conference on Artificial Intelligence (AAAI 2005), Pittsburg, PA (July 2005)

16. Pirttikangas, S., Fujinami, K., Nakajima, T.: Feature Selection and Activity Recognition from Wearable Sensors. In: Youn, H.Y., Kim, M., Morikawa, H. (eds.) UCS 2006. LNCS, vol. 4239, pp. 516–527. Springer, Heidelberg (2006)

17. Fukunaga, K.: Introduction to statistical pattern recognition, 2nd edn. Academic Press Professional, San Diego (1990)

Person Detection for Indoor Videosurveillance Using Spatio-temporal Integral Features

Adrien Descamps[1], Cyril Carincotte[2], and Bernard Gosselin[1]

[1] TCTS Lab, University of Mons, Mons, Belgium
[2] Multitel ASBL, 2 Rue Pierre et Marie Curie, Mons, Belgium

Abstract. In this paper, we address the problem of person detection in indoor videosurveillance data. We present a new method based on the state of the art integral channel features. This approach is extended to allow the use of temporal features in addition to appearance based features. The temporal features are integrated by a robust background subtraction method. Our method is then evaluated on several datasets presenting various and challenging conditions typical of videosurveillance context. The evaluation shows that additional temporal features are efficient and improve greatly the performance of the detector.

1 Introduction

Person detection in images and videos is a very active research topic in computer vision. It remains a challenging task, due to the huge variability of pedestrian appearance arising from changing pose, clothing, lighting and point of view. Inter-person occlusions, high background variability and/or small resolution images make the problem even harder in many real world scenarios.

In this paper, we address this problem in the particular context of indoor videosurveillance. Many recent works about person detection focus on automotive application [12,9,13], or on person detection in high resolution static images [10], but only a few of them have investigated the use of person detectors for videosurveillance and the particularities of this application [11]. The videosurveillance context has indeed some specific aspects compared to others applications : static background, relatively low resolution images, typical points of views, etc. These specific aspects impose constraints, especially the capacity to detect low resolution persons, and in densely occupied scenes. They also have advantages, the most important one being the static background, that allows use of methods like background subtraction to take into account the temporal aspect of the video data.

The method we propose integrates such temporal information into a classical appearance-based person detector. To do so, we extend integral channel features introduced in [14], and integrate a robust background subtraction method [7] in this algorithm.

We evaluate our method on various challenging data from public CAVIAR dataset [16] and a non-public real world dataset from the VANAHEIM project

R. Wichert, K. Van Laerhoven, J. Gelissen (Eds.): AmI 2011 Workshops, CCIS 277, pp. 110–118, 2012.

[18]. Our experiments show that temporal feature can improve greatly the performances of the detector, even in conditions in which they are generally considered unreliable, and that our method achieves performance similar to state of the art, with lower detection time.

The rest of this paper is organized as follows. A brief review of related works is presented in Section 2. Section 3 presents our approach : we describe the original integral features and their extension to temporal features. Experiments are described in Section 4 and results are reported in Section 5.

2   Related work

In the literature, some early approaches for persons detection were mainly based on background subtraction (see [3]), but these methods suffer from a high sensitivity to background variability, are limited to low density of persons and are not usable with moving camera.

On the other hand, the vast majority of recent methods are based on machine learning methods and use discriminative classifier scanned over the images. One of the first method achieving good performances was the Haar cascade proposed by Viola-Jones [1], which uses simple Haar filters as feature and a cascade of adaboost classifiers. The cascade of classifiers and the use of integral image to compute Haar feature allow to achieve a very fast detector.

The Histogram of Oriented Gradient feature, described in [4], has proven very effective for person detection. The HOG feature represents the intensity distribution of the gradient depending on its orientation, and model well the shape of the person.

In [11], covariance feature was shown to be effective and, combined with a background subtraction method, leaded to a fast and effective detector with good performances in videosurveillance context. The idea of utilizing both appearance and temporal features was also developed by [15], which utilize appearance features together with short-term (frame differencing) and long-term (background subtraction) motion information.

A new generic feature described in [14], called integral channel feature, consist of sums over local rectangular regions of multiple image channels computed using linear and non-linear transformations of the input image. Combined with a soft cascade adaboost classifier [8], this feature is shown to be fast and efficient despite its simplicity, and is a generalization of other features based on integral images, like Haar or HOG.

Several studies have been conducted to standardize procedures to assess performances and compare these methods with each other [10,12]. These studies show the overall prevalence of methods based on the HOG feature and the value of combining different features to improve performances. They also show that if the best methods reach good performance on high-quality and high-resolution images, they fail in the case of more realistic scenarios, with occlusions, variable quality images and variable background.

3   Algorithms and Method

3.1   Appearance Model

The basis of our method is the algorithm proposed in [14], which uses integral channel features based on appearance only. In this algorithm, for an input image I, a set of N channel images $C_i, i \in [1 : N]$ are computed by $C_i = F_i(I)$, where $F_i(I)$ can be any operation. Integral images of these channel images are then computed, and are denoted by C_i^I. The features are defined as sum of pixels in a rectangular region of a channel image for first-order feature, or a linear combination of such sums for higher-order feature. In this work, we only use first-order feature, as higher order features were reported to have very little impact on performances ([14]). Given the integral channel images C_i^I, any feature can be computed very efficiently by four accesses and three addition operations.

The parameters of each feature are thus the rectangular region (x_j, y_j, w_j, h_j) and the channel index i_j. A set of M features is generated by choosing these parameters randomly.Despite the high number of possible features, this strategy was shown to be efficient in [14].

A soft cascade adaboost classifier is then trained using these features. The soft cascade is a variant of the cascade of classifiers, in which a rejection threshold is used after evaluation of every weak classifier, instead of using multiple distinct cascade layers. A classical adaboost classifier using decision tree as weak classifiers is first trained. Then, using [8], the rejection thresholds are determined as the lowest values allowing to reach a given detection rate on a given dataset.

The parameters of the method are thus M the number of features, the parameters of the adaboost classifier, and most importantly, the channels used. The only constraint about these channels is that the generation function F_i must be translationally invariant, $T(F_i(I)) = F_i(T(I))$, T being any translation operation. In [14], the author tested many possible channels, and retained a configuration of ten channels, composed of three channels for the original image in the LUV color space, one channel for the gradient magnitude, and six channels for the Histogram of Oriented Gradients.

The HOG feature is composed by the normalized histogram of the gradient magnitude relative to its orientation over a subregion of the image. It can be computed with integral images as shown in [2], using one channel per histogram bin. The feature extracted from these channels are normalized a posteriori by the gradient magnitude channel, which corresponds to the L1 normalization in [4]. This feature has been shown to be very efficient to model shape of humans.

3.2   Temporal Information Extension

We propose to extend this method by using the temporal information of the video in the channels. For this, we extend the channel extraction function $C_i = F_i(I)$ to a more general one $(C_{i,t}, S_{i,t}) = F_i(I_t, S_{i,t-1})$, t being the time index. $S_{i,t}$ represents the state of the channel i at time t. This state allows the channel extraction function to use information about the previous frames of the video.

Given the new formula, we can integrate almost any video features into the method. This is illustrated in the following sections by integrating a background subtraction method.

Background Subtraction. We use the background subtraction algorithm described in [7], which uses a multi-layer model of background based on color and texture. In this case, the channel is a foreground probability image, providing the probability of each pixel to be part of foreground, and the state is the background model generated by the method. We have : $(C_{i,t}, B_t) = F_{i,t}(I_t, B_{t-1})$, B_t being the background model. Thus, at each frame, F_i is called with the current frame and the previous background model as input, and return a foreground probability image and an updated background model.

The foreground probability is an interesting feature which eliminates many false alarms, but is not discriminant in itself, since any moving object give similar response. The shape of the foreground is much more discriminant. We thus use, in addition to the foreground probability channel, one gradient magnitude channel and six HOG channels computed on the foreground image. These channels are computed similarly to those computed on the input image. However, unlike the classical HOG, we do not discard the information about the direction of the gradient. Indeed, this information is relevant for foreground image, because a person is supposed to appear as a high probability blob in a low probability background, and not the opposite.

Our final method can thus use up to 18 channels : 10 for appearance and 8 for background subtraction. A sample of these channels is presented at figure 1. It can be observed that the temporal channels bring important information about the presence and the shape of a foreground object. We can also see that foreground HOG channels are less noisy and represent better the shape of the person than appearance based HOG channels. These observations must be moderated by the sensitivity of the background subtraction method to occlusion, variable background and low-contrast persons, but they demonstrate the value of using temporal features in addition to appearance.

4   Experiments

4.1   Training and Testing Data

For training and testing our method, we use several public videosurveillance datasets and a dataset from Turin metro station coming from the VANAHEIM project. For training, around 9200 positive samples are extracted from CAVIAR, PETS2009, AVSS2007 and VANAHEIM datasets. These samples come with their corresponding foreground images. Negative samples are extracted by extracting 5000 random windows from a set of 88 background images coming from various datasets, collecting 5000 additional samples by bootstrapping once on these images, and 5000 more by bootstrapping a second time on training data containing persons. The aim of the second bootstrap is to collect hard negative samples

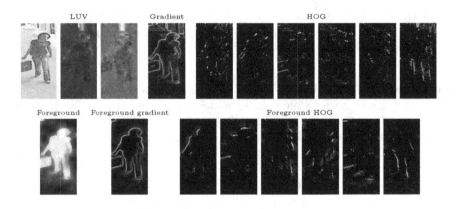

Fig. 1. Sample images of channels

that do not appear in images containing only background, like parts of persons or groups of persons.

We evaluate our method on CAVIAR and VANAHEIM data not used during training. The CAVIAR data contains two views of a shopping center, and we use 12 short sequences of each view containing 1400 annotations of persons (with high redundancy). The VANAHEIM data contains 17 views, with 2500 annotated persons. Note that these data present a high variability and challenging condition like changing light, moving escalators, ground reflections,or high density of persons.

The high proportion of persons is seen in very low resolution in these data, and this leads us to choose a detection window size of 18x36 pixel. We can note that this size is smaller than reported in most publications : for example, a window size of 64x128 was used in [4,10,9,14] (INRIA dataset [17]), and in ETHZ dataset ([6]), minimum person size is 60 pixels . Some authors [9,13] use the Daimler dataset, with a window size of 18x36 pixels, and report the difficulty to detect persons at such low resolution.

4.2   Evaluation Methodology

For the evaluation, we consider here that only unoccluded standing people must be detected. This hypothesis is of course limiting for applications, but is justified by the fact we don't use any occlusion handling method and the difficulty of the dataset. Other persons are marked as "hard" and are optional (they do not count as false positive if detected but do no need to be detected). Performances are evaluated for four category of persons: "far", which are less than 36 pixel high, "medium", which are between 36 and 72 pixels high, "near" which are more than 72 pixel high, and "global", which includes all the persons. The performances are evaluated following [12], by applying the detector on annotated images, performing a non maximum suppression to suppress multiple detections and matching detection bounding box with ground truth using PASCAL criterion, with an overlap threshold of 0.5. We use a simple non maximum suppression method ([14]) that suppresses the less confident of every pair of detections that overlap sufficiently according to the PASCAL criterion.

Original method, with only appearance channels (i.e. [14], referred further as Dollar), and our extension with foreground channels are evaluated. For comparison purpose, Opencv Haar cascade , Opencv LBP cascade, original HOG [4] and method based on covariance and background subtraction from [11] were also evaluated. Note that we use the same background subtraction algorithm as the covariance method, while other methods use only appearance. Except for covariance method, these methods are retrained with our dataset, and we used same training data and same parameters.

5   Results

Figure 2 shows performances of all methods on CAVIAR and VANAHEIM datasets. Note that VANAHEIM results are filtered using calibration and a ground plane hypothesis, but it doesn't influence their ranking.

The appearance methods, Haar, HOG and Dollar, give similar results, except for Dollar which outperforms slightly other methods in CAVIAR dataset. LBP method doesn't perform well on both datasets. The integration of background in Dollar improves performances greatly on both dataset and gives the best results in VANAHEIM.

The performances of the Covariance algorithm vary very much, being the best for CAVIAR, but very poor for VANAHEIM. However, this detector could not be retrained on the same dataset, due to the unavailability of the training code. This can affect greatly the results and make it difficult to draw conclusions, especially considering the CAVIAR dataset was used in the training stage [11].

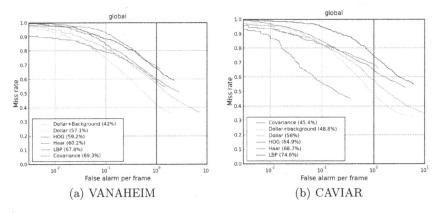

(a) VANAHEIM   (b) CAVIAR

Fig. 2. Global results on VANAHEIM and CAVIAR datasets

Finally, figure 3 shows performances evaluated globally on all the data, with curves for the different category of size defined above. Globally, we see the prevalence of methods which use temporal information: the Covariance method and our method with foreground. As expected, the curves show best results for near persons, and worst results for far persons. For medium and near persons, we see that foreground improves greatly performance. The gain due to foreground is especially high for medium scale, the near scale being already relatively well handled by appearance methods.

For far persons, we see that the integration background subtraction decrease performance slightly. A priori, it is for these far persons that temporal information should be the most useful, compensating the lack of appearance information. The results seem to indicate that foreground information is not discriminative enough at low scale to bring useful information.

Table 1 resume the results, showing the global detection rate at one false alarm per image, and the detection time of all the methods. The detection time is reported for VANAHEIM video, at 704x288 resolution. We see that our method with background subtraction gives the best compromise between performances and detection time.

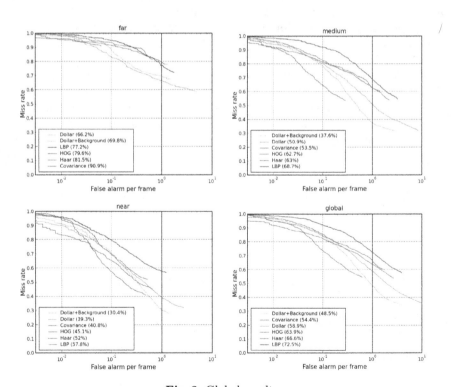

Fig. 3. Global results

Table 1. Global detection rate at one false alarm per image

Algorithm	VANAHEIM	CAVIAR	**Global**	Detection time (s)
Haar	39.8%	21.3%	33.4%	0.1
HOG	40.8%	35.1%	36.1%	3
LBP	32.2%	25.4%	27.5%	0.1
Covariance[1]	30.7%	**54.6%**	45.6%	2.5
Dollar	43.0%	42.1%	41.2%	0.5
Dollar+Background	**58.0%**	51.2%	**51.5%**	1.5

6   Conclusion

We presented a new pedestrian detector that integrates simply and efficiently appearance and temporal feature. The value of using temporal features for pedestrian detection in videosurveillance was demonstrated by evaluating the performance of our method on various and challenging data. However, performances achieved by the best detector are still far from those needed for real-world videosurveillance applications.

Many improvements of our method are possible. The first one is the addition of a tracking method to the detector, that should eliminate some false alarms and miss detections in persons trajectories. The features have still to be further investigated to find additional efficient temporal features, e.g. based on optical flow. Finally, the inter-person occlusions are an important problem in many cases in videosurveillance, and modelling explicitly these occlusions could help to improve greatly performances in such cases.

Acknowledgement. The research leading to these results has received funding from the European Communitys Seventh Framework Programme FP7/2007-2013 - Challenge 2- Cognitive Systems, Interaction, Robotics - under grant agreement n 248907-VANAHEIM.

References

1. Viola, P., Jones, M.: Rapid object detection using a boosted cascade of simple features. In: Computer Vision and Pattern Recognition (2001)
2. Porikli, F.: Integral histogram: A fast way to extract histograms in cartesian spaces. In: Computer Vision and Pattern Recognition (2005)
3. Ogale, N.A.: A survey of techniques for human detection from video. Master Thesis, University of Maryland (2006)
4. Dalal, N.: Finding people in images and videos. PhD Thesis, Institut National Polytechnique de Grenoble (2006)

---

[1] For covariance method, the curve doesn't reach the rate of one false alarm per image for CAVIAR and global datasets. The detection rate is thus reported at 0.3 and 0.7 false alarm per image respectively.

5. Zhu, Q., Avidan, S., Yeh, M.C., Cheng, K.T.: Fast human detection using a cascade of histograms of oriented gradients. In: Computer Vision and Pattern Recognition (2006)
6. Ess, A., Leibe, B., Van Gool, L.: Depth and appearance for mobile scene analysis. In: International Conference on Computer Vision (2007)
7. Yao, J., Odobez, J.M.: Multi-layer background subtraction based on color and texture. In: Computer Vision and Pattern Recognition (2007)
8. Zhang, C., Viola, P.: Multiple-instance pruning for learning efficient cascade detectors. In: Neural Information Processing Systems (2007)
9. Tuzel, O., Porikli, F., Meer, P.: Pedestrian detection via classification on riemannian manifolds. Pattern Analysis and Machine Intelligence (2008)
10. Wojek, C., Schiele, B.: A Performance Evaluation of Single and Multi-Feature People Detection. In: Rigoll, G. (ed.) DAGM 2008. LNCS, vol. 5096, pp. 82–91. Springer, Heidelberg (2008)
11. Yao, J., Odobez, J.M.: Fast human detection from videos using covariance features. In: Computer Vision Visual Surveillance Workshop (2008)
12. Dollar, P., Wojek, C., Schiele, B., Perona, P.: Pedestrian detection: A benchmark. In: Computer Vision and Pattern Recognition (2009)
13. Enzweiler, M., Gavrila, D.M.: Monocular pedestrian detection: Survey and experiments. Pattern Analysis and Machine Intelligence (2009)
14. Dollar, P., Tu, Z., Perona, P., Belongie, S.: Integral Channel Features. In: British Machine Vision Conference (2009)
15. Zhang, J., Gong, S.: People Detection in Low-Resolution Video with Non-Stationary Background. In: Image and Vision Computing (2009)
16. CAVIAR dataset, http://homepages.inf.ed.ac.uk/rbf/caviar/
17. INRIA dataset, http://pascal.inrialpes.fr/data/human/
18. VANAHEIM project (2010-2013), http://www.vanaheim-project.eu/

Person Authentication and Activities Analysis in an Office Environment Using a Sensor Network

Shuai Tao, Mineichi Kudo, Hidetoshi Nonaka, and Jun Toyama

Division of Computer Science, Hokkaido University, Japan
{taoshuai,mine,nonaka,jun}@main.ist.hokudai.ac.jp

Abstract. Person authentication and activities analysis are indispensable for providing various personalized services in a smart home/office environment. In this study, we introduce a person localization algorithm using an infrared ceiling sensor network, and realize person authentication anywhere and anytime. The key problem is how to distinguish different persons meeting at the same position. We solve this problem by different moving directions depending on individuals. Furthermore, with the locations and the known identities, multiple persons can be tracked and their interactive behaviors can be analyzed by our system.

Keywords: localization, person authentication, activities, sensor network, infrared sensors.

1 Introduction

Person surveillance and activity analysis have been applied to various circumstances, such as security control, person tracking, assisted living and human-computer interface (HCI), etc [1-6]. In recent years, along with the rapid development of computer vision and many kinds of network devices, person authentication, tracking and human-behavior understanding have become indispensable for providing many kinds of personalized services in response to the implicit/explicit demands of the users. In such a smart environment, the face, voice, gait, individual trajectories and other features are used to realize the recognition and real-time tracking of multiple persons. Meanwhile, recording the activities of multiple persons is an effective way to analyze the labor degree of individuals, to improve the room layout and to measure the ability of daily living of elderly persons.

Traditional authentication systems based on various biometric evidences, such as fingerprint, iris, speech and palm vain, can maintain a high level of security, but the cooperation of users is necessary. There have also been many studies using cameras for human activities analysis, however, to some extent, cameras might violate the privacy of users. In daily life, misidentification of users or misrecognition of activities does not cause a serious problem. While, physical/psychological disturbance should be seriously considered.

Video cameras and sensor networks have been used in many studies for person monitoring, tracking and behavior analysis [7-14]. Zhao et al. [7] succeeded in tracking

R. Wichert, K. Van Laerhoven, J. Gelissen (Eds.): AmI 2011 Workshops, CCIS 277, pp. 119–127, 2012.

persons with their modes of movements (e.g. walking, running) using several outdoor cameras. Sogo et al. [8] tracked two persons by multiple cameras. In another study, by the human shape model for gait, Yam et al. [10] tracked persons with a single camera in an outdoor environment. In these studies, vision is sometimes not obtained due to the existence of obstacles and greatly affected by light conditions. Schulz et al. [11] tried to use an ID badge for person localization and authentication. For many people, especially elderly people, such sensing devices might bring troubles to daily lives. The other studies realized the recognition of human activities by using cameras [12-13] and IR sensors [14].

In our previous work [15], an infrared ceiling sensor network has been used to keep tracking up to five persons in an office environment. However, the tracking/identification precision decreases with the pass of time, even though the degradation can be recovered if some other pieces of evidence are occasionally available. Recently, in order to increase the sampling rate and reduce the noise, we have developed an improved system using binary infrared sensors attached to the ceiling [16]. In this system, sampling rate of 80 Hz for up to 128 nodes using 250 kbps equilibrium line has been realized. By this system, we also proposed a novel method for person localization and soft authentication [17]. In the experiments, we confirmed that walking path and speed give useful information for authenticating the user. However, there are more problems to be solved. For example, due to the characteristics of infrared sensors, the information we obtain is still binary, that is, all we can know is if someone is under or just passed by the active sensor. Therefore, when multiple persons meet at one place, they cannot be distinguished anymore. We have to explore other pieces of evidence as supplemental information. In an office environment, it is natural that a person tends to go to his/her own desk immediately after entering the room or after meeting with someone, and walk straight after crossing with another person. Therefore, the moving directions, e.g. a direction from the entrance to his/her own desk, or a direction from a meeting point to his/her own desk are expected to provide reliable hints for person authentication.

2   Infrared Sensing System

We attach "pyroelectric infrared sensors", sometimes called "infrared motion sensors", to the ceiling [16]. This sensor detects an object with a different temperature from the surrounding temperature. The photographs of the sensor module and the interconnection of sensor nodes with cables are shown in Fig. 1. Such infrared sensors are easy to set up at a low cost ($20/unit). Light conditions and movable obstacles do not affect the performance.

Forty-three sensors were attached to the ceiling of our research room (15.0 m × 8.5 m) so as to cover all the area and not to produce any dead space. The average distance between each other is 1.5m. Figure 2 shows the layout of the room and the arrangement of the sensors. A binary response from each sensor can be read at the sampling rate from 1 Hz to 80 Hz.

Fig. 1. The sensor module and the interconnection of sensor nodes with cables

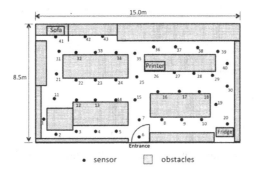

Fig. 2. Layout of infrared sensors

In our sensor network, motions of one person often make multiple sensors active. There is also a *get-out delay* of sensors in response to motions, that is, an active sensor keeps the active status for a few seconds after a person left the sensing area. There is no *get-in delay*. Another important fact is that the sensor sometimes cannot be active if the person is motionless or moves slightly, such as, keyboard typing or browsing with a mouse.

3 Person Localization Algorithm [17]

In the ceiling sensor system of our laboratory, we can assume that: (1) the walking speed of persons in our laboratory follows Gaussian distribution: $N(v, \sigma^2)$. So, we set the speed to v approximately in experiments; (2) detection area is a circle of radius R; (3) active status will be kept for D_{delay} (sec.) after the person getting off the detection area and D_{delay} does not depend on the speed v. In Fig. 3, we assume that the person enters the detection area with an incident angle α and the duration D of active status is decomposed as $D = t_e - t_s = D_{detect} + D_{delay}$ if the person gets out of the detection area at time frame t ($> t_e$).

From the sensor model in Fig. 3, we see that there are four cases to be considered: (1) at position P_0 (at time frame t_0 before detection), the distance from the sensor is $r_0 > R$, (2) at position P_1 (at time frame t_1 under detection), $r_1^2 = D^2v^2 + R^2 - 2RDv\cos\alpha$ ($D = t - t_s < \frac{2R\cos\alpha}{v}$), (3) at position P_2 (at time frame t_2 out of detection area but the sensor is still active), $r_2^2 = D^2v^2 + R^2 - 2RDv\cos\alpha$ ($\frac{2R\cos\alpha}{v} < D < \frac{2R\cos\alpha}{v} + D_{delay}$), (4) at position P_3 (at time frame t_3), the sensor becomes inactive again, and the distance from the sensor is $r_3 > R$.

For situations (2) and (3), with the expected value $\frac{2}{\pi}$ of $\cos\alpha$ in range $-\frac{\pi}{2} < \alpha < \frac{\pi}{2}$, we use the expected value of squared distance as $E(r^2) = D^2v^2 + R^2 - \frac{4}{\pi}RDv$.

Algorithm

(1) If a sensor S_i has already been active for duration D_i, we estimate the distance to the person by $r_i = \sqrt{D_i^2v^2 + R^2 - \frac{4}{\pi}RD_iv} = \sqrt{(D_iv - \frac{2}{\pi}R)^2 + (1 - \frac{4}{\pi^2})R^2}$.

(2) Gathering all the information D_i and thus r_i ($i = 1, \cdots, n$) from all active sensors, estimate the position $P_t = (x_t^*, y_t^*)$ at time frame t by solving

$$\min_{P_t} \sum_{i=1}^{n} (r_i - \|S_i - P_t\|)^2 = \min_{(x,y)} \sum_{i=1}^{n} \{r_i - \sqrt{(x_i - x)^2 + (y_i - y)^2}\}^2.$$

The solution (x_t^*, y_t^*) satisfies:

$$\begin{cases} x = \sum w_i x_i / \sum w_i \\ y = \sum w_i y_i / \sum w_i \end{cases} \quad w_i = \frac{\sqrt{(x_i - x)^2 + (y_i - y)^2} - r_i}{\sqrt{(x_i - x)^2 + (y_i - y)^2}}.$$

Therefore, with appropriate initial values, we can find the solution P_t by iteration.

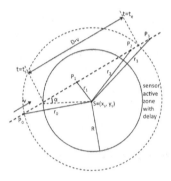

Fig. 3. The sensor model that contains four cases when a person passes by. Without generality, we may assume that he/she enters at the left end of x-axis.

4   Person Authentication

4.1   Entrance Authentication

Each person in an office room has individual living habits and tends to stay around some certain areas. By observation we found that persons tend to go to their own desks immediately after entering the room. Therefore, the walking directions are expected to hold information for recognizing multiple persons at the entrance. In our first

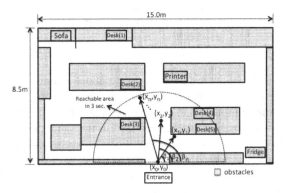

Fig. 4. The description of the directions. The direction of the person at time t is calculated by $\beta_t = arctan(\frac{y_t-y_0}{x_t-x_0}), t = 1, 2, \cdots, n$.

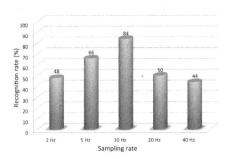

Fig. 5. Recognition rates of the entrance authentication

experiment, the walking direction for a short period (3 sec.) is used for identifying multiple persons. Here, we use only a short period because we want to identify entering users as soon as possible. The description of the directions is shown in Fig. 4.

In the experiment, five subjects (laboratory students) were asked to enter the room from outside and then to go forward to their own desks directly without stopping for twenty times. The locations of the five desks and the reachable area in 3 sec. are shown in Fig. 4. We used five kinds of sampling rate: 2Hz, 5Hz, 10Hz, 20Hz and 40Hz. The number of features is the product of the sampling time (3 sec.) and the sampling rate (2Hz-40Hz). The recognition rate was calculated by 20-fold cross-validation. The classifier was a support vector machine (SVM) with a radial basic kernel with default parameter values. The results are shown in Fig. 5.

From Fig. 5 we can see that the best recognition rate 84% of five persons is obtained at 10Hz sampling rate. The accuracy is not high enough, however, might prove the availability of the direction information for entrance authentication.

4.2   Distinguish Process

In our office environment, there are two typical situations required to distinguish persons from one active region (a connected region of active sensors). One situation happens when two persons approach to each other and pass through (Fig. 6(a)), in which they will share one active region and be localized to the same position. In this situation, we employ the empirical knowledge that a person tends to walk straight without changing direction after a cross with another person. The other situation happens when multiple persons meet at a place (Fig. 6(b)), in which they cannot be distinguished neither. At this moment, we rely on the knowledge that people tend to go back to their desks after meeting. The difference between above two situations is that the time duration when multiple persons have been localized at the same position. The duration of the latter one is longer according to the experience. We use $z_p = (x_p, y_p)$ to denote the estimate location of person p at the present time, use $z'_p = (x'_p, y'_p)$ to denote the estimate location one step before and use d_p to denote the desk of person p . The direction of person p at the present time is denoted by $\overrightarrow{\beta_p}$ and $D_{p_1p_2}$ describes the time steps that person p_1 and person p_2 were localized at the same position. The two situations are illustrated in Fig. 6. The distinguish algorithm is as follows:

for *person p_1, person p_2* **do**

    if $z'_{p_1} = z'_{p_2}$ and $z_{p_1} \neq z_{p_2}$ and $D_{p_1p_2} \leq 6$ (crossing case) **then**

        if $|\overrightarrow{\beta_{p_1}} - \overrightarrow{z'_{p_1}z_{p_1}}| + |\overrightarrow{\beta_{p_2}} - \overrightarrow{z'_{p_2}z_{p_2}}| > |\overrightarrow{\beta_{p_1}} - \overrightarrow{z'_{p_2}z_{p_2}}| + |\overrightarrow{\beta_{p_2}} - \overrightarrow{z'_{p_1}z_{p_1}}|$ (if the two persons tend to change their moving directions after the cross) **then**

            $z_{p_1} \leftarrow z_{p_2}, z_{p_2} \leftarrow z_{p_1}$

        end if

    end if

    if $z'_{p_1} = z'_{p_2}$ and $z_{p_1} \neq z_{p_2}$ and $D_{p_1p_2} > 6$ (meeting case) **then**

        if $|\overrightarrow{z'_{p_1}z_{p_1}} - \overrightarrow{z_{p_1}z_{d_1}}| + |\overrightarrow{z'_{p_2}z_{p_2}} - \overrightarrow{z_{p_2}z_{d_2}}| > |\overrightarrow{z'_{p_1}z_{p_1}} - \overrightarrow{z_{p_2}z_{d_2}}| + |\overrightarrow{z'_{p_2}z_{p_2}} - \overrightarrow{z_{p_1}z_{d_1}}|$ (if the two persons do not tend to move in the direction to their own desk after the meeting) **then**

            $z_{p_1} \leftarrow z_{p_2}, z_{p_2} \leftarrow z_{p_1}$

        end if

    end if

end for

According to the person localization algorithm, we can obtain the location of each individual person at any time. With the person authentication algorithms, all the persons in our office room can be recognized. Therefore, we can know who the users are and where they are at any time. If the location is connected to a special equipment, e.g., a printer, we might also get their behavior information.

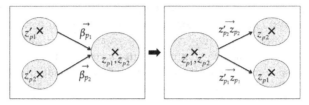

(a) The situation when two persons approach to each other and pass through

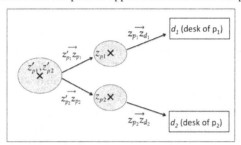

(b) The situation when multiple persons meet at a place

Fig. 6. The two typical situations required to distinguish persons from one active region

4.3 Experiments

We evaluate the assumptions in a more practical situation that up to five persons spent about half a day (more than four hours) in the laboratory room without any instructions. They behaved naturally because they were not aware that the system was in operation.

The experiment was conducted from 10 a.m. The behaviors of five persons were recorded. For about 1/4 of the period, they walked around or left/(re)entered, while, in the other 3/4 of the period, they stayed at their desks. The algorithms in Sec. 4.1 and 4.2 were used for realizing person authentication in different situations. The recorded numbers of different events and the identification results are summarized in Fig. 7.

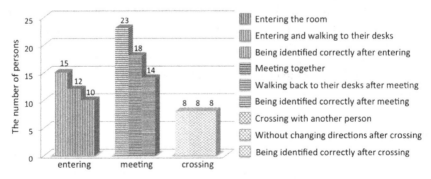

Fig. 7. The recorded numbers of different events and the person authentication results

From Fig. 7, we see that for the entering event, 12 of 15 persons (including the same persons) walked to their desks directly after entering the room, 10 of them were identified correctly. For the meeting event, 23 persons have met in different groups, 18 persons of them went back to their desks after meeting. Finally, 14 persons were correctly recognized. For the situation of crossing, all the 8 persons can be identified.

5 Discussion

In this study, we designed an improved system for person authentication and interactive human behaviors analysis. Our system consists of forty-three infrared ceiling sensors with low cost and easy installation. However, due to the simplicity of the binary sensors, the information we obtain is limited to the event that someone is under or just passed by the active sensor. Therefore, we have to explore other pieces of evidence as supplemental information for realizing person authentication and activities analysis.

Each person in our office room has an individual living habit. Persons tend to go to theirs own desks immediately after entering the room. We also find that persons always tend to go back to their own desks after meeting some others and a person tends to walk straight without changing direction after a cross with another person. In our study, the walking directions are expected to provide information for recognizing multiple persons.

On the basis of person localization and authentication, multiple persons can be tracked simultaneously and the activities of them can be recorded by our system. According to which, the interactive human behaviors can be analyzed in a convenient way. Usage of our system may reveal some groups of friends, redundant labor, and inefficient layout of equipments.

6 Conclusion

To realize localizing and authenticating multiple persons behaving naturally in a relatively large room, we have developed new algorithms to authenticate users at the entrance and to recover their lost identities because some of them have met at the same place. The idea is that every person tends to walk straight after a cross and return to his/her own desk after meeting, so the direction of walking gives us a strong piece of evidence. Indeed, our experiments showed that the current system is able to identify five persons and has the potential to track multiple persons and analyze their interactive behaviors.

References

1. Shankar, M., Burchett, J., Hao, Q., Guenther, B., Brady, D.: Human-tracking systems using pyroelectric infrared detectors. Optical Engineering 45(10), 106401(1)–106401(10) (2006)
2. Song, B., Choi, H., Lee, H.S.: Surveillance tracking system using passive infrared motion sensors in wireless sensor network. In: Information Networking, ICOIN 2008, pp. 1–5 (2008)

3. Zhou, J., Hoang, J.: Real time robust human detection and tracking system. In: IEEE Computer Society Conference on Computer Vision and Pattern Recognition Workshops, CVPR Workshops, pp. 149–156. IEEE (2005)
4. Sixsmith, A., Johnson, N., Whatmore, R.: Pyroelectric IR sensor arrays for fall detection in the older population. J. Phys. IV France 128, 153–160 (2005)
5. Toreyin, B., Soyer, E., Onaran, I., Cetin, A.: Falling Person Detection Using Multi-sensor Signal Processing. In: IEEE 15th Signal Processing and Communications Applications, pp. 1–4 (2007)
6. Hengstler, S., Prashanth, D., Fong, S., Aghajan, H.: Mesheye: a hybrid-resolution smart camera mote for applications in distributed intelligent surveillance. In: Proceedings of the 6th International Conference on Information Processing in Sensor Networks, IPSN 2007, pp. 360–369 (2007)
7. Zhao, T., Nevatia, R.: Tracking multiple humans in complex situations. IEEE Trans. Pattern Anal. Mach. Intell. 26(9), 1208–1221 (2004)
8. Sogo, T., Ishiguro, H., Trivedi, M.: Real-time human tracking system with multiple omnidirectional vision sensors. Syst. Comput. Jpn. 35(2), 79–90 (2004)
9. Lee, T.-Y., Lin, T.-Y., Huang, S.-H., Lai, S.-H., Hung, S.-C.: People Localization in a Camera Network Combining Background Subtraction and Scene-Aware Human Detection. In: Lee, K.-T., Tsai, W.-H., Liao, H.-Y.M., Chen, T., Hsieh, J.-W., Tseng, C.-C. (eds.) MMM 2011, Part I. LNCS, vol. 6523, pp. 151–160. Springer, Heidelberg (2011)
10. Yam, C., Nixon, M.S., Matsuo, J.N.: Automated person recognition by walking and running via model-based approches. Pattern Recognition 37(5), 1057–1072 (2003)
11. Schulz, D., Fox, D., Hightower, J.: People tracking with anonymous and id-sensors using rao-blackwellised particle filters. In: Proceedings of International Joint Conference on Artificial Intelligence (IJCAI), pp. 921–928 (2003)
12. Ramasso, E., Panagiotakis, C., Pellerin, D., Rombaut, M.: Human action recognition in videos based on the Transferable Belief Model. Pattern Analysis and Applications 11(1), 1–19 (2008)
13. Turaga, P., Chellappa, R., Subrahmanian, V., Udrea, O.: Machine recognition of human activities: A survey. IEEE Transactions on Circuits and Systems for Video Technology 18(11), 1473–1488 (2008)
14. Zappi, P., Farella, E., Benini, L.: Tracking Motion Direction and Distance With Pyroelectric IR Sensors. IEEE Sensors Journal 10(9), 1486–1494 (2010)
15. Hosokawa, T., Kudo, M., Nonaka, H., Toyama, J.: Soft authentication using an infrared ceiling sensor network. Pattern Analysis and Applications 12(3), 237–249 (2009)
16. Nonaka, H., Tao, S., Toyama, J., Kudo, M.: Ceiling sensor network for soft authentication and person tracking using equilibrium line. In: The 1st International Conference of Pervasive and Embedded Computing and Communication Systems (PECCS), pp. 218–223 (2011)
17. Tao, S., Kudo, M., Nonaka, H., Toyama, J.: Person Localization and Soft Authentication Using an Infrared Ceiling Sensor Network. In: Real, P., Diaz-Pernil, D., Molina-Abril, H., Berciano, A., Kropatsch, W. (eds.) CAIP 2011, Part II. LNCS, vol. 6855, pp. 122–129. Springer, Heidelberg (2011)

Using Human Motion Intensity
as Input for Urban Design

Esben S. Poulsen*, Hans J. Andersen, Rikke Gade,
Ole B. Jensen, and Thomas B. Moeslund

Department of Architecture, Design and Media Technology
Aalborg University Denmark
espo@create.aau.dk

Abstract. This paper presents a study investigating the potential use of human motion intensities as input for parametric urban design. Through a computer vision analysis of thermal images, motion intensity maps are generated and utilized as design drivers for urban design patterns; and, through a case study of a town square, human occupancy and motion intensities are used to generate situated flow topologies presenting new adaptive methods for urban design. These methods incorporate local flow as design drivers for canopy, pavement and furniture layout. The urban design solution may be configured due to various parameters such as security, comfort, navigation, efficiency, or aesthetics.

1 Introduction

For the first time in human history, more than half of the human population inhabits urban environments, and this now presents itself as 'second nature' to humans. The urban context is of a very complex nature and is composed by a multitude of different networks, infrastructures and volumes. The city has become the dominant 'scenery' for everyday life. As such it presents still greater design challenges for an improved urban spatial performance, and it creates more inspiring, efficient and stimulating public spaces. One must acknowledge that urban spaces are sites of movement and interaction that contain under-utilized potential [8,10]. If we can understand when the 'stages' are used in terms of human movement and occupancy, we can generate site-specific flow maps, which present a basis for new understandings of the dynamics of the different flow systems that can create a foundation for better and more sensitive/adaptive approaches to urban movement [7,9], to computer vision technologies and to new sensor technologies. It is an interdisciplinary design challenge to develop new analysis and design tools and methods that can improve urban performance and efficiency. By mapping everyday flow activities, it will be possible to generate site-specific representations, which present well functioning and unused regions

---

* Corresponding author.

R. Wichert, K. Van Laerhoven, J. Gelissen (Eds.): AmI 2011 Workshops, CCIS 277, pp. 128–136, 2012.

of urban space. This knowledge can be used to quality new flow topologies such as furniture placement, lighting, navigation patterns, or just as creative ingredients.

This paper will present the use of thermal computer vision as a method for automated human activity analyses in public places. The flow is presented as quantities of occupancy, groupings, and motion. Furthermore, this paper will present urban design scenarios for data driven design patterns and response strategies for adaptive urban environments. The tools are tested in the experimental setup at the central public square of Gl. Torv, Aalborg, Denmark (figure 1).

Fig. 1. View from the camera position, Gl. Torv in Aalborg, Denmark

2   Material and Methods

To approach this interdisciplinary research and design challenge, we employ the following models from the two scientific areas: computer-vision and parametric design [16]. The idea is to use thermal camera observations for the quantification of human activity in public spaces and later use the information as design drivers for parametric design "machines" [18] for urban spaces as illustrated in figure 2.

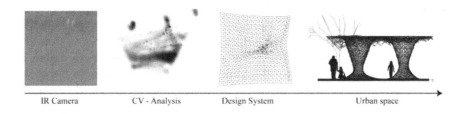

IR Camera   CV - Analysis   Design System   Urban space

Fig. 2. The processed maps from thermal camera observation, computer vision analysis, informed design system into urban design spaces

2.1   Generating Human Motion Intensity Maps

Detecting and tracking people is a large research area in computer vision; there are approaches, such as ours, using thermal cameras [1,5,2]. Thermal cameras are still quite expensive, but because of information security and privacy, it is not legal to film public places in Denmark. This is the primary reason to utilize thermal cameras. In this paper, the video material obtained from the thermal camera is analyzed in order to detect people and their activity in the public square. The people are detected in each frame by performing a running background subtraction and thresholding the image based on temperature difference. The position of each person is found using a homography that maps the image coordinates into the position at the square in world coordinates. The square is divided into 280 × 240 small areas and represented by a matrix, in which the detected persons are added as gaussian distributions with radii of 1 metre.

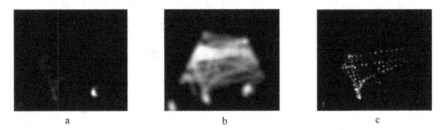

a   b   c

Fig. 3. Utilization of the square over a period of 30 minutes. a: Occupancy, b: Motion, c: Groupings.

Figure 3 illustrates the utilization of the square during 30 minutes of an ordinary Danish summer day. To calculate the occupancy map, each detected person is added to the corresponding area of the map. The intensity of each area of the map will therefore describe the total occupancy rate of the area during the observed time period. The motion map is found based on the difference between two successive frames. A gradient vector calculated for the position of each person gives a direction and magnitude describing the person's motion between the two frames. By summarizing the magnitude of these vectors, the motion map shown in figure 3 (b) is found. Groupings of people are found for each frame, by detecting areas where the gaussian distributions (representing people) overlap. These areas are added to the groupings map for the complete time period. Finally, the three maps are summed up to get a representation of the total utilization of the square as seen in figure 6.

2.2   Data Driven Urban Design Strategies

Because of the merger of technologies in the built environment [15], architecture has changed the scope from asking questions of what a building is to what a building does [11]. Today the very "face-expression" of the building can change to a wide range of success criteria. It is this process of adaptation, we need to qualify and articulate. If we can measure tendencies characterizing "good urban spaces", we are able to generate significant representations, which can afford better and more context-aware design solutions. In line with established theories in the field of urban design [3,13,4,20], we will argue that the creation of 'good urban spaces' has to do with functional requirements (access, capacities, legibility etc.), social dimensions (meeting points between different cultures and social groups, vivid and playful experiences etc.) as well as aesthetic dimensions (materials, urban furniture, surfaces etc.). In short, good urban spaces are spaces where the basic functions of the city (living, producing, and consuming) are fulfilled in an environment of socially creative and stimulating experiences.

Situated Design Patterns. During the last 10 years, computation has become a significant part of the architect's sketchbook and vocabulary; algorithmic [19], parametric [17], morphogenetic [6], animated [14], interactive, generative, responsive, adaptive, and performative [11]. All ways to qualify the specific use of computation in architectural design environments. The techniques apply advanced control algorithms, simulations and self-organizing generative algorithms, which allow designers to handle more information in design models and optimize e.g. structural and environmental performance. The techniques have had a tendency to stay inside the virtual domain without utilizing dynamic phenomena on-"site" as active design drivers. It seems to be of great relevance to take a step back and explore the qualities of the situated data and discuss how we can structure data into meaningful information and inform adaptive urban design systems; such as the intensity of the light, the pattern on the pavement or the three dimensional structures which provide shelter from the rain and the sun.

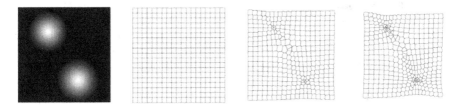

Fig. 4. Left weight image. The three right images, Voronoi variations of grid deformations with weight (0,4,8) of the weight image.

The computer vision data displays a differentiated high resolution bitmap of intensities of occupancy, groupings and motion in the urban space. This data is valuable information about its use and provides vital information for urban design. The different types of activities will afford different spatial requirement to the design, either for the static design of the place, e.g. pathways, furnishing, or for dynamic elements such as lighting, mediation etc.

3   A Case Study: "Gammel Torv" in Aalborg City

3.1   Experimental Setup

From a window placed on the 4th floor, a thermal camera films 24 hours of the activity in the square, Gammel Torv, in the city of Aalborg in Denmark. The camera films a crop of 70 × 50 meters of the total 300 × 70m square. The square is located in the center of the city and functions as an open, free space typically used for gatherings such as concerts, carnival, Christmas market etc. On ordinary days, however, it serves as a passage and a resting place between the two shopping streets in the city. The camera used in this setup is an AXIS Q1921-E with the following specifications: 10mm lens, 55° horizontal view, a resolution of 384 × 288, and a frame rate of 30 fps. The images include a primary flow path, a bench and a parking lot in the distance. The video was processed on a desktop computer using OpenCV for C++ and Matlab; the design patterns were generated in the parametric programming software Grasshopper for Rhino.

3.2   From Site Analysis to Urban Design Using Intensity Maps

First we need to understand the relationship between recorded data and architectural qualities. In the following, we will describe the spatial demands for places with high occupancy, primary flow lines, groupings and non-flow spaces.

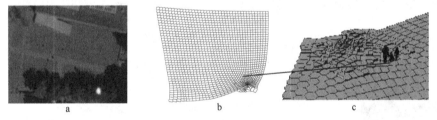

Fig. 5. a: Occupancy map. b: The tessellation in the Voronoi pattern is informed by the bitmap. c: The area of each Voronoi tile drives the high of the furniture structure, this gives many edges and height complexity in areas with long occupancy.

Occupancy. In places with high occupancy, there is often a need for places to stand, sit, lie or lean. Often, we do not occupy a space in the center of the square but seek towards the edges to cover our back. Our engagement is often directed towards other people, personal thoughts or fascination with the complex patterns of the tree crown or the dynamic patterns of the sky. It is a place for thoughtfulness. We prefer soft materials like grass, wood or plastic etc. Thus, we begin to have an idea of topologies and material properties for the region of occupancy. In figure 5, the occupancy map (30 min.) has informed a Voronoi tile. Intensity in the tessellation is controlled by the occupancy intensity on the map - places with high occupancy have a high amount of edges and complexity, whereas places with lower occupancy are less complex.

Primary Flow. The primary flow lines demand a frictionless movement - too many obstacles can cause a bad experience, and, in the worst cases, cause you to find another, faster route. When moving on the flow path you are observed and observing other people directly. The short eye-to-eye contact, body checking, ignoring etc. - this is the urban catwalk. It is a retreat for the high heelers, the person texting on the phone while running to the train or the fast moving skater etc.; indeed this space is a showroom. You do not want to stumble on the pavement or spend too much energy on navigation. The flow space is also the place to go when you are lost in the small spawns. When finding a route, it will always take you to a larger infrastructure, and as such you are connected to someplace you know. At night, this is the place where you want to see the heads of fellow pedestrians; it makes you feel calm and safe, because you can see the intentions. The space has an entrance and an exit; it has a direction, and the surface is plain but not slippery on rainy days. In the night time, the illumination is important.

Groupings. Places with a high amount of groupings could indicate meeting places or places with high friction. The grouping can be voluntary or involuntary; e.g. when waiting for a buss, standing in line or meeting your family or friends. Meetings in the public space are of informal groupings, and un-grouping is a very common social dynamic. The places are typically known as special places with special characteristics that somehow differentiate and become a common reference; e.g. under the clock or on the stairs by the water etc. It is difficult to present a single topology for this spatial character, but we can apply the principle of variation and differentiation in patterns, thus creating identity or exclusivity.

Non-flow Spaces. Regions with no or very little activity hold a potential for a new intervention that can improve the performance of the space. It is the first place to build a new design proposal, which facilitates new forms of occupancy; e.g. shelter from the sun, rain or wind, new facilities or maybe space for new architectural programs; such as kiosks, shops, restaurants etc. This presents potential places for new architectural footprints. In figure 6, one can see potential flow spaces; the red markings show the selected nodes. The placement can be more or less private (indicated by the amount of black in the circle). In figure 6, a column structure holds a potential canopy structure, which is raised towards the central flow paths and lowered around the more intimate sitting facilities. The pattern and the outline of the structure is informed by the intensities from the multilayered flow maps. As such, the pattern relates to one specific section of the square, underlining the novelty of that specific location.

Merging the four urban flow topologies presents a multilayered design matrix where different topologies and spatial qualities are separated by the analysis done from the existing site. Because of the nature of the data, it is possible to treat high-resolution data and create separations, not as lines but as gradient patterns. These are to be studied further together with the performative qualities of the urban flow topologies.

a   b

Fig. 6. a: White shows the collected flow regions. b: Selected canopy footprints (marked with +)

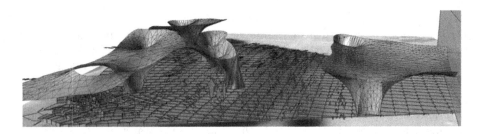

Fig. 7. Figure 5 & 6 are superimposed into a multilayered flow sketch

4   Discussion and Conclusion

The case study demonstrates that data from a thermal camera can be used as input in an urban design system, and by using computer vision techniques, it is possible to separate at least four types of flow: occupancy, flow, groupings and non-flow activity. The flow data maps are basis for a design case study where corresponding flow topologies are studied and formalized. The design scenario is one out of many possible design solutions, but it illustrates the intended data flow from between context, analysis, translation, representation, and into formalization. The outlined design methodology is linear, but if the project were realized; shape, texture, proportions, acoustics etc. would change the public "scene" and thereby change the way interactions unfold in the square. This is an iterative process. This looping process has a potential to visualize place usage, and present a foundation for a more intelligent selection of future design scenarios. The thermal camera images present tendencies, not individual actions, and they do not present accurate activities. The tendencies show how people are using (or not using) the public space, and this flow selection process indicates significant special qualities; is it a place you just pass through or a place where you check-in? Each of these activities has their own look and their own topology. As such, the image material gives us a better understanding of the spatial potentials and use of the space and presents valuable information for the designer or planner.

In this small project, we have used 30 minutes of recordings from a sunny summer day in mid July. These conditions are present 1495 hours [12] a year, which equals 17 %. This would give a snapshot of the existing flow patterns, which are in constant change and can never be predicted. We can collect more data by raising the chance of a good predication of human behavior, but it would always merely establish guidelines and tendencies. The flow tendencies are interlinked to the architectural setting, and when the light changes, the furniture moves, or a new tent is established, it will mobilize significant change in flow systems. These are the changes we have to evaluate to build better places for people. As such, we should discuss how the data could be a significant driver for future design decisions, and thereby close the feedback loop between real-world data and evaluated design effects. This study would need more than 30 minutes worth of snapshots, and the data would spread across seasons, for better qualifying new design proposals.

Redesigning the place, however, is a complex affair, and we still cannot tell the difference between a concert and a demonstration just by looking at the occupancy map. We still need an analytical eye interpreting the data. And what looks like unused spaces on the flow maps, could have other aesthetic qualities, e.g. the water surface (that appears as unused space on the heat map), the emergent ripple patterns on the surface, or the many-colored reflection of the sunset, which is the very reason to spend time on the riverbank - the unused space holds significant qualities, which can not be revealed from the maps. Therefore, it becomes important to treat urban design with due care before adding new edges in the city, but, indeed, the flow maps do add a significant and valuable design to the pencil case of the analytical planner.

References

1. Bertozzi, M., Broggi, A., Caraffi, C., Rose, M.D., Felisa, M., Vezzoni, G.: Pedestrian detection by means of far-infrared stereo vision. Computer Vision and Image Understanding 106(2-3), 194–204 (2007),
   http://www.sciencedirect.com/science/article/pii/S1077314206001858;
   Special issue on Advances in Vision Algorithms and Systems beyond the Visible Spectrum
2. Davis, J., Sharma, V.: Robust detection of people in thermal imagery. In: Proceedings of the 17th International Conference on Pattern Recognition, ICPR 2004, vol. 4, pp. 713–716 (August 2004)
3. Gehl, J.: Cities for people. Island Press, Washington, DC (2010)
4. Hajer, M., Reijndorp, A.: search of New Public Domain. Nai Publishers, Rotterdam (2001)
5. Han, J., Bhanu, B.: Human activity recognition in thermal infrared imagery. In: IEEE Computer Society Conference on Computer Vision and Pattern Recognition - Workshops, CVPR Workshops, p. 17 (June 2005)
6. Hensel, M., Menges, A.: Morpho-ecologies. Architectural Association, London (2006)

7. Jensen, O.B.: Facework, flow and the city - simmel, goffman and mobility in the contemporary city. Mobilities 2(2), 143–165 (2006)

8. Jensen, O.B.: Flows of meaning, cultures of movements - urban mobility as meaningful everyday life practice. Mobilities 4(4), 139–158 (2009)

9. Jensen, O.B.: Erving Goffman and Everyday Life Mobility, ch. 14, pp. 333–351. Routledge (2010)

10. Jensen, O.B.: Negotiation in motion: Unpacking a geography of mobility. Space and Culture 13(4), 389–402 (2010)

11. Kolarevic, B., Malkawi, A.: Performative architecture: beyond instrumentality. Spon Press, New York (2005)

12. Laursen, E.V., Rosenørn, S.: Technical Report 2-25: New hours of bright sunshine normals for Denmark, 1961-1990. Danish Meteorological Institute (2002), http://www.dmi.dk/dmi/tr02-25.pdf, ISSN 0906-897X, ISSN (online) 1399-1388

13. Lynch, K.: Good City Form. MIT Press, Cambridge (1981)

14. Lynn, G.: Animate form. Princeton Architectural Press, New York (1999)

15. McCullough, M.: Digital ground: architecture, pervasive computing, and environmental knowing. MIT Press, Cambridge (2005)

16. Schumacher, P.: Parametricism and the Autopoiesis of Architecture. Log 11, Los Angeles, lecture, SCI, Arc (September 2010), http://www.patrikschumacher.com/Texts/Parametricism %20and%20the%20Autopoiesis%20of%20Architecture.html

17. Schumacher, P.: The autopoiesis of architecture: A new framework for architecture, vol. 1. Wiley (2011)

18. Spuybroek, L.: NOX: machining architecture. Thames and Hudson, London (2004)

19. Terzidis, K.: Algorithmic Architecture. Architectural Press, Oxford (2006)

20. Whyte, W.: City. Rediscovering the Center. University of Pennsylvania Press, Philadelphia (1988/2009)

Sensor Based Monitoring for People with Dementia: Searching for Movement Markers in Alzheimer's Disease for a Early Diagnostic

Andre Hoffmeyer[1], Kristina Yordanova[3], Stefan Teipel[1,2], and Thomas Kirste[3]

[1] German Centre for Neurodegenerative Diseases, Rostock, Germany
andre.hoffmeyer@dzne.de
[2] University of Rostock, Department of Psychiatry, Rostock, Germany
[3] University of Rostock, Institute of Computer Science, Rostock, Germany

Abstract. We report on first results of using motion pattern behaviour as a possible diagnostics marker for detection and prediction of alzheimer diseases. We observed elderly subjects with and without dementia and recorded their motion behaviour with mobile sensors for 3 days. Additionally, we analyzed the sensor data offline and used probabilistic models (Hierarchical Hidden Markov Models) to differentiate between healthy subjects and subjects suffering form the disease. Our first results with 32 subjects achieve an accuracy of 91 percent.

Keywords: accelerometer, dementia, hidden markov model.

1 Introduction

Increasing life expectancy has a severe impact on the prevalence of age-associated diseases. Recent studies estimate that the worldwide number of subjects suffering from dementia will rise from 35 million at present to more than 65 million in 2030 – an increase of almost 100%. This increase of people suffering from dementia is accompanied by a parallel decrease in the number of of younger people that are available for care and nursing. One major challenge with dementia is the onset of behavioural symptoms that lead to institutionalisation of the patients and pose major costs on the health care system.

Abnormal motor behaviour and degeneration of the sleep-waking cycle are among the most severe behavioural symptoms. An early detection and even a prediction of these behaviours would allow a timely onset of therapeutical interventions that aim to delay the manifestation or exacerbation of symptoms and reduce the need of institutionalized care. To date, diagnostic and prognostic markers are unable to predict the onset of abnormal motor behaviour. Moreover, such markers may be useful to objectively evaluate the effect of current or future therapeutical interventions on the behaviour. Using behavioral cues as diagnostic instrument is interesting for two reasons: (i) data can be acquired in a persons everyday environment (ii) once behaviour analysis is in place, assistive

R. Wichert, K. Van Laerhoven, J. Gelissen (Eds.): AmI 2011 Workshops, CCIS 277, pp. 137–145, 2012.

functionality can be added for compensating errors in daily routine activities and for other forms of ambient assisted living.

2   Recent Work

Activity recognition plays a key role in assistive systems. The current activity or action of persons is necessary for a correct intention analysis. There are different approaches to realize activity recognition that can be differentiated into an indoor and an outdoor solution. An indoor solution can be for example a tracking system on wifi or ultrasound basis. It is also possible to use cameras [3], floor mats [8] or intelligent switches [15]. A disadvantage is that these systems need a local installation. As an outdoor solution the above mentioned points are not possible. Activity recognition outside for example is possible with the GPS system [9]. Furthermore combinations of different sensor types are explored. Hein [6] uses RFID and acceleration sensors to detect care activities.

Ambient Assisted Living (AAL) describes methods, systems, services that support the daily lifes of elderly people. The applications are manifold, a very good example is Oatfield Estates [1] in Oregon USA. This is a residential care home which is equipped with a variety of different sensors that make a wide range of information available. Thus, activity diagrams of the residents can be created allowing to analyze about sleep patterns, physical activity, but also the social activity. This information can be very helpful for treatment.

AAL Systems are mainly aimed at supporting independent and self-determined living for senior citizens. But there are also systems for the special needs of persons with dementia. These solutions can be classified into four groups. The compensation of cognitive skills [10], for example remember taking the medication[16], the support in the activities of daily living, for example washing hands [11], the stability of social contacts [13] and last the feeling of safety/security [12]. Kasteren [17] studied in his thesis temporal probabilistic models to recognize activities of daily living for eldery people by using different sensor types and wireless sensor network. The approach was verified in three houses and with Hierarchical Hidden Markov Models he gets the best classification results to recognize ADL.

Biological markers [5] for dementia are established in part to be explored in studies. A novel approach is to use methods from activity recognition as diagnostic marker. Kearns [7] used Ubisense, an indoor localization system, to record movement trajectories of people with dementia. In his studies the cognitive status of subjects correlated with the tortuosity of the movement trajectories.

3   Study Desgin

The DZNE is a research institute studying neurodegenerative diseases. One research topic in the DZNE Rostock is an early diagnosis of dementia in high risk populations and in subjects with demand for medical and social care support. This study has the following three aims:

- The prediction of problem behaviour in the stage of dementia: How strong is the abnormal behavior formed?
- The prediction of dementia in early stages: Is it possible to detect motion patterns which are typical for dementia in early stages?
- Review of the efficacy of therapeutic interventions.

To verify our aims we recruited elderly couples and divided the subjects into two groups of couples. In group A one partner suffers from dementia and the other is healthy, in group B both partners are cognitively healthy. To determine the cognitive performance of subjects we are using the CERAD battery [4].

The affected subjects were examined by a doctor and diagnosed with a light or mild dementia. Exclusion criteria for the study are diseases of Nervous system, neoplastic diseases, Restlesslegs-Syndrome or obstructive sleep apnea syndrome. The interesting point is that we can analyze the caregiver effect too. Are existing strains of healthy partners in group A measurable?

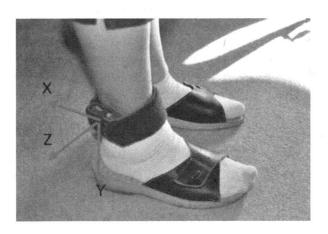

Fig. 1. The foot-mounted sensor worn by a volunteer. The bandage has a velcro closure and a opening for the sensor.

The record of the movement behavior of subjects is in their domesticity. Both partners have a motion sensor foot-mounted for round about 50 hours. We use this sensor position because it is the most comfortable position. As subjects wear the sensor for three days continuously a position at the hip for example is not acceptable because it would disturb the subject while sleeping. The combination with the foot position and comfortable bandage has been found to be the best alternative. Furthermore Atallah et. al. [2] evaluated different accelerometer positions(ear,chest,arm,wrist,waist,knee,ankle/foot-mounted) for detecting different activities of daily living. For low activities and the ankle position they got good results.

The shimmer sensor is a 3-axis accelerometer sensor. We used a 50 Hertz sampling rate and a range of -4/4G. The sensor operates autonomous. It requires

no infrastructure and the subjects can follow their usual activities. The data is
log on the sensor flash memory.[1]

4   Data Analysis Concept

Each subject of the study generated approximately 9 million data points (times-
tamp, and the x, y, z acceleration.) – a total of 900 MByte. Before the data is
used it is checked for its validity. So records are excluded where the sensor has
failed or the subject has not taken the device. Furthermore, the data is normalized by the raw sensor values in g.

The first step of any signal processing is to analyze the raw data before further
processing steps are made. Figure 2 presents a short-term Fourier transform
(window size = 256 samples/5.12 second) of a subject. The record includes 2
nights. Even at the different amplitude of the frequency spectrum it can be
distinguished between day and night. Walk sequences are also visible at a high
frequency. One advantage of the selected sensor position is that it is possible to
select features which are depending on a fix position. The sensor is located for
each subject always at the same position and the same orientation of the axes of
the accelerometer. Frequency features are normally very suitable for a feature.
But in the first step our focus is to find the best model for our issue.

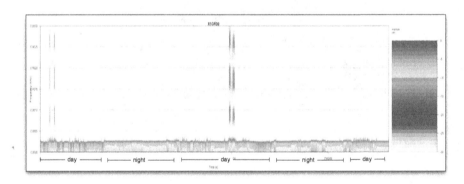

Fig. 2. The illustration shows a frequency analysis of a subject with the ground truth
of day and night. (Using R and seewave [14] for the illustration.)

The aim of this study is not to achieve an activity analysis of the subjects but
rather compare the daily routine between the healthy and demented subjects.
So the question is to find motion patterns that correlate with cognitive diseases
and is it possible to identify this motion pattern in a early stage before the
cognitive losses have been noticeable. Therefore, classical methods of activity

---

[1] The shimmer sensors have no ability for geo coding. We record no GPS data or
similar data. An important point for all subjects is that their privacy is always
protected.

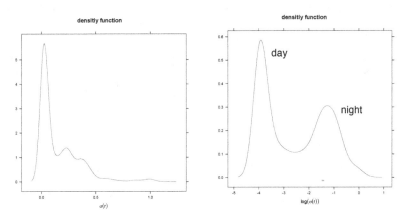

Fig. 3. Left: The density plot of $\sigma(r)$. Right: The densityplot of $log(\sigma(r))$

recognition such as decision trees or support vector machine are not suitable because they haven't the ability to analyze temporal structures. Thus we have chosen a Hidden Markov Model (HMM). HMMs have the advantage that they are able to reflect complex temporal properties. Furthermore they are human readable and adjustable and have well known algorithms for inference which also allows prediction. For the inference we built a toolkit that has the ability of filtering, smoothing and learning for HMMs and particle filter. The toolkit uses a flatten algorithm to handle Hierarchical Hidden Markov which creates a equivalent HMMs.

Our approach is as follows, we use for the classification two HMMs – healthy model mh and demented model md. Then we train the model mh with the datasets of the healthy subject and the model md with the dataset of the suffered subjects. When we want to classify an unknown subject we calculate the likelihood of both models. The highest likelihood (log odds) classifies the subject as healthy or suffering from dementia.

Before features from one dataset are calculated, the data size is reduced with a simple windowing without a sliding window algorithm. A window size of 2 minutes was chosen. After the windowing we only get 1500 windows with calculated features. For every feature we calculate the mean values and standard deviation σ from x, y, z and $r = \sqrt{x^2 + y^2 + z^2}$ (absolute value). With a small subset of 5 couples from group A (5 subjects suffering from dementia and 5 people that are cognitively healthy) we try different observations for the HMM. With a variance analysis we chose the $\bar{y}$ (normally distributed) and $\sigma(r)$ (lognormal distributed) (see figure 3) as features for classification. The advantage with a windowing is not only a data reducing. Rather it allows to analyze the daily structure of the subjects. This is due to the fact that a state $x(t)$ in a HMM depend only on its previous state $x(t-1)$. If we don't use a windowing the time difference between states is only 0.02 seconds. This minimal time difference makes an analysis of the daily structure impossible. The choice of 2 minutes is good compromise between long daily structure terms and short movement periods.

To find the best Markov model we tried different approaches. First we applied a two-state HMM with the $log(\sigma(r))$ as observation. With this first model we obtained two incorrectly classified subjects. A second two-state HMM, the observation $log(\sigma(r))$ and $\bar{y}$ got only one wrong classified subject. Adding more features does not improve the classification results. A third two-state HMM with the observations $log(\sigma(r))$, $\bar{y}$ $\bar{z}$ produces three incorrectly classified subjects.

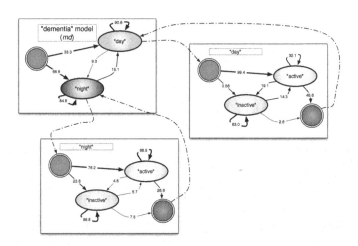

Fig. 4. Reconstruction of daily routine with the HHMM: The "dementia" model

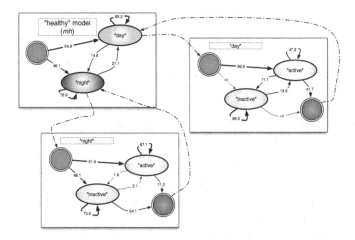

Fig. 5. Reconstruction of daily routine with the HHMM: The "healthy" model

The best results were received with two 2x2 Hierarchical Hidden Markov Model (HHMM) because the HHMMs are able to reproduce the daily routine from subjects. The choice of the features from the variance analysis is plausible.

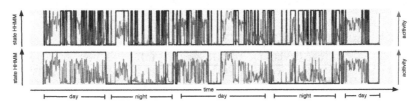

Fig. 6. Above: "dementia" model md Under: "healthy" model mh - The black lines represent the state transition in the first layer of the HHMMs. (see figure 4 and 5) The redlines each are the observation $\sigma(r)$. The output of both models were generated with the same data from a subject. The "healthy" model looks more stable and generate a typical daily structure. The "dementia" model looks less structured.

The mean of a feature y describes the body position in the best manner. The vector y (see figure 1) is the parallel vector to the acceleration of gravity when the subject stands and the orthogonal vector when the person lies. $\sigma(r)$ is a measure for the activity of the subjects.

Furthermore the HHMMs md and mh indicate first correlation between the cognitive status from the subject because the healthy model is significantly more stable. A very important point is that we used unlabeled data and no prior knowledge. Also the timestamps were not used by the HHMM. Figure 6 shows the states transition from the healthy and the demented model for one subject. Although the models have no prior knowledge about the time the model mh builds structure like the transition between day and night. (Note: In figure 4 and 5 the first layer is called just day and night.) The model md shows a very disturbed state transition behaviour. So the difference between the diseased and healthy daily routines is remarkable.

5 Running Study: First Results and Conclusion

At present we collect data from n = 32 subjects (16 pairs - Table 1) . In 9 of these couples one partner is suffering from dementia (Group A). In the other 7 couples both partners are cognitively healthy (Group B). All subjects were previously tested with the CERAD cognitive battery. All couples wear the sensor for about 50 hours in the domestics. The initial fears that the subjects have problems to wear the sensor were not confirmed. All subjects wore the sensor and no sensor has been lost. The worst mistake was a showered sensor for a short moment. One subject had the fear his heart pacemaker would be affected by the sensor. Altogether we can say that the subjects had no fear of contact with new technologies. Most subjects even have reported that they have not noticed the sensor over time. With our HHMM approach we get a classification precision of 91 percent (see figure 7). Two healthy subjects were classified as demented and one demented subject as healthy. The interesting point is that one incorrectly classified healthy subject had not good clinical findings in the

Table 1. Overview about the study group

	dementia	cognitive healthy
age average	80.1	73.4
age deviation	4.78	6.15
MMSE average	19.44	28.42
MMSE deviation	8.42	0.90

cerad test. It was just under the threshold to mild cognitive impairment. With a "leave one out" testing we still get an accuracy of 81 percent.

With our first experiments we wanted to verify the feasibility and if physical activity is correlated with dementia. For a small number of test subjects we have shown that it is possible to differentiate between healthy and suffering from dementia subjects only with mobile sensors. So we established an objective model to detect differences in movement behavior and now we are looking for typical motion patterns in dementia behavior. For our future work we intend to increase the number of subjects in Group A (20 couples) and complete the clinical recruitment. This is a preliminary study and we still have to investigate a number of aspects more closely. Conclusive statements about typical motion patterns can be made only at the end of the study.

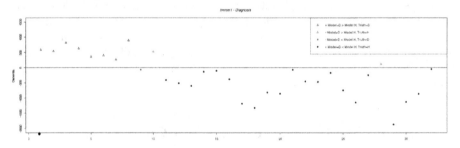

Fig. 7. Log-odds: automatic diagnosis from our Models

References

1. Assisted living and memory care in portland — elitecare.com (June 2011)
2. Atallah, L., Lo, B., King, R., Yang, G.-Z.: Sensor placement for activity detection using wearable accelerometers. In: Proceedings of the 2010 International Conference on Body Sensor Networks, BSN 2010, pp. 24–29. IEEE Computer Society, Washington, DC (2010)
3. Bieber, G., Hoffmeyer, A., Gutzeit, E., Peter, C., Urban, B.: Activity monitoring by fusion of optical and mechanical tracking technologies for user behavior analysis. In: Proceedings of the 2nd International Conference on PErvasive Technologies Related to Assistive Environments, PETRA 2009, pp. 45:1–45:6. ACM, New York (2009)

4. Morris, et al.: The Consortium to Establish a Registry for Alzheimer's Disease (CERAD). Part I. Clinical and neuropsychological assessment of Alzheimer's disease. Neurology 39, 1159–1165 (1989)
5. Hampel, H., Frank, R., Broich, K., Teipel, S.J., Katz, R.G., Hardy, J., Herholz, K., Bokde, A.L.W., Jessen, F., Hoessler, Y.C., Sanhai, W.R., Zetterberg, H., Woodcock, J., Blennow, K.: Biomarkers for alzheimer's disease: academic, industry and regulatory perspectives. Nat. Rev. Drug Discov. 9(7), 560–574 (2010)
6. Hein, A., Kirste, T.: A Hybrid Approach for Recognizing ADLs and Care Activities Using Inertial Sensors and RFID. In: Stephanidis, C. (ed.) UAHCI 2009, Part II. LNCS, vol. 5615, pp. 178–188. Springer, Heidelberg (2009)
7. Kearns, W.D., Nams, V.O., Fozard, J.L.: Tortuosity in movement paths is related to cognitive impairment. Wireless fractal estimation in assisted living facility residents. Methods of Information in Medicine 49(6), 592–598 (2010)
8. Klack, L., Möllering, C., Ziefle, M., Schmitz-Rode, T.: Future Care Floor: A Sensitive Floor for Movement Monitoring and Fall Detection in Home Environments. In: Lin, J., Nikita, K.S. (eds.) MobiHealth 2010. LNICST, vol. 55, pp. 211–218. Springer, Heidelberg (2011)
9. Liao, L., Fox, D., Kautz, H.A.: Extracting places and activities from gps traces using hierarchical conditional random fields. I. J. Robotic Res. 26(1), 119–134 (2007)
10. Meiland, F., Reinersmann, A., Bergvall-Kareborn, B., Craig, D., Moelaert, F., Mulvenna, M., Nugent, C., Scully, T., Bengtsson, J., Dres, R.: Cogknow development and evaluation of an ict-device for people with mild dementia. Studies in Health Technology and Informatics (7), 166–177 (2007)
11. Mihailidis, A., Boger, J., Craig, T., Hoey, J.: The coach prompting system to assist older adults with dementia through handwashing: An efficacy study. BMC Geriatrics 8(1), 28 (2008)
12. Patterson, D.J., Liao, L., Gajos, K., Collier, M., Livic, N., Olson, K., Wang, S., Fox, D., Kautz, H.: Opportunity Knocks: A System to Provide Cognitive Assistance with Transportation Services. In: Davies, N., Mynatt, E.D., Siio, I. (eds.) UbiComp 2004. LNCS, vol. 3205, pp. 433–450. Springer, Heidelberg (2004)
13. Rowan, J., Mynatt, E.D.: Digital family portrait field trial: Support for aging in place. In: Proceedings of the SIGCHI Conference on Human Factors in Computing Systems, CHI 2005, pp. 521–530. ACM, New York (2005)
14. Sueur, J., Aubin, T., Simonis, C.: Seewave: a free modular tool for sound analysis and synthesis. Bioacoustics 18, 213–226 (2008)
15. Tapia, E.M., Intille, S.S., Larson, K.: Activity Recognition in the Home Using Simple and Ubiquitous Sensors. In: Ferscha, A., Mattern, F. (eds.) PERVASIVE 2004. LNCS, vol. 3001, pp. 158–175. Springer, Heidelberg (2004)
16. Tsai, P.-H., Shih, C.-S., Liu, J.W.-S.: Mobile Reminder for Flexible and Safe Medication Schedule for Home Users. In: Jacko, J.A. (ed.) HCI International 2011, Part III. LNCS, vol. 6763, pp. 107–116. Springer, Heidelberg (2011)
17. van Kasteren, T.: Activity recognition for health monitoring elderly using temporal probabilistic models. Dissertation, Universiteit van Amsterdam (2011)

Functional Requirements for Assistive Technology for People with Cognitive Impairments and Dementia

F.J.M. Meiland[1], M.E. de Boer[2], J. van Hoof[3], J. van der Leeuw[4], L. de Witte[5], M. Blom[6], I. Karkowski[7], M.D. Mulvenna[8], and R.M. Dröes[1]

[1] Department of Nursing Home Medicine and Department of Psychiatry,
VU University Medical Center, Van der Boechorststraat 7,
1081 BT Amsterdam, The Netherlands
{fj.meiland,rm.droes}@vumc.nl
[2] Department of Nursing Home Medicine, VU University Medical Center,
Van der Boechorststraat 7, 1081 BT Amsterdam, The Netherlands
[3] Research Centre for Innovation in Health Care, Faculty of Health Care, Hogeschool Utrecht
University of Applied Sciences, Bolognalaan 101, 3584 CJ Utrecht, The Netherlands
[4] Vilans, Catharijnesingel 47, 3511 GC Utrecht, The Netherlands
[5] University of Maastricht, Hogeschool Zuyd, Postbus 550, 6400 AN Heerlen, The Netherlands
[6] Alzheimer Nederland, Kosterijland 3, 3981 AJ Bunnik, The Netherlands
[7] TNO, innovation for life, The Hague, The Netherlands
[8] School of Computing and Mathematics, University of Ulster, United Kingdom

Abstract. The amount of technological aids on the market to support people in their everyday functioning is increasing. For example mobile telephone, electronic diary, skyping and domotics. Many of these aids are too complicated to operate for people with cognitive impairments, like dementia. For technology to be practicable and useful for them, it will have to meet certain requirements. This paper addresses the needs and impairments of people with dementia, and the functional requirements for assistive technology for people with dementia.

Keywords: assistive technology, dementia, functional requirements.

1 Introduction

Today, in 2011, there are some 243,000 people with dementia in the Netherlands. This number will increase explosively to more than half a million people in 2040 due to increased life expectancy and population ageing. Dementia strikes not only the elderly, the disease can also emerge at a younger age. At this moment approx. 12,000 people under the age of 65 have the disease in our country [1].

The increase in numbers of people with cognitive impairments and dementia also increases pressure on the care and welfare services for this target group. This is aggravated by the anticipated relative decrease of available personnel in the care sector. In addition to carers, technological aids will therefore be employed more and more as alternative types of care and support in daily functioning. Technological aids may include, for example, remote care (telecare) and home automation (domotics), where

R. Wichert, K. Van Laerhoven, J. Gelissen (Eds.): AmI 2011 Workshops, CCIS 277, pp. 146–151, 2012.
© Springer-Verlag Berlin Heidelberg 2012

e.g. sensors can increase safety in the home, but also simplified mobile telephones, electronic diaries with automatic reminder systems, and videophoning using skype.

The expectation is that people can continue to function safely in their familiar living environment for a longer period of time. However, experience shows that technological aids are often too complicated to operate or learn to operate for cognitively impaired persons, like people with dementia. If they are to be able to use and benefit from the technology, it will have to meet certain requirements.

2   Needs of People with Cognitive Impairments and Dementia

To adequately support the growing group of people with cognitive impairment and dementia, it is necessary to understand their needs. Naturally these needs are related first of all to the specific cognitive impairment of the individual, such as memory complaints, problems with language expression and understanding, and problems performing complex tasks, and to the disease that may be causing them. In elderly persons symptoms of old age, such as difficulty walking and poor eyesight, can also play a role. In addition, personal and contextual factors, such as the way an individual deals with his complaints (coping strategies), what he or she considers most important for his/her quality of life and the amount of care one receives, determine what people need.

Research shows that people with dementia and their informal carers need support or assistance in various areas of everyday life, for example preparing food, household chores, memory problems, handling money and mobility. The most frequently mentioned unmet needs are [2]:

• support for memory problems
• information on one's condition and on care and support options
• social contacts and companionship
• monitoring health and safety
• daytime activities

Existing technology can already meet some of these needs [3]. Memory, for example, can be supported by 'electronic reminders' via mobile phone, television or computer ("Your daughter is visiting you this afternoon", "You have an appointment with the doctor at 10 o'clock"). To facilitate keeping in touch with family, friends and acquaintances there are simplified mobile phones and videophones. GPS systems can trace or assist people when they lose their way. And there are sensors that emit a signal when the person forgets to, for example, turn off the gas or the electric kettle, or that even automatically switch off appliances if needed.

Many of these developments are still in their infancy and are far from meeting every need of people with cognitive impairment and dementia (and their informal carers). In part the technology is insufficiently compatible with the possibilities and limitations of this target group.

3   Impairments of People with Dementia

Dementia is not one particular disease with one particular cause; it is a syndrome, i.e. an accumulation of symptoms, especially disorders in cognitive functions (including memory, attention, language, action), that together cause problems in daily functioning. In most cases of dementia, also in the most common type, namely Alzheimer's disease, there is a gradual decline in functioning. Roughly three stages can be distinguished, each with its particular characteristics.

In the first stage (early dementia), people may experience severe forgetfulness, concentration problems, problems with complex and new situations, difficulty managing finances, loss of sense of time, orientation problems, word finding problems and denial of problems.

In the second stage (advanced dementia) people may have no memory of most recent events, problems carrying out activities of daily living, problems with arithmetic, language problems (expression and understanding), personality and behaviour changes and diurnal rhythm disturbed.

In the final stage (severe dementia) symptoms are: loss of communication, largely unaware of surroundings, in need of assistance with most activities of daily living, not recognizing objects, problems controlling movement, incontinence, and loss of decorum.

For this target group, learning to use new aids is therefore (severely) complicated by memory and concentration problems, problems understanding instructions, recognizing objects/images, problems with verbal expression, and problems carrying out complex actions (apraxia). Also, psychological and behaviour problems can affect learning to use different types of assistive technology.

If assistive technology is to be useful for individuals in the different stages of dementia, these limitations must be taken into account when they are developed.

4   The Development of Assistive Technology

In the process of developing assistive technological aids the needs and wishes of the users have to be translated into technological requirements that the design of the assistive technology must meet, if it is to be practicable and useful for the target group (see fig. 1)[4,5].

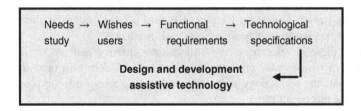

Fig. 1. Process from user wishes to design and development

An example of a functional requirement is that a reminder for a doctor's appointment must be repeated several times because of the user's short-term memory problems. How this reminder is displayed and how often it is to be repeated, must be determined by the engineers together with domain experts and also in consultation with the end users (people with dementia and the people close to them).

5   Needs, Aids and Functional Requirements

Below we present examples of electronic aids that could be used for the most frequently mentioned unmet needs of people with dementia (and their informal carers). For each of the listed aids we have added a brief description of the functional requirements that need to be taken into account when the future users are people with dementia, or their informal carers [6].

5.1   Need for Assistance with regard to the Symptoms of Dementia

a. Electronic compensatory aids for impairments such as memory problems in activities of daily living (ADL).

Example: Electronic Memory Aids.

➢ **Requirements.** Practicability, personal definition of reminders, informal carer controls reminders, repeat option. Interfaces in own language. Preferably multimodal, for example option for vibrate mode in combination with visual and auditory reminder in the case of visual or auditory impairment.

b. Flexible and individually customized electronic aids to support the informal carer in giving instrumental care to the person with dementia.

Example: Remote care services; support and education for informal carers via the internet and telephone.

➢ **Requirements.** Possibility to indicate personal preferences, integrated in personal environment.

c. Technological support for people with dementia and informal carers in dealing with behavioural and psychological changes.

Example: Websites; monitoring behaviour with sensors/cameras; influencing behaviour using music.

➢ **Requirements.** Easily accessible, integrate equipment in personal environment, possibility to indicate personal preference with a user-friendly interface in ones own language.

d. Emotional support for people with dementia and informal carers.

Example: Support via email groups; chat box on Alzheimer sites, etc.

➢ **Requirements.** Easily accessible, no codes or password, based on once-only registration and, for example, identification of the PC.

5.2   Need for Information on one's Condition and on Care and Support Options

a. Information on dementia
Example: Via Internet.
➢ **Requirements.** accessible texts and web design of Internet pages, not too childish, in ones own language and limited amount of information on a page.

b. Information on services, legal and financial matters and available care and welfare services.
Example: Digital social map of regional care and welfare services.
➢ **Requirements.** Supplied information is accessible and geared to the individual ('customized'); context specific and demand driven.

c. Information on personal condition, care appointments and planning of care.
Example: Electronic medical record, electronic patient record.
➢ **Requirements.** Remote consultation or at GP's: Actual and comprehensive record with information from most important professional carers.

5.3   Need for Social Contacts and Companionship

This concerns ways to stay in contact with family and friends and the social environment.

Example: Telecommunications systems such as simple mobile telephone/skype; touch-screen PCs; tele-visits; robot pets.

➢ **Requirements.** Intuitive operation must be possible; preferably the minimum number of buttons; design of operation screen geared to personal preferences.

5.4   Need for Health Monitoring and Experienced Safety

The need to be cared for and to be safe as the disease progresses is central here.

Example: Telecare/telemonitoring; fall detection and alert systems for, e.g. fall detection (sensors/cameras), monitoring sleep pattern or vital functions, detection of dangerous situations (e.g. forgetting electric kettle).

➢ **Requirements.** Geared to the needs of individual and informal carer; context specific; preferably full automatic (no direct input from person with dementia required); flexible and reliable feedback of detected (emergency) situations (depending on personal preferences alert is sent to person with dementia, informal or professional carer); with optimal user-friendliness for person with dementia (meaning also e.g. that professionals treat people well, good installation procedures).

5.5   Need for Daytime Activities

This is about being able to undertake activities to relax and to do something useful.

Example: GPS based tracking systems (e.g. a watch) to allow for outdoor activities (finding and guiding the way back home for people who lost their way); multimedia systems to look at photographs, listen to music or play games.

➢ **Requirements.** Geared to the needs of the individual; practicability (e.g. simple operation, taking into account memory, visual and auditory impairments); possibility of personalization; in own language; easy to take along; low battery usage.

Finally, it is important to investigate the (cost) effectiveness of the developed technology and, in the case of proven added value, to explore the possibilities of subsidies or reimbursement of costs for cognitively impaired people and their informal carers.

References

1. http://www.alzheimer-nederland.nl
2. Van der Roest, H.G., Meiland, F.J.M., Comijs, H.C., Derksen, E., Jansen, A.P.D., Van Hout, H.P.J., Jonker, C., Dröes, R.M.: What do community dwelling people with dementia need? A survey among those who are known by care and welfare services. International Psychogeriatrics 21(5), 949–965 (2009) (Epub July 15, 2009)
3. Lauriks, S., Reinersmann, A., van der Roest, H., Meiland, F.J.M., Davies, R.J., Moelaert, F., Mulvenna, M.D., Nugent, C.D., Dröes, R.M.: Review of ICT-based services for identified unmet needs in people with dementia. Ageing Research Reviews 6(3), 223–246 (2007) (Epub August 2, 2007)
4. Hettinga, M., Holthe, H., Andersson, A.L., Moelaert, F.: Managing the transition from user studies to functional requirements to technical specification. In: Mulvenna, M.D., Nugent, C.D. (eds.) Supporting People with Dementia Using Pervasive Health Technologies. Advanced Information and Knowledge Processing. Springer-Verlag London Limited (2010)
5. Meiland, F.J.M., Reinersmann, A., Sävenstedt, S., Bergvall-Kåreborn, B., Hettinga, M., Craig, D., Andersson, A.L., Dröes, R.M.: User-participatory development of assistive technology for people with dementia – from needs to functional requirements. First Results of the COGKNOW Project. Non-pharmacological Therapies in Dementia 1(1), 71–91 (2010)
6. Dröes, R.M., Bentvelzen, S.C.L., Meiland, F., Craig, D.: Dementia-related and other factors to be taken into account when developing ICT-support for people with dementia – Lessons from field trials. In: Mulvenna, M.D., Nugent, C.D. (eds.) Supporting People with Dementia Using Pervasive Health Technologies. Advanced Information and Knowledge Processing, ch. 8, pp. 113–130. Springer, London (2010) ISBN: 978-1-84882-550-5

Concept and Realization of an Individual Reminder Service for People Suffering from Dementia

Holger Storf, Mario Schmitt, Taslim Arif,
Wolfgang Putz, Michael Eisenbarth, and Özgür Ünalan

Fraunhofer Institute for Experimental Software Engineering (IESE),
Fraunhofer-Platz 1, 67663 Kaiserslautern, Germany
{Holger.Storf,Mario.Schmitt,Taslim.Arif,
Wolfgang.Putz,Michael.Eisenbarth,
Oezguer.Uenalan}@iese.fraunhofer.de

Abstract. Rendering and offering adequate reminder services in a situation-aware, proactive manner and providing information for diagnosis support is a major issue for Ambient Assisted Living systems when it comes to dealing with persons suffering from mild dementia. One great challenge therefore is to provide the reminders in context to the real situation, to minimize the number of reminder messages, and to individualize the reminder tasks. In the European project CCE (Connected Care for Elderly Persons Suffering from Dementia), this functionality is realized by a component called Dementia Diary. It is a central component of the overall CCE system with many interconnections to other components of the CCE system. This article gives an overview of the Dementia Diary and briefly describes its realization using rules.

Keywords: Reminder Service, Dementia, Drools.

1   Introduction

Demographic, structural, and social trends are driven by an increasing number of elderly people and single households in most industrialized countries. The consequences are that more and more elderly people are living alone longer. The resulting increase in emergency situations and missions, which will lead to a rise in health care costs in the coming years, will have dramatic effects on public and private health care, emergency medical services, and the individuals themselves..

In parallel, the number of people suffering from cognitive impairments, like MCI, dementia, or Alzheimer's, will also rise dramatically – whereas 1.3 million people are currently suffering from dementia in Germany, this will have nearly doubled by 2050 [1]. In last year's World Alzheimer Report, Alzheimer's Disease International estimated that there were 35.6 million people living with dementia worldwide in 2010; these numbers will increase to 65.7 million by 2030 and to 115.4 million by 2050 [2].

This fact motivates the development of special solutions based on new technologies for supporting cognitively impaired people in their daily lives. The

R. Wichert, K. Van Laerhoven, J. Gelissen (Eds.): AmI 2011 Workshops, CCIS 277, pp. 152–156, 2012.

corresponding research field is called Ambient Assisted Living (AAL) [3]. In the EU-funded project CCE (Connected Care for Elderly Persons Suffering from Dementia) [4], a system concept for supporting people suffering from dementia in their daily lives with the help of reminder services is being developed, implemented as a prototype, and validated.

People with dementia generally suffer from "gradual memory loss, decreasing ability to perform routine daily living tasks, impaired judgment, disorientation, personality changes, loss of language skills, and behavior disturbance" [5]. As the disease deteriorates, dementia sufferers find it more and more difficult to "comprehend language in written and spoken form" [6]. Short-term memory problems create further difficulties, as people become unable to follow a conversation, forgetting what was said just a little while ago. Furthermore, given that they become easily disoriented and distracted, it makes it very difficult to communicate when there are many people all talking at the same time.

The focus of CCE lies on providing assistance to people with cognitive impairments by giving them reminders regarding specific appointments or helping them interact with everyday devices, such as the door key before leaving the house, in order to prevent unpleasant situations. The reminders for appointments such as a visit to the doctor or the visit of a family member or neighbor should be seen as memory support. Besides these special appointments, people with dementia are also reminded to perform normal daily activities, the so-called ADLs [7], in order to follow their daily routines. The responsible component for triggering the reminders is the Dementia Diary.

The goal of this paper is to: (i) provide insights into the CCE system and the Dementia Diary, (ii) show the interconnections between the Dementia Diary and other components in the CCE system, and (iii) give a short example of the realization using the business logic platform Drools [8]. Finally, we provide an overview of the current status of the project and an outlook on future work.

2   The "Dementia Diary" in the CCE System

The so-called Dementia Diary is a core component of the CCE system and is located on the Home Gateway, which is in the apartment of the person suffering from dementia. The Home Gateway is connected to different other components. The person's physical activities can be detected via ambient sensors, like motion or contact sensors. The RFID Tray detects whether a specific device is located on the tray or not, and the Medication Dispenser reports if a medication has been taken or not. For visualizing the reminder messages, a tablet PC is attached, which can also trigger defined acoustical alerts. Critical notifications and characteristic information such as detected ADLs will be sent to the CentriHealth Corkboard for further interpretation, and the results can be seen by the person via the NetTV. The reminder services described below can be configured via a Web interface, which is also located on a server outside the apartment.

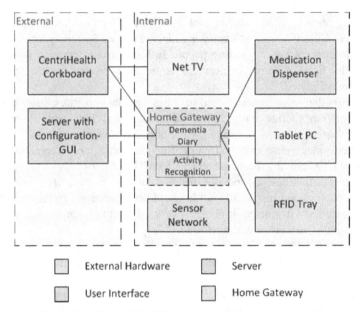

Fig. 1. Overview of the CCE System with the Dementia Diary

The Dementia Diary is of central importance and has interconnections with most of the other components. It offers two complementary communication methods. First, the synchronous/data-centric variant is based upon a central persistence unit (RDBMS, OR-Mapper, and data model), which maintains calendric information on past, present, and future appointments as well as planned tasks of the cognitively impaired person. Particularly such components of the CCE system that use this communication method provide interfaces to the different stakeholders (person with dementia, caregivers, relatives), i.e., Configuration UI, Tablet PC, and Corkboard access this predominantly static information directly.

In addition, the asynchronous/event-driven communication method uses an existing message-oriented middleware (MOM) implementation as an integration platform for employing a publish/subscribe message pattern on a domain-specific event topic model. Based on that MOM, the connected devices, i.e., the RFID tray and the Medication Dispenser, publish internal state changes, e.g., *take medication* or *take off/deposit a tray item* to the CCE system. The Dementia Diary receives those events along with events on detected activities published by the Activity Recognition component, which are later matched against planned activities and tasks. When such an activity or task is due, the Dementia Diary processes and synchronizes reminders for appointments and tasks on different user interfaces by publishing events to the relevant interaction devices. Besides its scalability, the major advantage of the approach taken is that producers and consumers are decoupled, meaning that the Dementia Diary might support an arbitrary number of end-user devices, even if they are tailored to other platforms.

3   Realization of the "Dementia Diary"

The general idea of the Dementia Diary is that the person suffering from dementia will be reminded to perform typical activities at home, like the activities of daily living (ADLs), in particular the preparation of meals, personal hygiene, or going to bed or getting up. Additionally, there are reminders for appointments that take place outside of the apartment - this may be a doctor's appointment, drinking tea with the neighbor, going shopping, etc. The reminders, which are shown on a tablet PC, can include additional information such as the location or the route description. The schedule can be configured by the relatives or caregivers with a web interface. Also connected to the Dementia Diary is a medication dispenser so that reminders can be triggered if the prescribed medication has not been taken. Another assistance service is that special items that are needed to perform the activity correctly, e.g., the door keys, wallet, insurance card, etc., can be connected to specific appointments. When the person wants to leave the apartment, the system checks whether the items have been taken. For this purpose, an RFID tag is attached to these items, and they are normally located on a special tray.

To realize this end user functionality, a Reminder Daemon service continuously scans the appointments at specific intervals to check for upcoming events. If it finds any upcoming appointment to be considered, it creates a Reminder Automata associated with the appointment. The Event Dispatcher receives all events from the Tray, the UI, the Medication Dispenser, and the Activity Recognizer and updates an existing appointment or sends the event to the Reminder Automata. The Reminder Automata then generates appropriate reminders and the reminder messages are shown on the UI. To model the application logic of the reminders, rules based on the business logic integration platform Drools [8] are used as shown in the following examples.

Example: initial reminder of an external appointment
```
rule "appointment reminder"
when
    Appointment(type:SOCIAL,status:in_approach,time_in_mins:30)
then
    Generate Reminder
      { Message : Appointment with Mr. Smith for tea at 4 pm }
      { Address of Mr. Smith is ...... }
      { Today's temperature is 5° Celsius, take your pullover }
end
```

Example: check of taken tray items
```
rule "forgotten tray items"
when
    Appointment( type: HEALTH_CHECKUP, status: is_active )
    Room( unit : MAIN_DOOR, status : opened )
    Tray( item : HEALTH_INSURANCE_CARD, status: in_place )
then
    Generate Reminder { Message: You've forgotten your health
    insurance card }
end
```

The pseudo-code of the first Drools example describes that the appointment is due in 30 minutes - the rule is reminding the person with the necessary information. In the second case, the person has an appointment with the doctor and is going out, but the health insurance card is still on the tray. The rule will remind him to take the card.

4   Discussion and Future Work

Drools appears to be a good choice for handling the application logic of the Dementia Diary because it is a mature, open-source business rule management system (BRMS) providing advanced features with respect to temporal reasoning and interval-based timers and schedulers.

Regarding the current status of the CCE project, the Requirements Engineering and realization concepts are finished and a lot of integration work is done. In parallel, the processes and the rules are being modeled. The plan is to run a feasibility study of the Dementia Diary in a controlled environment. For pre-testing and evaluation, the AAL test environment at Fraunhofer IESE will be used, which is a realistic apartment with a total of five rooms, equipped with furniture, sensors, and monitoring cameras. It is planned to install the overall CCE system in several test environments.

Acknowledgment. Part of this work has been funded by the European Commission under project ref. aal-2008-1-101 CCE [4].

References

1. Sütterlin, S., Hoßmann, I., Klingholz, R.: Demenz-Report 2011, Berlin-Institut für Bevölkerung und Entwicklung, Berlin, Germany (2011)
2. Alzheimer's Disease International (ADI), World Alzheimer Report 2010 - The Global Economic Impact of Dementia, p. 4 (2010)
3. Ambient Assisted Living Joint Program, http://www.aal-europe.eu (last visited August 23, 2011)
4. CCE, Connected Care for Elderly Persons Suffering from Dementia, EU project, http://www.cceproject.eu (last visited August 23, 2011)
5. Burgener, S., Twigg, P.: Relationships among caregiver factors and quality of life in care recipients with irreversible dementia. Alzheimer Disease and Associated Disorders 16(2), 88–102 (2002)
6. Haak, N.J.: Maintaining connections: Understanding communication from the perspective of persons with dementia. Alzheimer's Care Quarterly 3(2), 122 (2002)
7. Katz, S., Ford, A.B., Moskowitz, R.W., Jackson, B.A., Jaffe, M.W.: Studies of Illness in the Aged: The Index of ADL: A Standardized Measure of Biological and Psychosocial Function. Journal of the American Medical Association 185(12), 914–919 (1963)
8. Drools - The Business Logic integration Platform, http://www.jboss.org/drools (last visited August 23, 2011)

Graphical User Interface for an Elderly Person with Dementia

Christian Tamanini, Martin Majewski, Andreas Wieland, Christian Schlehuber,
and Felix Kamieth

Fraunhofer Institute for Computer Graphics Research IGD,
Fraunhofer Str. 5 64283 Darmstadt, Germany
{firstname.lastname}@igd.fraunhofer.de

Abstract. Developing Graphical User Interfaces for elderly people with dementia requires a special care for the needs of the target group. This paper addresses the requirements and the development of a Graphical User Interface for elderly people with dementia with the focus of developing a calendar-like application to support the elderly person in everyday life. Furthermore, it describes the design of an interface for caregivers to enter data into the system.

Keywords: GUI, dementia, calendar.

1   Introduction

The demographic change in the foreseeable future towards an age distribution which favors elderly citizens brings with it the challenge of dealing with the most common diseases associated with aging, including cognitive impairments. The occurence of dementia rises with age and it is thus predictable that in the future dementia will be a widespread phenomenon [1]. To tackle this problem, considering the predicted accompanying lack of health care personnel, support systems for people with dementia need to be developed, including input modalities which work with people with such impairments. This paper describes the creation process of such an interface and gives insights into the development of user interfaces for elderly citizens with dementia.

2   User Needs and Considerations, Interface Character

First considerations needed to be given to the end-user's needs as well as the purpose of the user interface. This required the analysis of the two distinct graphical user interfaces for the two different groups of users.

Caregiver Application
The caregiver application is more rational in the sense that it should provide the caregiver with factual data. It is warm since the data it provides is supposed to give the caregiver peace of mind. Similar to the assisted person application, the caregiver application is flexible. Users should be able to choose what services they want to use. The caregiver application has a "Pull UI", meaning that it is more in the background

R. Wichert, K. Van Laerhoven, J. Gelissen (Eds.): AmI 2011 Workshops, CCIS 277, pp. 157–161, 2012.

and expects the user to query for specific information. It may preselect information (especially, when it concerns alarms), but in general it is modest and does not make assumptions about the information the caregiver wants to have. The application does not guide the caregiver, but nearly informs about the status of their loved one. The caregiver will know best how to deal with the information provided, given their knowledge about the assisted person. Also, if we consider new caregivers, we presume that the communication service will facilitate knowledge transfer that the system by itself will not be able to surmount. The application offers lots of data, but is simple at the same time. Given that users are no computer experts or data analysts. The UI starts with generic information with the option for the caregiver to go more into detail. The caregiver application is passive and most often requires the caregiver to pull information from it. However, it does interpret the data to detect alarming situations. Finally the application is sober, sect, as to not distract the users from the essence of caregiving. The application conveys trustworthiness.

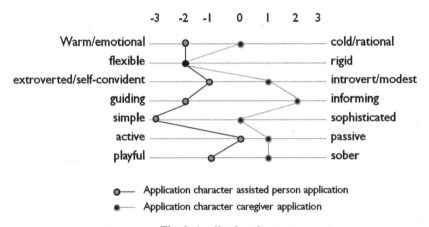

Fig. 1. Application character

End-User application

The assisted person application appears very friendly at initial contact to leave a sympathetic impression right from the beginning. It also radiates warmth to the patients, so they feel quickly comfortable in the presence of the system. This should increase the willingness to use the system and reduce its technical character. The system is able to react flexibly to the patient's behavior and doesn't just follow strict routines. Information will be shown at the patient's current location and be relevant to the respective context. In addition, the response – or even no response – of the patient will be recognized and considered dynamically. The character of the system can be described as rather extroverted. It's open-minded and tries to "activate" the patient. However it never tries to be in the center of attention, but will be on the spot if needed. Guidance is a central aspect of the UI, which is directly related to the idea of giving direct, helpful assistance. It "pushes" information to the patient when appropriate, but does not overwhelm the patient with non-pertinent information. Its purpose is to activate the patient, giving appropriate hints, rather than providing him/her with a choice of information.

A sequence is preferred to a list and assistance to self-service. The application is very simple in a sense of being easy to use and understand. This is in line with elicited user needs. The mental model is made abundantly clear. Sophistication is "hidden", but present; if there are choices, they are marked clearly and are explained sufficiently. Context is given where needed; the application uses simple language that the assisted person can understand. A localization of the application between the extremes "active" and "passive" leads to the middle ground between those extremes: The application is active when needed, "pushing" information; but also provides services if asked ("pull"). It stays in the background most of the time, like an attentive butler. Depending on the user profile, an overly active behavior would be considered too obtrusive or downright intimidating to most; too passive behavior is not helpful in most cases when assistance is needed. A fine balance must be maintained with the overarching goal of "attentive assistance". The application uses playful metaphors and language to overcome usage barriers and inhibitions. It comes across as a helpful friend with a joyful attitude, tackling the user need of happiness, fun and encouragement. Its language is uplifting and encouraging, never criticizing; when facts have to be stated, this is done in a friendly manner without "sugarcoating". In all of this, however, the application is not carefree, but trustworthy and dependable. All in all, the assisted person application can be described as a kind of "butler" -- a helpful, attentive "servant" who guides if necessary, but can stay in the background. He's self-confident, but at the same time knows his place in the household. He's playful, but at the same time never too emotional, keeping a cool head, and adapts to events and situations as needed and desired.

3   Graphical User Interface Development

3.1   Graphical User Interface End User

Visual Design
The visual design of the User Interface is mainly affected by the three characteristics "structured", "simple/reduced" and "sober". The main aim of the visual design was to avoid cognitive overload caused by too many information or a complex visual appearance.

Grid
All objects are aligned to a grid in order to achieve a clear structured appearance. Within this grid the objects are ordered according to their semantical meaning.

Visual Style
The visual style of the objects is sober and consists of simple shapes in order to reduce visual noise. In addition only the most important objects like appointments or the current time are highlighted in color. In order to get a first impression of the understanding of touch input, different kinds of buttons were tested with one elderly person.

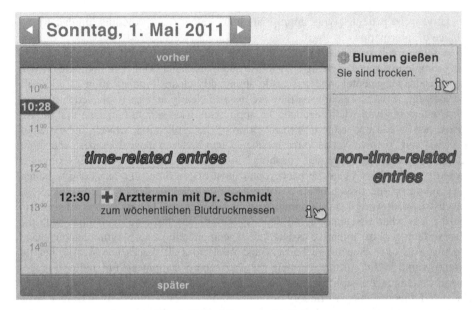

Fig. 2. Grid of the general interface

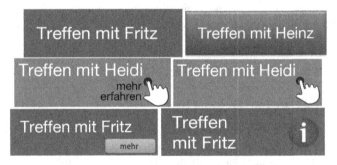

Fig. 3. Test for visuals of input buttons

The short test showed that even three-dimensional buttons don't make the use of the fingers clear to the elderly person. In contrast the buttons including a "hand"-icon made the touch input more clearly. Due to the result a "hand"-icon in combination with a usual "information"-icon is used to initially highlight the use of touch input.

Information Architecture

In order to reduce the cognitive workload and to keep up the feeling of self-determination, the information are presented according to the principle of "Progressive disclosure".

At the beginning the information are reduced to a minimal level of detail. The user got the possibility to request further information by selecting a certain object in order to open the detail page.

One example would be that the user wants to know the planned means of travel to get to an external appointment.

4   Summary and Outlook

This paper described the development of a graphical user interface for elderly people with dementia. Future work includes testing the developed interface with both experts and dementia sufferers with the goal of simplifying the interaction further. The results have been part of the work in the AAL-Joint-Programme [2] project CCE – Connected Care for Eldery Persons suffering from Dementia[3].

References

1. Sütterlin, S., Hoßmann, I., Klingholz, R.: Demenz-Report 2011, Berlin-Institut für Bevölkerung und Entwicklung, Berlin, Germany (2011)
2. Ambient Assisted Living Joint Program, http://www.aal-europe.eu (last visited August 10, 2011)
3. CCE, Connected Care for Elderly Persons Suffering from Dementia, AAL-JP Project, http://www.cceproject.eu (last visited August 10, 2011)

Empowering and Integrating Senior Citizens with Virtual Coaching
(Workshop Summary)

Andreas Braun[1], Peter H.M.P. Roelofsma[2], Dieter Ferring[3], and Milla Immonen[4]

[1] Fraunhofer Institute for Computer Graphics Research IGD, Darmstadt, Germany
andreas.braun@igd.fraunhofer.de
[2] VU University, CAMeRA, Amsterdam, The Netherlands
p.h.m.p.roelofsma@vu.nl
[3] Université de Luxembourg, Luxembourg
dieter.ferring@uni.lu
[4] VTT Technical Research Centre of Finland, Oulu, Finland
milla.immonen@vtt.fi

1   Background of the Workshop

With Europe's aging population and an increasing number of older people living alone or geographically distant from kin, loneliness is turning into a prevalent issue. This might involve deleterious consequences for both the older person and society, such as depression and increased use of healthcare services. Virtual coaches that act as friend in a para-social relationship but also as mentor that helps the elderly end-user to create meaningful relationships in his actual social environment are a powerful method to overcome loneliness and increase the quality of life in the elderly population. The AAL Joint Programme projects A²E² (AAL-2008-1-071) and V2me (AAL-2009-2-107) are exploring virtual coaches and their application in AAL scenarios, including the use of user avatars, virtual self-representations that allow the user to be represented in communication scenarios. Other European research projects that focus on social integration of the elderly are e.g. ALICE (AAL-2009-2-091) or WeCare (AAL-2009-2-026). Outside the European Union the negative implications of population aging can be observed in Japan, having an even larger proportion of senior citizens, using individual-centred devices, such as robot pets [1], to improve the quality of life of lonely elderly persons.

The user groups involved often are not acquainted with modern ICT systems and therefore it is a challenge to create intuitive, adaptive platforms that cater to the individual needs and allow the user to interact easily.

2   Aim of the Workshop

The workshop will discuss the effects of virtual coaches on elderly users and how they can be used to improve the quality of life by aiding in planning daily life activities and mediating meaningful relationships to maintain and expand the social network of the elderly persons. Additional applications of virtual coaches and avatars

R. Wichert, K. Van Laerhoven, J. Gelissen (Eds.): AmI 2011 Workshops, CCIS 277, pp. 162–165, 2012.

in AAL specific context will be discussed. Furthermore it will explore intuitive interaction between the user and virtual entities, leading to the following collection of topics:

- Realistic virtual characters in AAL applications
- Adaptive virtual self-representation in AAL applications
- Emotional expressiveness of virtual characters
- Intuitive interaction devices for elderly end-users
- User interface design for interaction with virtual entities
- Virtual entities in smart, sensor-equipped environments
- Mediating social contacts by means of virtual coaching
- Technology use and aging: Inhibiting and facilitating factors
- User experience and acceptance evaluation: Results of pilot studies and prototype testing from end-user perspective

3   Workshop Contributions

The workshop has attracted nine different contributions from six countries that covered a broad spectrum of the topics that had been defined in the call for papers.

Technology and Aging: Inhibiting and Facilitating Factors in ICT Use by Anja Leist and Dieter Ferring presented a literature review finding different characteristics of older adult users that explain the varying usage of ICT technology in this group.

How Older Adults Experience Wellness Monitoring? by Salla Muuraiskangas, Jaana Kokko and Marja Harjumaa performed a user experience study of a wellness monitoring system for older adult end users showing promising results in terms of acceptance rates.

How Avatar Based Communication Can Improve Decision Making Quality by Peter H.M.P. Roelofsma analysed the effect of Avatar-facilitated decision processes on the outcome. It was shown that Avatars do have a significant effect and might lead to more "risky" behavior by the user.

Preference for Combining or Seperating Events in Human and Avatar Decisions by Peter H.M.P. Roelofsma and Leo Versteeg presented a study researching the effect of Avatar facilitated communication on the "spreading of outcome" effect showing that it reduces the preference of spreading emotional impactful events over time.

Dynamic user representation in video phone application by Andreas Braun and Reiner Wichert presented different technical solutions and algorithmic approaches for realizing a dynamic user representation in video phone applications for mobile devices like smartphones and tablets.

Sex Differences in User Acceptance of Avatars by Leo Versteeg and Peter H.M.P. Roelofsma presented a study finding that male participants preferred younger female Avatars and female participants preferred older male graphical representations.

User-centered Design for and with Elderly Users in V2me by Kerstin Klauß and Peter Klein discussed the user-centered design process specific for older users on the example of the AAL JP project V2me.

Development of a Socio-Technical System for an Age-Appropriate Domestic Environment by Daniel Tantinger, Sven Feilner, Matthias Struck and Christian Weigand present a concept for a system comprised of a smart chair and a TV set dedicated to support training at home by means of bio-monitors and actuators in the chair and a virtual coach encouraging the user and guiding him through the training.

Using technology for improving the social and physical activity-level of the older adults by Milla Immonen, Anna Sachinopoulou, Jouni Kaartinen and Antti Konttila presents an overview of different social media technology systems that can support older adults in increasing their social network and improve their physical and mental health.

4   Workshop Discussions

The workshop continued with a moderated discussion round on the topic *The future of virtual coaches in applications for older adults*. Discussed questions include the level of detail future virtual coaches should strive for and accordingly the risks of facilitating the uncanny valley effect - that is the reduced perceived familiarity of entities with a human likeness when they approach high level of human likeness without reaching them, e.g. cartoon characters are considered more familiar than zombies. We concluded that human likeness is not always preferable since it may create expectations of a human-like behaviour and the user might project human attributes to the virtual entity that can't possibly be met. The detail level of avatars and virtual coaches should not be static - different applications might require different representation levels. However the logic behind has to be consistent. The coach should have one brain but provide various representations.

Another question discussed was about the role of a virtual coach in human-computer interaction, that is should it be the main interaction metaphor or if it is more feasible to use it only in certain situations or will it end up in niche applications. The discussion here was rather lively and concluded that this depends strongly on the target group of the system and furthermore the users always have to have the option of choosing their preferred interaction metaphor. Furthermore it is important to provide a suitable environment for the virtual coach to reach its potential. There has to be sufficient technology to support a real natural interaction with speech in various places and seamless transfer of the coach representation between different screens. The acceptance of virtual coaches will always depend on the user experience and the environment is a main part of that.

Another discussion point was to determine the main scenarios in which a virtual coach should be used in future and what the main functional requirements are. Intelligent coaches can be most effective if they allow for human performance modelling, that is having a vast behavioural knowledge and is able to infer potential actions and facilitate positive behaviour changes. We see the main application of virtual coaches in health & wellness monitoring, stepped care approaches, education and tutoring, social integration and mediating between organizations or other persons and the end user. Preliminary results show that virtual coaches might even lead to favourable results compared to actual human-human interaction in certain applications and for certain users.

5   Conclusion

The first international workshop on empowering and integrating senior citizens with virtual coaching brought together experts from different fields and lead to lively discussions about the future of virtual coaching and their application in systems for older adults. The discussions concluded that while much work already has been done in researching virtual coaches and user avatars there are numerous questions left unanswered that have to be tackled in focussed research efforts in the near future. A main question remains that while virtual coaches are prevalent in many laboratories and pilot sites around the world as of yet there is no wide-spread adoption yet. The technological limitations are mostly gone and it should be tried to bring innovative virtual coaching services into the hands of the user.

Technology and Aging: Inhibiting and Facilitating Factors in ICT Use

Anja Leist and Dieter Ferring

University of Luxembourg, FLSHASE, Route de Diekirch, L-7220 Walferdange, Luxembourg
{Anja.Leist,Dieter.Ferring}@uni.lu

Abstract. Extending a literature review, the paper gives an overview of inhibiting and facilitating factors associated with the use of information and communications technology (ICT) of older adults. The paper takes the position that there is no prototypical "elderly user" but that there is a wide heterogeneity of personal characteristics such as cognitive and motivational states and experiences in old age. Dependent upon various characteristics of the elderly user as well as the context of application, development and implementation of ICT should follow the desideratum of a differential technology implementation taking an integrative approach by reconciling individual and social as well as socio-political approaches.

Keywords: ICT - technology use - elderly users - psychological factors.

1 Introduction

Despite the evident benefits of modern technologies both on the personal as well as on the societal and economic level, technology solutions do not receive unequivocal acceptance by the potential end users. Since acceptance is directly linked to technology use, it is thus the essential characteristic of user experience. Technology acceptance is predetermined by several factors both at the individual as well as the societal level. Here, we will focus on the characteristics of the "elderly user" on the individual level without neglecting that the interaction of individual characteristics, the context of technology application, and the larger societal context may also play a significant role in explaining differences in individual use. Moreover, we will narrow the focus to the use of information and communications technology (ICT).

2 The "Elderly ICT User"

Despite the broad consensus that ICT in its various manifestations will bring benefits to elderly persons, there are at least three perseverant myths holding that elderly users show several limitations that can inhibit the use of these technologies [1]. The first myth concerns the *level of interest and negative attitudes towards technology* in elderly adults. Although there is evidence that older adults use information and electronic technology less often than other age groups, interest and willingness to acquire new ICT-related skills characterize the major part of older adults. A second

R. Wichert, K. Van Laerhoven, J. Gelissen (Eds.): AmI 2011 Workshops, CCIS 277, pp. 166–169, 2012.
© Springer-Verlag Berlin Heidelberg 2012

myth concerns the *learning capacity of elderly persons*, assuming to be limited due to decline in cognitive performance. Here, there is evidence that the young-old (age 60 to 74) and the old-old (age 75 and above) can readily acquire computer skills, navigate Web sites and maintain these skills over time [2]. Evidently, the most important factor within this context is the availability of training and continuous support of the elderly novice user [3]. Finally, a third myth holds that *negative attitudes and anxiety* may impact computer task performance of older adults. Results of several intervention studies are in favor of the benefits of training programs, showing that experience and training diminish anxiety [4].

These general findings may give the impression that there is some kind of a prototypical elderly ICT user; however this would simplify the heterogeneity of attitudes, motivational states, and experiences which constitute individuals in old age. In a representative European sample, the following typology of elderly ICT users was derived: (1) the *experienced front runners* who benefit from a lifelong expertise of computer use, (2) the *old age beginners* who use the computer less often than once a week, (3) the *technologically open-minded non-users* that are keen on learning about technology or wish to improve computer skills, and (4) the *digitally challenged non-users* who are not interested in learning or improving computer skills [5]. Whereas this user typology mainly relies on the factors 'technology experience' and 'current technology use', we postulate that various other characteristics also promote or hinder the use of ICT at the individual level. Some of the factors that have proven to be important in this context will be described in the following.

3   Inhibiting and Facilitating Factors of ICT Use – What We Know So Far

Earlier research has identified important user characteristics from a psychological point of view [6]. We will extend this line of thinking in suggesting to combine these characteristics in order to elaborate differential user profiles. When it comes to explaining differences in ICT use, it is important to underline that differences can be *inter-* as well as *intra*-individual: There are differences between individuals and one person may also show different profiles across time. Table 1 lists a non-exhaustive overview of several domains and indicators that are associated with differential ICT use at the individual level and may explain both kinds of differences.

The list starts with general *demographic characteristics*. Throughout the literature, high age, low educational attainment and low socio-economic status (SES), as well as being female are discussed as central features associated with low ICT use in old age. Although chronological age as a proxy of different functional and physical conditions may go along with a decrease in technology use, it is noteworthy that functional restrictions and age are not related to the *interest* in ICT. Moreover, cohort effects and the underlying different levels of expertise, knowledge and habits have more predictive validity for differences in ICT use than chronological age.

Table 1. Inhibiting and Facilitating Factors of ICT Use on the Individual Level

Domain	Exemplary Indicators
Demographics	Age, SES, education, gender
Physical and Functional Status	Visual and hearing impairments, morbidity and comorbidities
Performance Issues	Motor function, eye-hand coordination
Cognitive Status	Information processing (Perception - Attention - Memory)
Motivational Factors	ICT-related personal goals and motives
Personality Traits	Self-efficacy beliefs, control beliefs
Life Story	ICT-related autobiographical memories Technology experience
Social Cognition	ICT-related attitudes and beliefs Openness to ICT use

Besides demographic characteristics, differences in *physical and functional status* represent a further and evident category. This domain comprises visual and hearing impairments with their direct impact on ICT use as well as more systemic characteristics such as morbidities and comorbidities. Linked to this, we would also like to underline the importance of *performance issues* such as motor function including the coordination of fine and gross motor skills as further pre-determinants of ICT use. The *cognitive domain* and here the process of information processing is listed as a further central complex that explains differential ICT use. Information processing describes the interplay between attention, perception, and memory and thus the encoding and retrieval of information. All these processes play a dominant role in lifelong ICT use as well as in old age; it is also well documented that the speed of information processing decreases with age, although there are considerable interindividual differences. Impairments in attention span, perception or memory lead to a decreased efficiency in information processing and might thus hinder both the acquisition and application of knowledge on ICT use. Thus, information processing might even be considered as prerequisite for ICT use. *Motivational factors* are essential for both the short- and long-term commitment to technology use. We would like to underline the importance of individual needs for a given technology application: Only if the application serves – or is perceived as serving – a personal need, the person will be motivated to use a specific device or application. This notion exceeds the user gratification approach, since it considers both explicit and implicit motives and the fact that various different personal goals may underlie the use of a given specific application. Of course, for motivational factors to influence ICT use, the user needs basic knowledge about the functions and handling of a technology device, given that many users state that (a) they do not know why they should use a given tool or (b) they do not know that a given tool may serve a specific need. *Personality traits* as stable interindividual differences in specific dimensions are illustrated by self-efficacy and control beliefs, which represent central dimensions of ICT use: Only if a person believes that he or she can handle technology applications or that these will have an effect on his or her life, the person will be motivated to use specific technologies. Another domain represents the individual's *life story*. Here, we subsume autobiographical memories linked to ICT use and technology experience as the result of a lifelong learning history of technology use. Lastly, the domain of *social cognition* comprises all ICT-related attitudes and beliefs, stereotypes, and the general openness to ICT use. All these personal characteristics have shown to explain differences in ICT use in older adults.

4   Conclusion: The Need for a Differential Approach to ICT Use

Taken together, these factors represent important predictors of ICT use on the individual level, though factors might be of differential importance, interact in complex ways, or even counterbalance one another. High age, low education, and low SES characterize conditions of low ICT use despite a good functional status. However, even with major physical impairments, a person with high self-efficacy and control beliefs feeding upon a lifelong technology experience may be a frequent user. Both examples underline the importance of fine-grained *differential user profiles* to explain interindividual differences in ICT use. In knowing about different user profiles, technology applications in different fields (e.g., virtual coaching) can be manufactured accordingly to maximize user acceptance.

References

1. Rogers, W.A., Mayhorn, C.B., Fisk, A.D.: Technology in everyday life for older adults. In: Burdick, D.C., Kwon, S. (eds.) Gerotechnology: Research and Practice in Technology and Aging, pp. 3–18. Springer, New York (2004)
2. Morrell, R.W., Mayhorn, C.B., Echt, K.V.: Why older adults use and do not use the internet. In: Burdick, D.C., Kwon, S. (eds.) Gerotechnology: Research and Practice in Technology and Aging, pp. 71–85. Springer, New York (2004)
3. Ferring, D., et al.: Inhibiting and facilitating factors in ICT use in old age: A review (in preparation)
4. Kelley, C.L., Charness, N.: Issues in training older adults to use computers. Behaviour and Information Technology 14, 107–120 (1995)
5. Stroetmann, V.N., Hüsing, T., Kubitschke, L., Stroetmann, K.A.: Attitudes, expectations and needs of older people for telehealth: Results from the European SeniorWatch survey (2002), http://www.seniorwatch.de/download/presentations/SWA_Telemed2002.pdf (derived on November 8, 2011)
6. Oppenauer, C., Preschl, B., Kalteis, K., Kryspin-Exner, I.: Technology in Old Age from a Psychological Point of View. In: Holzinger, A. (ed.) USAB 2007. LNCS, vol. 4799, pp. 133–142. Springer, Heidelberg (2007)

How Older Adults Experience Wellness Monitoring?

Salla Muuraiskangas[1], Jaana Kokko[2], and Marja Harjumaa[1]

[1] VTT Technical Research Centre of Finland, P.O. Box 1100, 90571 Oulu, Finland
[2] Social and Health Services, City of Oulu, P.O. Box 37, 90015 Oulu, Finland
salla.muuraiskangas@vtt.fi, jaana.a.kokko@ouka.fi,
marja.harjumaa@vtt.fi

Abstract. Even though a lot of ICT is designed for the older adults, we still know little about this user group's abilities to interact independently with new technological devices and experiences the technology creates. In this paper, we explore user experience and long-term acceptance of a wellness monitoring solution in a real life setting. The solution collects data by asking questions about everyday life of the person through a touch screen PC. It also motivates users to perform their daily activities. From four to nine months field trial was conducted with nine users. The findings show that the older adults learned easily to use touch screen PC. Their sometimes doubtful attitudes towards technology might influence on the perceived usefulness and acceptance. The motivational features of the system had a positive influence on the user experience.

Keywords: older adult, wellness monitoring, touch screen, acceptance, user experience.

1 Introduction

There is an emergent need for novel solutions, which enable more independent living of the older adults with higher quality of life (QoL) [1]. This is because personnel resources and financial resources do not meet the growing number of the older adults who have a need for and who are entitled to different kind of services. One approach to solve this problem is wellness monitoring systems that would enable recognizing the needs of the customer and reacting faster to them. This would prevent small problems becoming big money consuming problems.

Designing technology for the older adults is challenging, because older people as a user group is not homogenous. Among users there is a lot of variation regarding their computer experience, attitudes toward technology, functional capacity (including physical, mental, and social), and wealth. Perception of the ease of use and usefulness of the technology has great influence to technology acceptance, simply put, user acceptance (UA) [2]. Therefore it is important to investigate user experience (UX) for creating solutions that will be used.

This paper explores findings from a study where nine older users adopted a wellness monitoring solution into their lives for several months. The objective was to study UX and long-term UA of this solution in real life settings.

R. Wichert, K. Van Laerhoven, J. Gelissen (Eds.): AmI 2011 Workshops, CCIS 277, pp. 170–174, 2012.
© Springer-Verlag Berlin Heidelberg 2012

2   Case Study

2.1   Prototype

A prototype of wellness monitor (WM) is created in Java for Windows OS and touch screen PC. The user interface is especially designed for the older users, e.g. font size and colour are carefully considered [3]. The functionality is designed according to persuasive design principles, namely personalization, reminders, social role and virtual reward [4]. The WM is a social "figure" without graphical appearance accompanying the day; politely wishing "Good morning Maria!" and then inquiring about the wellness with various questions through the day. The questions are personalized self-assessment questions used for collecting wellness data. Each answer has a numerical value and the system counts daily wellness value as the average of the answers. The WM rewards the user by thanking for answering and visualising the daily wellness value with a smiley. There are also personalized reminders which can relate, among others, to safety (e.g. "Please, check that your stove is not on."). The WM intends to motivate the user taking care of himself.

The collected wellness data can be viewed locally or remotely by any authorised person who is also able to modify the questions and reminders, e.g. the number of the reply options and the related wellness dimension. For creating comprehensive insight of the wellness, questions should cover all the wellness dimensions. The wellness model in the prototype is adopted from the Oulu wellness profile where the dimensions include independence, physical performance, mental performance, social networks, social exclusion, safety, self-rated health, lifestyle and self-rated QoL [5].

2.2   Participants and Methodology

Selected approach for the technology evaluation was field trial, experimenting with real users in their real home environments. It is suitable method for gathering understanding of how people use the service or application in real-life situations and what are the practical impacts on the user [6]. There were nine users; seven women and two men. They all were living in their homes or in a serviced flat. Their average age was 77.7 (from 69 to 87). One third of the users (3/9) had some prior experience of computers. Users reported having problems with eyesight (5/9) and with mobility (4/9). Also, some experienced problems with memory (2/9) and hearing (2/9).

The evaluation process was as follows. WM was brought to the user's home and the users were familiarized with the system. The self-assessment questions were created to the WM. One third or the users (3/9) had later internet connections that enabled remote monitoring. All users used the system (replied questions and reminders) from four to nine months. Researchers were in contact with the users during the research period, especially in the error situations. Long-term UA is studied monitoring the direct system use and UX [2]. As UX is subjective perception related to the use, various methods for collecting these perceptions from the user are used [7]. Users were encouraged to keep diary during the evaluation period and they were interviewed in the end. In addition, a questionnaire was sent for their close relatives.

3   Findings and Discussion

3.1   Long-Term User Acceptance

For estimating the use, monthly reply rate for the questions was calculated. The percentages for the first and fourth use month and the entire use period are presented in Table 1. The average reply percentage is 65. It seems users were replying in average more during the first month (73%) than in the fourth month (55%). When omitting data of the unexpectedly hospitalized user (U8) and one incomplete log (U2) the difference in reply behaviour decreased (68% and 61% respectively).

Table 1. Reply percentages in respective to the user (U)

U	1	2	3	4	5	6	7	8	9	Avg.
1st month	47.96	87.36	86.59	100.00	40.00	72.53	32.94	97.50	94.72	73.29
4th month	49.73	-[1]	90.96	80.47	33.00	34.16	50.91	14.00[2]	90.48	55.09
Avg.	48.43	75.63	89.13	83.04	30.91	36.51	45.79	84.33	89.94	64.86

Several reasons can be identified for explaining the use activity. After one user was hospitalized and came back home, the reply rate was remarkably lower than in the beginning (U6). The WM does not recognise whether the person is present or not when it displays the questions, so the percentage is lower for people who spend a lot of time outside the home. Timing of the questions is also important; one user had a high reply rate even if he was outgoing (U9) but another outgoing (U5) had low. It is also possible that user misses questions simply because he does not hear the signal of the arriving question from another room. This could be one additional factor explaining the low rate of U5 since she reported having a hearing problem. There could be various solutions for increasing the reply rate; presence detector, as suggested also by Kaushik et al. [8] or just turning the volume higher or displaying the questions in a mobile device that user carries around. Also, a checklist in the evening of the missed questions could be useful, as one user suggested. It was also reported that the questions were sometimes difficult to understand.

When asking whether the user would intend to use the WM often in future, one third (3/9) replied yes, four users replied more or less and two (U1 and U8) replied no. The reason why U1 would not use the WM could be that the system was not that useful for her because she had the carer living with her. Also, the interaction was problematic for her due to the mobility impairment. Even though U8 was living alone, practically bound to the house due to the mobility impairment, and was most thorough tester, he did not find the WM useful for him. Perhaps, it was not rewarding enough to have the visualized wellness for himself and there were no close ones to observe it either. If there are no relatives the information could go to neighbour or other close person, as one user suggested.

---

[1] Beginning of the log was missing due to system update.
[2] Hospitalization.

3.2   User Experience

Two thirds of the users (6/9) considered that the WM is useful for them and two thought it would be more or less useful. Also, all users were willing to recommend the WM to someone else. Users found many benefits in the system. The system motivates to take care of yourself *"because you know it will soon ask about it and you don't want to lie"*. It makes you feel important: *"As a close relative carer, it was like a surprise to think about your own wellbeing and the importance of it"*. Also *"It was pacing life"*. One user created a positive "relationship" with the system and commented that *"the machine became like a friend. You missed when it was not working for few days"*. One relative said that *"the reminders were good; the phone has not left open or medicines left without taking"*. Although smiley face visualisations for wellness were experienced positively, one user mentioned that he would prefer numerical evaluation. Therefore, it could be considered whether there should be complementary ways of presenting wellness data.

Learning to use WM was easy for most of the users (8/9). However, the hardware interaction was a problem in one case. In general, it was easy to learn control the system by touching the monitor even by inexperienced users. But it was slightly challenging for a user (U2) who suffered from memory loss. Interestingly, after keeping a paper note "touch the monitor" attached to the monitor for few days, even she learnt and the note could be removed. After learning phase, using the WM was easy for most of the users (8/9). One user (U1) found the use difficult because of the mobility impairment she could not easily access the monitor all times for replying the questions. Interestingly, another user in a wheel chair did not find the use difficult. It was discovered that the device should be located in a place that is in all times easily accessed. Also, complementary input device, such as remote control, could help in these situations.

Also some negative experiences were reported. Before use, it was discovered that users had fears and uncertainty about their abilities concerning technology use: *"I think I even said you can take that right back. I will never understand how to use it"*. During the use, fear of breaking the device was reported. *"I did not dare to touch it so it would not break down"* but these negative feelings changed positively after learning that the system is not easily broken and that they really are able to use it. The users were quite sensitive for the machine noise (e.g. crackle from the processing) and it made them worried. One computer was even changed because of the noise. One user had even fears that it would start up a fire and kept taking the plug out. The questions *"were difficult to understand"* and *"somehow the questions were set in a form that the replying was impossible"*. It cannot be emphasised enough that this kind of system must speak the user's language rather than only using the professional language [9]. Therefore, co-operating with the user in the personalization phase is crucial. Also the close ones, who would benefit from the system, should be heard. One relative appreciated the existing functionality of adapting the questions via internet by commenting that *"it is absolutely important to be able to add questions by ourselves so that the questions important for us come up"*. One user (U7) was especially afraid that computers would replace people in care work and criticised it through the field trial. This is a relevant issue and thus, it should be considered how technology could be used to increase the actual social contacts of the people.

As a whole, the UX evolved from fears to conquering most of them and giving users even some pleasure by being able to do something they thought they could not. Even though, the WM was perceived in many ways useful and easy to use, it was not ready to be adopted in a full scale. There may be various reasons. The implementation might not be attractive enough or it might not offer enough benefits for the user. Also, the users might not have enough motivation to use this kind of technology.

4   Conclusion

A system for wellness monitoring was developed and evaluated. The findings show that touch screen PC is easy to use, but users' sometimes doubtful attitudes towards technology might influence on the perceived usefulness and motivation to use the system and therefore the UA. The motivational features of the system seemed to have a positive influence on the UX and the meaning of personalized reminder messages was emphasized in the findings.

Acknowledgments. This work was conducted within Itea2 AmIE project which ended in 2010 [10]. We thank Juho-Pekka Pöyhtäri who was involved in developing and testing the system and made his master's thesis about the advanced version of the WM [11].

References

1. Lansley, P.: The promise and challenge of providing assistive technology to older people. Age and Ageing 30(6), 439–440 (2001)
2. Davis, F.: Perceived Usefulness, Perceived Ease of Use, And User Acceptance. MIS Quarterly 13(3), 319–340 (1989)
3. Kokko, J.: Elderly Online Wellness Monitoring (EOWM) Self-Assessment Tablet – User-Centered Interface Design. Oulu University of Applied Sciences, Department of Medical Engineering. Bachelor's thesis (2009)
4. Oinas-Kukkonen, H., Harjumaa, M.: Persuasive Systems Design: Key Issues, Process Model, and System Features. Communications of the Association for Information Systems 24, Article 28 (2009), http://aisel.aisnet.org/cais/vol24/iss1/28
5. Oulu Wellness Profile, http://www.ouka.fi/sote/projektit/OuluWellnessProfile.pdf
6. Faber, E., de Vos, H. (eds.): Creating Successful ICT-Services: Practical Guidelines Based on the STOF Method, Telematica Instituut. Enschede, The Netherlands (2008)
7. ISO 9421-210: Ergonomics of human system interaction – Part 210: Human-centred design for interactive systems (revises the ISO 13407)
8. Kaushik, P., Intille, S., Larson, K.: User-adaptive Reminders for Home-base Medical Tasks: A Case Study. Methods Inf. Med. 47, 203–207 (2008)
9. Nielsen, J.: 10 usability heuristics, http://www.useit.com/papers/heuristic/heuristic_list.html
10. AmIE project, http://www.itea2.org/call1_amie
11. Pöyhtäri, J.-P.: Online Self-Assessment Tablet for Wellness Management of the Elderly. University of Oulu, Department of Electrical and Information Engineering. Master's thesis (2010)

How Avatar Based Communication Can Improve Decision Making Quality

Peter H.M.P. Roelofsma

VU University Amsterdam, Faculty of Social Sciences
p.h.m.p.roelofsma@vu.nl

Abstract. This paper examines to what extent the use of avatars makes person's choices more optimal. Subjects were required to participate in choice tasks of decision problems that are well known for demonstrating sup-optimal choice behavior. Subjects participated in an experiment where a digital coach presented different decision problems. The participants were required to choose either themselves or through communication with their avatar, depending on the experimental condition. The results indicated that the use of an avatar significantly improved the decision quality of the subjects. When choosing through their avatar people demonstrated significantly more optimal choice behavior as compared to conditions without the avatar use. The results are explained by the use of decision framing and literature from the field of neuroscience.

Keywords: Virtual Agents and Avatars, Rational Choice Behavior, Framing, Elderly Decision Making.

1   Introduction

Virtual artificial agents can be equipped with intelligence in such a way that people can interact with them in ways, similar to human-to-human interaction. Virtual agents can replace other human informants and act as virtual coaches. They can also replace the person perspective of the decision maker itself, e.g. by using avatars which then act as self-representations of the human decision maker. The interaction between human and virtual agents has been the topic of many studies (Baylor, 2002, 2003, 2005, 2009; Baylor & Ebbers, 2003; Bailenson, Patel, Nielsen, Bajscy, Jung & Kurillo, 2008; Bicchieri & Lev-On, 2007; Bickmore & Pickard, 2005; Fox & Bailenson, 2004; Gulz, 2004; Isbister & Nass, 2000; Lim & Reeves, 2009; Skalski & Tamborini, 2007).

An interesting aspect of using virtual agents in human decision making is that they add new potential perspectives also called 'frames of reference' or 'framing effects' in the decision making process. More specifically, making a decision through an avatar changes the decision framing from a first person to a third person perspective. Such changes in person perspective may lead to different evaluation and choice. The results of a variety of experiments suggest that different parts of the brain are being

R. Wichert, K. Van Laerhoven, J. Gelissen (Eds.): AmI 2011 Workshops, CCIS 277, pp. 175–180, 2012.

activated when switching between person perspectives (Vogeley et al., 2001; Ruby & Decety, 2001; David et al., 2006; Decety & Jackson, 2004). Accordingly the first-person perspective is mostly linked with parts of the brain associated with the regulation of emotions (David et. al, 2006). The third-person perspective is said to activate parts of the brain associated with the making of (value-based) decisions, rational choice and self-reflection (Christopoulos et. al, 2009).

Research on decision-making has shown that people tend to make sub-optimal decisions when facing with decision problems under uncertainty using a first person perspective. For example in a series of classic studies of Tversky & Kahneman (1981) it was observed that subjects choose options with relatively lower expected value as a result of the framing of questions as gains or losses. People were asked to choose between: a sure gain of $240 or B: 25% chance to gain $1000 and 75% chance to gain nothing. 84% choose for option A and only 16% choose for option B, which is the option with the higher expected value.

One explanation is that Tversky's and Kahneman's choice frame triggered the emotional part of the brain which is very sensitive for certainty and risk. Following the notion of framing from the third person avatar perspective for the same choice problem a more reflective rational choice process would be aroused which should leading to choosing more options with a higher expected value.

The aim of this study is to examine to what extent such avatar framing effects lead to more optimal choice behavior in elderly persons. Our prediction is that by framing Tversky and Kahneman's problems from an avatar perspective this would lead to a more rational thought process and to the choosing of options with relatively higher expected value.

2   Method

Participants. Subjects were elderly persons, recruited from elderly care network end organizations in the Netherlands. Subjects were invited to the online experiment. A €125 reward was randomly given to one of the participants after the experiment. The age for the participant was from 60-78. 38% of the subjects were male and 62% were female.

Design and Procedure. A 2x2 between subjects factorial design was used to examine risky choice for gains and losses under the condition of use or non use of avatars. Participants were randomly assigned to one of the following four conditions.

Condition 1. Choosing between gain options without use of an avatar;
Condition 2. Choosing between gain options through an avatar;
Condition 3. Choosing between loss options without use an avatar
Condition 4. Choosing between loss options through an avatar.

The avatar was gendered, i.e. there was an same sex avatar for male and female participants. At the start of the experiment the gender was indentified to assign the corresponding sex identity. Subjects were then randomly assigned to the decision task. The task for the participant was to answer a question posed by a digital informant. Subject answered by using the mouse and the keyboard. In the non avatar condition they were asked what choice option they would select out of a binary choice option set. In the avatar condition subjects were asked what choice option their avatar would choose out of an identical choice option set. The participants received a welcome screen which explained they could win a price when participating in the online experiment. After the introduction screen subjects received an instruction screen explaining the procedure for each of the experimental conditions. Then they received two non related example questions to get them more acquainted with the experimental procedure. Next they received the experimental question. The choice problems in the experiment were selected from Tversky and Kahneman (1979; 1981). More specifically, the gain item consisted of a choice between

A: a certain gain (€240) or B: a 25% chance to gain €1.000 with a 75% chance to win nothing. The loss question was a choice was between A: a certain loss (€240) or B: 25% chance to lose €1.000 with a 75% chance to lose nothing. After answering the research questions the participants were given the opportunity to fill in their e-mail address to compete for the prize and they were thanked for their cooperation. An example of the condition 2 with choosing between gains though an avatar is given below.

Informant

Informant: "You have the choice between the following two options:

A. sure gain of €240
B. A 25% chance to gain €1000 and a 75% chance to gain nothing.

Which option does your avatar choose?

My avatar chooses:

A. A sure gain of €240 €1000 and a 75% chance

B. A 25% chance to gain to gain nothing.

Mijn avatar

3   Results

The results of the experiment are depicted below. First the results for the gain conditions (Condition 1 and 2) are presented and then the results for the loss conditions (Conditions 3 and 4). The raw data of the online experiment were lost and further calculations on the data are only possible on the frequencies presented below.

Decision Problem 1: Choosing between Gain options
A: Sure gain (€240)   B: a 25% chance to gain €1.000
                             and a 75% chance to win nothing.

Condition 1
No avatar   88%   12%
(n-100)

Condition 2
Avatar condition   46%   54%
(n-100)

Decision Problem 2: Choosing between Loss options
A: Sure loss (€240)   B: a 25% chance to lose €1.000
                             and a 75% chance to lose nothing.

Condition 3
No Avatar   23%   77%
(n-100)

Condition 4
Avatar condition
(n-100)   53%   47%

The results indicated that in the gain condition of making choices without using the avatar (Condition 1) subjects preferred the certain option (88%) over the uncertain option (12%), i.e. they would want to receive the certain option with the lower expected value. When the outcomes were transferred into losses (Condition 3) participants preferred however the uncertain loss (77%) over the certain loss (23%), i.e. they choose for the option with the more negative expected value with more uncertainty. This preference shift was highly significant ($\chi^2(1, N = 100) = 85.54$ $p < 0.001$). The results thus show the classic shift from risk-averse to risk-taking behavior in situations changing from gains to losses. These results are a reliable replication of the gain/loss asymmetry of Tversky and Kahneman (1979; 1981). This pattern of results changes drastically when the same choices are made through use of avatars as observed in condition 2 and 4. Then subjects choose the option with the higher expected value regardless of the uncertainty of the options. More specifically, in Condition 2 subjects' preference shifted more towards risk neutrality with 54% of the subjects choosing the uncertain option with a higher expected value and 46% choosing the certain option with lower expected value. This difference between condition 1 and 2 was strongly significant $\chi^2(1, N = 100) = 39.89, p < 0.001$. For conditions 3 and 4 similar pattern was observed. When choosing through their avatar, the preference shifted more towards the less negative expected value. 53% of the subjects choose the sure loss with lower negative expected value as compared to 47% choosing the more risky option. This difference is highly significant $\chi^2 (1, N = 100) = 19.10, p < 0.001$. The pattern of results of Condition 1 and 3 are similar to the condition 2 and 4. In both situations subjects choose the option with relative higher expected value when decision are made through their avatars.

4   Discussion

Several conclusions can be drawn from this experiment. First, additional support is found for the gain loss asymmetry for the situation of elderly person's choice behavior in situations *without* using avatars. In the domain of gains elderly subjects were observed to be risk aversive and in the domain of losses they appeared to be risk seeking. This is congruent with Tversky and Kahnemans findings using student populations. Second, it can be concluded that the addition of an avatar leads to a preference shift and choosing of options with higher expected value. In fact people tend to make relatively more optimal decisions when choosing through their own avatar, i.e. from a third person perspective compared to a situation where they choose directly for themselves, i.e. from a first person perspective. As proven in earlier research, differences in the framing of questions can cause a shift from risk aversion to risk seeking (Tversky & Kahneman, 1974; DeMartino, et al., 2006). In the current research the frame was shifted from the first-person perspective to the third-person perspective through an avatar manipulation, yielding significantly different results, i.e. people significantly chose the option with the higher utility, despite the uncertainty of the option. This can be attributed to the shift in framing – i.e. the shift in perspective – since this was the factor that was changed between the two conditions. It seems that the change in the context of the question successfully altered the judgment of that particular choice situation.

References

1. Bailenson, J., Patel, K., Nielsen, A., Bajscy, R., Jung, S., Kurillo, G.: The Effect of Interactivity on Learning Physical Actions in Virtual Reality. Media Psychology 11(3), 354–376 (2008)
2. Baylor, A.L.: Expanding Preservice Teachers' Metacognitive Awareness of Instructional Planning through Pedagogical Agents. Educational Technology Research and Development 50(2), 5–22 (2002)
3. Baylor, A.L.: The Split-Persona Effect with Pedagogical Agents. In: Proceedings of Workshop Embodied Conversational Characters as Individuals at Autonomous Agents & Multi-Agent Systems (AAMAS), Melbourne, Australia (2003),
   http://www.vhml.org/workshops/AAMAS2003/papers.shtml

4. Baylor, A.L.: The Impact of Pedagogical Agent Image on Affective Outcomes. Paper Presented at the International Conference on Intelligent User Interfaces, San Diego, CA (2005)
5. Baylor, A.L.: Promoting Motivation with Virtual Agents and Avatar: Role of Visual Presence and Appearance. Philosophical Transactions of the Royal Society Biological Sciences 364, 3559–3565 (2009)
6. Baylor, A., Ebbers, S.: The Pedagogical Agent Split-Persona Effect: When Two Agents are Better than One. In: Lassner, D., McNaught, C. (eds.) World Conference on Educational Multimedia, Hypermedia and Telecommunications 2003, pp. 459–462. AACE, Chesapeake (2003)
7. Bicchieri, C., Lev-On, A.: Computer-Mediated Communication and Cooperation in Social Dilemmas: an Experimental Analysis. Politics, Philosophy, & Economics 6, 139–168 (2007)
8. Bickmore, T., Picard, R.: Establishing and Maintaining Long-Term Human-Computer Relationships. ACM Transactions on Computer Human Interaction 12, 293–327 (2005)
9. Christopoulos, G.I., Tobler, P.N., Bossaerts, P., Dolan, R.J., Schultz, W.: Neural Correlates of Value, Risk, and Risk Aversion Contributing to Decision Making under Risk. The Journal of Neuroscience 29(40), 12574–12583 (2009)
10. David, N., Bewernick, B.H., Cohen, M.X., Newen, A., Lux, S., Fink, G.R., Shah, N.J., Vogeley, K.: Neural Representations of Self versus Other: Visual-Spatial Perspective Taking and Agency in a Virtual Ball-Tossing Game. Journal of Cognitive Neuroscience 18(6), 898–910 (2006)
11. De Martino, B., Kumaran, D., Seymour, B., Dolan, R.J.: Frames, Biases, and Rational Decision-Making in the Human Brain. Science 313(5787), 684–687 (2006)
12. Decety, J., Jackson, P.L.: The Functional Architecture of Human Empathy. Behavioral and Cognitive Neuroscience Reviews 3(2), 71–100 (2004)
13. Fox, J., Bailenson, J.N.: Virtual Self-Modeling: The Effects of Vicarious Reinforcement and Identification on Exercise Behaviors. Media Psychology 12, 1–25 (2004)
14. Gulz, A.: Benefits of Virtual Characters in Computer Based Learning Environment: Claims and Evidence. International Journal of Artificial Intelligence in Education 14, 313–334 (2004)
15. Isbister, K., Nass, C.: Consistency of Personality in Interactive Characters: Verbal Cues, Non-Verbal Cues, and User Characteristics. International Journal of Human Computer Studies 53, 251–267 (2000)
16. Lim, S., Reeves, B.: Computer Agents versus Avatars: Responses to Interactive Game Characters Controlled by a Computer or Other Player. International Journal of Human-Computer Studies 68, 57–68 (2009)
17. Ruby, P., Decety, J.: Effect of Subjective Perspective Taking during Simulation of Action: a PET Investigation of Agency. Nature Neuroscience 4(5), 546–550 (2001)
18. Skalski, P., Tamborini, R.: The Role of Social Presence in Interactive Agent-Based Persuasion. Media Psychology 10, 385–413 (2007)
19. Tversky, A., Kahneman, D.: Judgment under Uncertainty: Heuristics and Biases. Science 185(4157), 1124–1131 (1974)
20. Tversky, A., Kahneman, D.: Prospect Theory: An Analysis of Decision under Risk. Econometrica 47(2), 263–292 (1979)
21. Tversky, A., Kahneman, D.: The Framing of Decisions and the Psychology of Choice. Science 211(4481), 453–458 (1981)
22. Vogeley, K., Bussfeld, P., Newen, A., Herrmann, S., Happe, F., Falkai, P., Maier, W., Shah, N.J., Fink, G.R., Zilles, K.: Mind Reading: Neural Mechanisms of Theory of Mind and Self-Perspective. Neuroimage 14, 170–181 (2001)

Preference for Combining or Separating Events in Human and Avatar Decisions

Peter H.M.P. Roelofsma and Leo Versteeg

VUA University Amsterdam, Department of Social Sciences,
The Netherlands
p.h.m.p.roelofsma@vu.nl

Abstract. According to the Renewable Resources Model people have limited emotional resource capacity for making decisions. As a result people have a general preference for spreading outcome events over time (Linville and Fisher (1991). This study examines whether the introduction of avatars will alleviate limited emotional resources and result in increased preference for combining events. This hypothesis was tested using a 2x2 factorial between subjects design which systematically manipulated the decision outcome (gains versus losses) and avatar use (avatar mediated versus non avatar mediated decisions). Preferences for combining or separating positive and negative emotional impactful events were measured using choice problems of Linville and Fischer (1991). Results show a replication of Linville and Fisher (1991) but only in the non avatar condition. In contrast, in the avatar condition a significant increase of preference for combining events was observed as predicted. The results give support for the Renewable Resource Model.

Keywords: Avatar Mediated Communication, Limited resource model, Elderly Persons, Human decision Making, Time preference, Spreading of outcomes.

1   Introduction

Making choices and getting specific types and amounts of information can stress people out. Often choices are difficult to make, because of people's limited resource capacity. Especially choices or information that has a potential negative influence on individuals will cost energy and stress. For example, in the case of feedback, people tend to avoid negative feedback because they see it as ego-threatening or as an image burst (Ashford and Tsui, 1991; Janis and Mann, 1977; Miller, 1976; Baumeister, (2002); Baumeister, Smeichel, B.J., and Vohs, 2007).

As a result of such emotional factors Linville and Fischer (1991) have argued that people have a tendency to spread out outcomes over time. For example they prefer separating two gains in a week over receiving them on one day. According to Linville and Fisher Renewable Resource Model, this will result in the best gain-savoring resources to draw on, so each will be appreciated more fully. Similarly, losses will have a greater impact on people when they occur together, therefore two losses are also preferred on separate days in a week (Linville and Fischer, 1991).

R. Wichert, K. Van Laerhoven, J. Gelissen (Eds.): AmI 2011 Workshops, CCIS 277, pp. 181–183, 2012.
© Springer-Verlag Berlin Heidelberg 2012

One way to alleviate the limited emotional resources is to introduce an avatar into the decision-making process. Introducing an avatar into the decision-making process can make decision less stressful since the avatar can take over part of the user's self management. Instead of making decisions themselves, the avatar becomes partly 'responsible' for making decisions for the user.

The purpose of this study is to examine this notion. We examine the hypothesis that that the use of avatars in mediated decision processes will lead to a increase of combining positive and negative events over time.

2   Method

Subjects were elderly persons, recruited from elderly care network end organizations in the Netherlands. Subjects were invited to the online experiment. 200 subjects participated in the research project. The age range for the participant swas from 60-78. 41% of the participants were male and 59% were female.

Participants were randomly assigned to a 2 (Avatar, no Avatar) x 2 (Outcome Event: gain, loss) between subjects factorial design. Subjects preferences for combining or separating events (same or different days in a week, i.e Same/Diff) were measured. In the avatar condition subjects made their decision through mediation of their avatar self presentation. In the non avatar condition subjects made the decisions directly by themselves.

For the Gain condition the events were: 'Winning a €450 prize from a local store' and 'Winning €400 in a lottery sponsored by a local charity'. For the Loss condition the events were: 'Losing a non-refundable airline ticket worth €450' and 'Accidentally damage to your flat screen television computer stereo system. The repairs will cost €400'. Subjects were asked for the events to occur on the same day in the week or on separate days of the week.

3   Results

The results are presented in the Table 1 below. The results show that in the non avatar condition subjects demonstrated a preference for spreading of outcomes. 79% of the subjects preferred to separate outcomes in the Gain condition and 88% preferred to separate events in the Loss condition. This is a reliable replication of Linville and Fisher (1991). However, a change in the time preference pattern is observed when a comparison is made to the avatar mediated conditions. In the avatar mediated gain condition only 40% choose for the spreading of outcomes This difference is significant (χ^2, df = 1, n = 100, = 14,92 $p < 0.001$). In the avatar mediated Loss condition only 50% of the subjects choose for spreading of outcomes. Also this decline in preference for spreading is significant. (χ^2, df = 1, n = 100, = 16.88 $p < 0.001$). The raw data of the online experiment were lost and further calculations on the data are only possible on the frequencies presented below.

Table 1. A comparison between percentage of participants preferring same day and different days for the occurrence of gains and losses in the Non avatar condition and the Avatar condition

	Human decision Same/diff.	**Avatar Decision** Same/diff.
Gain	21% / 79%	60% / 40%)
Loss	12 % / 88%	50% / 50%

4   Discussion

Several conclusions can be drawn from this experiment. First, additional support is found for the spreading of outcome effect for the situation of elderly person's choice behavior in situations *without* using avatars. Both in the domain of gains and losses elderly subjects were observed to prefer the spreading of emotional impactful outcomes over time. This is congruent with Linville and Fisher's (1991) findings using student populations. Second, it can be concluded that the addition of an avatar leads to a significant preference shift and choosing of combining of outcomes over time. The result provide support for Limited Resource Theory and the Renewable Resource Model.

References

1. Ashford, S.J., Tsui, A.S.: Self-Regulation for Managerial Effectiveness: The Role of Active Feedback Seeking. The Academy of Management Journal 34(2), 251–280 (1991)
2. Baumeister, R.F.: Yielding to Temptation: Self-control failure, impulsive purchasing and consumer behavior. Journal of Consumer Research 28, 670–676 (2002)
3. Baumeister, R.F., Smeichel, B.J., Vohs, K.D.: Self-regulation and the executive function: The self as controlling agent. In: Kruglanski, A.W., Higgins, E.T. (eds.) Social Psychology: Handbook of Basic Principles, 2nd edn. Guilford, New York (2007)
4. Janis, L., Mann, L.: Decision making. Free Press, New York (1977)
5. Linville, P.W., Fischer, G.W.: Preference for separating or combining events. Journal of Personality and Social Psychology 60(1), 5–23 (1991)
6. Miller, D.T.: Ego involvement and attributions for success and failure. Journal of Personality and Social Psychology 34, 901–906 (1976)

Dynamic User Representation in Video Phone Applications

Andreas Braun and Reiner Wichert

Fraunhofer Institute for Computer Graphics Research - IGD, Fraunhoferstr. 5,
64283 Darmstadt, Germany
{andreas.braun,reiner.wichert}@igd.fraunhofer.de

Abstract. Video phone applications are growing more commonplace with integration into mobile smart phone platforms like Apple iOS or into online social networks like Facebook. However users may desire to not show their present mood or disorderly appearance while still desiring to use such applications. Virtual user representations are an option to hide the actual appearance while still participating in video phone calls. This paper discusses different approaches to using virtual characters in video phone applications, dynamic self-representation and user interface considerations.

Keywords: Virtual Self-Representation, Emotion Recognition, Graphical user interfaces.

1   Introduction

With available bandwidth increasing for both mobile and home devices connected to the internet, video phone applications that allow multiple users to communicate via video feed submission is growing more popular. The most popular smart phone platforms - Android and iOS - are supporting this feature for mobile devices. The majority of Notebooks and All-in-One PCs are factory-equipped with webcams. Facebook, currently the most popular social network is supporting video phone via plug-in.

With the extending propagation of video chat different user groups are targeted that have a different set of requirements than the tech-savvy early adopters. It is a reasonable assumption that many users that are participating in video chats do not want to share their current appearance, e.g. if they are not feeling well or have not completed their daily hygienic routine yet. The avatar principle, whereas someone uses a virtual representation that may or may not resemble the actual appearance, is commonplace in certain applications, most notably online games. Extending this principle to video phone applications poses various difficulties, ranging from computing complexity due to the real-time nature of this scenario to the control of this avatar.

This paper will discuss the problems related to video phone avatars, the state of modern virtual characters and how to control avatars in these scenarios.

2   Video Phone Applications

The transmission of a video signal via phone has been imagined very early in the history of telecommunication [1], leading to various commercial trials in the 20th

R. Wichert, K. Van Laerhoven, J. Gelissen (Eds.): AmI 2011 Workshops, CCIS 277, pp. 184–188, 2012.

century [2]. However the technology did not become economically feasible until the camera hardware and bandwidth became affordable enough for widespread adoption.

The current state includes ubiquitous availability of cheap camera hardware that is included in most smartphones and notebooks or can be added to regular PC systems at a minimal price. The required bandwidth for video phone applications is depending on the image quality to be achieved. Considering a high efficiency compression algorithm like H.264 any mobile device supporting UMTS and any PC connected to the internet with a speed of 1Mbit/s are sufficiently equipped for real-time video transmission. In conclusion the technical challenges for video phone applications can be considered solved nowadays.

Usage numbers of video telephony compared to regular phone and text messages is still very low [3]. Studies have shown that the interest of such systems is high for families that live far apart and have reduced opportunities for face-to-face communication and the deaf community, using such systems for communication in sign language [4].

3   Modern Virtual Characters and the Uncanny Valley

Within the last decade the graphical capabilities of mobile and home computers has increased greatly, leading to the ability of rendering figures in real-time in a quality similar to early computer generated movies that may have computed several days on a single image. The result is highly detailed virtual characters with emotionally expressive and realistic facial animation and gestures available on all platforms. A few examples can be seen in Figure 1.

Fig. 1. Facial rendering in modern game engines - from left: Half Life 2, Unreal Engine 3, Cryengine 3

The uncanny valley is a hypothesis postulated by Masahiro Mori in 1970 that expects a negative emotional response on human replicas that almost approach a human being in look and action [5]. On a graph showing familiarity and human likeness the area of negative response between almost human and fully human is called the uncanny valley (Figure 2). When designing applications with avatars this effect has to be considered.

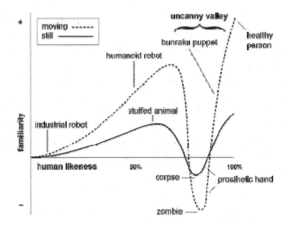

Fig. 2. Human likeness in robotics and their perceived familiarity

4   Explicit and Implicit Avatar Control

In many avatar applications, e.g. games, the user does explicitly control the movement and behavior of his virtual self. In video phone applications it is viable to offer different interaction metaphors, explicit UI based control to change the avatar behavior, as well as implicit interaction, e.g. through image analysis that provides a more immersive video phone experience without visible interface elements.

4.1   Dynamic User Representation

Dynamic user representation is the feature of letting the user select in real-time different levels of detail regarding his avatar for video phone applications. E.g. it can be envisioned to use a system providing four different levels of representation, an iconic representation, a two-dimensional static representation, a three-dimensional animated character and the actual unaltered video feed of the user. This gives the user explicit control over his appearance in the video call and therefore potentially increases the acceptance of video phone applications by providing choice.

4.2   Emotion Recognition

The recognition of emotion through analysis of images taken of the face has been researched extensively [6]. The required computations do require a certain hardware specification that is however matched by most modern smartphones and every common PC. The recognized emotion or mood can be used to implicitly control the user avatar, e.g. a detected smile of the user can be applied to the virtual character directly.

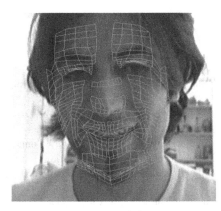

Fig. 3. Detection of facial expressions to gather information about the user's mood

4.3   Low Cost 3D Hardware - The Impact of Kinect

In late 2010 Microsoft made the Kinect system commercially available, a combination of infrared depth tracking and RGB camera that is powerful while being inexpensive. Researchers have shown examples how this technology can be used to create a 3D model from a regular person in real-time [7]. System like this may be used for generating avatars of the user for video phone applications with varying and dynamically changing levels of detail.

Fig. 4. 3D reconstruction of objects and false color texturing

5   Discussion

It can be concluded that the increasing bandwidth together with advancing computing capabilities and algorithms does allow using avatars in video phone applications that modify appearance and behavior according to the data gathered by sensors attached. Emotion recognition can be used to select from a variety of pre-determined animations while 3D hardware can be used to directly map recognized facial and skeletal features to the model. Both approaches can help to overcome the uncanny valley effect in video phone applications.

References

1. du Maurier, G.: Punch magazine (December 9, 1878)
2. Daly, E.A., Hansell, K.J.: Visual Telephony. Artech House, Boston (1999)
3. Press Release: Smartphone Video Call Users to reach 29 million by 2015 Globally, finds Juniper Research,
   http://juniperresearch.com/viewpressrelease.php?pr=209
   (retrieved August 28, 2011)
4. Kentucky School for the Deaf (KSD). DEAFinitely Connected: Bridging the Language Divide with Telecommunications, Computerworld Honors Program, Computerworld Information Technology Awards Foundation, Worcester, MA (2010) (retrieved August 28, 2011)
5. Mori, M.: Bukimi no tani The uncanny valley (MacDorman, K.F., Minato, T. (trans.)). Energy 7(4), 33–35 (1970)
6. De Silva, L.C., Miyasato, T., Nakatsu, R.: Facial emotion recognition using multi-modal information. In: Proceedings of 1997 International Conference on Information, Communications and Signal Processing (1997)
7. Zollhöfer, M., Martinek, M., Greiner, G., Stamminger, M., Süßmuth, J.: Automatic reconstruction of personalized avatars from 3D face scans. Computer Animation and Virtual Worlds 22(2-3), 195–202 (2011)

Sex Differences in User Acceptance of Avatars

Leo Versteeg and Peter H.M.P. Roelofsma

VUA University Amsterdam, Department of Social Sciences,
The Netherlands
p.h.m.p.roelofsma@vu.nl

Abstract. This presentation discusses some explorative observations on sex differences in user acceptance of Avatars. Elderly adults evaluated a male and a female avatar. Subjects were required to watch non verbal emotional and interactive expressions of these avatars. After the video the subjects were asked to which avatar they felt more connected and which avatar they would choose as their personal coach. Elderly men felt more connected to the woman coach and preferred the female coach and elderly women felt more connected to the male coach and preferred the male coach. The observations are discussed by differences in the perceived para-social relationship of the users with each of the avatars.

Keywords: Avatars, Sex differences, User acceptance, Non verbal emotional expression, Para-social Relations.

1 Introduction

The use of avatars is increasingly popular in ambient intelligence. Avatars are more and more introduced in a variety of ambient environments like, health and care, learning, work, and living. A crucial aspect in the success of the application of such technology is the level of user acceptance of the avatars . User acceptance is a important factor for sustained motivation in system use. Subjects may differ in their preference of avatar characteristics and such differences may lead to differences is system effectiveness. The field of human avatar interaction is an emerging research area and many issues and debates from dyadic human interaction research are relevant for human avatar interaction. One of these issues is the phenomenon of sex differences. Avatars may function as different cues for men and woman. In particular the perceived connectedness to these avatars may be different.

More specifically, when avatars are used as virtual coaches psychological factors may be at stake. Subjects may perceive coaching by same sex avatars as an ego threat. As a consequence the may prefer different sex type of virtual coaching. In addition, when living alone connectedness may be stronger to different sex coaching due to a contrast effect of adding difference to the environment. To explore this phenomenon field observations were made where elderly subjects watched digital coaches and answered questions concerning avatar connectedness and preference.

2 Method

60 eldery adults 30 males and 30 females with an age range of 65-79 were used in this field observation. The subjects were approached in the central hall of an elderly care

R. Wichert, K. Van Laerhoven, J. Gelissen (Eds.): AmI 2011 Workshops, CCIS 277, pp. 189–191, 2012.

institution and at an elderly care happening. Subjects were invited to participate in the study and sit at a table where they watched the interactive virtual coaches on a labtop PC. The subjects were required to watch non verbal emotional expressions of these avatars. The expression were: neutral, approval, denial, scorning, thinking, laughing, encouragement. After the video the subjects were asked to which avatar they felt more connected, the female or the male coach (*Do you feel more connected to the male or female avatar?*). In addition they were asked which avatar they would choose as their personal coach if they had to select one of them as virtual coach. (*If you had to choose one avatar as your coach, would you chose the male or female avatar?*). The male and female coaches are presented in Figure 1.

Fig. 1. The male and female virtual coaches used in this study

3   Results

The majority of the elderly men, 26 out of 30 (87%) felt more connected to the female avatar. 24 (80 %) choose the female avatar as their virtual coach over the male coach. This pattern is reversed in the elderly women group. The majority of and elderly women 25 out of 30 (83%) felt more connected to the male avatar. 21 choose the male avatar as their coach (70%).

4   Discussion

The explorative observations provide discussion for sex differences in the acceptance of virtual coaches. It seems that men tend to prefer female virtual coaches and women tend to prefer male virtual coaches. The study provides discussion that this variation may be related to the level of connectedness to the coaches. This connectedness could be explained by subjects differences in perceived para-social relationships with the coaches. The results have important implications for AAL system design that implement virtual coaching for human interaction. More controlled studies are needed to further examine these important potential relationships.

References

1. Jin, S.A.: The effects of incorporating a virtual agent in a computer-aided test designed for stress management education: the mediating role of enjoyment. Computers in Human Behavior 26(3), 443–451 (2010)
2. Thorson, K.S., Rodgers, S.: Relationships between blogs as ewom and interactivity, perceived interactivity, and parasocial interaction. Journal of Interactive Advertising 6(2), 34–44 (2006)

User-Centered Design for and with Elderly Users in V2me

Kerstin Klauß and Peter Klein

User Interface Design GmbH,
Ludwigsburg/Mannheim, Germany
www.uid.com

Abstract. Positive user experience is an essential precondition for making online technologies accessible for elderly users. The V2me team chose to develop along an iterative user-centered design process (UCD) in order to focus on the target group's needs and limitations. Interviews with potential users and workshops with professionals were conducted and requirements were derived from the gathered knowledge on the target group. Further the V2me team designed an interaction and screen design, made these concepts experienceable in a first demonstrator and conducted a usability study with potential users.

Keywords: user-centered design (UCD), AAL, elderly users, scenario-based design (SBD), user experience, user acceptance, online social networks.

1   Introduction

In the context of increasing social isolation among seniors the access to online communities and other ICT provides promising possibilities for elderly users to find new contacts and maintain existing ones. As many elderly users lag skills with ICT and perceive especially the online world with distrust and even anxiety [1] they cannot yet make advantage of it. In this case the usage of avatars as a virtual self-representation technique and a virtual coach as motivator and coach offer the possibility to enter the online world in a guided way and therewith decrease or prevent loneliness.

The access to the resources is provided by either a stationary (23" touchscreen) or a mobile system (7" tablet). When developing such a system the project team has to face the specific and at the same time multifaceted characteristics and individual life plans [2] of the target group. Besides few skills with ICT and a widespread avoidance of modern technologies many elderly persons have to deal with physical, cognitive and sensory limitations [3]. Therefore we chose a user-centered design process (UCD) according to DIN EN ISO 9241-210. This approach focuses on the needs and limitations of the target group. Following a UCD we iteratively develop along four phases: "analyze", "design", "experience" and "test". This paper will give an overview on which methods we chose in each phase dependent on the respective context during the first iteration.

R. Wichert, K. Van Laerhoven, J. Gelissen (Eds.): AmI 2011 Workshops, CCIS 277, pp. 192–195, 2012.
© Springer-Verlag Berlin Heidelberg 2012

2   Analyze – Collecting User Requirements

An extensive analysis phase at an early stage of the project provides a deeper understanding of the target group: their needs, their limitations and the context of use in which they will interact with the system. This includes information on the physical as well as on the social environment and allows deducting requirements that serve as a guideline for the whole development process. We chose two established methods to comprehend and understand the context of use: face to face interviews with residents of care centers and assisted living accommodations of the Diakonie (care provider) and workshops with professionals. Thereby we collected data from the users themselves as well as from the persons who are interacting with the target group day by day.

During the interviews and workshops the participants answered questions on the key factors for further specification of the target group: their currently existing social networks, their use of ICT and their general attitude towards technology. Moreover we asked for the residents' acceptance of current services and activities as well as the related problems and worked out possible solutions for the beforehand defined problems as well as future perspectives for the V2me system. Initial mock-ups helped gathering first feedback on three possible scenarios. To avoid starting from scratch we integrated results from other research projects [4] [5] and collected established design principles for the design for elderly [6]. As a next step we evaluated the quantitative and qualitative data and derived requirements to make them applicable, traceable and testable. The requirement "keep the user interface simple" for instance resulted from the interviews and workshops and moreover was affirmed by design principles like "minimize irrelevant screen information" or "clearly label keys" [6].

To help the multidisciplinary team designing from the users' point of view and supporting the communication in the project we wrote personas and scenarios based on the gathered requirements. Personas describe typical users with their needs, characteristics and attitudes towards ICT and typical tasks they have to perform in their daily life as well as the problems they have to face. Scenarios based upon the scenario-based design process (SBD) of Rosson and Carroll [7] tell stories from the users' lives. Scenarios facilitate communication and lead the project team through all phases of the UCD. They provide different degrees of details which allow the project team to document an abstract vision as part of documentation of the analysis phase as well as designing along these scenarios and feeding it step by step with more details.

3   Design – A User Interface for Elderly

Next we implemented these requirements in an interaction and design concept for elderly users. As "Facilitate direct social contacts – Virtual contacts cannot replace direct social contacts." was found to be one central requirement we selected a scenario along the friendship enrichment program of the University of Amsterdam (VUA) [8] for the first iteration. This program was originally meant to be conducted in group sessions. The friendship enrichment sessions aim at preventing people from getting lonely by improving existing friendships and developing new ones.

As a first step we adapted a typical session and wrote an information scenario based on it. Information scenarios describe the information displayed on each screen throughout a scenario. As a first step we focused on the user interface for the tablet [9]. In a design workshop we worked out the screen layout and screen types based on the requirements of the analysis phase and the requirements we derived from the information scenario. In a next step we detailed the existing information scenario with wireframes and described the possible interactions on each screen along the scenario. Based on exemplary wireframes of the central use cases we created a screen design which should meet the needs of elderly users and at the same time should be attractive and non-stigmatizing.

4   Experience – Implement a First Prototype

Early demonstrators are important steps in the UCD to enable potential users to experience the system at an early stage of the project. Most users cannot put themselves into concepts by means of mere theoretical descriptions. Therefore it is an important step in the UCD to implement design concepts in early demonstrators to enable potential users to experience the concepts, which is a precondition for valuable user feedback. For the first user research study we decided to create a functional but still limited prototype for the scenario described above.

Fig. 1. Screenshot of the mobile V2me element in a Virtual Coach session

5   Test – User Experience and User Acceptance

User experience and user acceptance studies at the end of each iteration circle ensured that the development team was still "on track" concerning the users' needs and mental models. Valuable feedback from potential users leads to possible improvements of the existing system and gives input for the further development of the system. We conducted a pilot study with one-on-one usability test sessions as well as workshops with potential users in Amsterdam. The participants performed typical tasks with the prototype and answered questions about the usage and their perception of the system. The mainly qualitative data gained by asking the participants to "think aloud" and by observation provided the V2me team with valuable information on weaknesses and strengths of the system. Moreover we derived possible improvements for the further development of the system.

6   Conclusion

A user centered design process focuses the development team on the users' point of view throughout the whole development process. Personas and scenarios support the UCD and appropriate means to facilitate communication in project teams, help to translate the requirements into designs and prototypes and make them testable with potential users. This paper describes the first iteration in a three year development process. Following the UCD a project team step by step adds and tests new functionalities.

References

1. Beckers, J.J., Schmidt, H.G.: The structure of computer anxiety: A six factor model. Computers in Human Behavior 17, 35–49 (2001)
2. Herwig, O.: Universal Design: Lösungen für einen barrierefreien Alltag. Birkhäuser, Berlin (2008)
3. SENIORWATCH Older people and information society technology. Factors facilitating or constraining uptake (2002), http://www.seniorwatch.de
4. Connected Care for Elderly Persons Suffering from Dementia (2011), http://www.cceproject.eu/
5. Förderung des Wissenstransfers für eine aktive Mitgestaltung des Pflegesektors durch Mikrosystemtechnik, WiMi-Care (2011), http://www.wimi-care.de/
6. Sears, A., Jacko, J.A.: The human-computer interaction handbook. Lawrence Erlbaum Associates (2008)
7. Rosson, B.M., Carroll, J.M.: Usability Engineering: Scenario-Based Development of Human-Computer Interaction. Morgan Kaufmann (1990)
8. Martina, C.M.S., Stevens, N.L.: Breaking the circles of loneliness? Psychological effects of a friendship enrichment program for older women. Aging & Mental Health 10(5), 467–475 (2006)
9. Wroblewski, L.: Why design for mobile first? In: User Interface 15 Conference, Boston (MA), USA (2010)

Development of a Socio-technical System for an Age-Appropriate Domestic Environment

Daniel Tantinger, Sven Feilner, Matthias Struck, and Christian Weigand

Fraunhofer Institute for Integrated Circuits IIS,
Image Processing and Medical Engineering Department,
Am Wolfsmantel 33, 91058 Erlangen, Germany
{daniel.tantinger,sven.feilner,matthias.struck,
christian.weigand}@iis.fraunhofer.de
http://www.iis.fraunhofer.de/med

Abstract. Being part of the social community is for many people a crucial part of their life. Unfortunately, many of the elder generation are not able to participate due to physical condition and lack of will power. These people often suffer from loneliness and depression. In order to overcome these issues a system is being developed with its main goal to be a motivator for these people. Closely related to this is the term of *primary prevention*.

Within an AAL living room scenario an armchair with integrated sensors monitors several vital signs and offers the possibility to perform exercises which both are displayed on a TV screen. In addition, by using a tablet the user is able to communicate with medical experts as well as social group members, relatives and friends.

The acquisition of vital data in combination with elements of (virtual) social networks prevents isolation, motivates to be (more) active and supports healthy aging with a high *joie de vivre*.

Keywords: AAL, vital signs monitoring, social connectivity, motivation.

1 Introduction

Within the context of the demographic evolution and the fact that physical activities have manifold positive effects on the elderly, the part who is doing sport regularly is dramatically low [1]. Furthermore, the discrepancy between the percentage of the population keen on doing sports and those being indeed sufficiently active shows the impact of one's weaker self. Especially elderly people suffer from this. As a consequence, it is crucial to identify the target group and how motivation concerning physical and even social activities occurs and targeted promotion can be given [2], [3].

A lot of people think that depression is part of the aging process. Loneliness coupled with depression among the elderly decreases the quality of their lives extremely. Frustration with the loss of memory and physical ability (e.g., the

R. Wichert, K. Van Laerhoven, J. Gelissen (Eds.): AmI 2011 Workshops, CCIS 277, pp. 196–200, 2012.

loss of hearing makes phone calls difficult, trouble by walking means no driving and exercise, vision problems mean no reading), death of a loved one and even financial problems are the main causes for depression and loneliness [4]. But these symptoms often remain misdiagnosed and untreated.

Several existing platforms support health monitoring, but they are lacking of interconnection with vital signs monitoring and activity incitation [5]. Especially the combination of daily used technologies and end devices (e.g., TV, tablets, etc.) with these platforms as well as the integration of sensor technologies for monitoring vital signs are missing.

Consequently, the main target is to find solutions and strategies to overcome the lack of will power - motivate the elderly to be more active, stay in contact with friends and relatives, and find groups of the same interests.

2   Concept and Vision

The system presented in this paper is one approach for *primary prevention* [6] where the elderly is encouraged and motivated to be more active. The complete system comprises of two main parts. On the on hand the *interactive* arm chair, which provides a variety of exercises to improve the users health status. Whereas, on the other hand the virtual coach covers the social aspects, like coordination of group activities or maintaining social connectivity with friends and relatives.

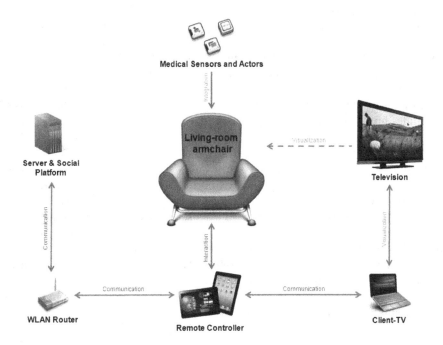

Fig. 1. Schematic representation of the overall concept

Both are means to motivate the user in a physical as well as in a social way. The system offers promising strategies and solutions for the motivation and activation of lonely and/or sport-passive elder people, even in their living room.

The concept shown in Fig. 1 consists of two core elements - a platform and a comfortable armchair. With the armchair (mounted on a carrier plate) it is possible to get passive and active feedback of the users. First, the elderly can perform exercises by using the chair (e.g., rowing or crunches) and second, vital signs can be measured on a voluntary basis. An important aspect is the inconspicuous integration of the armchair into the ambience of the living room design. Thus a high acceptance of the elderly concerning technical devices could be achieved. Beyond that, the user should not be aware of the measurements which should run automatically without any action of the user. Nevertheless, a comprehensive evaluation of the health status has to be ensured. In addition, the following (vital) parameters are acquired:

- Heart rate and single-channel ECG
- Oxygen saturation (SpO_2)
- Weight
- Respiratory rate

Hence, it is required to integrate the sensors in an unobtrusive way. For instance, in order to detect the weight distribution, four strain gauges were integrated into the carrier plate. Therefore, the detection and, ideally, the correction of the person's posture during the performance of different exercises (e.g., sit-ups, rowing, etc.) are possible (see Fig. 2).

Whereas the armchair is indeed part of the familiar environment of the user, the platform is rather the *invisible* core element of this system. The platform provides the health-related knowledge in order to process the vital signs recorded by the sensors integrated in the armchair. As a consequence, the system can provide useful hints for the elderly to improve his or her health condition.

This is realized by a *virtual coach* who acts as mediator and friend for the user and guides him or her through the system. The main function of this assistant is to motivate the elderly to be more active. This means that he suggests exercises according to a schedule set up by a physician and/or by the user himself.

At the same time, he acts as a mediator for existing and potential social relationships. He initiates communication with other users of the social network and encourages social activities (e.g., visiting a concert or going to the theater). In this context the assistant is a mediator of the user's social network, connecting to different groups of the same interests (e.g., playing chess or Nordic walking) and updating the user regularly with incoming news, appointments and requests. The *virtual coach* will manage the assets of the user and enable communication with friends, relatives and even health care services and professionals. As a consequence, this assistant motivates the elderly to be more active both, in a physical and a social manner.

The above mentioned data, vital signs and activity profile, are stored on the server (under persistence, data security and privacy aspects) and can be displayed on the TV screen. For this interaction a mobile device (e.g., tablet PC) is

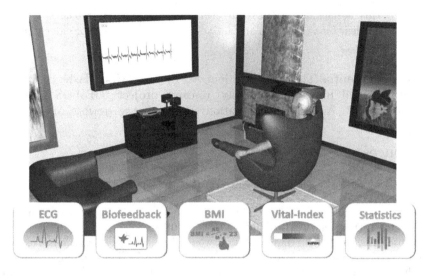

Fig. 2. System integration in the home environment

used as a remote control. This device offers the possibility to navigate through the application - selecting an exercise, get in contact with friends, display the measurements and the vital signs.

In addition, the data can be transmitted via the platform to medical experts or other service providers of the health care sector in order to maintain medical care.

Within this system standardized components and communication also have to be accounted and thus standards, like WLAN (IEEE 802.11) or W3C standards for Internet applications, have to be considered.

3 Conclusion and Outlook

In this work the overall concept was pointed out and the technical approach was presented. The term of *primary prevention* was described and on its basis the principal purpose, increasing the motivation of the older population to do more exercises, was specified. Hence, the social connection will be made possible again over physical and social components. But what is even more achievable: the technology should prevent to loose this connection. This is to be achieved with a system, which disturbs the domestic environment in no way and thus as technical aid reaches a broad acceptance by the elderly.

The upcoming steps - after the integration of the sensor technology into the armchair - consist of comprehensive laboratory tests and user evaluation during pilots. On the one hand this serves the iterative optimization of the system. On the other hand target-oriented evaluation of the armchair and the measuring system both, from user and medical view, is enabled.

Finally, this assistant enriches the user's life and increases the social and physical activities. As a result, an attractive living environment for elderly people is being created.

Acknowledgments. This work was founded by the BMBF (Federal Ministry of Education and Research, Germany) research project "GEWOS - Gesund Wohnen mit Stil". Additional information: http://www.gewos.org

References

1. Denk, H., Pache, D.: Die Bonner Alterssportstudie. Sportwissenschaft 29, 324–342 (1999)
2. Moritz, E.F., Erdt, S., Schulz, T., Strehler, M., Struck, M.: Kampf dem Schweine-hund. In: 4. Deutscher AAL-Kongress, Berlin (2011)
3. Friedrich, M., Gittler, G., Halberstadt, Y., Cermak, T., Heiller, I.: Combined exercise and motivation program: Effect on the compliance and level of disability of patients with chronic low back pain: A randomized controlled trial. Archives of Physical Medicine and Rehabilitation 79(5), 475–487 (1998)
4. Stapleton, C.: Loneliness, depression and aging, Palm Beach Post, http://www.palmbeachpost.com
5. TK Gesundheitscoach - TK Health Coach, http://www.tk.de/tk/online-filiale/meine-services/ tk-gesundheitscoach/38516
6. Moritz, E.F., Strehler, M.: Innovationspotenziale in der primären Prävention. In: Sport und Gesundheit in der Lebensspanne, pp. 48–52. Feldhaus, Hamburg (2008)

Using Technology for Improving the Social and Physical Activity-Level of the Older Adults

Milla Immonen, Anna Sachinopoulou, Jouni Kaartinen, and Antti Konttila

VTT Technical Research Centre of Finland, Kaitoväylä 1, 90571 Oulu, Finland
{Milla.Immonen,Anna.Sachinopoulou,Jouni.Kaartinen,
Antti.Konttila}@VTT.FI

Abstract. Social media and internet technologies are regularly used by young and adult population. Older adults are using social media rarely, even though these technologies have the potential to ease and enrich their lives. This article discusses different possibilities for the use of technologies to enrich the lives of older adults by activating them socially and physically. Technology can also support the maintenance of close relationships with relatives and care givers and ease their workload.

Keywords: Social motivation, social media, Internet, older adults, exercise.

1 Introduction

This article describes the ways that the new technologies can help older adults enjoy their pension years, focusing on social networking, socially motivated hobbies and physical exercises. Although today's recently pensioned persons have little experience on computers and social media, they are often willing to learn how to use new technologies. They are motivated to do so by their wish to be more aware of the life of their children and grandchildren, to be informed about interesting events, discussions and social networking. Even though traditional methods for communication, such as telephone, are valued among the elderly people [1], they also value peripheral awareness of friends and family. Older adults also tend to associate using a method of communication in a specific situation primarily with its advantages or benefits [2].

This article will describe potentially suitable and modifiable technologies for elderly use and present some ideas for the use of these technologies. User interaction methods for the older adults will not be discussed here. It is the belief of the authors that most of the described technologies will need modifications in order to accommodate with suitable user interfaces for older adults.

2 Valuable Everyday Life

Depression in old age is an important public health problem. Among others, depression in elderly persons has been associated with social deprivation that may rise from health or other reasons [3]. For example, unexpected death of a spouse or

R. Wichert, K. Van Laerhoven, J. Gelissen (Eds.): AmI 2011 Workshops, CCIS 277, pp. 201–205, 2012.
© Springer-Verlag Berlin Heidelberg 2012

expected death after a long stressing caregiving period increases the chances for depression among the surviving spouses [4]. A solution to this problem can be given by new technologies that can be combined and modified for the use of older adults and support a more social and thus happier life. While designing user interfaces and usability for elderly persons, the earlier, already familiar technologies should be kept in mind to improve the acceptance [2], [5], and [6]. Different possibilities for the use of Internet technologies are visualized in Figure 1.

Fig. 1. Possibilities for the use of Internet technologies for the older adults in communication with relatives, services such as banking and travelling, and socializing, e.g. sharing experiences and keeping up with events and carpooling.

2.1   Information Sharing

Older adults very often have children and grandchildren whom with they are willing to share daily thoughts, images and videos. The need is bigger if the relatives live in a different city or country and they don't meet very often. The information sharing can be made easy by direct or indirect communication technologies. Direct communication technologies are those resembling the telephone and that can be provided at a cheaper price through the Internet. Indirect communication technologies are for example the social media where users provide updates about their life, thoughts and feelings which are then available for their "friends" to read. In both cases, technology can add value to everyday life and improve the elderly quality of life. One important issue, especially addressed by the elderly users [7] is security. Information sharing should happen only with the people intended to see the information and it should be made easy for the elderly users to choose who they communicate with. Shared information can also include care instructions or hints for the different aspects of life, for example healthier life. Also car-pooling saves money, resources and environment and can be easily arranged through social media technologies.

2.2   Social Networking

After the working years, the social activities are reduced and it is not easy to find new friends. According to previous research [8], older adults are willing to find new friends, preferably from the close surroundings. Keeping contact with former colleagues and life time friends is still essential but becomes more difficult. An online system, that will connect people through interest groups and discussion forums, could help older adults to maintain long-term relationships but also find new friends. It has been shown in recent studies, that videoconferencing makes older adults happier, more connected and less isolated [8] thus adding to their quality of life.

2.3   Time Scheduling

Online digital calendars can support time scheduling for older adults and their relatives. The help of grandparents in child care is valuable and important for the family. By using online calendars, suitable times can be suggested by the parents and the grandparents can accept or reject them. It can be also easy for them to see what activities their grandchildren have and from where they will have to pick them up. Such calendar can also be used in scheduling online the care times or visiting times between relatives of the elderly person, so that the person is visited often enough.

Remembering of important days, i.e. birthdays, is important for the older adults and their relatives. The calendars could be used for reminding these days too.

2.4   Social Motivation

Despite the known benefits of exercise for older adults, the majority of these individuals do not exercise regularly. Although the benefits of the exercising are the main motivation for doing so, the social aspects also are important. Hearing about other older adults exercising, or seeing others exercising, can be highly motivating. Shared stories about gained benefits, such as better coping with daily activities or less falls than earlier, are also important. Knowing that someone is interested in or following your activity level or exercise program can be also motivating. Social media has potential to play an important role in social activation. The information of the benefits of the exercising or different hints and guides for exercising can be shared through the social media. Even if the user of social media does not result in increasing the exercise regime of elderly persons, they at least motivate them to be socially active and encourage him or her to contact people, organize meetings and go out of the house.

3   Suitable Technologies

3.1   Skype and Other Live Communication Technologies

Skype is a communication tool among the information technology and web communication tools that is most favored by the elderly persons. [9] It is thought that this is due to its simplicity as well as its resemblance to a normal phone, a concept familiar to everyone. However, there are some characteristics that require attention in order to make the tool easier for use by elderly persons. Skype's user interface is easy to use as it is, but it could be modified to be more usable and similar to older technologies, to be more acceptable by the older adults. For example, initializing connection with someone could be directly put under an icon of a traditional phone. The quality of the Skype video calls leaves still much to be desired. Other live communication tools are not as popular as Skype, and mostly share the same difficulties. In some cases the open source tools are preferred, because Skype's developer license doesn't allow development on mobile or tablet platforms.

3.2   Facebook and Google+

Although social media platforms, as Facebook and Google+, are popular, reported usage level among the older adults is very low. One reason may be the fact that the function of Facebook and Google+ is not well understood. It is often challenging to realize who is seeing one's statuses, photos, pictures etc. and what ones sees on his wall, or how one should react to what is shown. Security issues are one of the most worrying issues for the older adults in the Internet use [5], [6]. Since there is no precedent technology that can relate to Facebook and Google+, another paradigm should be found in order to make it easy for the older adults to understand what is Facebook and Google+.

It is possible to develop applications that use Facebook or Google+ in the background. Facebook provides an open source software development kit (SDK) for website development for both JavaScript and PHP [10]. Similarly, Google+ has an API, which can be used for integrating Google+ with other applications [11]. These developer API's enables using Google+ in a more friendly way. Facebook and Google+ could be used for information sharing, scheduling and motivation.

4   Conclusions

Social media technology can benefit elderly users by making them more active and more social. There exist already some tools that are being used by few elder users but need to be further developed in order to increase usability and acceptance by a vaster elder community. Some new tools such as online agendas and calendars can also be beneficial.

References

1. Romero, N., van Baren, J., Markopoulos, P., de Ruyter, B., IJsselsteijn, W.: Addressing Interpersonal Communication Needs through Ubiquitous Connectivity: Home and Away. Ambient (Cmc), 419–429 (2003)
2. Melenhorst, A.-S., Rogers, W.A., Caylor, E.C.: The Use of Communication technologies by Older Adults: Exploring the Benefits from the User's Perspective. In: Proceedings of the Human Factors and Ergonomics Society 45th Annual Meeting (2001)

3. McDougall, F.A., Kvaal, K., Matthews, F.E., Paykel, E., Jones, P.B., Dewey, M.E., Brayne, C.: Prevalence of depression in older people in England and Wales: The MRC CFA Study. Psychological Medicine 37(12), 1787–1795 (2007)
4. Burton, A.M., Haley, W.E., Small, B.J.: Bereavement after caregiving or unexpected death: Effects on elderly spouses. Aging and Mental Health 10(3), 319–326 (2006)
5. Chou, W.-H., Lai, Y.-T., Liu, K.-H.: Decent Digital Social Media for Senior Life: A Practical Design Approach. In: Proceedings of the 3rd IEEE International Conference on the Computer Science and Information Technology, ICCSIT (2010)
6. Goswami, S., Köbler, F., Leimeister, J.M., Krcmar, H.: Using Online Social Networking to Enhance Social Connectedness and Social Support for the Elderly. In: Proceedings of the International Conference on Information Systems ICIS, Saint Louis, MO, USA (2010)
7. Tieto- ja viestintätekniikan käyttö, Official Statistics of Finland (2010) (in Finnish), http://www.stat.fi/til/sutivi/2010/ sutivi_2010_2010-10-26_fi.pdf
8. Savolainen, L., Hanson, E., Magnusson, L., Gustavsson, T.: An Internet-based videoconferencing system for supporting frail elderly people and their carers. Journal of Telemedicine and Telecare (2008)
9. Study of elderly persons using Skype and Facebook, http://www.dailymail.co.uk/sciencetech/article-1385330/Rise- silver-surfers-Grandparents-using-Skype-Facebook-stay-touch- family-record-numbers-seen-before.html
10. Facebook developer API's: https://developers.facebook.com/
11. Google developers API's: http://code.google.com/

Workshop: Integration of AMI and AAL Platforms in the Future Internet (FI) Platform Initiative

Antonio Kung[1], Francesco Furfari[2], Mohammad-Reza Tazari[3],
Atta Badii[4], and Petra Turkama[5]

[1] Trialog, Paris, France
[2] ISTI-CNR, Pisa, Italy
[3] Fraunhofer-IGD, Darmstadt, Germany
[4] U.Reading, UK
[5] U.Aalto, Finland
antonio.kung@trialog.com, francesco.furfari@isti.cnr.it,
saied.tazari@igd.fraunhofer.de, atta.badii@reading.ac.uk,
petra.turkama@aalto.fi

Abstract. The digital agenda of the European Commission includes plans for the building of Information and Communication Technology (ICT) based on a new generation of networks, or the Internet of the Future. To this end, the Future Internet Private Public Partnership (FI-PPP) has been established with the help of the European Commission. It will involve the building of a proof of concept FI platform in the coming two years. One of the main challenges of this platform is to be generic while serving the needs of specific application sectors. This workshop focused on the challenges of integrating Ambient Intelligence (AmI) and Ambient Assisted Living (AAL) platforms with this kind of platform. Participants in the workshop involved members of the AmI/AAL platform community andmembers of the FI community.

Keywords: AmI, AAL, Future Internet, Platforms.

1 Workshop Context

In March 2008, the ICT community in Europe produced the Bled declaration calling for a concerted European action to redesign the Internet [1]. The result was the Future Internet Public Private Partnership programme (FI-PPP) [2] which is coordinated by the CONCORD facilitation project [12]. It includes three phases as shown in Figure 1 and will involve a public budget of 300 MEuro. The first phase has started in April 2010 and consists of a technology foundation project focusing on the provision of an FI platform that will be used by up to eight use case scenario projects. The second phase will focus on further validation of this platform through five use case scenario pilots. The third phase will be dedicated to the expansion and enlargement of many test beds and pilots.

Ambient Assisted Living refers to "intelligent systems that will assist elderly individuals for a better, healthier and safer life in the preferred living environment and

R. Wichert, K. Van Laerhoven, J. Gelissen (Eds.): AmI 2011 Workshops, CCIS 277, pp. 206–212, 2012.
© Springer-Verlag Berlin Heidelberg 2012

covers concepts, products and services that interlink and improve new technologies and the social environment" [3]. AAL is supported by the European Commission's ageing well action plan [4] as well as a series of measures that involve more than one billion Euros in research and development between 2006 and 2013. Realising that many collaborative projects were dedicating resources to the development of platform features, the European Commission decided in 2009 to launch a call for proposals for the development of a common platform. This led to UniversAAL, an FP7 project [5] which is now coordinating AALOA, an initiative for an open source platform [6]. In parallel, work related to accessibility has led to the launch of the OpenURC initiative [7]. AAL is a compelling use case scenario for the Future Internet. Furthermore, the AAL community has accumulated a wealth of platform requirements [8,9] that could directly benefit the Future Internet. The vision of the FI-PPP is that the technology foundation project will provide generic enablers which would be associated with specific enablers developed within a domain to allow for the design, development and deployment of applications. The question is, can the FI-PPP enablers give leverage to the AAL community?

Further to technical integration, the FI PPP and AAL communities share the same development priorities: smartness, sustainability and inclusiveness, as well as similar social, regulatory and economic implementation barriers. This workshop discussed joint methodologies and instruments for collaborative research, development and innovation contributing to the European growth strategy. Such methods include user driven open innovation, public sector innovation, policy coordination methods, as well as living lab experimentation.

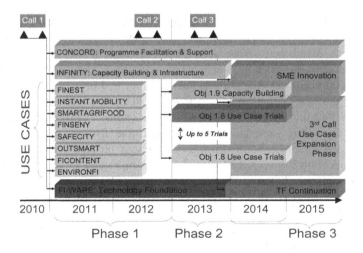

Fig. 1. FI-PPP Phases

2   Workshop Content

This workshop focused the challenges of integrating AmI and AAL platforms with the FI-PPP initiative. In this respect the workshop provided information on concrete means to engage with the FI PPP future calls and experiments, either as a user or as a co-developer. A secondary objective was to explore the opportunities for joint statements and declarations addressing the grand societal challenges of aging, e-inclusion and e-competences, as well as the implementation of Digital Agenda.

The following topics were discussed:

- Architecture of an FI platform. Challenges from an FI viewpoint.
- Architecture of existing and to come AmI/AAL platforms. Challenges from an AmI/AAL viewpoint.
- How can integration take place? What are the hurdles?
- What are the means of experimentation? Can AAL be a usage area for the Future Internet?
- What is the impact of evaluation? How can we move towards a European digital single market?
- Identification of measures and instruments.
- Actions.

Participants of the workshop included members of the AmI/AAL platform community and members of the FI community.

3   Session 1: The AAL Initiative

The session, chaired by Atta Badii (University of Reading) started with two movies [13, 14]. The chair presented a check list concerning user needs using inputs provided by Elizabeth Mestheneos from Age platform: rapidity of innovation, role of consultation, cost, user-friendly, standards of accessibility, digital literacy, specialized versus general needs, acceptability. He also commented on five points: lip service, gimmicks (pretending), shallow valued packing, old age/disability, mainstreaming.

Sabine Wildevuur (WAAG) presented Express2connect [15] where the *Play with your life* story telling game has been developed. She also presented the Health-lab living lab [16] in Amsterdam (focusing on solutions for care). She emphasized the need to work with the user (rather than for the user) and to work out in parallel business models.

Francesco Furfari (CNR-ISTI) presented AALOA [6] as a community to help coordinate development related to open platforms for AAL. He presented a number of coordinated work such as EvAAL [17] that focuses on evaluation and comparison of AAL solutions by exploiting Living Labs infrastructure, or Zb4osgi [18] that focuses on the integration of Zigbee networks with IP-based applications. Such networks are important enablers of healthcare scenarios.

Antonio Kung (Trialog) presented the context that led to this workshop, including the Lecce declaration [19] (which calls for the creation of ecosystems based on open common platforms), and the current preparation of a strategic implementation plan for the European Innovation Partnership on Active and Healthy Ageing [20].

4   Session 2: The Future Internet Initiative

Session 2 was chaired by Mikko Riepula (Aalto University). He provided an overview of the programme, consisting of eleven projects: one technology foundation/software platform project, FI-WARE [21] bearing some resemblance and analogies to UniversAAL [5]; 1 capacity/testbed cataloguing project (Infinity [22]), 8 use cases (number and scope to be redefined for 2013 onwards; this is also where Health, Wellbeing and Active Ageing could fit in as a vertical domain), and finally, CONCORD [12] as the programme facilitation and support project for the whole FI PPP programme. FI PPP is a 5-year programme that started half a year ago, and opportunities exist for joining later (cf. open calls).

Thierry Nagellen (Orange Labs) then introduced the central FI-WARE platform itself, emphasising how it is to be an open specification with open source components for the reference implementation. Partners have not started from scratch, but each have brought their background IPR to the table. The resulting platform should of course be such that the partners can commercially extract revenue from their implementations later on. The so-called technical chapters include e.g. trust and security, Internet of Things (IoT) and cloud hosting, which should many be of interest also to AAL. At the same time, some components of IoT specifically are missing in this early stage of the FI-WARE project, which could be a opportunity for UniversAAL to feed in.

Josema Cavanillas (ATOS) presented some of the vertical use case domains in more detail. (ATOS is a project partner in several use cases in addition to FI-WARE).

Finally, Takis Damaskopoulos (EIIR) elaborated on the need for studies and recommendations to the EC on policy, regulations and governance when it comes to the access to, storage and use of, and disposal of various kinds of data and services, as may be implied by the term "Future Internet" and specifically the Public-Private partnership focus of the FI PPP programme. FI PPP/CONCORD tries to see policy, regulation and governance from two perspectives: policy, regulation and governance as seen from a 'technology perspective' and technology as seen from a 'policy, regulation and governance perspective'. The possibilities of the aging population using the Future Internet to their benefit is certainly a policy/regulation/governance item, since the business models are largely missing from free markets.

The discussion further revealed that it might be beneficial to formulate a future use case around Ambient Intelligence as a more widely applicable topic than to propose the scope of AAL anew in the open calls for new use cases.

5   Session 3: Panel on Technical Coordination

This session was chaired by Antonio Kung (Trialog) with questions prepared by Saied Tazari (Fraunhofer IGD).

Francesco Furfari (CNR-ISTI) presented the technical work achieved in the universAAL. He showed how the results of previous AAL projects on platforms have been consolidated into a common understanding from which the technical concept of

AAL space has emerged. He presented a number of application scenarios where this concept was used. Discussions in the panel led to two conclusions: first, there was a need of harmonizing technical terminology between the AAL and the FI technology communities, and secondly, the concept of AAL spaces could be a contribution as an enabler of a FI platform.

Antonio Kung presented slides prepared by Jan Alexanderson (DFKI) on URC. URC is an ISO standard (ISO24751) for personalized user interfaces based on dynamic adaptation capabilities, i.e. deploying interfaces plug-ins matching personal profiles. The OpenURC alliance [7] has been established in a move to further coordinate the growing URC community (200 partners directly or indirectly using URC technology as of today). OpenURC would therefore be a coordination representative of URC based technology within AALOA. OpenURC would also support applications domains where user interfaces were needed (e.g. public transport), in particular developments associated with GPII [23], an initiative calling for the adoption of personalized interfaces in public infrastructures. Discussions in the panel led to the following conclusions: first, URC based technology could be considered as an enabler for accessibility, and secondly, this enabler was currently not implemented in FI technology community currently.

Questions prepared by Saied Tazari were addressed. It was confirmed that (1) FI-Ware connects cloud computing to the internet of things, (2) universAAL brings the concept of AAL spaces, (3) OpenURC is a generic approach for accessibility. The panel concluded with a discussion on the technical feasibility of joining forces. It was concluded that in order to integrate AAL enablers (including URC) four short term milestones had to be reached (1) terminology harmonization, (2) architecture harmonization, (3) defining an approach for long term interoperability, (4) defining an approach for long term support.

6   Session 4: Panel on Opportunities for Collaboration

The session was chaired by Antonio Kung. Martin Potts (Martel) presented the Infinity project [22] and how it would collect and coordinate the provision of information on FI related undertakings. Gaby Lenhart (ETSI) explained the role of standards and the involvement of ETSI in technological development. Ana Garcia (ENoLL or European Network of Living Labs) presented the role of ENoLL [24] in coordinating Living labs communities and provided examples of AAL living labs.

The panel first debated issues related to ecosystems based on open platforms. On coordination between AAL, OpenURC and the FI technologies, Thierry Nagellen said that FI-WARE is defining a methodology for defining integrating enablers. On coordination between AAL, OpenURC and the FI communities Martin Potts reported that Infinity is also defining a methodology (using in particular a *common description framework*). On the possibility that living labs use common platforms, Ana Garcia said that the presence of ENoLL as a partner of Concord would ensure that the FI undertaking is well integrated and taken into account by the living lab community. She also pointed out the need for flexibility and customizability, and the need to allow for diversity. On how standardization could be anticipated at platform level, Gaby Lenhart provided two advices, first taking into account the issue of backward compatibility and secondly ensuring a good knowledge of the state of the art in order to identify gaps.

The panel then moved to discuss applications. Blanca Jordan (ATOS) confirmed the relevance and suitability to integrate AAL applications into a wider vision of active healthy ageing (AHA) combining eHealth, AAL and other aspects. Ana Garcia confirmed that ENoLL could act as a front door to find and engage living labs developing applications in the AHA area. Gaby Lenhart also widened the issues of standardisation to metrology, terminology and ontology, interoperability. A discussion then took place on policies for interoperability. It was agreed that while it should not be mandatory to be interoperable, it was mandatory to be able to express its intention (e.g. using a commonly understandable description). It was finally agreed that long term support was needed (e.g. ensuring that support provided by Infinity currently would be available after the project completion).

The panel finally discussed actions towards a MoU between the FI and the AAL communities. Identified area for collaboration were terminology, architecture, approach for interoperability, approach for support, and understanding of FI-PPP methodologies (i.e. FI-Ware methodology used to integrate a technology enabler, Infinity methodology used to describe capabilities). The proposed timeline was January 2012 for terminology and understanding methodologies, October 2012 for architecture understanding and possible agreements for convergence, and April 2013 for an approach for interoperability and for community support. This would be synchronized with the FI-PPP timeline (i.e. First release of FI-WARE platform in April 2012, second release in April 2013). Persons involved in the preparation of the MoU would be Mikko Riepula or Petra Turkama, Juanjo Hierro, Patrick Gatellier, Thierry Nagellen on the FI-PPP side and Antonio Kung, Saied Tazari, Francesco Furfari on the AAL side.

7   Conclusion of the Workshop

Session 1 showed that the AAL community is well structured, with in particular the support of AALOA which coordinate efforts related to open platforms. Session 2 showed that FI community was also well structured, with in particular the support of FI-Ware to build a platform, the support of Infinity to interface with projects and the involvement of ENoLLto interface and integrate user communities (developers, SMEs, citizens, etc). Both communities are engaged into undertakings to create mainstream sustainable ecosystems, with initial contributions coming from the living labs community. The opportunity for having collaboration between ENoLL and AALOA was identified during the workshop as AALOA was in effect coordinating the development of enablers that could be used by living labs. An MoU or statement of intent will now be discussed on an identified list of topics with a proposed 18-month timeline.

References

1. Bled declaration, http://www.future-internet.eu/publications/bled-declaration.html
2. Future internet FI-PPP, http://www.fi-ppp.eu/, http://ec.europa.eu/information_society/activities/foi/lead/fippp/index_en.html
3. Ambient Assisted Living Roadmap. AAliance, http://www.aaliance.eu
4. Action Plan on Information and Communication Technologies and Ageing (June 14, 2005), http://eur-lex.europa.eu/LexUriServ/site/en/com/2007/com2007_0332en01.pdf, http://ec.europa.eu/information_society/activities/einclusion/policy/ageing/action_plan/index_en.html
5. UniversAAL IST project, http://www.universaal.org/
6. AALOA, http://www.aaloa.org
7. OpenURC, http://www.openurc.org
8. Kung, A., Jean-bart, B.: Making AAL Platforms a Reality. In: de Ruyter, B., Wichert, R., Keyson, D.V., Markopoulos, P., Streitz, N., Divitini, M., Georgantas, N., Mana Gomez, A. (eds.) AmI 2010. LNCS, vol. 6439, pp. 187–196. Springer, Heidelberg (2010), http://portal.acm.org/citation.cfm?id=1926762
9. Fagerberg, G., Kung, A., Wichert, R., Tazari, M.-R., Jean-Bart, B., Bauer, G., Zimmermann, G., Furfari, F., Potortì, F., Chessa, S., Hellenschmidt, M., Gorman, J., Alexandersson, J., Bund, J., Carrasco, E., Epelde, G., Klima, M., Urdaneta, E., Vanderheiden, G., Zinnikus, I.: Platforms for AAL Applications. In: Lukowicz, P., Kunze, K., Kortuem, G. (eds.) EuroSSC 2010. LNCS, vol. 6446, pp. 177–201. Springer, Heidelberg (2010), http://portal.acm.org/citation.cfm?id=1940178
10. MonAMI project: http://www.monami.info/
11. CompanionAble: http://www.companionable.net/
12. CONCORD: http://www.fi-ppp.eu/projects/concord/
13. Charlie and Marie: a tale of ageing, http://www.youngfoundation.org/publications/reports/charlie-and-marie-a-tale-ageing-february-2011
14. The AAL joint program, http://www.youtube.com/user/AALJP?feature=mhsn
15. Express2connet project, http://www.express2connect.org
16. Health-lab living lab, http://health-lab.nl/
17. Evaal, http://evaal.aaloa.org
18. Zb4osgi, http://zb4osgi.aaloa.org
19. Lecce declaration, http://www.aalforum.eu/group/leccedeclaration
20. EIP-AHA, http://ec.europa.eu/research/innovation-union/index_en.cfm?section=active-healthy-ageing
21. FI-Ware, http://www.fi-ware.eu/
22. Infinity, http://www.fi-infinity.eu/
23. Global Public Inclusive Infrastructure, http://gpii.net/
24. European Network of Living Labs, http://www.openlivinglabs.eu/

Ambient Gaming and Play: Opportunities and Challenges

Janienke Sturm[1,2] and Ben Schouten[1,2]

[1] Dept. Industrial Design, Eindhoven University of Technology, P.O. Box 513, 5600MB Eindhoven, The Netherlands
[2] Serious Game Design / Ambient Intelligence & Design lectorate, Fontys University of Applied Sciences, P.O.Box 347, 5600AH Eindhoven, The Netherlands
{j.sturm,bschouten}@tue.nl

Abstract. During the workshop on Ambient Gaming (AmGam'11) at the International Conference on Ambient Intelligence in Amsterdam, 16-18 November 2011, 17 participants from 8 different countries discussed emerging research topics around Ambient Gaming. With ambient games and play we denote playful activities that are seamlessly integrated within our daily lives in such a way that the boundaries between other activities and play disappear or blur. Ambient games blend the virtual and real world and are interacted with through multiple ubiquitous devices. Ambient games and play have a strong motivational character and may offer more natural and improved interaction. However, we are also faced with many challenges, not only technological, but societal and ethical as well.

Keywords: Ambient gaming, playful interactions, ambient intelligence, open-ended play, persuasive technology.

1   Introduction

In many historical works about play, the definition of play is restricted to a specific 'time and place', separated from ordinary life (i.e. play takes place in a 'magic circle') [1,2]. Digital play, however, can be more integrated in a spatial, temporal and social sense [3] owing to new media, social networks, modern technology and (social) interaction. This enables us to design for playful activities that are seamlessly integrated within our daily lives in such a way that the boundaries between other activities and play disappear or blur; we call this ambient games and play.

Ambient games blend the virtual and real world and are interacted with through multiple ubiquitous devices. They incorporate ambient intelligence characteristics [4], which means being surrounded by 'smartness'. Ambient intelligence environments may sense who is present, where they are, what they are doing, and when and why they are doing it. In line with this, ambient games offer context-aware and personalized features. They also allow players to move around freely, without being bound by a computer screen or another device, by using information coming from sensors embedded in the environment. By their nature, they allow players to play

R. Wichert, K. Van Laerhoven, J. Gelissen (Eds.): AmI 2011 Workshops, CCIS 277, pp. 213–217, 2012.
© Springer-Verlag Berlin Heidelberg 2012

throughout the day, as play and games may be incorporated in everyday objects and routines [5].

In this sense, ambient gaming and play changes the traditional notion of 'game', as governed by a well-defined set of rules, impenetrable to our everyday interactions, and bounded in terms of time, space, and participation, by expanding it in spatial temporal and social sense. Spatially, the traditional physical context is transformed into an omnipresent, dynamic, responsive and reconfigurable space for play [6]. See for instance the work on urban gaming and designing playful mechanics for interacting though and with the augmented city [7, this volume] in which the city serves as an environmental game interface that is augmented by transparent technologies. Vatavu et al. [8, this volume] describe how smart sensors and recognition algorithms enable people to use every day objects as active elements in their games, so that they are no longer confined to a single location to play, but can walk about freely and use a toy gun or a wooden stick as a weapon in the game. In this way, ambient gaming technologies lead to unrestricted and natural interaction. Extension in a temporal sense means that ambient games can be played throughout the day in an active or passive way. For instance, the ambient game that is described by [9], plays on even if the players are not actively playing. Finally, in the social sense, rules in ambient games are more likely to be socially constructed, and emergent patterns of play arise, much more like the free, unstructured play in traditional playgrounds, yet triggered and enabled by the artifacts of the ambient play space [6]. For instance, Rosales [10, this volume] describes how free play experiences can be improved and encouraged by adding technology to everyday objects such as clothes, accessories and toys that children wear all the time. The same holds true for the Intelligent Playground [11, this volume] which provides opportunities for open-ended play, based on intelligent sensors, adaptivity and embodiment. Free or open-ended play with interactive objects promotes children's social and personal skills. Also, ambient gaming redefines the role of the players themselves, as everyone present in the ambient play may become part of the activity. Space. Players, onlookers, and passers-by may move in and out of the ambient play space and influence what happens even unaware [3]. Playful interactions in ambient play spaces are thus likely to lead to more social involvement, as compared with traditional, bounded play environments.

2   Opportunities

Ambient gaming and play can be an effective means to persuade people to take part in certain activities, such as educational activities or physical exercise. For instance game-based learning tools could help to improve the learning process by creating a motivating, dynamic and entertaining forum to both teach and learn [, this volume]. In the PlayFit project [13, this volume] opportunities for play are created throughout the day, aimed at reducing the amount of time teenagers spend sedentary. As another example, the Ubitheragames [14, this volume] intend to offer handicapped people in a smart environment playful tools to do their exercises. By integrating smart sensors and actuators in daily objects such as wheelchairs and walkers, and by providing opportunities to play in a smart environment handicapped people are stimulated in a playful and ambient way to do their daily exercises. The motivation for people to take part in these ambient health games is high, because of their playful character.

Moreover, the threshold to take part is very low, because the activities are intertwined with peoples' daily activities and routines (e.g. taking the bus to school, having lunch, or having a daily walk).

Using ambient intelligence in games and play offer opportunities for more natural and improved interaction, because they are no longer confined to a television or computer screen, but can extend to the real world, using everyday objects as interaction devices [8,11]. In addition, ambient technology enables advanced awareness and personalization. This leads to more engaging experiences and increased flow, because the magic and suspension of disbelief are not broken by real world hurdles. In this way, in ambient gaming and play interaction moves from a more functional, goal-oriented role, to a playful experience that goes beyond usability, deriving meaning from its context.

Designing ambient games and designing for ambient play requires a different role of the designer. Design processes move to co-creation, participatory design and other design methods where the user and the environment play an important and active role, reflecting the change to interaction as the creator, facilitator or mediator of experiences [10].

3   Challenges

From a technological perspective, ambient gaming and open-ended, free play require smart sensors that can be embedded in every day objects, such as clothes, walls, furniture, street lamps, the human body, etc. Intelligent algorithms are required that are able to detect, recognize and interpret data coming from different sensors in the environment. On the basis of the analyzed sensor data, adaptation and personalization should take place and relevant and adequate feedback should be provided to the user [14].

Ambient gaming is closely linked with gamification, a recent phenomenon that entails adding playful elements to non-game applications, in order to make them more fun and engaging. Gamification is already applied many different contexts, for instance in education, health and commercial organizations. Obviously, not every activity is more effective when cast in the form of a game, but gaming has several assets (e.g. intrinsic motivation, challenge, flow) that do work. However, although the strong motivational power of games has been proved in many different cases, it is unknown what the effects are in the long run. For instance, it is well-know from psychological studies that punishments and rewards can stop being effective when used for a longer period of time. Therefore, gaming mechanisms like competition and punishments and rewards should be used with caution, they should not be an end in itself. For instance in open-ended or free-play environments there are no predefined and fixed rules and goals, it is the experience of playing in itself and the social interaction that takes place around play that is rewarding.

Finally, in terms of control and privacy, it is important to allow players to make informed choices about their engagement. Especially when the boundaries between play and non-play are blurred, as they may be in ambient games, the user may become part of a game unaware and unwillingly. Also, when play is no longer restricted to a defined place in front of the television, or computer screen, data about players and players' actions may become publicly visible. This calls for a fine balance between control and engagement.

4   Conclusion

In the workshop on Ambient Gaming (AmGam'11) at the International Conference on Ambient Intelligence in Amsterdam, 16-18 November 2011, 17 participants from 8 different countries discussed emerging research topics around Ambient Gaming. Originally, ambient intelligence was designed to be 'calm' and non-intrusive technology [15]. Some of the criticism on ambient intelligent systems is focused on privacy and human control. Digital play and gaming as a process for user awareness and participation and creation [6] could balance this criticism, the disruptive nature of play. Other challenges are to facilitate open-ended and free play in smart environments, a big challenge for human behavior analysis. Finally, until now, the quality of interaction has mainly focused on usability and functionality of 'cause and effect'; this needs to be changed into dimensions of social interaction and experience, sometimes inefficient, emotional or counter-productive. The workshop contributed to a fruitful discussion and the organization of a network for ambient play research institutes.

References

1. Huizinga, L.: Homo Ludens. A Study of the Play Element in Culture. Beacon Press, Boston (1955)
2. Caillois, R.: Man, Play, and Games. Thames and Hudson, London (1962)
3. Montola, M., Stenros, J., Waern, A.: Pervasive games: theory and design. Morgan Kaufmann (2005)
4. Aarts, E., Marzano, S. (eds.): The New Everyday: Visions of Ambient Intelligence. 010 Publishers, Rotterdam (2003)
5. Sturm, J., Tieben, R., Deen, M., Bekker, T., Schouten, B.: PlayFit: Designing playful activity interventions for teenagers. In: Proceedings of Digra 2011, Hilversum, The Netherlands, September 14-17 (2011)
6. Schouten, B.: The Role of Play. Inaugural Speech Professor of Playful interaction. Eindhoven University of Technology (2011)
7. De Luca, V., Bertolo, M., Zannoni, M.: Around Play. Play and Interaction Design Research Group. In: Proceedings of the First Workshop on Ambient Gaming (AmGam 2011), Amsterdam, The Netherlands (2011)
8. Vatavu, R.-D., Zaiti, I.-A.: Exploration for Gaming Applications. In: Proceedings of the First Workshop on Ambient Gaming (AmGam 2011), Amsterdam, The Netherlands (2011)
9. Eyles, M., Eglin, R.: Ambient Games, Revealing a Route to a World Where Work is Play? International Journal of Computer Games Technology (2008)
10. Rosales, A., Arroyo, E., Blat, J.: Evocative Experiences in the Design of Objects to Encourage Free-Play. In: Proceedings of the First Workshop on Ambient Gaming (AmGam 2011), Amsterdam, The Netherlands (2011)
11. Rijnbout, P., de Valk, L., de Graaf, M., Bekker, T., Schouten, B., Eggen, B.: i-PE: A Decentralized Approach for Designing Adaptive and Persuasive Intelligent Play Environments. In: Proceedings of the First Workshop on Ambient Gaming (AmGam 2011), Amsterdam, The Netherlands (2011)

12. Hjert-Bernardi, K., Hernández-Leo, D., Melero, J., Blat, J.: Do different hint techniques embedded in a digital game-based learning tool have an effect on students' behavior? In: Proceedings of the First Workshop on Ambient Gaming (AmGam 2011), Amsterdam, The Netherlands (2011)
13. Tieben, R., Sturm, J., Bekker, T., Schouten, B.: Playful moments of activity. In: Proceedings of the First Workshop on Ambient Gaming (AmGam 2011), Amsterdam, The Netherlands (2011)
14. Madeira, R.N., Postolache, O., Correia, N.: Gaming for Therapy in a Healthcare Smart Ambient. In: Proceedings of the first workshop on Ambient Gaming (AmGam 2011), Amsterdam, The Netherlands (2011)
15. Weiser, M., Brown, J.: Designing Calm Technology. Powergrid Journal 1 (1996)

Around Play and Interaction Design Research

Vanessa De Luca[1], Maresa Bertolo[2], and Michele Zannoni[3]

[1] SUPSI, Laboratory of Visual Culture - Interaction Design Lab,
Department for Environment Constructions and Design (DACD)
vanessa.deluca@supsi.ch
[2] Politecnico di Milano, School of Design, dep. INDACO
(Industrial Design, Arts, Communication and Fashion)
maresa.bertolo@polimi.it
[3] University of the Republic of San Marino
michele.zannoni@unirsm.sm

Abstract. The paper presents an inter-faculties experience stemming from the common interests of researchers and designers in ludic interactions between people and interfaces. The new territories mapped by the game and Ambient Intelligence (AmI) paradigms in everyday communication interfaces are a shift in how design incorporates new functions and meaning. Design itself has become a way to play with artifacts, complex systems and networks. Moving beyond formal and aesthetical use of games, it is possible to bring different competences to reflect together on the interviewing of game and play elements in the design of the daily spaces, objects and activities. The question is how the play paradigm can improve the relationship between people and ambients and, as a consequence, the issues of Interaction Design in the AmI field of study. In this paper we present our initiative to build a multidisciplinary design group. From our synergy three particular areas have been identified as new design sectors in which games are involved in person's environments.

Keywords: Interaction Design, Game Studies, Urban Games, Board Game analysis, Alternate and Augmented Reality Games.

1   Introduction

Nowadays, the daily-life environment can be looked as an overlapping of different realities populated by people, digital networks, hybrid practices and ubiquitous technologies. At the same time, technologies that are integrated into a person's environment or on a person's body as well are central in the Ambient Intelligence discourse. Systems that are sensitive to individuals, responsive to human intervention, able to adapt their function and stimuli around us, nonintrusive, ubiquitous and intelligent probably will constitute our near future sensor-based interface. In our opinion, the scenario configured conveys the human participation as a voluntary act to play and start a conversation with an interface system. This inkling can be applied through the game design approach. The real world empowerment with engaging interfaces - gesture, tangible or sensors equipped - and gameplay elements - such as

R. Wichert, K. Van Laerhoven, J. Gelissen (Eds.): AmI 2011 Workshops, CCIS 277, pp. 218–223, 2012.

metaphors, rewarding mechanics, narrative paths, as well as winning contexts - can have a positive impact in designing everyday interactions. This background moves Around Play research and addresses the group members design and teaching activities for envisioning the forthcoming interfaces. Through the investigation of the interviewing of interaction design and game-play design the group purpose is to meet and explore the contemporary mixed people expectations in an unobtrusive manner.

Without overlooking critical and ludic approaches to design and behaviourism the Around Play glances at the Ambient Gaming as an opportunity to understand how multiple competences could be conveyed in a meaningful way.

2   Why Do Research Around Play? Objectives and Challenges

In the contemporary world we live in, tangible and hybrid can be noticed as two important aspects that characterize the everyday interfaces. In this reality, the Around Play research group investigates the positive impact of the game-play elements in the design practice of future human interactions in environmental interfaces augmented by transparent technologies.

Walking around Play and Interaction Design field of studies the research group is focused on the exploration of a multidisciplinary areas discovering and experimenting the interconnected domains of knowledge.

In this way, the research activity dwells upon the relationship between the game system and the human play attitude; a wide area, where Around Play Research Group follows a compass built on our studies and research, constantly growing, looking for answers to many different questions, such as:

- In which way game mechanics engage people?
- What are the game constructive components?
- How the game and play elements can enrich non-game environments?
- How can ludic engagement (and consequence) influence user behaviours?
- How can we use the Play paradigm to stimulate the lateral thinking capabilities and to improve user involvement in the interaction dynamics?

3   Areas of Interest

The Around Play areas of interest involve different topics, such as board games analysis and design, gamification concept and clues, ambient and urban games, alternate and augmented reality, the playful values of interactive systems and extended game interfaces.

Our knowledge base is further enriched and shared in a truly inter-disciplinary space, peripheral as well as dynamic. Being an inter-faculty research group, we foster activities and projects for encouraging reflections and discussions around the game and play design field of studies in different domains, ranging from basic action rules and mechanics to aesthetic aspects of game elements and interfaces.

Each member of Around Play group is involved in her/his Faculty research projects and teaching activities, being able to coordinate local occupation with this inter-athenaeum group interests.

Group members are locally engaged in different projects, where Interaction Design, in its many declinations and shapes, is always involved. For instance, a topic of great interest is the deep analysis of mixed games spatiality dimensions; how the real space perception can change within the play experience, and how the game environment itself can affect the user's spatial experience.

Our approach to classroom activities is strongly project-oriented, being them Ateliers, Laboratories as well as Design Courses. During our teaching activities we juxtapose practical experience to theoretical lectures, giving reinforcement to the learning process, and often we use student's works as critical instrument for starting the discussion on the mutual comparison and game design reflections in classrooms.

The Around Play research areas draw on the experiences and projects of the research members which address the cultural, social and design issues in the development of meaningful exchanges between the Play and Interaction Design field of studies. We are now focused in three main projects:

3.1   Playful in Motion Experience

This project aims to integrate and coordinate research and practical workshop experiences on the areas of Exercise Games by managing many disciplines and professional knowledge involved and design-based backgrounds. The core concept starts from the noticed interests on mobility and personal healthy experiences linked to the wide research on the gaming platforms and the social network potentials. While the experiences on fitness and sport activities supported by digital technologies are mostly limited on the training and coaching practices, stimulating solely physical aspects, next-gen gaming consoles are now developing persuasive and also wearying entertaining application. In this current situation we are investigating how to improve exercise activities though the ludic engagement and a more complete motion experience suited to merge both physical and mental aspects in order to give users a motivational context for a playful exercise practice. In this way the ongoing project includes workshop initiatives that aim to structure a network of inter-sharing between researchers and industry professionals.

3.2   Urban Games for the Augmented City

This research area explores and experiments the play-factor as a stimulus to design playful mechanics for interacting with and through the augmented city. It investigates how to support the contemporary urban gamer lifestyles combining several aspects: psychogeography, pervasive games, social games, methods and techniques for the city investigation, transmedia storytelling and cultural aspects of urban life as flânerie and rhabdomancy. The group's empirical study is supported by design concepts and educational activities with the main focus on the game-interaction design.

[GIUC-MI] is a project conceived in this direction. It structures an urban game for the social and territorial communication of the city of Milan. The project designs a system for the tourists immersion in the city quarters involving several artisan workshops of Milan and their identities and historical backgrounds, that would otherwise remain unknown. During the city exploration the players have to hunt the workshops and interact with the artisan dwellers in order to reach points and discover the hidden side of Milan. The project includes QRcodes located outside each place and a web supporting system holding game materials and data.

3.3   Game Analysis and Design

Games and overall social games have the potential to predispose users for learning - dynamics, context or contents - in a playful way. This powerful focus point move the research group to test methods and processes involved in the design practice. As simulation of realities, each game can be adopted as interactive microcosm and used to understand bigger interaction system in many different design areas. In this regard we have found the Laboratory of Game Analysis (LGA) in which multicultural approaches, analytical and interpretative tools are adopted for structuring reusable models and to test game prototypes. The LGA is a recurrent collective game analysis session which offers to heterogeneous focus groups a variety of game-play opportunities for approaching projects in a design perspective. People, students, friends as well as designers and researchers participate at the play-sessions where we open discussions on the play experience associate to the analysis of the design elements and relationship rules trigged by the game experience. LGA initiative is mainly oriented to board games and analog games for the understanding and the consequent definition of patterns and constructive game elements.

4   The Research Group

The Around Play and Interaction Design Research Group is an inter-faculty and international research team focused on the design and evaluation of games and play challenges, promoting a cross-sectional approach to research in Interaction Design and Game Studies. It aims to enable and provide efficacious support to students, makers and researchers in undertaking novel meaningful approaches to design interactive environments (digital, analogical and mixed). Team activities are intended to facilitate culturally and qualitatively oriented game design research, providing both traditional and experimental ways for investigating and exploring game elements and player's engagement.

The group takes birth in the long-term research and teaching relationship among the three founders; they share interests and approaches although referring to different athenaeums: Laboratory of Visual Culture - IDLab - SUPSI (Switzerland), INDACO Department and School of Design - Politecnico di Milano (Italy) and the University of the Republic of San Marino (San Marino).

Main members are:

Vanessa De Luca
Vanessa is a researcher and designer. She completed a Ph.D. in Industrial Design and Multimedia Communication at the Politecnico di Milano (2009, Italy) where she has started to investigate the game paradigm in interaction design field of study. Her current research centers on: player's experience in non-ordinary game environments, urban gaming and the intertwining of the game/play elements and mechanisms in the daily life.

Maresa Bertolo
After her academic degree in Computer Science in the field of Computer Graphics and Animation, the interest for Interaction Design brought her to the Politecnico di Milano, where she is now tenured researcher; her research fields are Computer Graphics and Animation (2D, 3D and S3D); Stereoscopy; Game Studies; Interaction Design.

Michele Zannoni
He graduated at the University Institute of Architecture in Venice, with an experimental thesis entitled "Digital Didactic Modules". He has taught at the universities of Politecnico di Milano and IUAV of Venice (Italy). He is a professor of "Digital Representation" at the University of the Republic of San Marino. As designer he works at the "Studio Visuale", where his activities and scientific research are focused on new media and interaction design projects.

References

1. Around Play Research Group, http://www.aroundplay.net
2. Aureggi, M., Bertolo, M., De Luca, V., Pillan, M.: Training new designers for interaction: GINA, a game design workshop for improving sensitivity toward interactive dynamics and synaesthetic perception. In: 8th European Academy of Design Conference. The Robert Gordon University, Aberdeen (2009)
3. Bellotti, V., Back, M., Edwards, W.K., Grinter, R.E., Henderson, A., Lopes, C.: Making Sense of Sensing Systems: Five Questions for Designers and Researchers. In: CHI 2002, pp. 415–422. ACM Press, Minneapolis (2002)
4. Benford, S., Schnädelbach, H., Koleva, B., Anastasi, R., Greenhalgh, C., Rodden, T., Green, J., Ghali, A., Pridmore, T., Gaver, B.: Expected, sensed, and desired: A framework for designing sensing-based interaction. ACM Transactions on Computer-Human Interaction (TOCHI) 12(1) (2005)
5. Caillois, R.: Les Jeux et les hommes: le masque et le vertige. Gallimard, Paris (1958)
6. De Luca, V., Bertolo, M.: Urban Games to design the augmented city. In: Proceeding of Future and Reality of Gaming (FROG 2011), Eludamos top-paper candidate, Vienna (2011)
7. De Luca, V., et al.: Undesigned for: re-thinking interactions through game-play design. In: Proceeding of 2010 SDN Swiss Design Network Symposium, Design Fiction, Basel (2010)

8. De Luca, V.: Play Design: A collaborative design space based on digital game project. In: The Inter-Society for Electronic Arts (ISEA). Ulster University, Belfast (2009)
9. De Luca, V., Suteu, I.: Design Instrument for Learning Games: Shaping the motivation of play. In: International Technology, Education and Development Conference (INTED), Valencia (2008)
10. Gaver, W.: Designing for ludic aspects of everyday life. ERCIM News 47 (October 2001)
11. Mariani, I.: Giuc[MI], a playful approach to local identities communication. Poster. In: Future and Reality of Gaming (FROG 2011), Vienna (2011)
12. Nijholt, A., Reidsma, D., Poppe, R.: Games and entertainment in ambient intelligence environments. In: Aghajan, H., Delgado, R., Augusto, J.C. (eds.) Human-Centric Interfaces for Ambient Intelligence. Elsevier (2009)
13. Suits, B.: The Grasshopper: Games, Life and Utopia. Broadview Press, Toronto (2005)
14. Suteu, I., De Luca, V.: How to construct and express the creative thought. Understanding the communication mechanisms of the collaborative design teamwork. In: IASDR, Seoul (2009)
15. Zimmerman, J., Forlizzi, J., Evenson, S.: Research through design as a method for interaction design research in HCI. In: Proceedings of the Conference on Human Factors in Computing Systems, pp. 493–502. ACM Press (2007)

Gaming for Therapy in a Healthcare Smart Ambient

Rui Neves Madeira[1], Octavian Postolache[2], and Nuno Correia[3]

[1] Escola Superior de Tecnologia de Setúbal, IPS, Setúbal, Portugal
rui.madeira@estsetubal.ips.pt
[2] Instituto de Telecomunicações, Instituto Superior Técnico, Lisboa, Portugal
octavian.postolache@gmail.com
[3] Interactive Multimedia Group, DI/FCT/New University of Lisbon, Mt. Caparica, Portugal
nmc@di.fct.unl.pt

Abstract. Games elements are transcending the usual boundaries of their medium to enhance user experience and user engagement in non-game applications. Therapeutic serious gaming allows a patient to execute specific exercises while engaging with a game, trying to achieve its goals related to therapeutic activities. A ubiquitous therapeutic game corresponds to adding these elements into a context-aware smart ambient. This paper presents a proposal towards the use of therapeutic serious games in a pervasive healthcare assistive ambient. We are implementing these games to be used in the rehabilitation of both cognitive and motor deficits, taking advantage of the infrastructure developed for assisting and monitoring elderly and disabled people. The work's research will also be used on studies to improve the system's effectiveness through personalization.

Keywords: Pervasive, personalization, therapeutic games, smart ambient.

1 Contextualization

The concept of serious gaming refers to the use of computer games to teach something to users or help them developing specific skills, without the main purpose of pure entertainment altough maintaining it [6]. Games and related technologies are increasingly transcending the usual boundaries of their medium leading towards gamification, an informal umbrella term for the use of game elements to enhance user experience and user engagement in non-game applications [3]. A main example is therapy based on serious games (theragames), with several studies and projects demonstrating the efficiency of this approach in domains such as rehabilitation after spinal cord injury and stroke [6]. Theragames allow a patient to execute specific exercises to achieve its goals and levels related with rehabilitation purposes, while playing and engaging in a game context.

Furthermore, ubitheragames combine theragames with ubiquitous computing, usually a context-aware smart ambient, mixing a digital environment with real world elements [4]. Within the last decade, new systems concepts related with pervasive healthcare [1] brought several new solutions that offer chances to create ubitheragames. Pervasive technologies permit develop interesting theragames using

R. Wichert, K. Van Laerhoven, J. Gelissen (Eds.): AmI 2011 Workshops, CCIS 277, pp. 224–228, 2012.

lightweight and convenient devices for tracking users' activities, RFID technology for identification of users and objects, biosensors to measure physiological vital signals, and ambient displays to deliver feedback, among other possibilities. This combination can offer valuable contributions to develop more effective games as assistive instruments for diagnosis and therapeutics monitoring in the rehabilitation field.

Motivated by the aforementioned, this paper presents a proposal towards ambient therapeutic gaming in a pervasive healthcare assistive environment (PAE) [5]. This environment serves the purpose of having a starting working system to apply the design of our theragames model proposal. It presents the following main features:

- Integrates smart objects, such as wheelchairs that have embedded sensors to measure physiological parameters and mechanical quantities (e.g., Acceleration).
- RFID technology is used to identify the patients on the wheelchairs and to locate the latter within the indoor space of application.
- An android-based tablet PC is attached to the wheelchair for information presentation and user interaction.
- The integration of ambient displays is also important to offer new opportunities for collaboration and a better resolution for combination of information, as it is being seen in healthcare environments [2].

2   The Ambient Gaming Model Design

We propose a model of gameplay criteria and principles to be followed in the design of ubitheragames based on the PAE previously presented. However, this model can be followed in the implementation of theragames in other pervasive healthcare spaces. Table 1 sketches the model presenting its principal features.

Table 1. Model's principles and gameplay criteria

Principles	Gameplay Criteria
Present Simple and Persuasive UIs	Rehabilitation Area
Consider the Patients	Game Genre
Give Performance Feedback	Game Interface Type
Apply Adaptability/Personalization	Game Modes
Register Users Interactions	Game Portability
Support Casual Play	Technologies

As a first principle, the interfaces of the games should be simple, easy to understand, user-friendly, persuasive and informative, since they are usually directed for elderly patients. Therefore, the development of these games has to take into account both patients' specificities and practitioners' needs, with a high level of acceptance by patients and therapists and demonstrating efficiency when compared to classical therapies. Another important issue is the performance feedback. The patient should receive feedback about her/his performance during the gametherapy, so s/he can have measures of the progress in achieving goals, or in their skills, over time [6]. This also increases the motivation of the patient that can receive suggestions and tips.

Scoring mechanisms should be implemented as would be in a classic computer game. However, the score can be based on monitored accuracy or effort, thus reinforcing the correct gesture and attitude.

Ubitheragames have real conditions to enable dynamic adaptation of therapeutics according to the patient's performance and capabilities because of their context-aware nature, maintaining the engagement and entertainment in playing. The designed theragames should take into account the adaptability element, the capability to adapt dynamically the game difficulty and proposed challenges. The system should self-adapt to the patient as she/he improves. This is a principle closely related with personalization aspects. The first time a patient plays a game should encounter a low level of challenge/difficulty. Then, games should offer increasingly difficult levels that give the player the sense of challenge in his progress.

The games system should allow saving the results of patients' interactions, which is important as input for the personalization process. It is also used for progress monitoring, closely related with operations that should be available to the therapist, such as: setting up exercises, loading them into the game system to tailor activity to the patient's needs; and receiving results/scores reports to evaluate the effectiveness of the treatment. Additionally, the proposed games should support casual play, being as much as possible seamlessly integrated with daily activities.

Available technologies and their selection are essential for the gameplay criteria definition. In terms of technologies that can be used for interaction and context-aware sensing, we consider mainly motion tracking devices, RFID, physiological sensors, situated ambient displays, tablets mounted on wheelchairs and mobile phones. Webcams can be used for tele-rehabilitation monitoring. We consider both cognitive rehabilitation and motor rehabilitation regarding the application area. Another important gameplay criteria is the game genre, which can vary depending on the goal, such as evaluation of the movement (catch, reach and grasp), and motion, simulations, cognitive strategy, or a combination of several. The game interface should be initially a two-dimensional (2D) one, but this kind of environments presents potential for three-dimensional (3D) implementations. The design should consider both single player (single) and multi-player (multi) as game modes. The engagement with therapeutics goals can result through an individualized approach or in a group with collaboration and/or competition settings, which can potentiate engagement.

In relation to game portability, the developed theragames can be used in any environment (e.g., home for elderly, hospital) that has the elements used by them. It is important that the patient does not need to carry the digital tools/devices for the gametherapy wherever s/he goes. Therefore, the games design should take into account preferably elements pervasively embedded in the environment.

3   Implementation of Ambient Gaming Prototypes

The main game is still in development and uses the movement and location of the user's wheelchair as main feature for gameplay. It is designed to stimulate elderly patients to move within the space of application, promoting a more pro-active attitude and working mostly on the cognitive field. It integrates sub-games developed both for cognitive and for motor rehabilitation.

The game's main mode presents an indoor map in the wheelchair's tablet. We have defined three gameplay scenarios as can be seen in Table 2. The choice of the map and games depends on the desired configuration, which depends on the patients that are doing therapeutics in the space of application. Elements of the three scenarios can be combined to create gameplay variants.

Table 2. Game scenarios

Game Scenario	Description
1	Virtual objects appear at specific positions of the map. They should be "caught" by patients through the physical movement of the wheelchair passing on their corresponding physical positions.
2	Circuits are marked on the map indicating which physical path should be performed by the patient on wheelchair.
3	The map highlights positions/spots to where the patient should proceed in the wheelchair in order to play adaptive sub-games.

In scenario 1, the patient sees virtual objects appearing in the map, which have to be "caught" through the physical movement of the wheelchair. So, the patient should "pick-up" only the objects associated with a certain category, such as family or cooking. Scenario 2 is focused on forcing the patient to follow a path, in order to recognize a sequence of positions, simulating a race game. Time limits can be included. Finally, the third scenario indicates positions to where patients should go in order to play cognitive or motor activities that are launched as sub-games. We already have a first functional sub-game, which combines elements of both memory and mahjong kind of games. It addresses clinical situations where semantic categorization and auditory and reading comprehension are impaired in aphasia and alexia, the most common speech and language disturbance in stroke and head trauma. It is integrated as a sub-game of the third scenario of the main game, but it can be independently used by patients.

With this type of game, patients can combine virtual spaces and objects with physical presence in real-time and using sensory modalities. RFID tags on the floor are used to mark the paths, the virtual objects' positions, and the activities spots. The wheelchair's LF RFID reader tracks and identifies the floor's tags. The usage of the physiological sensors enables the capture of patients' physical and physiological data as biosignals, not only for monitoring purposes but also as input to the personalization process. Combined with the patients' current performance scoring (and therapeutic scoring history) and goals, they are used for setting up levels and activities (e.g., adaptation of GUI and information) and for difficulty adaptation (e.g., game flow such as maps design and selection, time limits, tips presentation). The games are personalized according to the mentioned points, but also taking into account results of questionnaires posed to the therapists and patients.

An additional interface of the game will be designed for the ambient displays. Therefore, while the patient will see his/her presence in the virtual map displayed in the tablet, a therapist will be able to follow the global action with the visualization of the general map (and represented wheelchair(s)) in the ambient display.

4   Conclusions

We have proposed a model of gameplay criteria and principles to be followed in the design of ubitheragames. The approaches to game development presented here can potentially enhance treatment outcomes with engagement in playing. However, much research is still needed to provide the adequate methodologies and frameworks to ensure efficacy. The development of these games has to take into account both patients' specificities and practitioners' needs, presenting a high level of acceptance.

Our main goal is to identify and study technological and therapeutics challenges to facilitate the development of ambient gaming especially for elderly patients on wheelchairs. We want to use them for personalization studies related with interactions between users and pervasive healthcare systems. Future research is important in the design of evaluation methods for testing them in real environments, such as clinics and homes for the elderly.

In terms of current development, we are studying how to best integrate the ambient displays, which can be a new form of motivating multi-player therapy with collaboration and competition settings.

References

1. Arnrich, B., Mayora, O., Bardram, J., Tröster, G.: Pervasive healthcare: paving the way for a pervasive, user-centered and preventive healthcare model. Methods Inf. Med. 49(1), 67–73 (2010)
2. Bardram, J.E., Hansen, T.R., Mogensen, M., Soegaard, M.: Experiences from Real-World Deployment of Context-Aware Technologies in a Hospital Environment. In: Dourish, P., Friday, A. (eds.) UbiComp 2006. LNCS, vol. 4206, pp. 369–386. Springer, Heidelberg (2006)
3. Deterding, S., Sicart, M., Nacke, L., O'Hara, K., Dixon, D.: Gamification: using game-design elements in non-gaming contexts. In: Proc. of the 2011 Annual Conference Extended Abstracts on Human Factors in Computing Systems (CHI EA 2011), pp. 2425–2428. ACM Press, USA (2011)
4. Lindt, I., Ohlenburg, J., Pankoke-Babatz, U., Ghellal, S., Oppermann, L., Adams, M.: Designing cross media games. In: 2nd International Workshop on Gaming Applications in Pervasive Computing Environments (2005)
5. Postolache, O., Madeira, R.N., Correia, N., Girão, P.: UbiSmartWheel – A Ubiquitous System with Unobtrusive Services Embedded on a Wheelchair. In: Proc. ACM PETRA 2009, pp. 1–4. ACM press (2009)
6. Rego, P., Moreira, P.M., Reis, L.P.: Serious games for rehabilitation: A survey and a classification towards a taxonomy. In: Proc. CISTI 2010, June 16-19, pp. 1–6 (2010)

Evocative Experiences in the Design of Objects to Encourage Free-Play

Andrea Rosales, Ernesto Arroyo, and Josep Blat

Carrer Tanger 122-140
08018 Barcelona, Spain
andrucha@gmail.com, {ernesto.arroyo,josep.blat}@upf.edu

Abstract. In the near future technologies will be even more present in every day objects, which should add a playful value for children, to make use of their natural interest to play while being socially and physically active. We have moved towards this direction by building on free-play experiences identified through a face-to-face ethnographical study conducted over 4 months. The study shows that, beyond the increase of screen based entertainment, children have scarce opportunities for free-play (leading to them being more sedentary). Moreover during free play, they combine the interest of an individual activity, with a personal challenge, while collaborating and competing. Based on these findings we propose augmenting accessories with sensor systems giving feedback while doing specific body challenges. We have developed and tested two prototypes based on this concept: shoes that blink while jumping and a fanny pack that blinks while moving.

Keywords: free-play, social skills, motor skills, multi-experiences, ubiquitous, augmented technologies.

1   Introduction

It is expected that technologies will be even more present in everyday objects in near future. Technologies for children could be introduced in clothes, accessories, simple toys and playgrounds, and some of them can be used to sparkle children's creativity, stimulate face-to-face interaction and free-play to promote social and personal skills, for instance. Researchers have been working around these issues, mostly creating brand new ideas, but alternative approaches could lead to innovative products for final users. We have taken the route of understanding successful free-play experiences through ethnographic lenses to build on successful free-play experiences. This way, technology would add a new level to the existing free-play experiences.

Free-play encourages children to practice social skills, as they have to come up with new ideas together, they have to express, negotiate and collaborate with each other. Free-play occurs when kids spontaneously get together to play, when they are physically active, specially when they choose what to do, and do not have a concrete objective or a rigid set of rules [1], [3], [6], [4]. In spite of this, many factors increase or decrease the opportunities for free-play [8], such as the high interest of kids for

R. Wichert, K. Van Laerhoven, J. Gelissen (Eds.): AmI 2011 Workshops, CCIS 277, pp. 229–232, 2012.
© Springer-Verlag Berlin Heidelberg 2012

screen based entertainment, the increasing number of extracurricular activities or a hectic life style [3].

In this paper we describe the evocative design process of free-play oriented interactive objects. The first phase of the process includes the use of ethnographic methods for understanding children's relation with free-play in specific living contexts. Through this phase we identified objects and activities related with free-play as well as routines and spaces that might influence their free-play. We chose to elicit new ideas with ethnography methods as it provides "a way of getting a first hand view of the ground realities of everyday life" beyond what people say or do and can be captured through surveys or focus groups [1].

The second phase of the process includes applying the evidences emerged from the ethnographic phase in the conceptual design of new objects to build on successful free-play experiences.

According to this process we have created Playful Accessories; clothes that act as playful objects, that children wear all the time and that encourage free-play in unexpected moments.

2   Evocative Design Process

2.1   Ethnographic Studio

The ethnographic study was carried out throughout 4 months observing around 240 kids playing in parks, schoolyards and homes in three districts of Barcelona (Spain). The observations were conducted to understand objects, activities and routines related with free-play.

We collected contextual evidences in real life situations using participation-observation, note taking, and informal interviews [1]. We analyzed the data through Grounded Theory [9]: we read our field notes, generated an initial list of open codes, and grouped them into initial categories. The four main categories that emerged include:

"*Let's jump!*": Kids in this age get involved in physical challenges, playing with strength, speed, gravity, coordination, etc. Beyond playing with a airplane, a ribbon or with a pebble they are facing physical challenges.

"*I've got no time to play*": The daily routine is full of curricular and extracurricular activities and gives no room for free-play.

"*I'm bored*": There are a lot of boring moments, such as going to the supermarket, or visit grandparents. However, being bored can be opportunity to sparkle children's imagination and boredom is more easily overcome with a suitable object within reach.

"*Can I play with you?*": While playing with body challenges such as scooter races or climbing a wall, kids mix this individual activity, with collaborative and competitive social patterns.

2.2   Design Concept

Based on ethnographic findings we have defined the design concept of playful accessories to encourage free-play.

We aim at designing playful accessories that give feedback to children's actions to encourage free-play. These sensor-augmented accessories can react to specific body's actions and movements, and, according to the ethnographic study, kids are highly interested in body challenges.

Moreover, this playful added value on everyday clothes or accessories can be put into practice by children in unexpected situations or in the different and multiple *I'm bored* moments happening every day (identified in the ethnographical study). The free-play is encouraged – even if *there is no time to play*.

We also seek that the augmented accessories offer a combination of individual activities and personal challenges with the possibility to collaborate or compete with others, which is a key social pattern identified during our observations of free-play in real-life settings.

Our proposal takes advantage of current sensing technologies to create smart clothes adding a relevant value Steffen [5] by add a playful one for smart clothes for children.

2.3 Prototypes

We have designed, developed and tested two Playful Accessories: Statue and FeetUp.

Statue: is a fanny pack that blinks and makes sound whenever the user moves. Statue stimulates children to play games related with being a statue or moving without being noticed, which are commonly played by children, according to our ethnographical observations. It is inspired in many folk games, which include being statue. According to our evaluations, the accessory added a new condition in their everyday settings that encouraged transforming their frequent games. Social interaction emerged by slightly modifying the rules in a social dynamics that challenged power, leadership and creativity, they also practiced body language, imitations and small talks.

FeetUp: is a pair of shoes that blinks and makes sound whenever the user jumps, or is off the ground. FeetUp stimulates children to play against gravity, one of their most frequent activities during free-play. According to our evaluations, with FeetUp each found his/her personal style to play with the accessory; doing ballet, capoeira, handstands and so on. This led children to associate with someone with whom they had a common interest, shared their knowledge and tried to improve their performance together, generating challenging social experiences.

3   Conclusion and Future Work

We suggest using ethnographic methods to study children's relation with free-play in specific contexts, where children's life happens. Ethnographic explorations may be used to build on existing evidence of factors that facilitate or restrict the opportunities for free play to design evocative objects that encourage free-play.

According to our ethnographic explorations we propose add a playful value to clothes or accessories children wear all the time, to make use of their playful attitude and their infinite interest to improve body challenges.

We have designed 2 playful accessories: FeetUp and Statue. Both are wearable objects that encourage free-play in unexpected situations everywhere and all the time.

Future work includes compare the evaluation of both accessories to understand how the different features of each design influenced the experience, and define a set of design opportunities, that can be taken into account in the design of future objects to encourage free-play.

References

1. Bekker, T., Sturm, T., Eggen, B.: Designing playful interactions for social interaction and physical play. J. Pers. Ubiquit. Comput. 14, 385–396 (2010)
2. Blomberg, J.: An Ethnographic Approach to Design. In: Jacko, J.A., Sears, A. (eds.) The Human Computer Interaction Handbook, pp. 969–987. Lawrence Erlbaum Associates Publishers, New Jersey (2003)
3. Creighton, E.: Jogo An Explorative Design for Free Play. In: 9th International Conference on Interaction Design and Children, pp. 178–181. ACM, Barcelona (2010)
4. Nachmanovitch, S.: Free Play: Improvisation in Life and Art. Penguim Putnam, New York (1990)
5. Steffen, D., Adler, F., Marin, A.W.: Smart semantics Product semantics of smart clothes. In: 3th World Conference of Design Research IASDR, pp. 79–88 (2009)
6. Santer, J., Griffiths, C., Goodall, D.: Free Play in Early Childhood. National Children's Bureau, London (2007)
7. Turkle, S.: Falling for science: objects in mind. MIT Press (2008)
8. Veitch, J., Salmon, J., Ball, K.: Individual, social and physical environmental correlates of children's active free-play: a cross-sectional study. The International Journal of Behavioral Nutrition and Physical Activity 7 (2010), http://www.Springerlink.com
9. Charmaz, K.: Constructing Grounded Theory: A Practical Guide through Qualitative Analysis. SAGE, London (2006)

Playful Moments of Activity

Rob Tieben, Janienke Sturm, Tilde Bekker, and Ben Schouten

Eindhoven University of Technology, Department of Industrial Design, Postbus 513, 5600 MB Eindhoven and Fontys University of Applied Sciences, Serious Gaming lectorate, Rachelsmolen 1, 5612 MA Eindhoven

Abstract. In our design-research studies, we aim to persuade teenagers to engage in playful moments of casual activity. In this article, we present one explorative prototype: walk-of-fame, a multimedia installation that creates virtual avatars in a corridor, depending on the walking style of passers-by. We intend to create playful active moments throughout the day, independent of time or location, supported by mobile and ambient technologies.

Keywords: Playful interaction, persuasive technology, design research, teenagers, ambient gaming.

1 Introduction

In the PlayFit project, we aim to persuade teenagers to engage in playful moments of casual activity throughout the day. This project is a collaboration between Eindhoven University of Technology and the Fontys University of Applied Sciences. In this four-year design research project we closely cooperate with serious-game designers, exergame companies, and governmental sports and health organisations [1].

Our aim is to create playful experiences that connect to the teenagers' daily interests and activities. To achieve this, we examine their lives to ensure that our designs fit in with their lifestyle, and we study the influence of our designs on their lifestyle [2]. We intend to create playful and active moments throughout the day, independent of time or location, supported by mobile and ambient technologies.

2 Ambient Play

In order to offer playful activities throughout the day, we have several design challenges that we intend to address:

— How can we implement playful activities at various locations, or even in a location-independent way?
— How can we create play that is seamlessly integrated in the daily activities?
— How can we repeatedly elicit curiosity and interest for the playful activity, and make sure it remains enjoyable over a longer period of time?

These challenges are all related to our vision on ambient play, turning everyday activities into opportunities for play. We will explain this in more detail below.

R. Wichert, K. Van Laerhoven, J. Gelissen (Eds.): AmI 2011 Workshops, CCIS 277, pp. 233–237, 2012.

2.1   Using AmI Principles

We can derive new qualities for an enriched gaming experience from the Ambient Intelligence properties [3]:

1. *Context-aware*: (game) devices can recognize users and their situational context
2. *Personalized:* the functionality is tailored to users' needs and preferences (short timescale, e.g. installing personal settings)
3. *Adaptive:* the system can change/adapt in response to users and their environment (adjustments resulting from longer monitoring)

An example that clarifies the use of the AmI qualities in playful situations is the *Kinect Avatar* [4,5]: the Kinect system recognizes a player, loads a profile with settings, and creates a matching avatar. Technologies such as face recognition, expression analysis, speech recognition and motion recognition translate the player's movement into a personal Avatar. In addition, the Kinect uses a combination of context-awareness and adaptation to setup the sound output: a special learning algorithm adapts the sound output to the physical characteristics of the room, including the position of the players and objects.

Pervasive and *locative* games are another example of games that use aspects from ambient intelligence. These games blend the virtual and real world and are interacted with through multiple ubiquitous devices. A location-based game (or location-enabled game) is one in which the gameplay evolves and progresses through a player's location. Thus, location-based games almost always support some kind of localization technology, for example by using satellite positioning (GPS).

Urban gaming or *Street Games* are typically multi-player, location-based games. The playground is the city itself. An example of such a pervasive game is Geocaching [6], treasure hunting with the help of GPS, a popular activity in which players search hidden caches around the world. The caches and puzzles have been created by other players. In Parallel Kingdom [7], players use their location-aware telephone to conquer different areas of the map. The playground is the current real-world location of the players; the playground is constantly changing by players that travel around in the real world.

Fig. 1. Pervasive and locative games: Geocaching (2000) [6], finding hidden caches throughout the world using GPS; Parallel Kingdoms (2010) [7], conquering areas depending on your physical location; and Head Up Games (2010) [8], playing games depending on your proximity to other players and game objects

2.2   Explorations and Implementations

In our own project [9], we are exploring the design and implementation of AmI-empowered prototypes, in order to elicit playful activities throughout the day – in other words, we try to enable ambient play. At the moment, we focus on play in the context of a school: we try to motivate teenagers to be active in a corridor or hall, while walking through, on repetitive encounters.

One example that we are currently implementing is the *Walk-of-Fame*: an interactive corridor in which specific types of walking are translated in various characters and actions. Walk-of-Fame is a playful installation in a corridor, consisting of a group of connected cameras and a display that covers the span of the wall. The system detects teenagers walking through the corridor and analyzes their way of walking. A digital avatar is visualized on the display, walking alongside the passer-by; which avatar is shown depends on the person's way of walking.

John walks slug and slowly through a corridor in his school, bored with his upcoming mathematics class. On his left, he sees a flicker of movement, and suddenly Marvin the Paranoid Robot walks alongside him through the corridor, on the video screen. Curious, he retraces his steps and starts walking through the corridor with exaggerated heavy movements. Now, B.A. Baracus of the A-team appears! Laughing, he enters the main hall, showing B.A. to his classmates who are watching.

Over time, groups of friends start walking in their specific way, always activating their preferred characters. At certain moments, the system records a movie of the passers-by and their avatars, and uploads it to Facebook; this way, the interplay of watching, walking, and being watched broadens to the network sites.

This installation uses several AmI principles; it is, in a way, personalized and adaptive. At the same time, it is not fully 'ambient', as it is bound to a fixed location. In the near future, we want to connect this installation to other ambient play activities: for example, actions on interactive seats on the schoolyard, or in a mobile game, could influence the displayed characters.

Fig. 2. Walk-of-Fame detects teenagers walking through the corridor and analyses their way of walking. A digital avatar is visualised on the display, walking alongside the passer-by; which avatar is shown depends on the person's way of walking.

3   Conclusion and Future Work

We envision that games and AmI will become more and more intertwined in the nearby future. As we also argue in [10], gaming will become more context-aware, adaptive, personalized and anticipatory. Games will be developed that allow us to move freely, not depending on a central computer but supported by sensors embedded in play objects and toys. Gaming will be more playful, open-ended such that rules can easily be altered and supportive to other activities.

However, before this vision can become reality, technological and design problems need to be solved; the questions posed in this article are just a small part of the complexities involved in this ambient sort of gaming. Besides those contextual questions, we face several larger issues or trade-offs:

- mobile vs. intelligent environments: how do we use mobile applications, that interact with the user independent of the user's location, and interactive environments? How can mobile technologies support and enrich intelligent environments, and create a synthesis of the two? What is the 'best' solution for enabling ambient play?
- digital vs physical vs hybrid: how will the interaction, and the content, be presented on a physical or digital layer? Or, is the combination of the two, in a hybrid equilibrium, the best solution for AmI-enriched interactive play? Will we play at our computer, mobile phone, and with our body, or do we want to separate these elements?
- Ethical and privacy issues: besides the privacy and ethical issues commonly associated with the AmI vision, we face other issues: do we want or need to protect the users from sharing actions in playful activities? Can immersion in a physical-yet-digital game lead to embarrassing situations, and if yes, is this a problem?

References

1. PlayFit project, http://www.playfitproject.nl (retrieved on June 1, 2011)
2. Tieben, R., Sturm, J., Bekker, M.M., Schouten, B.A.M.: Eliciting casual activity through playful exploration, communication, personalization and expression. In: Proceedings of CHIsparks 2011, Arnhem, Netherlands (2011)
3. Aarts, E., Marzano, S.: The new everyday: Views on ambient intelligence. 010 Publishers (2003)
4. Microsoft Xbox Kinect (2010), http://en.wikipedia.org/wiki/Kinect (retrieved on February 01, 2011)
5. Microsoft Xbox Kinect Avatar (2011), http://www.xbox.com/en-us/kinect/avatar-kinect (retrieved on March 02, 2011)
6. GeoCaching (2000), http://www.geocaching.com (retrieved on October 12, 2010)
7. Parallel Kingdom (2010), http://www.parallelkingdom.com (retrieved on October 12, 2010)

8. Soute, I., Kaptein, M., Markopoulos, P.: Evaluating outdoor play for children: virtual vs. tangible game objects in pervasive games. In: Proceedings of the 8th International Conference on Interaction Design and Children, pp. 250–253. ACM (2009)
9. Sturm, J., Tieben, R., Deen, M., Bekker, M.M., Schouten, B.A.M.: PlayFit: Designing playful activity interventions for teenagers. In: Proceedings of DIGRA 2011 (2011)
10. Schouten, B.A.M., Tieben, R., van den Ven, A., Schouten, D.W.: Human Behavior Analysis in Ambient Gaming and Playful Interaction. In: Salah, A.A., Gevers, T. (eds.) Computer Analysis of Human Behavior. Springer (2011)

i-PE: A Decentralized Approach for Designing Adaptive and Persuasive Intelligent Play Environments

Pepijn Rijnbout, Linda de Valk, Mark de Graaf,
Tilde Bekker, Ben Schouten, and Berry Eggen

Department of Industrial Design, Eindhoven University of Technology
P.O. Box 513, 5600 MB Eindhoven, The Netherlands
{p.rijnbout,l.c.t.d.valk,m.j.d.graaf,m.m.bekker,
b.schouten,j.h.eggen}@tue.nl

Abstract. This paper presents the approach of the intelligent Play Environments (i-PE) project. The aim of this project is to develop design guidelines for designing interactive environments that stimulate social and physical play. We want to create an environment that supports this play behavior and emphasizes on the flow of play by offering freedom in interaction. In this position paper, we describe our approach for designing such a play environment. We will introduce two focus areas for our research: playful persuasion and adaptation.

Keywords: Intelligent play environment, decentralized systems, open-ended play, playful persuasion, adaptation.

1 Introduction

The Dutch historian Huizinga describes play as a voluntary act, situated outside of everyday life, with no direct benefit or goal but capable of totally absorbing the player [7]. Within play, a temporary perfect world is created with its own boundaries and rules [7]. For children, playing is also a way of practicing skills and exploring imaginary worlds [2].

The i-PE project is a Dutch design research project that joins together knowledge institutes and creative companies and aims at stimulating social and physical behavior through play. We follow a research-through-design process in which we want to ground our design principles and better understand play dynamics in relation to interactive designs, resulting in design guidelines. We use the term Intelligent Play Environment for an environment "with one or more interactive objects that use(s) advanced technology to react to the interaction with the children and actively encourage children to play" [11]. Previous research has shown that interactive play objects can extend traditional play opportunities for children as they can allocate meaning to the diverse interaction properties [3].

In this paper, we describe our new approach to play environment development which combines decentralized systems and open-ended play. Furthermore, the focus areas of playful persuasion and adaptation are introduced as directions for further

R. Wichert, K. Van Laerhoven, J. Gelissen (Eds.): AmI 2011 Workshops, CCIS 277, pp. 238–244, 2012.

research. Overall, we believe this is a promising approach that can lead to both attractive designs and design guidelines. We will first provide examples of related work to create a non-exhaustive overview of the current state of art, both commercially and scientifically. Secondly, we will present our approach and two focus areas – as mentioned earlier – playful persuasion and adaptation. Then, we will illustrate these focus areas by two initial design ideas.

2   Related Work

In both the commercial and the scientific field many examples of interactive play designs can be found. This section describes several examples, relevant for the development of our approach and choice of focus areas.

Recent commercially available interactive play products focus on facilitating an environment where several pre-defined games can be played. An example is Sona (by Yalp). Sona (www.sonaplay.com) consist of a playfield and a large orange arch over it containing a camera. Sound feedback is used for a number of pre-defined games. These games mostly combine physical and social play. Multiple players compete against each other, e.g. in DanceBattle the players are divided over two teams and have to dance the best they can. This example shows some limitations of these products concerning the play opportunities: in order to play, the player has to choose one of the pre-defined games. Also, there is only one way to play the game; the system does not adapt to e.g. the amount of players or the personality of the player. The games have fixed rules with pre-defined possibilities. With our design, we want to go beyond pre-defined games and offer an environment that supports play and provides more opportunities for players to shape their play.

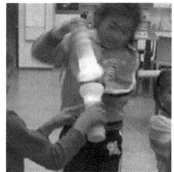

Fig. 1. Sona   **Fig. 2.** ColorFlare

The ColorFlare [3] is an example of an open-ended play object created for design research purposes. Players can roll the ColorFlare to change its color and shake it for flashing. In flash mode, the ColorFlare can influence the color of another ColorFlare using infrared communication. No game is pre-defined; players can create games by defining their own play rules. Although the open-ended aspect of the ColorFlare offers many play opportunities, its behavior and interaction opportunities do not change during play. We think an adaptive design can offer even more diverse play experiences and stay engaging for a longer period of time. Furthermore, the ColorFlare does not attract players when no-one is playing. Only when children start to play, it becomes interactive. In that sense the ColorFlare is a rather non-inviting object.

3   Approach

In this paper we suggest a new approach for designing intelligent play environments. We aim at developing environments for open-ended play in which intelligence is embedded in spatially divided interactive objects. Below we discuss the aspects of open-ended play and decentralized system design.

When designing for open-ended play, the design does not offer concrete goals and rules but provides local interaction opportunities that lead to games the players create themselves [3]. Through this open-endedness the environment elicits a dialogue with and between the players. Players can create their own game goals and rules, and are stimulated to social interaction: negotiating ideas and interacting with other players. The system should follow what we call *the flow of play*. The term flow can be interpreted in two ways. Firstly, it refers to the flow experience of being totally absorbed by an activity as described by Csikszentmihalyi [4]. Secondly however, play has its own dynamics; it evolves in time. From this point of view flow refers to the overall play development instead of the user experience. With the flow of play we refer to the latter, although we expect the two are closely related.

We believe that a certain amount of intelligence is needed to cope with this flow of play, which has a high degree of uncertainty and unpredictability. With intelligence we mean that the environment can somehow sense certain factors of players and adapt to the current situation in the play environment. This is closely related to the vision of Ambient Intelligence [1], which describes five key principles: context awareness, embeddedness, personalization, adaptation, and anticipation. We want to propose a decentralize system approach. A decentralized system contains a number of separated autonomic devices that can somehow interact with each other or with the shared environment [6]. We expect that the scalable, robust and can be self-organizing properties of a decentralized systems, as described by [6], provide opportunities for the use in a play environments and fit the principles of Ambient Intelligence.

4   Focus Areas

Within the described approach we want to focus our research into intelligent play environments on the areas of playful persuasion and adaptation. These areas will lead to research questions for future exploration. In this section we will describe the two focus areas in more detail.

4.1   Playful Persuasion

Playful persuasion refers to applying playful mechanisms in a design with the aim to change people's attitudes and behaviors [10, 12]. These mechanisms can support playful experiences while users interact with the design, in this way persuading users to become physically and socially active. We believe playful persuasion can be used in the different stages of the play process [9]: invitation, exploration and the actual play experience, which we call immersion. These different stages are not always linear and some play experiences may not involve all three stages. These different stages can be linked to playful user experiences, such as curiosity, exploration and challenge [8]. Concerning the invitation stage, the design has to persuade people to actually become players. This phase is clearly linked to the playful experience of curiosity: the design elicits curiosity by being interactive and actively encouraging potential players to interact with the design. The exploration stage should give players the chance to investigate the rules and the playing field. This exploration, another playful experience, is supported by simple interaction opportunities and clear feedback. Lastly, the immersion stage should be challenging to be fun and stay fun for a longer period of time. Important aspects for this stage are time constraints and possibilities to give meaning to different interactions.

Possible research questions for this area are: How can curiosity be used to attract players to the playground? How can exploration be supported to help players understand the rules and interaction possibilities by playing? How can the play environment remain challenging for a longer period of time?

4.2   Adaptation

Play is an unpredictable process that cannot be captured easily in fixed scenarios [5]. We aim at designing a play environment with interactive elements that supports different types of play and which follows the flow of play. Instead of defining a system that supports one form of play, we believe the system should have adaptive properties. For example: a situation with several interactive elements can react slowly and timidly on quiet and slow forms of play. When players in this environment show more physical active play, the system can adapt by speeding up and creating more explicit output. The adaptive approach also fits to the described playful persuasion mechanisms; the different stages of the play process ask for other play dynamics.

Possible research questions for this area are: How can adaptation be used to support the persuasive mechanisms described above? How to design an effective adaptive environment? How to implement adaptive properties in a decentralized system so that it supports the flow of play?

5   Initial Concepts

Our aim is to design and build an intelligent play environment applying the approach as described above, with playful persuasion and adaptation as our main research topics. In this section we describe two initial ideas called *FlowSteps* and *Space*

Blocks. As a first step, we aim at a fixed play environment of similar proportion as a traditional playground, supporting physical play for various numbers of players.

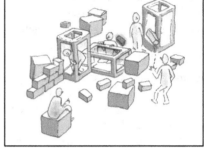

Fig. 3. FlowSteps   **Fig. 4.** Space Blocks

5.1   FlowSteps

Two boys like physical forms of play. One of them takes a couple of FlowSteps and makes a path with the mats. When he jumps on the first mat, the FlowSteps light up one after another. The other boy starts to run and tries to catch the light. They start to add more FlowSteps to their playing field. When they run faster, they notice it becomes harder to catch the light. Eventually they manage to catch the light, and they hear a score sound and give each other a high five.

FlowSteps consists of a large number of flexible interactive mats that players can use to throw, flip, jump or sit on. In this way, players can create their own games by placing the mats in any position they like. The design does not communicate a clear function; the embodiment is rather neutral. It provides players with opportunities to design their own play, creating playgrounds that support their diverse forms of play.

5.2   Space Blocks

A group of children enjoy playing fantasy games. Within the Space Blocks environment they are engaged in a serious fight with a dragon. One of the children yells: "We have to collect firestones and hide ourselves!" He starts picking up small blocks which twinkle in blue light, and crawls in a large hollow block. The others follow. The 'firestones' provide bright light flashes when they are thrown at the imaginary dragon.

Space Blocks is inspired by the notion that play can be created with loose material ("trash") lying around the playground. By offering different sizes of interactive cubes or rectangular blocks that players can stack, roll, throws, sit on or crawl inside, players can create a variety of fantasy and/or physical games. Within this idea, the embodiment of the objects becomes a much more important factor in determining the play opportunities.

6   Conclusion

In the previous sections we have discussed our design approach for designing decentralized play environments. We described two areas we focus on: *playful persuasion* and *adaptation* in order to design an environment that supports the flow of play in a natural way. For this, we use the research through design process. Eventually, this should provide us with design guidelines that can support the design of intelligent play environments in the future.

A next step is to further develop our initial ideas into one or more feasible design concepts and validate these designs with potential users. At this point we are extending our overview on the area of play design. We are interested in ways to analyze the playability of our designs and the quality of interaction. We are curious to see what different design approaches imply and how they conflict or complete our approach as described above.

Acknowledgments. The i-PE project is part of the CRISP program, funded by Dutch government FES funding. The authors would like to thank our partners in this project for their contributions so far. For a complete list of partners, see www.crispplatform.nl/projects/i-pe.

References

1. Aarts, E., Marzano, S.: The New Everyday: Visions of ambient intelligence. 010 Pubslishers, Rotterdam (2003)
2. Acuff, D.S., Reiher, R.H.: What kids buy and why; the psychology of marketing to kids. Free Press (1997)
3. Bekker, M., Sturm, J., Eggen, B.: Designing playful interactions for social interaction and physical play. Personal and Ubiquitous Computing 14(5), 385–396 (2010)
4. Csikszentmihalyi, M.: Flow; the psychology of optimal experience. Harper and Row, New York (1990)
5. Deen, M., Schouten, B.A.M.: Let's Start Playing Games! How games can become more about playing and less about complying. In: Proceedings of the 3rd International Conference on Fun & Games (Fun and Games 2010), Leuven, Belgium (2010)
6. van Essen, H., Rijnbout, P., de Graaf, M.: A Design Approach to Decentralized Interactive Environments. In: Nijholt, A., Reidsma, D., Hondorp, H. (eds.) INTETAIN 2009. LNICST, vol. 9, pp. 56–67. Springer, Heidelberg (2009)
7. Huizinga, J.: Homo Ludens: A Study of the Play Element in Culture. Beacon Press, Boston (1955)
8. Korhonen, H., Montola, M., Arrusvuori, J.: Understanding playful experiences through digital games. In: Proceedings of the 4th International Conference on Designing Pleasurable Products and Interface (DPPI 2009), pp. 274–285 (2009)
9. Polaine, A.: Developing a language of interactivity through the theory of play. Doctoral dissertation, Faculty of Arts & Social Sciences, Sydney University of Technology (2010)

10. Romero, N.A., Sturm, J., Bekker, M.M., de Valk, L., Kruitwagen, S.: Playful Persuasion to support older adults' social and physical activities. Special Issue on Inclusive Design, Interacting with Computers 22(6), 485–495 (2010)
11. Sturm, J., Bekker, T., Groenendaal, B., Wesselink, R., Eggen, B.: Key issues for the successful design of an intelligent interactive playground. In: Proceedings of Interaction Design and Children (IDC 2008), pp. 258–265 (2008)
12. Sturm, J., Tieben, R., Deen, M., Bekker, T., Schouten, B.: PlayFit: Designing playful activity interventions for teenagers. In: Proceedings of DiGRA 2011 Conference (2011)

An Investigation of Extrinsic-Oriented Ambient Exploration for Gaming Applications

Radu-Daniel Vatavu and Ionuţ-Alexandru Zaiţi

University Stefan cel Mare of Suceava, 13, Universitatii, Suceava 720229, Romania
`vatavu@eed.usv.ro, ionutzaiti@yahoo.com`
`http://www.eed.usv.ro/~vatavu`

Abstract. Measurements of the grasping hand can be used in order to infer properties about grasped objects such as shape, size, and even object id. Therefore, ambient exploration and ambient information collection can also be accomplished by recognizing hand postures and gestures while users grasp and manipulate real-world objects. We show how such an extrinsic-oriented exploration scenario can be used for designing ambient games. The approach encourages freedom of interaction by allowing players to immediately use any object present in the environment as an active element inside the game.

Keywords: hand measurements, posture recognition, gestures, ambient gaming, ambient intelligence, games, data glove, wearable computing.

1 Introduction

The human hand represents a remarkable instrument for interacting in the real-world by manipulating objects, sensing the environment, and conveying meaningful information through semiotic gestures. Extensive studies exist in psychology, kinesiology, and rehabilitation that have thoroughly investigated the motor and sensing capacities of the human hand [1]. Also, with the advances in acquisition and recognition technology, the human hand has also been investigated by computer scientists for robotics applications and human-computer interaction [3].

In psychology, MacKenzie and Iberall [1] look at the grasping hand as a general purpose device due to its multiple capacities for sensing, communicating, and changing the environment. The sensing property can be re-used in computing applications by considering the hand as an automatic tool that extracts information from the objects being grasped. This information can be further processed in order to infer object properties or user actions. Such a technique of collecting information has been demonstrated before at various levels and in various research domains. For example, in motor control research, Santello and Soechting [6] showed that it is possible to discriminate between concave and convex objects by using just the relative flexure between the fingers. In ubiquitous computing, Paulson et al. [3] showed that hand posture can be used to discriminate between several actions in an office setting. We call such strategy of collecting ambient information via hand posture measurements *extrinsic-oriented exploration*. This opposes to *intrinsic-oriented exploration* in which environmental objects have been enhanced with sensing and communication capacities which allow them to share

R. Wichert, K. Van Laerhoven, J. Gelissen (Eds.): AmI 2011 Workshops, CCIS 277, pp. 245–248, 2012.

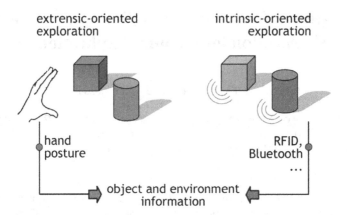

Fig. 1. Extrinsic vs. intrinsic-oriented object exploration. In extrinsic exploration, there is no need for sensors or tags to be attached to objects. Instead, measurements of the human hand are used to infer object properties.

information via various technologies such as radio-frequency identification (RFID) or Bluetooth/wireless communication. Figure 1 illustrates the difference between these concepts.

The main advantage of extrinsic-oriented exploration consists in the absence of any sensors or tags that would otherwise be attached to objects in the intrinsic-oriented approach. Of course, limitations do exist with regards to the amount and accuracy of the retrieved information when comparing with intrinsic techniques such as using RFID tags [4]. However, such limitations can be controlled by working with more generic object properties (such as identifying shape and size) rather than exact object id or by associating actions with grasping styles rather than with specific objects. In the end, the application scenario determines the right association method to be used. The great advantage that the technique brings is freedom in interaction by allowing the user to select any real object from the environment and re-use it for interaction purposes. One of the problems in gesture interface design is represented by the difficulty to find a good correlation between functions and gestures [2]. This time however, rather than designing gestures to fit the function, the exploration naturally allows users to perform unconstrained hand movements during object manipulation rather than memorizing and recalling gesture sets.

2   Object Recognition Using Hand Posture Measurements

We describe in the following an implementation of the extrinsic-oriented exploration scenario. In order to acquire hand measurements, the 5DT Data Glove 14 Ultra[1] was connected to a ultra mobile PC[2] via the USB interface. The glove has 14 sensors that measure finger flexure (2 sensors per finger) and abduction between fingers (4 sensors).

---

[1] http://5dt.com/products/pdataglove14.html

[2] Wibrain at http://en.wikipedia.org/wiki/Ultra-mobile_PC

The system including the glove and PC can be easily worn as it only weights 500 grams and is small in size (19 x 8 x 3 cm). Each sensor of the glove was calibrated to give a response in the $[0..1]$ interval with 1 denoting maximum flexure/abduction. Therefore, the hand posture at a given moment can be specified by a 14-vector of normalized sensor measurements: $posture = (p_1, p_2, ...p_{14})$. The nearest-neighbor recognition rule was used in order to classify a hand posture as previous research showed good results of the technique [3]. The rule classifies a posture by assigning it to the class of its closest sample from a training set with respect to some distance in the sensor space. The Euclidean distance was used in order to measure the dissimilarity between two posture measurements p and q:

$$d(p,q) = \left(\sum_{i=1}^{14} (p_i - q_i)^2 \right)^{1/2} \tag{1}$$

The training set was constructed by associating hand postures with objects shapes and sizes during a training procedure. An initial experimentation with 18 objects and 12 users showed a robust recognition rate above 95%.

3   Ambient Gaming Opportunities

We describe in the following several gaming opportunities that use the concept of extrinsic-oriented exploration:

- **First Person Shooter.** One of the most common game genres is first-person shooter (FPS) in which a player takes on adversaries using various weapons. Augmented Reality researchers have investigated the use of such genres in outdoor environments [5] however, although a mix between real and virtual was obtained for visualization, the game playing techniques remained practically unchanged. Common weapons for FPS include a stick, a hand grenade, or a pistol gun. In the extrinsic-oriented exploration, the selection of a new weapon can be performed by detecting the corresponding hand posture needed to grasp it. The stick weapon can be trained by holding any cylinder-like object; the grenade by using a round shaped object; and the pistol by holding a toy gun or by simulating the trigger gesture with the index finger. Such actions which are classically performed using different combinations of keys and mouse clicks can be achieved using hand grasps performed on any object in the environment making the gaming experience more realistic;
- **Arcade games: Snow Balls.** The objective of the Snow Ball game is to hit targets or to defeat opponents by throwing virtual snow balls. The snow balls in the game are associated with soft balls in the real environment. The size of the ball which can be determined from the hand posture being used during grasping can serve as a parameter which controls the amount of damage the ball would cause when thrown and hit the target. The goal of the game is to reach the destroy threshold for each target.

4   Conclusions

The paper discussed the opportunity of using extrinsic-oriented exploration of ambient environments for designing gaming applications. The main advantage of using such an exploration consists in extracting information about grasped objects by only using hand postures without the need of attaching tags or embedding sensors in the environment. Future work will consider evaluations of the user experience in such scenarios. We hope that the approach will appeal to game designers in building ambient games that naturally re-use objects from the environment.

References

1. Makenzie, C.L., Iberall, T.: The Grasping Hand. North-Holland, Elsevier Science B.V, Amsterdam, The Netherlands (1994)
2. Nielsen, M., Störring, M., Moeslund, T.B., Granum, E.: A Procedure for Developing Intuitive and Ergonomic Gesture Interfaces for HCI. In: Camurri, A., Volpe, G. (eds.) GW 2003. LNCS (LNAI), vol. 2915, pp. 409–420. Springer, Heidelberg (2004)
3. Paulson, B., Cummings, D., Hammond, T.: Object interaction detection using hand posture cues in an office setting. International Journal of Human-Computer Studies 69, 19–29 (2011)
4. Philipose, M., Fishkin, K.P., Perkowitz, M., Patterson, D.J., Fox, D., Kautz, H., Hahnel, D.: Inferring Activities from Interactions with Objects. IEEE Pervasive Computing 3(4), 50–57 (2004)
5. Thomas, B., Close, B., Donoghue, J., Squires, J., Bondi, P., Piekarski, W.: First Person Indoor/Outdoor Augmented Reality Application: ARQuake. Personal and Ubiquitous Computing 6(1), 75–86 (2002)
6. Santello, M., Soechting, J.F.: Gradual Molding of the Hand to Object Contours. Journal of Neurophysiology 79(3), 1307–1320 (1998)

Challenges of Human Behavior Understanding for Inducing Behavioral Change

Albert Ali Salah[1] and Bruno Lepri[2,3]

[1] Boğaziçi University, Department of Computer Engineering,
Istanbul, Turkey
salah@boun.edu.tr
[2] FBK, via Sommarive 18, Povo,
Trento, Italy
lepri@fbk.eu
[3] MIT Media Lab, 20 Ames Street, 02-139 Cambridge,
MA, USA

Abstract. We summarize the contributions presented at the 2nd International Workshop on Human Behavior Understanding (HBU'11) and the subsequent discussions. The scientific contributions focused on techniques and algorithmic aspects of human behavior analysis, including visual and audio modalities, as well as the design aspect of persuasive systems. One important conclusion of the workshop is that while persuasive systems and carefully designed persuasive messages form the crux of inducing behavior change, the design of systems informed by large-scale analysis of human behavior can also lead to engineered contexts for affecting behavior, at different resolutions ranging from an individual level (e.g. mobile platforms or smart homes) to urban level (e.g. carefully planned cities).

1   A Short Discussion of the HBU Workshop

The focus topic of the HBU'11 was "inducing behavioral change", where we discussed theories and technologies to analyze human behavior to create systems that can induce or promote positive behaviors [2]. Such analysis typically targets human pose and gestures, actions, activities, social interactions, vocal and visual expression of emotions and affective states. While theories of psychology and sociology prove to be valuable tools in forming models in this domain, signal processing, pattern recognition and machine learning approaches are essential to drive data analysis [1]. Placing the HBU Workshop in the broader context of ambient intelligence also highlighted the **design and user experience aspects** of systems that use these technologies.

It is obvious that we have much more real-time data available to analyze human behavior patterns, through the improvements in sensor technology and their ubiquitious usage. Nonetheless, most systems rely on careful interaction design and less on real-time behavior analysis for personalization and adaptation. Many reasons can be conceived for this choice. Based on the discussions at HBU'11,

R. Wichert, K. Van Laerhoven, J. Gelissen (Eds.): AmI 2011 Workshops, CCIS 277, pp. 249–251, 2012.

we believe that the problem ultimately lies with the inadequate channels over which the data are collected. We put forward two arguments for this.

We observe that machine learning and pattern recognition approaches dominate the field of human behavior analysis. This usually implies that the correlation structure of extracted features from the sensed modalities is what receives the most attention during analysis. There is however a need to go deeper in the models, and look at causalities to model more complex and subtle behaviors. For such behaviors, annotation of data is a significant issue.

What we apparently lack at the moment are **appropriate tools of recording and annotation** to measure natural behaviors and interactions. Traditional cameras and microphones are extensively used, and more recent sociometric badges and wearable sensors provide further modalities, but natural interactions and social signals contain much richer information, and more extensive and non-intrusive sensor sets are required to measure these without affecting the process itself. Mobile phones have emerged as a suitable medium to partly answer this need. Data collection via phones can occur automatically through the sensor set of the phone itself, or through software programs that allow recording and annotation of arbitrary experiences by the user. The interactive experience assessment (INEA) framework was presented at the Workshop as an example of this latter type of tools.

On the individual scale, psychophysical measurements can be potentially used to interpret and annotate data collected from humans. Nonetheless, the dataset explosion that occured in for instance object recognition community did not happen in this field yet, with the possible exception of urban computing. Urban computing approaches gather and use behavioral patterns (e.g. mobile phone usage, or public infrastructure usage) on a grander scale and look at the behavior of masses instead of individuals. Annotation and interpretation of such data requires expert knowledge and cross-linking of external information to provide context and semantics. The benefits are improved infrastructures and digitalization of cities, but there are significant challenges in real-time analysis of large volumes of data, which also need to be collected, stored and protected against misuse.

Human behavior analysis finds applications in health and ambient intelligence, interactive artifact design, robotics, entertainment, human-computer interfaces, and many more. We spend more and more of our daily lives in presence of computers and devices with computational capabilities, on virtual platforms, connected to other people over mobile phones or the Internet, and using the computers for tasks ranging from work to entertainment. Churchill stated that "we shape our buildings, thereafter they shape us". The influence of the technology-suffused environment on the human psyche is perhaps much more relevant with regards to digital platforms which have gained prominence in our everyday life. Human behavior analysis provides us with insights to assess this influence, but more than that, it allows harnessing it for beneficial purposes. To give a simple example, take computer games. Games can be motivational tools. What is covered in **serious gaming** is when the game is designed to serve a purpose different than solely entertainment, without neglecting the latter. But any domain can undergo gamification, which is the approach of making novel behaviors rewarding in terms of psychological needs, rather than associating external rewards to them. Games and gamification emerge as useful tools of inducing behavioral change, by virtue of the interaction they afford.

A very important trend in HBU is the **analysis of nonverbal signals**. Thin slices of behavior are revealing genuine and rich information about humans, both in terms of their transient affective states and in terms of more prevalent characteristics of personality. The automatic analysis of these signals serves to improve computer systems to be more natural, responsive, successful, etc., but also stands to help to mediate novel ways of human communication.

Social media affected a transformation of social relations, where people have many more brief but less intimate contacts with their social connections. Over this novel modes of exchange, we see a loss of nonverbal signals that carry the bulk of communication in ordinary social contacts, primarily because the channels of social media are not responsive to these messages. Furthermore, even the signals that are transmitted undergo a change; the perception of social signals depend on the media of transmission. The goal of **socially emotional computing** is to make emotions available to other people through channels that are designed to do the translation in both ways. This is in contrast to **affective computing**, where the goal is to make emotions available to artificial systems in a useful form. Both are active areas of research in HBU.

Socially emotional computing simplifies the process by removing the requirement that the computer should be able to make sense of the presented emotions on the one hand, but introduces a further layer of complexity on the other hand by requesting human-readable analysis and synthesis, as well as affective interaction design. The affective signal that is transmitted need not be symmetrical at the two human ends of the communication channel. The example provided by Dr. IJsselsteijn during his keynote presentation was a huggable interface (e.g. a teddy bear equipped with sensors) to send someone a "hug" over social media channels, as opposed to clicking a "hug" button on a web page. This asymmetry is also usefully employed in asymmetrical game design, where participants can assume different roles, encompassing different interaction patterns, and requiring different skill sets.

The Second HBU Workshop largely dealt with challenges of human behavior analysis in ambient intelligence applications. The next HBU will shift the focus to another application area, and deal with human behavior analysis for robotics.

References

1. Salah, A.A., Gevers, T., Sebe, N., Vinciarelli, A. (eds.): HBU 2010. LNCS, vol. 6219. Springer, Heidelberg (2010)
2. Salah, A.A., Lepri, B. (eds.): HBU 2011. LNCS, vol. 7065. Springer, Heidelberg (2011)

Human Behavior Understanding for Inducing Behavioral Change: Social and Theoretical Aspects

Bruno Lepri[1,2], Albert Ali Salah[3], Fabio Pianesi[1], and Alex Sandy Pentland[2]

[1] FBK, via Sommarive 18, Povo,
Trento, Italy
{lepri,pianesi}@fbk.eu
[2] MIT Media Lab, 20 Ames Street, 02-139 Cambridge,
MA, USA
pentland@mit.edu
[3] Boğaziçi University, Department of Computer Engineering,
Istanbul, Turkey
salah@boun.edu.tr

Abstract. The 2nd International Workshop on Human Behavior Understanding (HBU'11) focuses on inducing behavioral change via computer systems that can analyse human behavior and communicate persuasive messages accordingly. While analysis techniques that involve pattern recognition, signal processing and machine learning are very relevant to this aim, the underlying psychological and sociological aspects of inducing behavioral change cannot be neglected. This paper provides a framework for assessing the impact of social factors for these applications, and discusses the role of social mediation of behaviors and attitudes.

1   Introduction

People routinely engage in relationships whereby they influence and are influenced by other humans but they are just starting confronting with machines that have this capability, due to the recent attempts at building persuasive systems. Most of the research on persuasive technologies is comprised under the umbrella of the term 'captology' [20], which refers to the study of machines designed to influence people's attitudes and behaviors. A notable difference between persuasion in human-human interaction as opposed to human-machine interaction, is the limited (if any) resort of machines to real-time understanding of people's individual traits, activities and social dynamics. As a consequence, most of the current persuasive systems lack flexibility and cannot personalize and adapt their message to the broader context the target person(s) is (are) in.

The automatic analysis of human behavior, in turn, has been progressing in the last few years, thanks to the shared awareness that computer systems can provide better and more appropriate services to people only if they can understand much more about their attitudes, preferences, personality, social relationships etc., as well as about what people are doing, the activities they have been engaged in the past, their routines and lifestyles.

R. Wichert, K. Van Laerhoven, J. Gelissen (Eds.): AmI 2011 Workshops, CCIS 277, pp. 252–263, 2012.
© Springer-Verlag Berlin Heidelberg 2012

This paper proposes a set of social and theoretical perspectives and considerations to develop systems and applications that rely on human behavior analysis for inducing behavioral change. These systems have the potential to re-define the relationship between the computer and the human, moving the computer from a passive observer role to a socially active one and enabling it to drive interactions that influence the attitudes and behaviors of people in their everyday environments [51].

In a quite general sense, the goal of this paper is to contribute to further advancing ubiquitous information societies where computers and humans are part of one and the same ecosystem. One crucial property of entities living in the same ecosystem is that they mutually influence and affect each other's behavior, as well as internal states (e.g., attitudes) in a host of different ways and through varied means, including implicit and indirect ones whose mechanisms are not necessarily fully grasped by the target.

It seems to us that there is still a good deal of reluctance in facing the puzzling possibility that, in order to approach autonomous human-like behavior, machines must, among other things, also be able to use different means to affect human behaviors and attitudes. Yet, this possibility is intrinsic to the overall vision of machines as autonomous agents in constantly changing environments, which lies at the heart of research areas such as artificial intelligence, cognitive systems, embedded systems, ambient intelligence, pervasive and ubiquitous computing, and so on. Such capabilities are also an essential ingredient of applications that aim to turn those technological and scientific advances into valuable services for the users.

This paper is structured as follows: Section 2 proposes a possible approach to social influence and computer-induced behavioral change. Section 3 deals with the possibility of endowing machines with the skills needed to social perception, and underlines the importance of personality assessment. Section 4 shortly discusses the sensing modalities for social behavior, and provides pointers for further reading. Section 5 discusses the technological, scientific and societal impact of the discussed framework. Finally, the last section draws our conclusions.

2   Bringing about Change: Perspectives on Social Influence

In an attempt to lay the foundations of a theory for computer-induced human change, we will operate under several assumptions that incidentally set this work apart from most current efforts in the same direction. First of all, our focus is on the modifications of the social structure and dynamics of small and large groups (friends, colleagues, families, students, and so on) and on changes in individuals (behaviors and attitudes) that occur because of their membership in social entities. Social settings are, in most respects, more challenging than those based on a single individual because of the dynamic and bidirectional individual-group relationships: in many respects, understanding a group's characteristics implies understanding the characteristics of its members, and social change implies individual change.

In social psychology, researchers study the psychological processes involved in persuasion, conformity, and other forms of social influence, but they have seldom modeled the ways influencing unfolds when multiple sources and multiple targets interact over time [43]. On the other hand, researchers in sociology, economics, network science and physics have developed models of influence flow in populations and groups without relying on any detailed understanding of the participating individuals. For example, the social diffusion phenomenon, in which a behavior spreads over a social network, is explained by a mechanism of behavioral cascading whereby the probability for a group member to adopt a behavior is affected by the adoption behavior of the other group members. In many aspects, this approach is similar to a popular model of spreading epidemics: subject X adopts the same behavior as the other group members if his/her exposure to it exceeds a given threshold [10,13,24,57]. Obviously, at this level of modeling, details of individuals are neglected.

Recently, some proposals have been advanced to incorporate a detailed micro-level understanding of influence processes derived from social psychology within the broader picture of multidirectional, dynamic influences typical of social network studies [43,21]. For example, Friedkin proposed to merge social-psychological approaches to the attitude-behavior link with the behavioral cascades diffusion models [21]. The attitude-behavior link, in turn, is accounted for by means of the Theory of Planned Behavior (TPB) [2]. In a simplified form, TPB maintains that actual behavior is explained by behavioral intentions that, in turn, are influenced by (i) the specific attitudes toward that behavior (e.g., attitude towards smoking); (ii) subjective norms (beliefs concerning how the people one cares about view the behavior in question); and (iii) perceived behavioral control (e.g., whether people think it will be easy for them to stop smoking).

Once the relationships from attitudes to behavior is accounted for, the reverse link, from behavior back to attitudes, can be modeled using, e.g., the Self Perception Theory (SPT) [8]. According to SPT, the behavior-attitude link is activated in situations where people do not already have clear ideas about their own attitudes, so that they rely on external observations to infer about then. For instance, STP's view of the behavior-attitude link fits well situations in which individuals' attitudes are not yet well formed.

Another possible shift in the conception of computers as actors of social change is the idea that they behave as a sort of peripheral device, exploiting different kinds of minimalist strategies to bring about change through the smallest amount of human-computer interaction. Minimalist strategies are motivated by the desire that even in the presence of a change inducing system, the main activity of people (their 'primary task') remain that of interacting with other people (e.g. friends, colleagues, relatives, and so on). Minimalist strategies for change could exploit the accumulating evidence about behaviors occurring automatically and without conscious effort [5,11]. For instance, people who were unconsciously exposed (primed) to the stereotype of an elderly person walked slower than a control group [6] and participants listening to male-typical words while driving drove faster than participants listening to neutral words [54]. Importantly, direct investigations about the participants' perception of their own behavior revealed that they were not aware of these induced changes.

Because of its pervasiveness, the so-called direct perception-behavior link [11] can be exploited to bring about desired behavioral changes by means of priming procedures (based on gender-related, cultural, age-related, etc., stereotypes) and/or by facilitating *mimicry*, the tendency to mimic other individuals' behaviors without awareness or intent. One might also venture that at least some of the phenomena usually addressed under the rubric of *behavioral cascades* and *social contagion* (i.e. the propagation of behaviors and attitudes in a socially mediated manner) can be profitably addressed by means of the concept of mimicry and of the perception-behavior link.

The idea of agents that pursue change through indirect and minimalist strategies is also related to the peripheral route to persuasion of the Elaboration Likelihood Model (ELM) [46]. This often-discussed socio-psychological model of behavioral/attitudinal change posits two ways in which attitudinal and behavioral change can take place: a central route and a peripheral route, respectively. The **central route** requires that the influencee attentively attends to an argumentative communication and thinks about the arguments presented. The efficacy of this communication depends on the coherence, logic, and depth of the arguments presented, as well as the knowledge and reasoning abilities of the receiver. The **peripheral route**, in turn, involves strategies that influence people by means of peripheral cues, e.g., the status of the communication source, its attractiveness and credibility, etc.

Some recent works have attempted at exploring these ideas by devising systems that present members of a working group with information about their own social behavior, with the goal of changing it and making it more conducive to better group dynamics [16,33,47,56]. Moreover, an interesting and recent work [1] tested an experimental intervention for inducing changes in fitness-related, physical activities and habits. The intervention was based on a novel social mechanism in which subjects were rewarded based on their peers' performance rather than their own. The results suggested that (i) social factors have an effect on physical activity behavior over time, (ii) social incentives strengthen social influence among subjects, and (iii) a phenomenon similar to contagion emerges as it relates to the pre-existence of social ties among the subjects. This work is a good example of the way two of the general concepts discussed so far can work to drive behavioral chenges: (i) the importance of social factors in inducing individual changes and (ii) the effectiveness of strategies based not on argumentation and logical reasoning but on mimicking and learning through imitation of the others' behavior.

3   Understanding Social Behavior

From the discussions of the previous section, two major dimensions emerge that characterize change in our framework: (i) social vs. individual change and (ii) attitudinal vs. behavioral change.

Regarding the first dimension, we pursue both social and individual change, with the latter addressed through the mediation of the group. It therefore pops up with all its importance the goal of endowing behavior-inducing systems with the ability to understand social behaviors and social relations.

It is impossible to mention here the many cognitive and social psychology theories that have been formulated to account for human social behavior. It is more important to point out that some of these theories are already providing the backbone to computational models and are going to be used in change-inducing systems. A telling example in this respect are dominance and other dimensions related to social verticality [22]. Dominant behavior, in fact, is a key determinant of a group's social structure and dynamics [7]. Quite straightforwardly, the recognition of dominant people could be useful to decide about the right subjects to address in order to maximize the chance of success of group persuasion attempts.

Following the lead of much work in social psychology [25,44], computer scientists focused their attention on studying dominance and role-based status cues [27,28,31,49,50] and functional social roles [59,?] in small-group, task-oriented meetings, using audio-visual nonverbal

Another important piece of knowledge that can be used to to build effective change-inducing systems is personality: people, in fact, react differently to persuasive stimuli according to their personality. For instance, studies about the relationship between the trait of self-esteem and susceptibility to social influence have reported that people with low self-esteem are most easily influenced and those with high self-esteem are much less so [29,30]; other works found that people with medium self-esteem values are most open to influence [26,14]. Locus of Control, too, has been found to empirically relate to social influence susceptibility. *Internals*, who believe they control their behavioral outcome during their lifetime, seem to be more resistant to social influence than *externals*, who attribute their behavioral outcome to external factors such as fate, luck, or powerful others [26,14].

Moreover, the relative efficacy of one or the other persuasive route in the ELM model might also depend on the personality of the target subject: for instance, people who are deemed as "in need for cognition", a trait indicating that people enjoy thinking about complex problems [9], are more amenable to persuasion through the central route than people who score low in such a trait [9,46]. Conversely, people with low need for cognition are more susceptible to be persuaded using unconscious stimuli (e.g. mimicry and priming strategies).

On the computational side, several works have started exploring the automatic recognition of personality, mostly targeting the Big Five model [41,42,37,36,47,12] and/or traits such as the Locus of Control [36,47], using different sources of behavioral data, e.g. visual and acoustic cues and mobile phone data. All these approaches to the automatic recognition of personality more or less implicitly share the so-called 'person perspective' on personality [19]: for a given behavioral sample, they attempt to classify whether that sample belongs to an extrovert or introvert (or equivalently, to a neurotic or an emotionally stable person, and so on). The problem with this approach is that it assumes a direct and stable relationship between, e.g., being extravert and acting extravertedly. Extraverts, however, can sometimes act introvertedly, while introverts can at times exhibit extraverted behaviors. Similarly, people prone to neuroticism need not always exhibit anxious behavior, while agreeable people can sometimes be aggressive. While the person perspective has often dismissed these fluctuations of actual behavior as statistical noise, it has been recently suggested by Fleeson [19] that they can be meaningful. The social psychology literature has coined the term *personality states* to refer to concrete behaviors (including ways of acting, feeling and thinking) that can be described as having a similar content to the corresponding personality traits. In other words, a personality state describes a specific behavioral episode wherein a person behaves more or less introvertedly/extravertedly, more or less neurotically, etc. Personality can then be reconstructed through density distributions over personality states, with parameters such as means, standard deviations, etc., summarizing what is specific to the given individual. Recently, this paradigm shift has started being considered by computational approaches, as by Staiano *et al.* who investigated the automatic recognition of personality states in small group meetings [55].

Regarding the second dimension, a change inducing system could aim to modify individual minds by changing their attitudes towards the relevant issues (or person, group of people, etc.). It might also try to change people's behavior directly. We note that the distinction between mental and behavioral modifications is not unlike the differences in effect durations; mental modifications last longer than those that affect only behavior.

Recently, some works started to model behavioral and attitudinal changes in individuals [38,40,39]. In [40], the authors described the use of mobile phones to model and understand the link between exposure to peers and weight gain among a group of undergraduate students, where a positive correlation was established between the change in an individual's Body Max Index (BMI) with face-to-face exposure to social contacts who themselves gained weight. Along the same direction, Madan et al. [39] measured the spread of political opinions (republicans vs. democrats) during the 2008 US presidential election campaign to model specific behaviors and changes in political opinions.

4   Sensing Social Signals

The previous section showed that we can endow machines with the skills to understand and predict human social behaviors, individual characteristics and attitudes. In this section, we reviews ways we can provide them with the ability of perceiving and sensing the social signals upon which such an understanding can be built. Research on first impression formation has demonstrated that even when observing a person in social interactions for only a short amount of time and even without knowing him/her, we are capable to accurately assess aspects of his/her personality [3,23], emotions, motives and intentions, cognition, future behavior and the types of social relationship he/she is used to get involved in [53,25]. This quite precise "zero-acquaintance" appreciation (or rapid cognition) of the internal properties of another person is based on short sequences of expressive behavior called "thin slices of behavior" [4], is almost automatic and largely exploits nonverbal behavior [3,32], such as posture, position, facial expressions, location, prosodic features, and so on.

There is encouraging evidence that computers can be made capable of exploiting thin slices of behavior to detect individual traits such as personality [35,47] and dominance [27,28,31], group properties like social roles [17], interactions' outcomes [15,36], etc. Many of these works have employed so-called 'honest signals' - social signals that, being too difficult for humans to control, can provide a reliable source of information about socially relevant aspects [58,45].

In [51], the authors have discussed the different modalities used to sense signals pertaining to individual behavior or social behavior. Traditional sensors like cameras and microphones provide valuable information, yet sensing social data almost invariably is more challenging than sensing the behavior of a single individual, and temporal dynamics is found to be of the utmost importance for social signals [52]. For instance turn-taking behavior, interruptions, relative sound energy, usage of gaze and attention, are all found to be relevant in transmitting status and dominance [22].

Recently, the rich sensor sets installed in smartphones have been harnessed to transform the smartphone into veritable data mines for assessing social interaction information. Not just the usage patterns of these phones (as in the reality mining study of Eagle and Pentland [18]), but also proximity and communication data have been found to be useful [38,40,39]. Other types of sensors have been packaged into wearable units, the so-called 'sociometric badges', to specifically target small-group interactions [34].

These developments allow for a cost-effective, real-time, extensive, and (mostly) unobtrusive monitoring of human social signals, and open up the way to the implementation of new socially sensing machines.

5   Technological, Scientific and Societal Impact

The framework proposed here contributes to transform science, technology and societies in several different ways, and it is difficult to underestimate the societal impact of computer systems that induce behavioral change. Such systems can contribute to enforce individual and social values by helping individuals reach target behaviors through interaction and immersion. Apart from technological challenges, these systems require careful preservation of privacy and the maintenance of appropriate levels of control by the users. The enormous potential impact is partly due to the ubiquity and informality of such systems; they can be everywhere and can function through subtle and inconspicuous influences. It is also due to the richness of the application domain, as these technologies stand to transform vital sectors such as healthcare, organizational and individual psychology, management, education, entertainment, commercial advertising, politics, and many more. The societal impact will not be limited to the offer of new and revolutionary technologies, as the relationship between systems and users will change in fundamentally different ways. Once the ethical and legislative framework is set in place, researchers from different fields will have access to first hand, empirical data on how computer-induced change works in realistic contexts, as well as models and paradigms to initiate new projects of behavioral change.

The marriage between social sciences that systematically chart out principles of human behavior and computer-related disciplines (such as multimodal analysis, signal processing, pattern recognition, machine learning) that aim to provide computer systems with the ability of automatically analyzing behavior, can produce long-lasting effects on both sides. Social psychology and social sciences have worked out much of the theoretical foundations for the issues discussed in this work. However, present approaches like TPB, thin slices in rapid social cognition, the perception-behavior link, peer pressure, social contagion, etc., are mostly descriptive frameworks that lack formal and computational modeling. The framework proposed in this paper is mostly geared towards laying the foundations of computational modeling of psycho-social and sociological concepts and theories with the goal of actually incorporating them in working real-world systems.

The combination of psychology and technology at this level is a major departure from the tradition and practice of captology. Although the Computer as a Social Actor (CASA) framework [48] has convincingly argued that we tend to attribute computers characteristics that are typically human, it has done so in quite restricted scenarios, mostly limited to single computer-single human settings. The tradition of captology has taken the media equation and CASA as enabling factors for computer-induced change. By exploiting concepts such as the peripheral route to attitude, the automaticity of behavior, the peer pressure of cascade models, we depart from this tradition, requiring forms of sociality in the human-computer relationship, and subsequently filling a gap in our understanding of the social/non-social continuum in human-machine interaction.

6   Concluding Remarks

Throughout the paper, we have been stressing the importance of social and personality factors for building systems that interact with individuals in ways that would result in behavioral change. When we design 'persuasive' systems, the dialectic nature of human-computer interaction cannot be ignored, and we converge, in many respects, onto models of human-human interaction, i.e. the twin domains of psychology and sociology.

The influencing of a single person can happen via different routes. It is possible to directly influence a certain behavior, or to cause changes in an attitude that will in time result in the modification of a certain behavior, or start a behavioral cascade, where the behavioral change in the individuals social circle (for instance through the dominant people in the group) will eventually cause the individual to adapt to its environment by accepting the same behavior change.

The persuasive message can require conscious processing and elaboration, or it may be subliminal and peripheral. We have cited many empirical studies, which establish that there is no general methodology that can be adopted for persuasion, but each individual will, depending on his or her personality, his or her context and other such factors, be influenced by different strategies to differing extents.

A point of consideration is that even very short expressions of behavior can be extremely useful in selecting the appropriate strategies. These cues can give us the key to detecting dominant people in groups or personality traits of interacting individuals, thereby laying the foundation for inducing behavioral change. Old and new sensor technologies are combined in innovative ways to capture these social signals. It is our firm belief that the resulting systems will have a significant impact on the confluence of humans and computational systems.

Acknowledgments. Bruno Lepri's research is funded by PERSI project inside the Marie Curie COFUND – 7th Framework.

References

1. Aharony, N., Pan, W., Ip, C., Khayal, I., Pentland, A.: Social fMRI: Investigating and shaping social mechanisms in the real world. Pervasive and Mobile Computing (2011)
2. Ajzen, I.: From intentions to actions: A theory of planned behavior. In: Kuhl, J., Beckmann, J. (eds.) Action Control, from Cognition to Behavior, pp. 11–39. Springer (1985)
3. Ambady, N., Hallahan, M., Rosenthal, R.: On judging and being judged accurately in zero-acquaintance situations. Journal of Personality and Social Psychology 69(3), 518–529 (1995)
4. Ambady, N., Rosenthal, R.: Thin slices of expressive behavior as predictors of interpersonal consequences: A meta-analysis. Psychological Bulletin 111(2), 256–274 (1992)
5. Bargh, J.A.: The automaticity of everyday life. Lawrence Erlbaum Associates Publishers (1997)
6. Bargh, J.A., Chen, M., Burrows, L.: Automaticity of social behavior: Direct effects of trait construct and stereotype activation on action. Journal of Personality and Social Psychology 71(2), 230 (1996)
7. Barsade, S.G.: The ripple effect: Emotional contagion and its influence on group behavior. Administrative Science Quarterly, 644–675 (2002)
8. Bem, D.J.: Self-perception theory. Advances in Experimental Social Psychology 6, 1–62 (1972)
9. Cacioppo, J.T., Petty, R.E.: The need for cognition. Journal of Personality and Social Psychology 42(1), 116–131 (1982)
10. Centola, D., Macy, M.: Complex contagions and the weakness of long ties. American Journal of Sociology 113(3), 702 (2007)
11. Chartrand, T.L., Bargh, J.A.: The chameleon effect: The perception–behavior link and social interaction. Journal of Personality and Social Psychology 76(6), 893 (1999)

12. Chittaranjan, G., Blom, J., Gatica-Perez, D.: Who's who with big-five: Analyzing and classifying personality traits with smartphones. In: Proc. 15th Annual Int. Symp. on Wearable Computers, ISWC (2011)
13. Christakis, N.A., Fowler, J.H.: The collective dynamics of smoking in a large social network. New England Journal of Medicine 358(21), 2249–2258 (2008)
14. Cox, D.F., Bauer, R.A.: Self-confidence and persuasibility in women. Public Opinion Quarterly, 453–466 (1964)
15. Curhan, J.R., Pentland, A.: Thin slices of negotiation: Predicting outcomes from conversational dynamics within the first 5 minutes. Journal of Applied Psychology 92(3), 802–811 (2007)
16. DiMicco, J.M., Bender, W.: Group Reactions to Visual Feedback Tools. In: de Kort, Y.A.W., IJsselsteijn, W.A., Midden, C., Eggen, B., Fogg, B.J. (eds.) PERSUASIVE 2007. LNCS, vol. 4744, pp. 132–143. Springer, Heidelberg (2007)
17. Dong, W., Lepri, B., Cappelletti, A., Pentland, A.S., Pianesi, F., Zancanaro, M.: Using the influence model to recognize functional roles in meetings. In: Proc. 9th Int. Conf. on Multimodal Interfaces, pp. 271–278. ACM (2007)
18. Eagle, N., Pentland, A.S., Lazer, D.: Inferring friendship network structure by using mobile phone data. Proc. National Academy of Sciences 106(36), 15274–15278 (2009)
19. Fleeson, W.: Toward a structure-and process-integrated view of personality: Traits as density distributions of states. Journal of Personality and Social Psychology 80(6), 1011–1027 (2001)
20. Fogg, B.: Persuasive technologies. Communications of the ACM 42(5), 27–29 (1999)
21. Friedkin, N.E.: The attitude-behavior linkage in behavioral cascades. Social Psychology Quarterly 73(2), 196–213 (2010)
22. Gatica-Perez, D.: Automatic nonverbal analysis of social interaction in small groups: A review. Image and Vision Computing 27(12), 1775–1787 (2009)
23. Gifford, R.: A lens-mapping framework for understanding the encoding and decoding of interpersonal dispositions in nonverbal behavior. Journal of Personality and Social Psychology 66(2), 398–412 (1994)
24. Granovetter, M.: Threshold models of collective behavior. American Journal of Sociology, 1420–1443 (1978)
25. Hall, J., Coats, E., LeBeau, L.: Nonverbal behavior and the vertical dimension of social relations: A meta-analysis. Psychological Bulletin 131(6), 898 (2005)
26. Harvey, O.J., Consalvi, C.: Status and conformity to pressures in informal groups. The Journal of Abnormal and Social Psychology 60(2), 182–187 (1960)
27. Hung, H., Jayagopi, D., Yeo, C., Friedland, G., Ba, S., Odobez, J.M., Ramchandran, K., Mirghafori, N., Gatica-Perez, D.: Using audio and video features to classify the most dominant person in a group meeting. In: ACM Multimedia, vol. 3. Citeseer (2007)
28. Hung, H., Jayagopi, D., Ba, S., Odobez, J., Gatica-Perez, D.: Investigating automatic dominance estimation in groups from visual attention and speaking activity. In: Proc. 10th Int. Conf. on Multimodal Interfaces. pp. 233–236. ACM (2008)
29. Janis, I.L.: Personality correlates of susceptibility to persuasion. Journal of Personality 22(4), 504–518 (1954)
30. Janis, I.L.: Anxiety indices related to susceptibility to persuasion. The Journal of Abnormal and Social Psychology 51(3), 663 (1955)
31. Jayagopi, D.B., Hung, H., Yeo, C., Gatica-Perez, D.: Modeling dominance in group conversations using nonverbal activity cues. IEEE Transactions on Audio, Speech, and Language Processing 17(3), 501–513 (2009)

32. Kenny, D.A., Horner, C., Kashy, D.A., Chu, L.: Consensus at zero acquaintance: Replication, behavioral cues, and stability. Journal of Personality and Social Psychology 62(1), 88–97 (1992)

33. Kim, T., Chang, A., Holland, L., Pentland, A.: Meeting mediator: enhancing group collaborationusing sociometric feedback. In: Proc. 2008 ACM Conf. on Computer Supported Cooperative Work, pp. 457–466. ACM (2008)

34. Kim, T., Olguín, D.O., Waber, B.N., Pentland, A.: Sensor-based feedback systems in organizational computing. In: Proc. Int. Conf. on Computational Science and Engineering, vol. 4, pp. 966–969. IEEE (2009)

35. Lepri, B., Mana, N., Cappelletti, A., Pianesi, F.: Automatic prediction of individual performance from thin slices of social behavior. In: Proc. 17th ACM Int. Conf. on Multimedia, pp. 733–736. ACM (2009)

36. Lepri, B., Mana, N., Cappelletti, A., Pianesi, F., Zancanaro, M.: Modeling the Personality of Participants During Group Interactions. In: Houben, G.-J., McCalla, G., Pianesi, F., Zancanaro, M. (eds.) UMAP 2009. LNCS, vol. 5535, pp. 114–125. Springer, Heidelberg (2009)

37. Lepri, B., Subramanian, R., Kalimeri, K., Staiano, J., Pianesi, F., Sebe, N.: Employing social gaze and speaking activity for automatic determination of the extraversion trait. In: Int. Conf. on Multimodal Interfaces and the Workshop on Machine Learning for Multimodal Interaction, ICMI-MLMI, pp. 7:1–7:8. ACM, New York (2010)

38. Madan, A., Cebrian, M., Lazer, D., Pentland, A.: Social sensing for epidemiological behavior change. In: Proc. 12th ACM Int. Conf. on Ubiquitous Computing, pp. 291–300. ACM, New York (2010)

39. Madan, A., Farrahi, K., Gatica-Perez, D., Pentland, A.S.: Pervasive Sensing to Model Political Opinions in Face-to-Face Networks. In: Lyons, K., Hightower, J., Huang, E.M. (eds.) Pervasive 2011. LNCS, vol. 6696, pp. 214–231. Springer, Heidelberg (2011)

40. Madan, A., Moturu, S.T., Lazer, D., Pentland, A.S.: Social sensing: obesity, unhealthy eating and exercise in face-to-face networks. In: Wireless Health 2010, WH 2010, pp. 104–110. ACM, New York (2010)

41. Mairesse, F., Walker, M.: Automatic recognition of personality in conversation. In: Proceedings of the Human Language Technology Conference of the NAACL, pp. 85–88. Association for Computational Linguistics (2006)

42. Mairesse, F., Walker, M.: A personality-based framework for utterance generation in dialogue applications. In: Proc. of the AAAI Spring Symposium on Emotion, Personality and Behavior (2008)

43. Mason, W.A., Conrey, F.R., Smith, E.R.: Situating social influence processes: Dynamic, multidirectional flows of influence within social networks. Personality and Social Psychology Review 11(3), 279 (2007)

44. Mast, M.S.: Dominance as expressed and inferred through speaking time. Human Communication Research 28(3), 420–450 (2002)

45. Pentland, A.: Honest signals: how they shape our world. The MIT Press (2008)

46. Petty, R.E., Cacioppo, J.T.: The elaboration likelihood model of persuasion. Advances in Experimental Social Psychology 19(1), 123–205 (1986)

47. Pianesi, F., Zancanaro, M., Not, E., Leonardi, C., Falcon, V., Lepri, B.: Multimodal support to group dynamics. Personal and Ubiquitous Computing 12(3), 181–195 (2008)

48. Reeves, B., Nass, C.: The Media Equation: How people treat computers, television, and new media like real people and places. CSLI Publications, Cambridge University Press (1996)

49. Rienks, R., Heylen, D., van der Weijden, E.: Argument diagramming of meeting conversations. In: Multimodal Multiparty Meeting Processing, Workshop at the 7th Int. Conf. on Multimodal Interfaces, pp. 85–92 (2005)
50. Rienks, R., Zhang, D., Gatica-Perez, D., Post, W.: Detection and application of influence rankings in small group meetings. In: Proc. 8th Int. Conf. on Multimodal Interfaces, pp. 257–264. ACM (2006)
51. Salah, A.A., Lepri, B., Pianesi, F., Pentland, A.S.: Human Behavior Understanding for Inducing Behavioral Change: Application Perspectives. In: Salah, A.A., Lepri, B. (eds.) HBU 2011. LNCS, vol. 7065, pp. 1–15. Springer, Heidelberg (2011)
52. Salah, A.A., Pantic, M., Vinciarelli, A.: Recent developments in social signal processing. In: Proc. IEEE Int. Conf. on Systems, Man, and Cybernetics (2011)
53. Schmid Mast, M., Murphy, N., Hall, J.: A brief review of interpersonal sensitivity: Measuring accuracy in perceiving others, pp. 163–185. University of the West Indies Press, Trinidad (2006)
54. Schmid Mast, M., Sieverding, M., Esslen, M., Graber, K., Jäncke, L.: Masculinity causes speeding in young men. Accident Analysis & Prevention 40(2), 840–842 (2008)
55. Staiano, J., Lepri, B., Kalimeri, K., Sebe, N., Pianesi, F.: Contextual modeling of personality states' dynamics in face-to-face interactions. In: Proc. IEEE Social Computing (2011)
56. Sturm, J., Herwijnen, O., Eyck, A., Terken, J.: Influencing social dynamics in meetings through a peripheral display. In: Proc. 9th Int. Conf. on Multimodal Interfaces, pp. 263–270. ACM (2007)
57. Watts, D.J., Dodds, P.S.: Influentials, networks, and public opinion formation. Journal of Consumer Research 34(4), 441–458 (2007)
58. Zahavi, A., Zahavi, A., Balaban, A., Ely, M.: The handicap principle: a missing piece of Darwin's puzzle. Oxford University Press, USA (1999)
59. Zancanaro, M., Lepri, B., Pianesi, F.: Automatic detection of group functional roles in face to face interactions. In: Proc. 8th Int. Conf. on Multimodal Interfaces, pp. 28–34. ACM (2006)

Privacy, Trust and Interaction in the Internet of Things

Johann Schrammel[1], Christina Hochleitner[1], and Manfred Tscheligi[1,2]

[1] CURE – Center for Usability Research and Engineering, Vienna, Austria
{Schrammel,Hochleitner,Tscheligi}@cure.at
[2] ICT&S Center, University of Salzburg, Salzburg, Austria
Manfred.Tscheligi@sbg.ac.at

Abstract. This document presents a summary of the AmI-11 workshop about privacy, trust and interaction in the Internet of Things. In this workshop researchers and practitioners from different backgrounds and interests, ranging from social sciences to engineering participated. Workshop-papers covering related topics in the area of privacy and trust were presented.

Keywords: HCI, Privacy, Trust, IoT.

1 Overview

This workshop aims to integrate the user directly in the trust chain, guaranteeing transparency of the underlying security and reliability properties of the Internet of Things (IoT). The information security properties of the IoT are often difficult to understand for its users, because they are hidden in pervasive systems and small devices. Trustworthiness, security functions and privacy implications are vast, and must be assessable to users and consumers. These topics are also elaborated within the uTRUSTit project, from which this workshop originated.

The ideas presented within the workshop cover a wide area, ranging from trust strategies to RFID as a key technology in the Internet of Things. Fritsch et al. [1] describe situations where end-users of IoT systems encounter different situations and services, where they need to decide which trust strategy they want to apply. A more technical approach to trust – trust from a developer's perspective – was presented by Fugard et al. [2]. Gudymenko et al. [3] discuss privacy concerns of RFID technology, one of the main enablers in the Internet of Things. Putting the user back in control is the main topic of the work presented by Hoepman [4]. Privacy challenges in pervasive social networks were addressed by Mabrouki et al. [5].

2 Discussed Topics

Following the presentation of the workshop papers, a vivid discussion emerged, in which different important aspects and issues were identified. In detail the following topics were addressed as part of the discussions:

R. Wichert, K. Van Laerhoven, J. Gelissen (Eds.): AmI 2011 Workshops, CCIS 277, pp. 264–266, 2012.

Privacy: For most users the primary objective is to achieve their goal, e.g. buying something online. Thus, privacy and security issues are secondary to them. Users do not want to be constantly reminded about possible privacy issues. Therefore there is a trade-off between putting users in control and providing too much information.

Trust: The concept of trust is a current topic, present in many scientific publications. Nevertheless, various definitions of the term and the context of trust currently exist. Therefore a unified definition of trust is needed. Moreover, the context the definition is applied to needs to be clarified.

Interaction: Providing users with the right amount of feedback to be able to make informed trust-decisions is very important for them. Nevertheless, the IoT environment complicates and limits the possibilities to do so. Because of the pervasive nature of the IoT, the interfaces might range from embedded screens to everyday appliances such as pens. Therefore providing feedback, given the various and also limited interaction possibilities is an environment-based challenge that needs to be overcome.

At the end of the workshop the focus was placed on identifying privacy and interaction factors influencing the success of the IoT. This was achieved as a collaborative group effort and the following key factors were identified:

- **Transparency:** When interacting with the Internet of Things, users need transparency about the devices' functionality and their benefits from using it, as well as transparency about information transmission and the employed privacy policies.
- **Simplicity:** The information should be displayed in an understandable way, concerning the screen design as sxsx x well as the wording.
- **Control:** Users must always be in control of their information.
- **Management Tools:** Users should be provided with management tools to put them in control of their data.
- **Information Ownership:** Users need to be informed about who has access to their information and potential delegation of ownership.
- **Withdrawal:** Users need to have the possibility to opt-out, revoke their consent and remove or even delete information.
- **Feedback:** In combination with the previously mentioned factors, users need to be given feedback about the underlying processes.

Summarizing, the workshop has indicated that all treated topics (privacy, trust and interaction) are important in an IoT context and need to be addressed by future research. Given the different backgrounds of researchers in this area, a unified definition of trust is needed and the influencing factors on trust in the IoT need to be clearly identified and further researched.

Acknowledgments. This work was funded by the European Union Seventh Framework Programme (FP7/2007-2013) under grant 258360 (uTRUSTit; see http://www.utrustit.eu/).

References

1. Fritsch, L., Groven, A.K., Schulz, T.: On the Internet of Things, Trust is Relative. In: Wichert, R., Van Laerhoven, K., Gelissen, J. (eds.) AmI 2011Workshops. CCIS, vol. 277, pp. 267–273. Springer, Heidelberg (2012)
2. Fugard, A.J.B., Beck, E., Gärtner, M.: How will Software Engineers of the Internet of Things Reason about Trust? In: Wichert, R., Van Laerhoven, K., Gelissen, J. (eds.) AmI 2011 Workshops. CCIS, vol. 277, pp. 274–279. Springer, Heidelberg (2012)
3. Gudymenko, I., Borcea-Pfitzmann, K., Tietze, K.: Privacy Implications of the Internet of Things. In: Wichert, R., Van Laerhoven, K., Gelissen, J. (eds.) AmI 2011 Workshops. CCIS, vol. 277, pp. 280–286. Springer, Heidelberg (2012)
4. Hoepman, J.H.: In Things We Trust? Towards Trustability in the Internet of Things (Extended Abstract). In: Wichert, R., Van Laerhoven, K., Gelissen, J. (eds.) AmI 2011 Workshops. CCIS, vol. 277, pp. 287–295. Springer, Heidelberg (2012)
5. Mabrouki, O., Chibani, A., Amirat, Y.: Privacy in Pervasive Social Networks. In: Wichert, R., Van Laerhoven, K., Gelissen, J. (eds.) AmI 2011 Workshops. CCIS, vol. 277, pp. 296–301. Springer, Heidelberg (2012)

On the Internet of Things, Trust is Relative

Lothar Fritsch, Arne-Kristian Groven, and Trenton Schulz

Norsk Regnesentral – Norwegian Computing Center,
Gaustadallen 23a/b, Kristen Nygaards hus, NO-0373 Oslo, Norway
{Lothar.Fritsch,Arne-Kristian.Groven,Trenton.Schulz}@nr.no
http://www.springer.com/lncs

Abstract. End-users on the Internet of Things (IoT) will encounter many different devices and services; they will need to decide whether or not they can trust these devices and services with their information. We identify three items of trust information that end-users will need to determine if they should trust something on the IoT. We create a taxonomy of the likely scenarios end-users will encounter on the IoT and present five trust strategies for obtaining this trust information. Upon applying these strategies to our scenarios, we find that there is no strategy that can work efficiently and effectively in every situations; end-users will need to apply the strategy that best fits their current situation. Offering multiple trust strategies in parallel and having this information transparent to end-users will ensure a sustainable IoT.

Keywords: Internet of Things, trust, trust strategies, mobile Internet, usability, accessibility, privacy.

1 Introduction

The Internet of Things (IoT) will be composed of many interacting, federated devices that communicate over many different communication networks [1]. Users in the Internet of Things will use a variety of objects and services from different providers. This requires users to exchange their information to many different "trusted" devices owned by different entities. The user perception of the IoT here is assumed to be a "thing" that is part of a one or several devices and device federations. However, there is a great potential for harm through privacy violation in the IoT [2], and in addition there are other security issues with mobile and ubiquitous services [3]. We argue that the most important trust information for end users in the IoT are:

1. recognition or identification of the federation of "things" one connects to,
2. ability to identify the owner, controller, or legally responsible person behind a federation, and
3. transparency concerning functionality, and security and privacy assurance information.

R. Wichert, K. Van Laerhoven, J. Gelissen (Eds.): AmI 2011 Workshops, CCIS 277, pp. 267–273, 2012.

There are five strategies that users can apply to get this information, but these strategies are not sufficient by themselves. Extra information must be available so that users can select the best strategy based on their situation.

Our argument is based on taxonomy of four different scenarios and five strategies for approaching trust. We show how these strategies can be applied to scenarios we selected to get the trust information. We also show how, without extra information, these strategies can break down if applied blindly.

2   Taxonomy and Trust Strategies

Let us begin by taking a look at how end-users interact with the IoT by breaking it up into a taxonomy. We can then take a look at the trust strategies end-users can apply when interacting with the IoT.

2.1   The Internet of Things—Taxonomy

We presume that an end-user normally connects to the IoT through the user's own, personal device. A device is anything from a simple smart card tag to a sophisticated terminal like a smart phone. In our discussion, we ignore secondary channels such as point-of-sale terminals and stationary computers. A federation is a special binding between "things" that organizes them into, e.g., trusted circles, or application-specific federations [4]. For example, an application-specific federation could be an electronic ticketing system made of RFID tickets, RFID readers, sales terminals, NFC mobile phones, and a background network for sales and validation. As we focus on the end-user experience, the user-perceivable IoT configurations can be classified into four basic scenarios:

1. User connects to an anonymous device or network; e.g., using a smart phone to connect to a public information terminal at a railway station.
2. User connects to a device or network that is owned or managed by a known person; e.g., using a tablet computer to connect to a friend's digital music player.
3. User connects to a personalized federation; e.g., a group of game enthusiasts that update their playing location through their equipment to their friends to make it easier to find each other.
4. User is surrounded by several, possibly overlapping, federations that form a conglomerate application federation with several circles of trust; e.g., a user use a smartphone for electronic public transport ticketing, mobile payment, as an electronic door opener, and a personal navigation device against various service federations.

2.2   Trust and Trust Strategies

Trust is about reliance of other agents, humans, or technology. A trust decision should lead to an answer of the following questions: is an agent representing something or someone in question worthy of trust? Is it trustworthy? Usually one expects this to be either a "yes" or a "no." Yet, various more fine-grained scales of strengths between "yes" and "no" could be applicable. Trust is our response to uncertainty. Trust is related to someone's or something's behavior or related to the knowledge they have: you can trust someone's knowledge about European history, but not let that person mange your savings. Trust decisions based on false assumptions might cost us dearly. Therefore, choosing the right strategy depending on the case or scenario is crucial. In addition, risks are associated with the context or circumstance where trust decisions are made: a trust decision is often associated with, e.g., time or group pressure on making a decision about whether to trust or not.

There is a set of basic trust strategies applicable in our daily lives regardless of technology use. Yet, they can be related to technology application, especially in the network communication domain like the Internet, IoT, mobile Internet, and ad-hoc networks. O'Hara, Alani, Kalfoglou, and Shadbold [5] list trust strategies for the semantic web that are also applicable to Internet of Things:

Optimistic Strategy Assume all agents are trustworthy unless proven otherwise.

Pessimistic Strategy Assume all agents are untrustworthy unless proven otherwise.

Centralized Strategy Trust information is managed by and obtained from centralized institutions.

Investigative Strategy Check and evaluation of agents to determine their trustworthiness.

Transitive Strategy Analyzing networks of agents to determine their trustworthiness.

The Optimistic Strategy is a simple strategy. One agent will trust another agent, even if its performance is uncertain, unless there are real reasons for not trusting it. So, an agent will accept the bona fides of other agents offering services by default unless they fail one or more tests. Looking at our three points of trust information, we can see that an agent using the optimistic strategy will not be concerned with the recognizing or identifying the federation, who is legally responsible, or the assurances of security or privacy. The agent will only be checking to make sure that the federation is not part of a known bad federation.

Using the Pessimistic Strategy restricts interactions with agents unless there is a reason to trust them. The Pessimistic Strategy corresponds to trust through personal acquaintances in the offline world, which is the basic model of trust (local trust or trust in small). Looking at our three points of trust information again, an agent using the Pessimistic Strategy would be the opposite of the Optimistic one. The agent would dismiss any federation unless it was one of the previously known good federations.

The Centralizing Strategy involves deferring the costs of interacting with and investigating agents to a central, third party authority. That authority can certify a particular agent as willing and able to act in some specified way. If the agent bears a certificate, then it can, following this strategy, be trusted. The agent having to make a trust decision now only needs to trust the authority. Trusting the authority is dependent on belief in the authority's ability to investigate potential agents thoroughly and to sanction betrayals effectively. In our three points of trust information, an agent using the Centralized Strategy would ask the federation to present its certificates to identify itself, the legally responsible party, and its terms of service and assurances. The agent would then look at the information and who had issued the certificates. If the agent trusted the authority, it would use the federation based on the agent's requirements.

The Investigation Strategy tries to reduce uncertainty by investigating or evaluating other agents to determine some salient details of operation. It is not passive; it actively tries to discover aspects of the environment—as events unfold—that are relevant to reduce uncertainty. In some ways it is a compromise between the Optimistic and Pessimistic strategies, neither blindly accepting nor denying information, but instead investigating to find the truth. Using the three points of trust information, an agent using the Investigative Strategy would try to find out information about the federation through multiple sources. It might join the federation and use the federation's services to see how they work—likely using different, perhaps fake, data—until the agent could determine that federation was trustworthy. Yet, it would periodically investigate again to ensure this trust is still justified. All this investigation would require large resources.

An agent using the Transitive Strategy asks whether another agent is trustworthy. The network of acquaintances of the requesting agent will then either send back an opinion based on experience, or pass the message onto the networks' acquaintances, many of them will be unknown to the first agent. The aim is to increase the scope of a single agent's knowledge by exploring the network feature of agents' communities to bring in information from other, unknown, agents. Using the three points from above, an agent applying the Transitive Strategy would check other agents' experiences with the federation before joining. Considering the responses from the other agents, the agent would determine the trustworthiness of the federation, the federation's legally responsible party, and federation's assurances.

3   Analysis of Trust Strategies Related to the IoT End-User Scenarios

One thing to keep in mind with the scenarios is the context of the trust decision. Your potential loss of engaging in transactions with others will influence your selection of trust strategy. If the result of a bad transaction might be negative to you (economically or in other ways), you will probably act differently compared to a situation where the outcome is benign, e.g., loosing ten minutes of your time. Trust should therefore be analyzed by its potential for negative effects.

3.1   First Scenario: Use an Offering from Anonymous Things

In this scenario, the strategy to apply is based on what is at stake. If the anonymous thing is just providing some information, such as how many people have passed by the things, the Optimistic Strategy seems to be the right choice, at least if the potential for negative effects is low. With higher stakes, such as serious privacy issues that have a serious affect on the end-user or vast financial loss, other strategies should be used. One basic assumption is the focus on the trust in the underlying anonymous services. This can be achieved either through the Centralized, Investigative, or Transitive trust strategies.

3.2   Second Scenario: Use an Offering from Personalized Things with a Known Owner

The use and offering of personalized things between actors and owners known to each other assumes a trust relation. This trust could have been established through any of the five trust strategies. The exchange of personalized information or resources represents a larger downside potential. Assuming proper authentication, the exchange of information could be based on the Optimistic Strategy. The distance and complexity between the actors should be subject to a trust strategy as well. If complex infrastructure is used, the question of trust expands beyond the two parties. The parties need to examine the infrastructure between them to ensure that it is trustworthy. This may require multiple trust strategies.

3.3   Third Secnario: Federation of Things, a Trusted Circle of Friends

A federation of things defines an arena or a context, e.g., a context of interest where trust is established between actors depending on their previous actions on that arena. You might be a merited actor in the arena sharing privileges with other merited actors, or you might be an ordinary actor: fully accepted by the merited actors, but not in every respect. Alternatively, you might be a newcomer: not recognized as trustworthy by the ordinary or merited actors until you have proven yourself otherwise. This building of trust between a set of actors, can be described as the Pessimistic Strategy (local trust or trust in small), which is trust based on your historic actions or merits. You do not know the identity of the other actors sharing common arenas, but they become your friends.

Assuming you have trusted cycles of friends, you might be using the friends of your friends in some situations where you want to establish trust relations to an unknown agent; that is, by asking if any of your friends, friend of friends, or friend of friend of friends, etc., have good or bad experience with a certain agent. Hence, you will be following a Transitive Strategy.

While these strategies work, the Optimistic Strategy may be dangerous to the circle if the wrong actors are allowed in. Suppose an optimistic merited actor in the circle just accepts anyone into the circle or promotes actors. These newly accepted or promoted actors are not trustworthy and cause damage in the circle.

As this is repaired, likely by using the Investigative Strategy, the optimistic actor may eventually find circle access revoked since the optimistic actor is deemed "untrustworthy."

3.4 Fourth Scenario: Multiple IoT Federations with Known and Unknown Owners

IoT "web services," involving exchange of personal information in this complex scenario, should establish trust in the communication channels, e.g., by using the Centralized Strategy. This trust strategy should also be used towards the owner of the IoT service if it is an unknown owner. As the end-user switches between collaborating federations, the end-user might be interested in the Investigative Strategy as well, particularly to exercise end-user's privacy rights. Depending on the downside potential, other strategies could be used, e.g., the Transitivity Strategy. Often, however, a human actor will use the Optimistic Strategy, because it is too complex to find all information. The Pessimistic Strategy would not work here at all unless the end-user knew all the federations, which is unlikely. It would keep the end-user safe, but it would mean ignoring the service and missing any of its advantages.

4 Conclusion

As seen above, the choice of one single trust strategy for the IoT is not always possible. Different strategies work in different situations, and there are dependencies to non-technological issues. These dependencies have an impact on stakes and influence the choice of trust strategies. The application area, the stakeholders, and the transactions to be performed all influence the trust needs. To complicate matters, the chosen trust mechanism might get compromised, such that there is a need to switch to another trust strategy. Considering these insights, we doubt that there will be one dominant "one-size-fits-all" trust strategy for the IoT nor will there be one dominant trust technology as the prescribed "best model" for IoT trust management.

We foresee that any sustainable IoT federation must offer as many of the five trust strategies as possible in parallel, and in alternative modes of overlapping operation. They should be transparent to end-users and usable by them. We think that, ultimately, only end users can assess the stakes at risk, especially concerning privacy. They will need to make decisions about switching over to another trust strategy, e.g., after one of the user's "friends" in the trusted federation is no longer trustworthy, a certificate authority providing the trust chaining gets compromised, or an IoT scenario turns into a hostile scenario calling for adjustments [6]. We therefore urge development of adaptable and flexible trust management systems that have usable user interfaces within the IoT and offer several trust strategies that relate to end user's real-life needs and strategies when they deal with their personal trust decisions. Vendors and operators of IoT infrastructures will contribute to more sustainable infrastructures and use fewer resources on redeployment. But, any user-directed measure will only be successful if it is designed in accessible and usable ways and keeps in mind that there is a limitation in complexity and resources users are willing to spend on reconfiguration issues [7]. This calls for good usable and inclusive design of the IoT trust mechanism portfolio.

Acknowledgments. This research is funded as part of the uTRUSTit project. The uTRUSTit project is funded by the EU FP7 program (Grant agreement no: 258360).

References

1. Bassi, A., Horn, G.: Internet of Things in 2020: A Roadmap for the Future. European Commission: Information Society and Media (2008)
2. Maghiros, L., Punie, Y., Delaitre, S., Hert, P.D., Gutwirth, S., Schreurs, W., Moscibroda, A., Friedewald, M., Linden, R., Wright, D., Vildjiounaite, E., Alahuhta, P.: Safeguards in a world of ambient intelligence. In: Intelligent, E. (ed.) 2nd IET International Conference on Intelligent Environments, vol. 2. IEEE Computer Society, Athens (2006)
3. Naumann, I., Hogben, G., Fritsch, L., et al.: Security issues in the context of authentication using mobile devices, Mobile eID (2008)
4. Walter, T., Bussard, L., Roudier, Y., Haller, J., Kilian-Kehr, R., Posegga, J., Robinson, P.: Secure mobile business applications – framework, architecture and implementation11IST-Programme / KA2 / AL: IST-2001-2.1.3. Inf. Secur. Tech. Rep. 9, 6–21 (2004)
5. O'Hara, K., Alani, H., Kalfoglou, Y., Shadbolt, N.: Trust Strategies for the Semantic Web. In: ISWC 3rd International Workshop on Trust, Security, and Reputation on the Semantic Web (2004)
6. Fritsch, L.: Business risks from naive use of RFID in tracking, tracing and logistics. In: RFID Systech 2009 – 5th European Workshop on RFID Systems and Technologies. VDE Verlag (2009)
7. Fritsch, L., Fuglerud, K.S.: Time and Usability as Upper Boundary in Friend and Family Security and Privacy, vol. DART/11/2010, p. 11. Norsk Regnesentral, Notat (2010)

How Will Software Engineers of the Internet of Things Reason about Trust?

Andrew J.B. Fugard, Elke Beck, and Magdalena Gärtner

ICT&S Center, University of Salzburg
Sigmund-Haffner-Gasse 18, 5020 Salzburg, Austria
{Andy.Fugard, Elke.Beck, Magdalena.Gaertner2}@sbg.ac.at
http://icts.uni-salzburg.at

Abstract. The Internet of Things (IoT) will consist of everyday physical objects communicating with each other via massively distributed service-oriented architectures (SOAs). One neglected area of research is how engineers developing software underlying the IoT will decide whether the services they use and compose are trustworthy. We sketch how a formal socio-cognitive theory of trust can guide empirical research on the topic, and report preliminary results from 25 engineers who were asked how they currently reason about software component trustworthiness.

Keywords: trust, software engineers, components.

1 Introduction

The Internet of Things (IoT) promises to be everywhere, from light bulbs and garden sprinklers to door locks and medicine bottles [4]. Artefacts on the IoT will use massively distributed and dynamically adapting service-oriented architectures (SOAs) [1] in which composable software services interact with each other via message passing. Given the pervasiveness of the things connected by the IoT, trust will be central. An important neglected question is: how will engineers of the software realising this future vision reason about the trustworthiness of the services they use and compose? For instance, how might a fire alarm software engineer trust software services for automatically unlocking doors in the event of a fire? The present paper addresses the question by empirically exploring how software engineers who use third-party components currently decide whether the components they choose are trustworthy. The main focus is on exploring how socio-cognitive processes beyond the technical SOA domain influence decisions made and impact on trust.

To investigate trust requires some theory of what trust is. According to Castelfranchi and Falcone [2], trust is a relation, $trust(X, Y, c, \tau, g_x)$, denoting that X (the trustor) trusts Y (the trustee) in context c to perform the tasks, τ, necessary to achieve X's goal, g_x. There are three main stages to trust in the theory:

1. The *evaluation* of the trustee on the basis of available information, including reputation and previous personal experience of the trustee. There are two

R. Wichert, K. Van Laerhoven, J. Gelissen (Eds.): AmI 2011 Workshops, CCIS 277, pp. 274–279, 2012.
© Springer-Verlag Berlin Heidelberg 2012

main types of evaluation, one involving implicit decisions (e.g., based on prior experience and routine), and the other a more explicit deliberation of reasons. The two types are not independent. Although it may be possible to find very general notions of trustworthiness, such as honesty and efficiency, the evaluation is always with respect to a particular goal.

2. An *intention* to delegate to the trustee. This is a positive evaluation, i.e., that Y is good for achieving the goals by carrying out the required actions.

3. The trust *decision*, a 'leap of faith' [6] whereby X delegates the tasks to Y and depends on Y., i.e., the actual action of trusting. This has happened when, for instance, the system goes live with a particular trusted service being used as an integral part.

Cognitive agents, defined as agents with goals and beliefs, play a special role in this theory: only they can be trustors, so, e.g., a software engineer can trust but a software service cannot; also whether a cognitive trustee is trusted can influence how trustworthy they are, whereas a software service cannot care. However the trustee (Y) need not be a cognitive agent, so, matching intuitions, it is possible according to the theory to trust a software component.

Most goals people want to achieve depend on tasks carried out by others. Correspondingly, people often work on tasks to enable others to achieve their goals. It might therefore come as no surprise that a major set of socio-cognitive processes concerns representing and drawing inferences about the goals of others [5]. We hypothesized that the trust decisions made by software engineers are influenced by a range of socio-cognitive factors beyond the technical domain. There is some anecdotal evidence of this, e.g., Dijkstra [3] argued (and warned) that software engineers often reason about software as if it had goals and intentions:

> The anthropomorphic metaphor is perhaps even more devastating within computing science [...]. Its use is almost all-pervading. To give you just an example: entering a lecture hall at a conference I caught just one sentence and quickly went out again. The sentence started with 'When this guy wants to talk to that guy...'. The speaker referred to two components of a computer network.

We designed a semi-structured questionnaire-based study to explore how software engineers choose software components and what impact their choices have on how trustworthy they think the component is.

2 Method

2.1 Participants

Participants were 25 (5 female) European software developers or designers. Their mean age was 34 years ($SD = 5.3$), with 4.7 years ($SD = 2.7$) in their current profession and 10 years ($SD = 5.1$) working in a software-related field.

Table 1. Types of goals engineers wanted to achieve

Goal type	N	Example responses
Functionality	19	'correct implementation of communication standards'
		'parse and store my data'
Reliability	6	'only do what I told it to do'
Performance	6	'time of response'
		'to be able to cope with a large number of queries'
Security	5	'not modifying data and not disclosing that data to third
		parties'
Consistency with	4	'Work as expected based on the documentation'
documentation		'be correctly implemented according to the . . . API'
Stability	1	'other alternatives were unstable'
Maturity	1	'other alternatives were . . . research prototypes'
Documentation clarity	1	'it had clear interfaces'
Simplicity	1	'A simpler solution would have been better'

2.2 Questionnaire

A web-based semi-structured questionnaire was developed. Participants were asked to consider a time they had chosen to use a software component. Questions concerning this choice were formulated to address each of the following entities and relationships: a software engineer (or set of engineers), X, trusts a software service (non-cognitive trustee), Y, developed by another engineer (or engineers; cognitive trustees) Z, to perform a sequence of tasks, τ, in context c, leading (X hopes), to the satisfaction of X's goal g_x. There are two trustees, one cognitive (the component developer) and the other not (the component). See the Appendix for the questions asked.

3 Results and Discussion

3.1 Software Domains

Participants chose examples from the following domains: semantic storage, banking, network management, data analysis, encryption, and simulation. These are representative of domains the IoT will involve. For instance a device might gather data from sensors, storing it in a semantic database or analyse it on the fly, and then send it encrypted across a network to a bank.

3.2 Engineers' Goals

Table 1 shows the main goals participants wanted to achieve. The most important concern was that the component achieves the participant's primary functional goals. This corresponds with results found elsewhere for non-engineers' uses of technology. Trustors have a primary goal, e.g., ordering a gift online, and issues such as reliability and security are secondary [7]:

Trustors initiate transactions with a primary goal in mind – order the birthday gift that is delivered in time, to pay a credit card bill before incurring a penalty. Discharging the tasks required to reach these goals in a secure manner – i.e. a way that does not put your credentials at risk – is a secondary goal.

3.3   Subjective Trustworthiness

Participants were asked, 'How trustworthy do you think the component is?' on a scale from 0 (= completely untrustworthy) to 5 (= completely trustworthy). A central claim of trust theories is that there must always be a 'leap of faith' [6], otherwise trust would be unnecessary. This was reflected in the responses people gave (see Figure 1(a)), with most respondents giving the assessment 4 out of 5. Several respondents chose to use a component, even though they gave it quite a low score (2 or 3). This illustates the distinction between trust *evaluation* and the trust *decision* introduced earlier. It is possible to delegate a task to a trustee even if inferred trustworthiness is low. In one case the component's results were always monitored, so the trustor's goals could still be achieved even though the trustee was seen as untrustworthy.

Given the important role of cognitive agents in the trust theory, we asked if participants had any contact with the component developers. We expected that contact would have had an impact on trustworthiness, for instance making it possible to increase perceived trustworthiness. Only 8 out of 25 participants answered in the affirmative. Contact was via mailing lists and forums (3), email (3), bug tracking systems (1), and training courses (1). Contrary to expectations, those who did have contact gave a slightly lower trustworthiness evaluation than those who did not ($t(9.9) = 2.3$, $p = .047$; non-parametric Wilcoxon rank sum test $W = 94$, $p = .048$; see Figure 1(b)). There is a plausible explanation for this difference: all of the contact concerned problems, e.g., problems installing

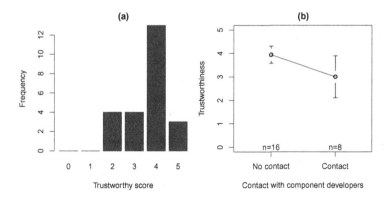

Fig. 1. (a) Distribution of trustworthiness ratings (0 = completely untrustworthy; 5 = completely trustworthy) and (b) mean trustworthiness (and 95% uncertainty intervals) as a function of whether the component's user had contact with its developers

software, incompatibility between different library versions, bug reports, so, in this sample, the act of initiating contact was a signal of untrustworthiness.

3.4 Processes to Infer Trustworthiness

There were two main technical approaches mentioned. Unsurprisingly, various types of software testing were most important. Testing is a technical analogue of experience building seen when non-engineers decide to trust [6]. Occasionally source code was also inspected.

Two non-technical approaches were mentioned. Chatting with colleagues was seen as important, e.g., other team members, project partners, and the boss or project/team leader. This illustrates another case of delegation, that of the very decision to trust. Engineers trust their peers and team leads to help them choose which components to trust. Finally reputation was important, e.g., positive feedback on developer forums, a component being 'well-established'.

4 Conclusions

Guided by a formal trust theory, we explored how software engineers think about trust. As hypothesized, in addition to using technical approaches, software engineers rely on the same basic socio-cognitive processes as do non-engineers, e.g., reasoning informally about reputation, making a 'leap of faith', focusing on primary functional goals. Better understanding the role of these socio-cognitive processes will help ensure the Internet of Things is trustworthy. Future work should investigate how interactions between service producers and consumers might have a positive influence on trust, e.g., by interaction design enabling positive contact when everything is working as hoped in addition to queries in the event of problems with a service.

Acknowledgements. This work was funded by the European Union Seventh Framework Programme (FP7/2007-2013) under grant 257930 (ANIKETOS; see http://www.aniketos.eu/).

References

1. Atzori, L., Iera, A., Morabito, G.: The Internet of Things: A survey. Computer Networks 54(15), 2787–2805 (2010)
2. Castelfranchi, C., Falcone, R.: Trust Theory: A Socio-cognitive and Computational Model. John Wiley and Sons Ltd., Chichester (2010)
3. Dijkstra, E.W.: On anthropomorphism in science. Tech. rep. (1985), http://www.cs.utexas.edu/users/EWD/ewd09xx/EWD936.PDF
4. Gershenfeld, N., Krikorian, R., Cohen, D.: The Internet of Things. Scientific American 291(4), 76–81 (2004)
5. Kilner, J.M., Friston, K.J., Frith, C.D.: Predictive coding: an account of the mirror neuron system. Cognitive Processing 8, 159–166 (2007)

6. Möllering, G.: Trust: Reason, Routine, Reflexivity. Elsevier, Oxford (2006)
7. Riegelsberger, J., Sasse, M.A.: Ignore these at your peril: Ten principles for trust design. In: Proceedings of Trust 2010: 3rd International Conference on Trust and Trustworthy Computing (2010)

Appendix: Semi-structured Questionnaire

1. Consider a time you have chosen to use a software component. What was its function?
2. In what programming language(s) was it written (leave blank if you don't know)?
3. 'Trust' and 'trustworthiness' have many different meanings. In the context of the software component you have in mind, what exactly did you trust it to do (or not to do)?
4. Did you have any contact with the developers of the software component? [Yes/no.]
5. How did you get in contact?
6. Why did you communicate with the developers? Briefly describe what you discussed.
7. What kind of software did the component become part of?
8. Approximately how many people (including you) worked on the project?
9. Why did you choose to use the selected component and not another component? Briefly describe any reasoning behind the decision.
10. With whom did you speak to help decide whether to use the component? (Leave blank if nobody.)
11. Did you perform any kind of real-time monitoring or checking of the component in the live project?
12. Please describe the real-time monitoring or checking that was performed.
13. Is there a situation or context in which you would not trust the component? [Yes/no.]
14. In what situation/context?
15. How trustworthy do you think the component is? [Rated from 0 = completely untrustworthy to 5 = completely trustworthy on a discrete scale.]
16. What (if anything) would have changed your mind about the trustworthiness of the component?
17. What would the consequences have been if the component had turned out not to be trustworthy? (Try to be as specific as possible.)
18. In retrospect, is there anything you believe you should have done to decide how trustworthy the component was?
19. Do you have any general comments you think might be of relevance?

Privacy Implications of the Internet of Things

Ivan Gudymenko, Katrin Borcea-Pfitzmann, and Katja Tietze

Dresden University of Technology
Department of Computer Science, Chair of Privacy and Data Security
Nöthnitzer Str. 46, 01187 Dresden
ivan.gudymenko@gmail.com, {katrin.borcea,katja.tietze}@tu-dresden.de

Abstract. The Internet of Things (IoT) is likely to become one of the milestones which is going to determine the technological advance for the future. At the same time, new privacy concerns arise which might seriously impede the adoption of such systems. In this paper, we provide for our view on privacy implications of IoT focusing on RFID technology as one of its main enablers and suggest possible solutions to developing IoT systems in a privacy-respecting and secure way.

Keywords: IoT, privacy, RFID.

1   Introduction

The authors of [1] describe IoT as " [...] a world where things can automatically communicate to computers and each other providing services to the benefit of the human kind". It is desirable that communication protocols are standardized since this greatly facilitates the process of worldwide adoption and implementation of IoT and thus encourages the process of transition from numerous local proprietary solutions to the ubiquitous ones with a qualitatively new level of interoperability. Such a process is likely to initially converge into IPv6, namely IPv6 over Low-Power Wireless Personal Area Networks (6LoWPAN) [2], since it has a potential of leveraging the two basic concepts which brought success to the conventional Internet, namely packet switching and the "end-to-end" principle. The latter suggests that "[...] the behavior of the network should be determined by what is connected to it rather than by its internal construction [...]", and given the heterogeneity of end devices of IoT should help to "solve the problem of connecting heterogeneous devices rather than heterogeneous networks" [3].

The very prospective area of IoT, however, raises serious concerns over individual privacy in the new environment of smart things. The reason for this is that thanks to the omnipresent intelligence-integrated artefacts, the process of sampling and distribution of information in IoT can be practically carried out anywhere. Ubiquitous connectivity through Internet access aggravates the problem because, unless special mechanisms are considered (encryption, authentication, etc.), personal information might become worldwide available.

In this position paper we express our concerns over privacy issues of IoT and outline possible solutions to this problem. The main focus is made on privacy

R. Wichert, K. Van Laerhoven, J. Gelissen (Eds.): AmI 2011 Workshops, CCIS 277, pp. 280–286, 2012.
© Springer-Verlag Berlin Heidelberg 2012

implications of RFID technology as it is fairly considered to be one of the main enablers of the IoT paradigm.

2   Privacy Implications of IoT

Privacy issues are often left unconsidered during the development of IT systems and are frequently implemented later as an add-on rather than a built-in solution. That might result in immaturity of privacy compliance of the end product and consequently endanger privacy of its users [5]. Therefore, we argue that it is highly important to pay proper attention to privacy issues because the maturity of privacy management mechanisms and availability of robust security solutions[1] will to a large extent determine the level of acceptance of the IoT concept among users. The authors of [1] claim that "People will resist the IoT as long as there is no public confidence that it will not cause serious threats to privacy". In [5] we have already discussed the privacy implications of UbiComp, which to a large extent intersect with the ones of IoT. In this position paper, we would like to focus on IoT and also present our view on its privacy implications.

Radio Frequency Identification (RFID) is quite often seen as the major and possibly the most suitable technology which is going to enable IoT. Low-cost, mass production and the ability to attach RFID tags to almost every possible artefact makes them truly pervasive. This surely raises serious privacy concerns because, in such a scenario, the IoT technology has the potential to penetrate everybody's everyday life and affect not only the individuals who directly use the service, but also those, who are simply unaware of the fact that they are the "passive" users. For example, in [6,7], a scenario of integrating RFID tags into clothes was described. For logistic purposes and returns tracking a chip can be sewn into garments during the manufacturing process and remain in operation even *once the item has been sold*. This raises serious concerns over privacy of customers who happen to use the RFID system in a subtle way without their consent. Equipping garments with RFID tags may enable remote tracking of customers and therefore paves the way to illegal profiling introducing another case of privacy violation.

That is why Weber mentions in [8] that the EU Commission is going to seriously consider the "right to silence of the chips" and the possibility of the individuals to be able "to disconnect from their networked environment at any time". This closely relates to the problem of the "disability to opt-out" discussed in [5] where it was explicitly mentioned that one of the key requirements to provide for a privacy-respecting system is the support of opt-in/opt-out according to the user's choice (i.e. carefully considering the individual's consent).

The ability of mass producing RFID tags and their wide distribution, which ensures the ubiquitous presence of computing and its pervasive penetration into daily life aggravate the problem. According to [6], around 15 million chips were shipped to the retail company by 2003. This demonstrates the large scale of

---

[1] Security provides for the necessary basis for implementing and ensuring privacy and is, therefore, an integral part of the underlying mechanisms of privacy management.

this initiative. Moreover, the authors of [7] inform that some firms are going to release *handheld* devices capable of reading RFID tags (including the ones, woven into the garments). That means that it has become much easier not only to disseminate personally identifiable information (PII) to the infrastructure (fixed readers) but also to perform *reading* from mobile[2] readers which have become relatively small and unobtrusive. If such devices are further equipped with the function of transforming the RFID-specific data (obtained from the query) into an IP-compatible format (i.e. acting as a gateway) and have access to the Internet, then the queried PII can be made worldwide available without necessarily allowing the affected individuals to have any control over this, or perhaps not even informing them of such data distribution.

The authors of [1] argue that "[...] there will be an amazing number of occasions for personal data to be collected" putting a so-called "right to be forgotten" in question because the intelligent artefacts can now gather the PII and save it for an indefinite length of time.

3   Possible Solutions

It is always desirable that privacy and security are considered through a cross-layered approach. That is why we suggest introducing privacy protecting solutions into IoT across several layers[3]. At the application layer, access control policies, and enforcement thereof should enable privacy management, as has been demonstrated in [4]. At the lower layers, privacy middleware should provide for the necessary interfaces which can be used up the stack and therefore bridge the specific communication mechanisms between the smart things and their high-level representation.

Finally, inherent privacy implications, which directly result from the specific technology of smart things production, should be considered as well. For example, the ability to perform a remote reading of an RFID tag from a large distance or, if it is possible to permanently deactivate a tag with a guarantee that it can not be reactivated in future.

Moreover, the means of technical privacy enforcement applied directly to end devices (e.g. RFID tags) play an important role in privacy protection. The following list describes several techniques, which from our point of view are the main components of technical privacy enforcement in the IoT, focusing on their implementation in RFID:

- *Anonymization.* Given the ubiquity of RFID tags distribution and the constantly increasing likelihood of their pervasive presence in daily life, it is important to provide for protection against data linking and profiling. The authors of [17], for example, described a scheme allowing an RFID tag to answer with a different ID to each new request of the reader[4]. Since a

---

[2] RFID readers are usually fixed or mobile but not handheld.

[3] Analogous to the OSI Basic Reference Model [16].

[4] This procedure is based on the randomization algorithm implemented in the tag's circuitry.

legitimate reader is connected to the system database where the ID sets of each tag are stored, tag identification by legitimate parties is enabled while an adversary is prevented from doing so.

- *Encryption.* Personally identifiable information (PII)[5] residing in the tag is subject to protection. Lightweight implementations of encryption can protect sensitive information from illegitimate exposure. The authors of [19,18], for example, have already demonstrated the feasibility of AES[6] and ECC[7] implementation in constrained environment of RFID.
- *Hash functions.* In order to ensure that an RFID tag offers its functionality only to a legitimate reader, hash functions can be utilized. For example, the authors of [22] suggest a concept of an "unlock key" implemented through a hash function which ensures that only a reader possessing such a key can have its request processed by a respective tag.
- *Tamper resistant modules.* Critical data (e.g. encryption and identification keys) can be stored in the protected memory area of a tag, which has a tamper-resistance property. The utilization of such areas, however, may significantly raise the cost of a tag and given the scale of production process, the overall cost of a system.
- *Disabling a tag.* A very straightforward but effective approach: physically shielding a tag when not in use (e.g. Faraday cage), temporarily disconnecting RFID antenna (by using, for instance, the "clipped" tags principle described in [23]) or plainly killing a tag by destroying its antenna.

Technology alone will not be able to provide for full-fledged privacy protection mechanisms. Additionally, legal issues should be considered. Thus, privacy regulation and *legal enforcement* of privacy rights is an important part of privacy management mechanisms in the IoT.

The European Commission expressed its concerns over privacy in RFID-based applications and issued a recommendation "on the implementation of privacy and data protection principles in Applications supported by Radio Frequency Identification" — the so-called framework for privacy and data protection impact assessments (PIA) [9]. This framework is targeted at facilitating the process of establishment and maintenance of compliance with the privacy and data protection laws and regulations as well as risk management in RFID systems. It also provides for privacy assessments at early stages of RFID system development. Thus, we consider PIA as one of the key steps for developing IoT systems according to the "Privacy by Design" paradigm [10].

The development of such a framework is a decent step towards the creation of a competent and widely acceptable means of privacy assessment of an RFID system, which can be understood by all parties involved. Furthermore,

---

[5] The information stored in the tag which can be used for inference allowing to obtain PII falls into this category as well. Consider an example of a unique ID of a tag woven into clothes combined with the name of a customer who has purchased the respective garment.

[6] Advanced Encryption Standard [20].

[7] Elliptic Curve Cryptography [21].

having created the appropriate legal basis, it might be possible to oblige organizations, which utilize RFID technology for business purposes, to carry out PIA assessment with, for example, subsequent certification. The resulted report can be provided for an external review by the respective authorities enhancing the transparency and contributing to the overall process of privacy protection.

Surely, such a framework can be efficient only if it is based on the results of a decent research on underlying technological principles of RFID systems and privacy implications of these.

In order to approach privacy issues in the IoT based on RFID technology, we suggest that the following requirements are considered:

- *Assessment of privacy compliance of an RFID system*: It should be possible to provide for competent privacy assessment of the RFID system in question in a way, that can be understood by all parties involved (e.g., based on PIA).
- *Ability to opt-out*: By default, the users should be provided with an opportunity to prevent communication of their devices with the RFID infrastructure at any time.
- *Ability to permanently disable the tag* [8]: some of the tags are constructed in such a way that they can be remotely reactivated again after having been sent the deactivation command ("kill" command). Thus, it might be useful to certify the utilization only of those tags the processing and transmission functions of which can be permanently disabled (e.g., by a strong electromagnetic impulse which *physically* destroys the tag's circuitry).
- *Marking the intelligence-enabled artefacts*: The fact of intelligence being integrated into certain artefacts should be made visible to *all* individuals who might be directly and indirectly affected by the RFID system (e.g., attaching special markers to the smart things which indicate their IoT activity. Whenever this is not possible (e.g., in case of RFID transceivers sewn into clothes, see [6,7]), this kind of information should be included into the terms of use supplied along with the goods containing the IoT device/s.
- *Considering M2M Privacy*: Machine-to-machine (M2M) privacy should be specifically addressed. Current EU Directives only consider natural persons as objects of privacy laws [13]. In IoT environments, however, smart artefacts quite often can be directly associated with their owners or even with other individuals in their vicinity and thus to a large extent affect the individual privacy. Moreover, one of the definitions of the IoT itself indirectly introduces the notion of M2M: "Things *having identities* and *virtual personalities* operating in smart spaces using intelligent interfaces to connect and communicate within social, environmental, and user contexts" [1]. This results into smart things possessing their own privacy derived from that of an individual. Since smart things can communicate with each other (M2M communication, see [14,15]), this form of privacy can be called M2M privacy.
- *RFID usage restriction*: Critical areas should be protected by prohibition or at least restriction of the use of RFID technology [8]. This is because some areas (e.g., AIDS centers, etc) succumb to particular regulations with respect to the privacy of the individuals.

- *Support for security goals*: Confidentiality, integrity, and availability should be provided for in IoT systems. The authors of [12] claim that to a certain extent it is already feasible to solve this problem, for example using the AES/CCM encryption (see [11] for details).

Moreover, the current legal regulation on privacy in the EU is rather coarse-grained and hence inflexible. Weber claims in [8] that "[...] only "extreme" warranties are legally guaranteed [...]". That is why a lot of effort should be targeted at fine-tuning the legal privacy regulations. These, from our point of view, can be realized only in cooperation with IT specialists who can provide for the necessary technological basis highlighting the peculiar privacy threats inherent in the IoT systems.

4 Conclusion

IoT is a very promising and challenging paradigm. Modern communications are steadily evolving and IoT is one of the milestones which is going to determine the technological advance for the future. The dynamic environment of IoT introduces unseen opportunities for communication, which are going to change our perception of computing and networking. At the same time, the privacy and security implications of such an evolution should be carefully considered to prevent the promising technology from being transformed into a pervasive surveillance tool.

References

1. Atzori, L., Iera, A., Morabito, G.: The internet of things: A survey. Comput. Netw. 54, 2787–2805 (2010)
2. Hui, J.W., Culler, D.E.: Extending IP to low-power, wireless personal area networks. IEEE Internet Computing 12(4), 37–45 (2008)
3. Krikorian, R., Gershenfeld, N., Cohen, D.: The Internet of Things. Scientific American, 76–81 (October 2004)
4. Welbourne, E., Battle, L., Cole, G., Gould, K., Rector, K., Raymer, S., Balazinska, M., Borriello, G.: Building the internet of things using RFID: The RFID ecosystem experience. IEEE Internet Computing 13(3), 48–55 (2009)
5. Gudymenko, I., Borcea-Pfitzmann, K.: A Framework for Transforming Abstract Privacy Models into Implementable System Requirements. In: 1st International Workshop on Model-based Interactive Ubiquitous Systems (2011)
6. Benetton to tag 15 million items (March 2003),
   http://www.rfidjournal.com/article/view/344 (accessed on July 18, 2011)
7. Gonsalves, A.: Privacy concerns hinder RFID rollout (January 2000),
   http://www.itnews.com.au/News/
   11417,privacy-concerns-hinder-rfid-rollout.aspx (accessed on July 18, 2011)
8. Weber, R.H.: Internet of things - new security and privacy challenges. Computer Law & Security Review 26(1), 23–30 (2010)
9. Report: Privacy and data protection impact assessment framework for RFID applications (January 2011) (accessed on May 25, 2011)

10. Cavoukian, A.: Privacy by Design. Take a challenge. Electronic Resource (2009),
    http://www.privacybydesign.ca/content/uploads/2010/03/
    PrivacybyDesignBook.pdf
11. Whiting, D., Housley, R., Ferguson, N.: Counter with CBC-MAC (CCM). Internet
    Ingineering Task Force (2003)
12. Schelby, Z., Bormann, C.: 6LoWPAN: the Wireless Embedded Internet. Wiley
    (2009)
13. European Parliament and Council Directive: Directive 2002/58/EC of the Euro-
    pean Parliament and of the Council: concerning the processing of personal data
    and the protection of privacy in the electronic communications sector (Directive
    on privacy and electronic communications). Official Journal of the European Com-
    munities (2002)
14. Cha, I., Shah, Y., Schmidt, A.U., Leicher, A., Meyerstein, M.V.: Trust in M2M
    communication. IEEE Vehicular Technology Magazine 4(3), 69–75 (2009)
15. Wu, G., Talwar, S., Johnsson, K., Himayat, N., Johnson, K.D.: M2M: From mobile
    to embedded internet. IEEE Communications Magazine 49(4), 36–43 (2011)
16. Day, J.D., Zimmermann, H.: The OSI reference model. Proceedings of the
    IEEE 71(12), 1334–1340 (1983)
17. Cichon, J., Klonowski, M., Kutylowski, M.: Privacy Protection in Dynamic Systems
    Based on RFID Tags. In: Fifth Annual IEEE International Conference on Pervasive
    Computing and Communications Workshops, PerCom Workshops 2007, pp. 235–
    240 (March 2007)
18. Hutter, M., Feldhofer, M., Wolkerstorfer, J.: A Cryptographic Processor for Low-
    Resource Devices: Canning ECDSA and AES Like Sardines. In: Ardagna, C.A.,
    Zhou, J. (eds.) WISTP 2011. LNCS, vol. 6633, pp. 144–159. Springer, Heidelberg
    (2011)
19. Hutter, M., Joye, M., Sierra, Y.: Memory-Constrained Implementations of Elliptic
    Curve Cryptography in Co-Z Coordinate Representation. In: Nitaj, A., Pointcheval,
    D. (eds.) AFRICACRYPT 2011. LNCS, vol. 6737, pp. 170–187. Springer, Heidel-
    berg (2011)
20. NIST. Specification for the Advanced Encryption Standard (AES). FIPS 197
    (November 2001)
21. Koblitz, N.: Elliptic Curve Cryptosystems. Mathematics of Computation 48(177),
    203–209 (1987)
22. Weis, S.A., Sarma, S.E., Rivest, R.L., Engels, D.W.: Security and Privacy As-
    pects of Low-Cost Radio Frequency Identification Systems. In: Hutter, D., Müller,
    G., Stephan, W., Ullmann, M. (eds.) Security in Pervasive Computing. LNCS,
    vol. 2802, pp. 201–212. Springer, Heidelberg (2004)
23. Karjoth, G., Moskowitz, P.A.: Disabling RFID Tags with Visible Confirmation:
    Clipped Tags are Silenced. In: Proceedings of the 2005 ACM Workshop on Privacy
    in the Electronic Society, WPES 2005, pp. 27–30. ACM, New York (2005)

In Things We Trust? Towards Trustability in the Internet of Things*
(Extended Abstract)

Jaap-Henk Hoepman[1,2]

[1] TNO Information and Communication Technology
jaap-henk.hoepman@tno.nl
[2] Institute for Computing and Information Sciences (ICIS)
Radboud University Nijmegen
jhh@cs.ru.nl

Abstract. The Internet of Things is nothing new. Yet the imminent confluence of cyberspace and physical space into one ambient intelligent system still poses fundamental research challenges in the area of security, privacy and trustability. We discuss these challenges, and present new approaches that may help to overcome them.

1 Introduction

The Internet of Things is nothing new. First introduced as Ubiquitous Computing by Mark Weiser [28] around 1990, the basic concept of the "disappearing computer" has been studied as Ambient Intelligence or Pervasive Computing in the decades that followed. Today we witness the first large scale applications of these ideas. We see RFID technology being used in logistics, shopping, public transport and the like. The use of smart phones is soaring. Many of them have GPS localisation capabilities. Some phones already have NFC (Near Field Communication) capabilities, allowing them to communicate with objects tagged with RFID directly. Combined with social networking (like Facebook or Twitter), this gives rise to advanced location based services, and augmented reality applications. In fact social networks interconnecting things as well as humans have already emerged. Example are Patchube, a web-based service built to manage the world's real-time data[1] and Flukso, a web-based community metering application[2].

As the full ramifications of the Internet of Things start to unfold, this confluence of cyberspace and physical space is posing interesting new and fundamental

---

* This research is supported by the research program Sentinels (www.sentinels.nl) as project 'Identity Management on Mobile Devices' (10522). Sentinels is being financed by Technology Foundation STW, the Netherlands Organization for Scientific Research (NWO), and the Dutch Ministry of Economic Affairs.

[1] https://pachube.com/
[2] http://www.flukso.net/

R. Wichert, K. Van Laerhoven, J. Gelissen (Eds.): AmI 2011 Workshops, CCIS 277, pp. 287–295, 2012.
© Springer-Verlag Berlin Heidelberg 2012

research challenges. In particular, as we will argue in this essay, it has a huge impact on security, privacy and trustability. As Bruce Schneier puts it in a recent issue of CryptoGram [19] (discussing IT in general)

> "[...] it's not under your control, it's doing things without your knowledge and consent, and it's not necessarily acting in *your* best interests."

The question then is how to ensure that, despite these adverse conditions, the Internet of Things is a safe, open, supportive and in general pleasant environment for humans to live in.

2   The Vision

What exactly is the Internet of Things? Many definitions can be given. At a basic level the Internet of Things is a dynamic global network infrastructure with self configuring capabilities where physical and virtual "things" have identities, physical attributes, and virtual personalities and use intelligent interfaces, and are seamlessly integrated into the information network [23]. Such "things" could be a pair of jeans (with an RFID tag attached), a light switch, a light bulb, a fridge, a washing machine, or any other sensor or actuator. The list of things is basically endless. All these things become first class members of the Internet, sharing their data with the world, and using the world's data for their own purposes.

But far more interesting is the envisioned applications of the Internet of Things to realise the Ambient Intelligence (AmI) concept. This concept

> ...provides a vision of the Information Society future where the emphasis is on userfriendliness, efficient and distributed services support, user-empowerment, and support for human interactions. People are surrounded by intelligent intuitive interfaces that are embedded in all kinds of objects and an environment that is capable of recognising and responding to the presence of different individuals in a seamless, unobtrusive and often invisible way. [8]

In an ambient intelligence world, devices work in concert to support people in carrying out their everyday life activities, tasks and rituals in easy, natural way using information and intelligence that is hidden in the network connecting these devices [1, 12].

Applications areas of the AmI concept are housing (home automation, smart washing machines), smart cities, mobility (traffic management systems, congestion control, support for multi-modal transport, public transport ticketing), commerce (inventory management, marketing and advertising, store personalisation), education (digital libraries, digital museums), and health (self-treatment, long-distance monitoring) [8].

3   The Problem

The vision of the Internet of Things outlined above is certainly an attractive one. However, the very same components used to build this vision can also be used to create a totally different future. To prevent this vision to become our worst nightmare, basic guarantees have to be implemented that will protect our privacy and will maintain security.

3.1   Privacy

Privacy — sometimes loosely defined as the 'right to be let alone' [25] — is considered a fundamental human right in many societies. It is "essential for freedom, democracy, psychological well-being, individuality and creativity" [20]. Privacy has many dimensions (corporeal, relational, etc.), but for the purpose of this essay we focus on the data protection aspect of it. We wish to stress that data protection is not the same as keeping personal information confidential. Data protection laws and regulations are much broader. They determine the conditions under which businesses and governments are allowed to collect, process and use personal information (proportionality and subsidiarity). They empower citizens to determine how personal data about them is used even after it is collected by third parties. They allow them to be informed about the use of their personal information, and give them the right to correct personal information about themselves.

In a world of sensors and actuators that surround us and support us in our day to day activities, privacy is obviously a big concern. In order to achieve the vision of the Internet of Things, sensors need to collect large amounts of data, that are often of quite personal nature. Sensors will be everywhere, in our offices, cars, homes and bedrooms. The data from these sensors will have to be collected, analysed and perhaps combined with data elsewhere to generate the desired overall system behaviour. As a consequence, privacy protection in the Internet of Things [9, 14] involves much more than data minimisation techniques like using pseudonyms and the like. In fact, the vision of an Internet of Things that intelligently supports us in our day to day activities *needs* to collect large amounts of personal information... The challenge is to accommodate this need for personal data, while maintaining privacy guarantees.

3.2   Security

Serious integrity, authenticity, and availability concerns arise too when the Internet of Things has gained in popularity.

Consider the use of RFID tags in supply chain management as an example. If the logistics of a company critically depends on the correct bookkeeping of items in stock through RFID tags, then inserting fake or wrong tags in the system can do serious damage. Radio interference or outright radio jamming may make inventory scanning impossible or highly inaccurate. Swapping tags on items in stock may allow customers to defraud store owners.

When the Internet of Things expands to other application areas, like health care, smart grids, and the like, the Internet of Things itself becomes a critical infrastructure. This is especially the case when the nodes are not merely sensors but also actuators, whose actions control critical components. This imposes strong security requirements. Not so much regarding confidentiality (although this is a concern with respect to industrial espionage related to supply chain information), but the more so regarding integrity, authenticity, and availability of the Internet of Things [14].

3.3   Trustability

An even more principal issue, that partly underlies the security and privacy problems associated with the Internet of Things, is that of trust, or rather, trustability. In sociology, trust is defined as follows [10]

> When an actor trusts another actor, he or she is willing to assume an open and vulnerable position. He or she expects the other to refrain from opportunistic behaviour even if there is the possibility to show this behaviour.

A paradigm shift is needed away from a paternalistic 'trust us' implementation of the ICT infrastructure that surround us, to a more user-centric 'trustability' approach where the infrastructure allows the user to built up trust using personal tools and other means. It is an interesting question how techniques from identity management (and solutions to its associated problems [2]), and the trusted computing paradigm [16] can be re-applied in this new context.

4   Solutions

Most research so far has focused on techniques to minimise data collection, by implementing certain forms of authentication and access control while respecting the resource constraints inherent to RFID based systems. We do not discuss these here, but instead focus on alternative approaches and future research directions.

4.1   Alternative Approaches

Spiekermann *et al.* [21] observe that although there are many protocols and proposals for limiting access to RFID tags (either by killing them completely or by requiring the reader to authenticate), few systems have been proposed that allow effective and fine grained control over access permissions. Recent research efforts have tried to bring the user back into control. Notable examples are agency tools like the RFID Guardian [18] and the Privacy Coach [7], as well as the "resurrecting duckling" [22] principle of Stajano and Anderson.

Design philosophies. The "resurrecting duckling" [22] security policy model of Stajano and Anderson is an example of a general design philosophy applicable to the Internet of Things, that aims to put the user in better control of the devices that he owns or the devices that surround him. The principle is based in analogy to the biological principle of *imprinting* discovered by Lorentz [15], which describes the initial bonding process between hatched ducklings and their (supposed) parents. In this model a device is in two possible states: *imprintable* or *imprinted*. When imprintable, anyone can take ownership of the device. In doing so, the device becomes imprinted. Only the owner of an imprinted device may cause the device to 'die', bringing it back to its imprintable state (and resetting all other settings to default, essentially bringing the device back in a virgin, new-born, state). Additionally, an owner of a device may change security policies on the device, granting certain rights to other users. This allows an owner of a device to lend the device to another user, and delegate a subset of its power to this user.

Agency tools. The RFID Guardian and the Privacy Coach can be classified as *agency tools*: tools that support the user to make choices and to impose those choices on the world [5]. These tools put the user at the centre of the Internet of Things.

The RFID Guardian [18] is best understood as a personal firewall between the RFID tags a user carries, and the world of RFID readers that surround the user. The user programs the RFID guardian to grant or deny access to specific tags from certain readers, possibly depending on the current context. The RFID Guardian performs this task by selectively jamming radio signals if it detects a reader that tries to access a tag for which access is denied.

The Privacy Coach [7] puts the user in control in a different way. It is an application running on a mobile phone that supports users in making privacy decisions when confronted with RFID tags on items they buy (or otherwise obtain). The Privacy Coach itself does not block or prevent any privacy infringements. Instead it informs the user of the possibility of this happening when purchasing goods tagged by RFID. The mobile phone should be equipped with a reader that can read RFID tags. Certain such NFC enabled phones are currently on the market. The Privacy Coach functions as a mediator between customer privacy *preferences* and corporate privacy *policies*, trying to find a match between the two, and informing the user of the outcome.

The idea is that a user programs his own personal privacy preferences in his mobile phone, through the Privacy Coach application. Typical preferences are: "I do not want the purchase of a tagged item to be linked to my personal profile", or "I do not mind if I receive offers based on the possession of a tagged item". Producers of goods tagged by RFID will similarly store the company privacy policy associated with these tags in a central database. Alternatively, consumer organisations may create such privacy policies for companies that do not provide these policies themselves. When picking up an item tagged by RFID, the mobile phone of the user reads the tag, and looks up the corresponding privacy policy in the database. It uses a mobile Internet connection to do so. The Privacy Coach then matches the found policy against the user's privacy preference, and tells the user whether they match or not. In the latter case, the Privacy Coach displays the aspects on which the privacy policy and the user preference do not match. Based on this information, the user decides to keep the item, or not.

4.2 Future Challenges

Many challenges remain that need to be addressed if we want to realise a 'friendly', i.e., secure, privacy friendly and trustable Internet of Things.

Privacy beyond data minimalisation. Current approaches to protect our privacy focus on data minimalisation. This is as counterproductive in the Internet of Things as it is in social networks: both only 'work' if you are willing to share your data. This is not to say that in order for the IoT to be useful, your personal data needs to be shared with *everybody*. Like in social networks, context [17] will play an important role in the Internet of Things as well. But simply refusing to share your data with anybody will not be possible (although in certain cases, anonymity mechanisms may still be applicable).

This means that privacy enhancing technologies need to be developed that prevent the abuse of personal data once it is collected [11], and that prevent the leakage of information from one context to the other (thus maintaining contextual integrity [17]). Design philosophies, and derived design patterns, for the Internet of Things need to be developed that accomplish this. Moreover, a common privacy engineering practise based on these principles needs to be established. These privacy preserving approaches need to be applicable to heterogeneous sets of devices [23], and need to be user friendly. This adds to the research challenge already present.

Several approaches can be followed to achieve this. One approach is to collect and maintain user profiles and preferences on a personal device held by the user (like a mobile phone) instead of by the infrastructure directly. The core data needed to make the ambient infrastructure intelligent is then still under control of the user. The infrastructure can query the user profile through standard interfaces provided by the personal device. Here the personal device operates as a personal firewall. This approach is somewhat similar to recent studies into privacy enhanced profiling of website visitors. These techniques aim to implement targeted advertising on websites [3, 24] without the usually associated privacy problem of collecting user profiles centrally.

Alternatively, user profiles can be split into many small parts and stored and many different, uncorrelated, locations. This can even be done in such a way that wrong information is encoded in some of these parts. The parts can be combined using secret sharing techniques. In case of wilfully distributing wrong information, the wrong data can be filtered out using majority voting and other fault tolerant techniques [13] once all the parts (correct and incorrect ones) have been collected.

Security. The main security properties that are relevant for the Internet of Things are integrity, authenticity, and availability. These need to be achieved in an environment where the endpoints are mostly very resource constrained. Endpoints are typically tags, sensors and actuators, that need to be produced at the lowest possible cost (because a proper implementation of the Internet of Things will need so many of these nodes to be deployed). These endpoints have little memory, little processing power, and slow, short range and unreliable communication links. These security properties (and also the aforementioned privacy-enhancements) therefore need to be built upon resource efficient cryptographic primitives. This remains a challenging area of research.

Also, the Internet of Things will lack a single central authority. This calls for models for decentralised authentication [23], including strategies for revocation and key-distribution in an ad-hoc fashion. In general, security measures need to support the requirements of multiple stakeholders (e.g. fairly balance privacy protection and accountability), in order to support multilaterally secure cooperations [27], and should be designed in such a way that they can be used by casual users. This has to be achieved without the coordinating role of a central authority trusted by all stakeholders.

Establishing trustability. Establishing trust in the Internet of Things should go beyond the mere user perception side of the issue, but instead focus on measurable ways to establish trustability, and on tools to support and measure this. Trustability aims to answer questions like: How well does the infrastructure safeguard the data you entrust to it? What are the future consequences of its use? How clearly and openly do infrastructure providers advise you of your rights and responsibilities? What guarantees of future reliability and availability does the infrastructure give you?

Very few of these tools exist to help the user to determine the trustability of the infrastructure it is engaging in. The issue is much more complex than simply determining whether a certain public terminal is authentic before entering your PIN code on it [4] (although certainly knowing the terminal is authentic helps to some extent). Methods based on direct anonymous attestation [6] using Trusted Computing Modules (TPM) (that establish that a certain device is a known good state) are of limited value. The sheer heterogeneity of the devices that make up the Internet of Things make it impossible to enumerate all the good states each of these devices can be in. Moreover, because the IoT has no central authority, and as context matters, the question is who to turn to determine what a good state of a certain device is in the first place.

Most importantly though, establishing trust is a process, a process that progresses over time in which users adjust their trust assessment in the devices and infrastructures they engage in with every transaction they perform with them. The use of personal, mobile, devices and applications (cf. [26]) to support the user in this process need to be developed. These could for instance be used to predict the future consequences of current engagements with the Internet of Things (cf. [11]). These ideas could build upon the results obtained in the Smart Products[3] project that aim to embed "proactive knowledge" into the IoT and consider e.g. usability and security in access control mechanisms based on machine learning techniques to make the configuration of the IoT manageable by casual users.

---

[3] http://www.smartproducts-project.eu/

Acknowledgements. I would like to thank the members of Council[4] (Rob van Kranenburg, Erin Anzelmo, Cristiano Storni, James Wallbank, Tijmen Wisman) and the members of IFIP WG 11.2[5] (Denis Trcek, Stefan Georg Weber, Igor Ruiz-Agundez) for their input to this essay.

References

[1] Aarts, E., Harwig, R., Schuurmans, M.: Ambient intelligence. In: Denning, P. (ed.) The Invisible Future: The Seamless Integration Of Technology Into Everyday Life. McGraw-Hill (2001)

[2] Alpár, G., Hoepman, J.-H., Siljee, J.: The identity crisis. Security, privacy and usability issues in identity management, eprint CoRR cs.CR:1101.0427 (January 2011)

[3] Androulaki, E., Bellovin, S.M.: A Secure and Privacy-Preserving Targeted Ad-System. In: Sion, R., Curtmola, R., Dietrich, S., Kiayias, A., Miret, J.M., Sako, K., Sebé, F. (eds.) FC 2010 Workshops. LNCS, vol. 6054, pp. 123–135. Springer, Heidelberg (2010)

[4] Asokan, N., Debar, H., Steiner, M., Waidner, M.: Authenticating public terminals. Computer Networks 31(8), 861–870 (1999)

[5] Bandura, A.: Social cognitive theory: An agentic perspective. Annual Review of Psychology 52, 1–26 (2001)

[6] Brickell, E.F., Camenisch, J., Chen, L.: Direct anonymous attestation. In: Atluri, V., Pfitzmann, B., McDaniel, P.D. (eds.) ACM Conference on Computer and Communications Security, pp. 132–145. ACM (2004)

[7] Broenink, G., Hoepman, J.-H., van 't Hof, C., van Kranenburg, R., Smits, D., Wisman, T.: The privacy coach: Supporting customer privacy in the internet of things. In: Pervasive 2010 Conference Workshop on What can the Internet of Things do for the Citizen?, Helsinki, Finland, May 17, pp. 72–81 (2010)

[8] Friedewald, M., Costa, O.D.: Science and technology roadmapping: Ambient intelligence in everyday life (amilife). Tech. rep., JRC/IPTS - ESTO (2003)

[9] Garfinkel, S.L., Juels, A., Pappu, R.: RFID privacy: An overview of problems and proposed solutions. IEEE Security & Privacy, 34–43 (May-June 2005)

[10] Hardin, R.: Trust & Trustworthiness. Russell Sage Foundation, New York (2002)

[11] Hildebrandt, M.: Behavioural biometric profiling and transparency enhancing tools. FIDIS Deliverable 7.12

[12] ISTAG. Ambient intelligence: from vision to reality. Tech. rep., ISTAG (2003)

[13] Jalote, P.: Fault Tolerance in Dsitributed Systems. Prentice Hall (1994)

[14] Juels, A.: RFID security and privacy: A research survey. IEEE Journal on Selected Areas in Communications 24(2), 381–394 (2006)

[15] Lorenz, K.: Er redete mit dem Vieh, den Vögeln und den Fischen. Borotha-Schoeler, Wien (1949)

[16] Mitchell, C.J. (ed.): Trusted Computing. The Institution of Engineering and Technology (November 2005)

[17] Nissenbaum, H.: Privacy as contextual integrity. Washington Law Review 79(1), 119–158 (2004)

---

[4] http://www.theinternetofthings.eu
[5] http://www.cs.ru.nl/ifip-wg11.2

[18] Rieback, M.R., Gaydadjiev, G., Crispo, B., Hofman, R.F.H., Tanenbaum, A.S.: A platform for RFID security and privacy administration. In: LISA, pp. 89–102. USENIX (2006)

[19] Schneier, B.: Security in 2020. CryptoGram (January 2011)

[20] Solove, D.J.: Understanding Privacy. Harvard University Press (2008)

[21] Spiekermann, S., Evdokimov, S.: Critical RFID privacy-enhancing technologies. IEEE Security & Privacy 11(2), 56–62 (2009)

[22] Stajano, F., Anderson, R.: The Resurrecting Duckling: Security Issues for Ad-hoc Wireless Networks. In: Malcolm, J.A., Christianson, B., Crispo, B., Roe, M. (eds.) Security Protocols 1999. LNCS, vol. 1796, pp. 172–182. Springer, Heidelberg (2000)

[23] Sundmaeker, H., Guillemin, P., Friess, P., Woelffl, S.: Vision and Challenges for Realising the Internet of Things. Publication Office of the European Union, Luxembourg (2010), Clusterbook of CERP-IoT, ISBN 978-92-79-15088-3

[24] Toubiana, V., Narayanan, A., Boneh, D., Nissenbaum, H., Barocas, S.: Adnostic: Privacy preserving targeted advertising. In: 17th Ann. Network and Distributed System Symposium, San Diego, CA, USA (February 2010)

[25] Warren, S.D., Brandeis, L.D.: The right to privacy. The implicit made explicit. Harvard Law Review IV(5), 193–220 (1890)

[26] Weber, S.G., Martucci, L.A., Ries, S., Mühlhäuser, M.: Towards trustworthy identity and access management for the future internet. In: The 4th International Workshop on Trustworthy Internet of People, Things & Services (Trustworthy IoPTS 2010) Co-located with the Internet of Things 2010 Conference, Tokyo, Japan (November 2010)

[27] Weber, S.G., Mühlhäuser, M.: Multilaterally Secure Ubiquitous Auditing. In: Caballé, S., Xhafa, F., Abraham, A. (eds.) Intelligent Networking, Collaborative Systems and Applications. SCI, vol. 329, pp. 207–233. Springer, Heidelberg (2010)

[28] Weiser, M.: The computer for the 21st century. Scientific American (February 1991)

Privacy in Pervasive Social Networks

Olfa Mabrouki[1,2], Abdelghani Chibani[2], and Yacine Amirat[2]

CityPassenger SA, Avenue de l'Atlantique
Les Conquérents BP 903, 91976 Courtaboeuf Cedex, France
omabrouki@citypassenger.com
Université Paris-Est Créteil (UPEC), LiSSi Lab, E.A. 3956
120-122 rue Paul Armangot, 94400 Vitry sur seine, France
{olfa.mabrouki,chibani,amirat}@u-pec.fr

Abstract. In this paper, we study privacy challenges in Pervasive Social Networks as a new field of research. We highlight the main issues to consider for having a better privacy protection. Then, we give an idea about existing privacy researches.

Keywords: privacy, pervasive computing, social networks.

1   Introduction

A new concept has emerged when the paradigms of Pervasive Computing and Social Networks have been associated: it is Pervasive Social Networks (PSN). According to Ben Mokhtar et al. in [15], PSN present a new vision that aims to complement virtual interactions with physical ones. This new notion enables users who are both socially and physically related to find each other and perform activities of common interest. In another work [14], the PSN are, also, called Mobile Social Network (MSN). It is considered as a novel computing paradigm deriving from the convergence of Pervasive Computing and Web 20. Social networking services (e.g. Facebook, MySpace, and Twitter).

In Pervasive Computing Environment (PCE), mobile users interact with services provided by their surrounding physical environment (e..g. mobile devices, display screens, multimedia services). In PSN, users interact with people among their social relations, especially, among their direct relations (e.g, friends) or indirect (e.g. friends of friends). Normally, users are in relationship with other that share similar preferences/interests. In PSN, these descriptions mentioned previously are joined to allow users discovering people sharing the same interests with them and are physically proximate unlike Web 2.0 services that connect people related only by exploring their social connections.

The key challenge of PSN environment is user privacy. These environments promise to have profound effect on person's interactions with members, devices or even physical spaces while people are claiming their right to have a better privacy protection. In this paper, we study privacy in Pervasive Social Networks as a new field of research. We discuss related works from literature in section 2.

R. Wichert, K. Van Laerhoven, J. Gelissen (Eds.): AmI 2011 Workshops, CCIS 277, pp. 296–301, 2012.

Then, we present privacy challenges in section 3. We only attempt to highlight relevant recent research that is good starting points and any omissions are inadvertent. Concluding remarks and future work are given in the final section.

2 Related Works

There were many attempts for user privacy protection in PCE and PSN separately. Privacy management techniques surround access controls models, privacy languages and semantic privacy models. In [15], Ben Mokhtar et al. proposed a social networking middleware service. This one dynamically combines both social and physical proximity relations between mobile users to accurately recommend them people with whom to perform activities of common interest. In another work [9], the proposed privacy architecture was implemented for the evaluation of context-dependent preferences. While in [2], privacy model is based on the P3P language to specify user privacy preferences. At the same time, the model is represented by ontology. We consider that the corresponding application due to the use of ontology. We notice that privacy model based P3P is, almost, oriented Web application architecture. In addition, in most cases, authors proposed a static privacy management technique. Basically, the design of privacy is done just one time in the design phase of pervasive application.

However, users' needs, profiles, contexts and situation are constantly changing. This rapid change makes researchers facing a great issue of privacy which is dynamic character. Other works have focused on the access control mechanisms. For example, an e-Wallet was developed in the context of MyCampus project [6]. A case study "restaurant concierge" is implemented to illustrate the use of the e-Wallet. The academic domain is the application fields of "MyCampus" project [6].In [18], both of context and situation information are used in the pervasive application. Context is classified into physical context (obtained from various sensors, devices, actuators, and other smart objects that are distributed in the environment) and logical relationship that the user has with the environment and other entities such as social relationship). Two approaches are used for assigning privacy weights to the context elements: user centric and system. Additionally, a Context-Privacy Graph (CPG) is created with the privacy setting of the system as the root and the context elements at the lowest level. It could be considered as dynamic. Dynamic rules are modeled using the knowledge of user activity and behavior.

3 Privacy Challenges in Pervasive Social Networks

Protection of user privacy is becoming more and more difficult. The presence of sensors and actuators in PCE makes them smarter, especially, with important capacities of information processing. Indeed, contextual information gathered by these sensors and the integrated equipments can be adapted even personalize offered services to its users based on their context and preferences. However, this ease of access to user data threatens, seriously, their privacies that can be exploited by malicious or even by the curious system administrators.

Therefore, pervasive systems are becoming the "big brother". Their main role is to capture the maximum of information about users and track him. For example, in the case of hospitals, clinics and homes where there is an abundance of sensitive personal information and reviews that must be protected and secured. Moreover, in some situations, people refuse to be followed but these systems keeping track of their personal information.

Some of privacy challenges are, already, highlighted in many works. For example in [20], Campbell et al have pointed out the multilevel, transparency, context-awareness, interoperability, extended boundaries and scalability as challenges of privacyware systems. We agree with them for all of these challenges. However, we note that an important privacy challenge in PCE like "Situation-awareness" is not taking into account. Researchers handle context-awareness rather than situation-awareness. In the following part, we list the different challenges related to privacy issue in the pervasive social networks.

Generally, privacy presents many challenges especially as individuals vary widely in their concern over privacy and information control. In our case, privacy challenges include those of pervasive computing environments [17] and social networks [13] at the same time. In other words, we have to surround privacy challenges in pervasive social networks. Hence, in this section, we define from the point of our view privacy challenges in PSN applications.

3.1   One Person for Many Profiles in Many PSN

People can no more surpass themselves of social networks. They are members in several social networks on Internet. These online social networks are over than 250, nowadays. By using them, people are looking for communicating and sharing information with their lists of contact (friends, family, and colleagues) or even with strangers for some purpose (e.g blogging, business, pets, religious, entertainment, and friends). This situation constitutes a key challenge for privacy protection. Having at least one profile in one or many socialware(s) aggravates privacy settings as user can be lost in his initial setting. He has to update privacy setting each time or it is not the case. Actually, user is looking for the easiest way to enhance his privacy protection in Web socialwares without being disturbed. There is, also, the problem of data redundancy. People are obliged to put, approximately, the same information in different socialwares and sometimes different privacy preferences.

3.2   User-Centric Privacy Management

Users don't have a choice to protect their privacy unless through available applications tips or using existing privacy settings. Allowing user to make a decision about his security is not an easy task. It, even, proves to be very complicate. User is too demanding. He wants to be involved in the decision making about his privacy, controlling and at the same time not be disturbed in every decision. Thus, we consider that proposing a user-centric privacy approach is a challenge to be taking in account to enhance privacy protection.

3.3   Semantic and Expressiveness

We should worry about the semantic and expressiveness of privacy concepts. Actually, there are a wide range of PSN applications users. They come from different backgrounds and different jurisdictions. Thus, privacy model must be well-defined semantics. Consequently, many PSN applications in different PCE can understand and interoperate with each other correctly.

3.4   Context and Situation Control

Traditional privacy is static and context/situation insensitive. Pervasive computing integrates context and situational information. Temporal boundaries should be considered in this case. This makes the PCE into a sentient space. What is not private in past might become in future and vice versa. In addition, when the information is being persistent much of the actions done in past cannot be undone. Otherwise, we should also consider special circumstances. Context data provide important information for intrusion detection mechanisms. In otherwise, we have to consider context and situation concerns when handling privacy issue in PSN.

3.5   Simplex Relationship vs. Multiplex Relationship

In our lives or what is called the off-line world, human relationships are far more complicated than just friends. Multiple relationship types exist in our societies. Normally, PSN environments should simulate the off-line world to support multiplex relationships. Providing such a relationship space for social interaction can facilitate the control of access level and information flow, leading to better preservation of information privacy.

3.6   Individual Level vs. Group Level Interaction

On some abstraction levels, e.g., individual-to-group, group-to-group, group-to-network, etc., can avoid certain detail of information being disclosed. Subsequently, accommodating relationships at various abstraction levels for interaction is required. This problem can potentially lead to the problem of relationship structure, i.e., the ability to manage hierarchical relationships and utilize them for privacy preservation.

3.7   Access Level Control

The problem of access level control ensures for users a best control of their private information by granting different levels of access for their social contacts. Mainly, it is due because of the need of various relationships with others in PSN at different level of granularity.

3.8 Protecting Information Disclosure

Inspired by the proposition of Cardoso and Issarny in [21], we underline that only data strictly necessary during a service access must be disclosed in PSN applications. Decisions about which data has to be disclosed, for what purposes and how it should be disclosed can be agreed upon beforehand, through the use of labeling protocols. Systems have to disclose only necessary personal and contextual data required by the transaction and nothing else. Cardoso and Issarny proposed three techniques to adjust personal data resolution: modification, multiplication and generalization.

The idea for the first technique "Modification" is that it substitutes the requested information for different information. The second technique "Multiplication" replaces requested information with a set of data where the requested information is contained and generalization substitutes the requested information with another less specific data. This one could correspond to different values of the requested information. Many techniques were developed to change the resolution of location data, modifying [10], [3], generalizing [1] or multiplying them [8], [12]. Images are also sensitive data, and there are techniques that enable modification [7] and generalization [11], [4], [22], [16] of specific kinds of images (such as the face of a person recorded by a webcam). Finally, identity information can also be generalized to avoid connections between data and individuals [19], [5].

4   Concluding Remarks and Future Work

In this work, we've studied the main privacy challenges in Pervasive Social Networks. Based on this study, we aim to propose, in the future, a modular and extensible ontology supporting reasoning about privacy. We aim to take into account user privacy preferences regrading his context and situation. Consequently, only a member of PSN will have the whole control of his privacy.

References

1. Al-Muhtadi, J., Campbell, R., Kapadia, A., Dennis Mickunas, M., Yi, S., Dennis, M., Yi, M.S.: Routing through the mist: Privacy preserving communication in ubiquitous computing environments (2002)
2. Babbitt, R., Wong, J., Chang, C.: Towards the modeling of personal privacy in ubiquitous computing environments. In: Proceedings of the 31st Annual International Computer Software and Applications Conference, COMPSAC 2007, vol. 02, pp. 695–699. IEEE Computer Society, Washington, DC (2007)
3. Beresford, A.R., Stajano, F.: Location privacy in pervasive computing. IEEE Pervasive Computing 2, 46–55 (2003)
4. Boyle, M., Edwards, C., Greenberg, S.: The effects of filtered video on awareness and privacy. In: Proceedings of the 2000 ACM Conference on Computer Supported Cooperative Work, pp. 1–10. ACM (2000)
5. Brands, S.A.: Rethinking Public Key Infrastructures and Digital Certificates: Building in Privacy. MIT Press (2000)

6. Cas, J.: Privacy in pervasive computing environments - a contradiction in terms? IEEE Technology and Society Magazine, 24–33 (2005)
7. Crowley, J.L., Coutaz, J., Bérard, F.: Perceptual user interfaces: things that see. Commun. ACM 43, 54–64 (2000)
8. Duckham, M., Kulik, L.: A Formal Model of Obfuscation and Negotiation for Location Privacy. In: Gellersen, H.-W., Want, R., Schmidt, A. (eds.) PERVASIVE 2005. LNCS, vol. 3468, pp. 152–170. Springer, Heidelberg (2005)
9. Edwards, J.: Location privacy protection act of 2001 (2001)
10. Gruteser, M., Grunwald, D.: Anonymous usage of location-based services through spatial and temporal cloaking, pp. 31–42 (2003)
11. Hudson, S.E., Smith, I.: Techniques for addressing fundamental privacy and disruption tradeoffs in awareness support systems. In: Proceedings of the 1996 ACM Conference on Computer Supported Cooperative Work, pp. 248–257. ACM (1996)
12. Kido, H., Yanagisawa, Y., Satoh, T.: An anonymous communication technique using dummies for location-based services. In: ICPS 2005, pp. 88–97 (2005)
13. Shan, C., Mary-Anne, W.: Privacy in social networks: a comparative study. In: PACIS 2009 Proceedings, pp. 81–93 (2009)
14. Mokhtar, S.B., Capra, L.: From pervasive to social computing: Algorithms and deployments. In: Proceedings of the ACM International Conference on Pervasive Services (ICPS 2009) (July 2009)
15. Mokhtar, S.B., McNamara, L., Capra, L.: A middleware service for pervasive social networking. In: Proceedings of the International Workshop on Middleware for Pervasive Mobile and Embedded Computing, M-PAC 2009, pp. 2:1–2:6. ACM, New York (2009)
16. Neustaedter, C., Greenberg, S.: The Design of a Context-Aware Home Media Space for Balancing Privacy and Awareness. In: Dey, A.K., Schmidt, A., McCarthy, J.F. (eds.) UbiComp 2003. LNCS, vol. 2864, pp. 297–314. Springer, Heidelberg (2003)
17. Palen, L., Dourish, P.: Unpacking "privacy" for a networked world. In: CHI 2003: Proceedings of the SIGCHI Conference on Human Factors in Computing Systems, pp. 129–136. ACM, New York (2003)
18. Pallapa, G.V.: A Privacy Enhanced Situation-aware Middleware Framework For Ubiquitous Computing Environments. PhD thesis (December 2009)
19. Rivest, R.L., Shamir, A., Tauman, Y.: How to Leak a Secret. In: Boyd, C. (ed.) ASIACRYPT 2001. LNCS, vol. 2248, pp. 552–565. Springer, Heidelberg (2001)
20. Pasquale, F., Al-Muhtadi, J., Naldurg, P., Sampemane, G., Mickunas, M.D.: Towards Security and Privacy for Pervasive Computing. In: Okada, M., Babu, C. S., Scedrov, A., Tokuda, H. (eds.) ISSS 2002. LNCS, vol. 2609, pp. 1–15. Springer, Heidelberg (2003)
21. Cardoso, R.S., Issarny, V.: Architecting Pervasive Computing Systems for Privacy: A Survey. In: Sixth Working IEEE/IFIP Conference on Software Architecture: WICSA 2007, Mumbai, Maharashtra, Inde, p. 26 (2007)
22. Zhao, Q.A., Stasko, J.T.: Evaluating image filtering based techniques in media space applications. In: Proceedings of the 1998 ACM Conference on Computer Supported Cooperative Work, pp. 11–18 (1998)

Self-adaptive Architectures of Building Management Systems: Approaches, Methods, Algorithms

Aliaksei Andrushevich[1], Ralf Salomon[2], and Alexander Klapproth[1]

[1] CEESAR-iHomeLab, Lucerne University of Applied Sciences and Arts, Technikumstr. 21,
6048 Horw, Switzerland
{aliaksei.andrushevich,alexander.klapproth}@hslu.ch
[2] University of Rostock, 18051 Rostock, Germany
ralf.salomon@uni-rostock.de

Abstract. This paper describes the ideas, approaches, first results derived from ongoing research in the area of adaptive Building Management Systems (BMS).

Keywords: Self-adaptive architectures, building management systems, Ambient / Building Intelligence, user interaction, autonomic computing

1   A Clear Formulation of the Research Question

Humans have a very limited natural environment acceptance range first for survival and second to feel comfortable. The methods for keeping environmental parameters at human-acceptable levels are always dictated by the level of available technologies.

The Building Management System (BMS) is a modern method / technology to control the building comfort parameters by orchestrating the available Building Automation Systems (BAS) composed of energy distribution and transformation devices, heating-ventilation and air conditioning (HVAC) systems, lighting, window / door controls, white ware, consumer electronics, etc.

The approaches, methods and algorithms to solve the conflict between user comfort and energy consumption / efficiency of buildings and houses are the grounding question of my research. Increasing the energy efficiency of buildings means delivering the same user comfort level as modern BMS does while reducing the amount of energy consumed.

2   Identification of the Significant Problems in the Field of Research

In my research, I address the question of user-oriented and energy efficient control of the comfort level in buildings. More concretely, I come to the following three significant problems of the modern BMS based on the background described in Section 1:

R. Wichert, K. Van Laerhoven, J. Gelissen (Eds.): AmI 2011 Workshops, CCIS 277, pp. 302–307, 2012.
© Springer-Verlag Berlin Heidelberg 2012

1. *Lack of adaptability.* Daily operation of modern BMS / BAS is nowadays mostly based on rules and schedules that are typically pre-configured during the construction commissioning phase. However, fixed and static control rules usually do not consider individual building users' preferences, their behavioral changes or the current state of the external environment.
2. *Little focus on interaction between user and building, or Human-Building Interaction (HBI).* The user is not properly informed about BMS actions or the information coming from BMS often requires significant understanding and interpretation efforts. Moreover, the user does not often have the control to influence the system. As a result, the user acceptance factor is rather low.
3. *Lack of self-managing properties.* Typical modern BMS often requires technically qualified personnel for its installation, configuration and maintenance. As a result the BMS operation costs are rather high.

3   Current Knowledge of the Domain, the State of Existing Solutions

The research area of adaptive BMS is highly interdisciplinary and is composed of knowledge from the domains of Building Information Modeling and Simulation, Ambient Intelligence (AmI), Knowledge Representation, Semantic Web, Multi-Agent Systems, User Behavior Models, Autonomic Computing, Context-Aware Middleware, and Wireless Sensor Networks to name a few. Here I will only elaborate on the most relevant developments to the newly proposed approaches in Section 4.

The concept of context awareness and its implementation as context-aware systems [1] create the basic input for improving adaptability, interaction and self-managing. Service Oriented Architectures (SOA) is the state-of-the art for implementation of open flexible architectures. Practically, researchers from the AmI field [2] adopt algorithms and methods from Artificial Intelligence (AI) research, such as machine learning and pattern recognition [3], into the low-power low-cost distributed sensing and actuating infrastructure offered by research in pervasive / ubiquitous computing.

As possible technical approach, the IBM's autonomic computing (AC) [4] paradigm formalizes and systemizes the key features of self-adaptive systems. Further, the usage of multi-agent systems (dynamic) combined with ontologies (static) is a common implementation method for distributed ad-hoc smart environments [5].

Ideologically, AmI research is user-centric and hence heavily focused on the user interaction and positive user experience. One of the recent developments [6] is an open distributed framework for adaptive user interaction developed within the PERSONA project considering implicit vs. explicit interaction, used modalities, interaction objects, device choice, scheduling, goal vs. function oriented interaction.

According to [7], the user acceptance is strongly dependent on the system's ability to adapt to individual user preferences and interactions. The basic idea for considering user preferences is to integrate the user behavior and interaction in building performance. Earlier static building models had already tried to incorporate the user activities in the past [8]. Also industry foundation classes contain person static descriptions. More recent developments introduced the modeling and simulation of the dynamic individual user behavior [9] and validate it with real user activities in buildings. The interesting hypothesis in [10] claims that addressing the individual user means to model and simulate the extreme behavior limits instead of average user preferences that are often used in building performance simulations nowadays.

4   Preliminary Ideas, Proposed Approach and the Results So Far

To address the problems of *adaptability* and *self-management* I introduced the architecture of Semantic Buildings [11]. The SB functional core uses a multi-agent architecture for goal-driven service allocation and control. The goal is to unite the comprehensive view for the diversity of building automation (BA) applications. The new semantic view in BA allows viewing buildings as autonomic intelligent entities with their own semantic goals like comfort, energy efficiency, safety and security. A reasoning and resolution engine for optimal service allocation is based on a service semantics description and uses classification, association and mapping of higher goals stored in semantic goals ontology.

The information retrieval framework [12] for Semantic Buildings based on fuzzy logic is meant to contribute to solving the *HBI* problem by providing user support through helpful recommendations and information preceding a search for context-aware data. The system concept is thought to generate user-readjusted answers on umpteen conditions. Another motivation behind is to diminish the user information overload through adaptive information filtering based on current user context.

The property of self-adaptability can be implemented using the paradigm of Autonomic Computing (AC). Researchers have already shown ways to use AC in grid architectures, pervasive computing and power management [4]. My contribution is to use the AC paradigm for a functional implementation of the intelligence component of the semantic layer in Semantic Buildings [13].

Combinatorial approaches for system composition, allocation and evolution mainly target the *self-management* problem. The suggested idea to apply hierarchical morphological multi-criteria approach for modular composition and improvement of building automation systems demonstrates [14, 15] the design process on realistic numeric example of Building Automation System (BAS).

The interaction quality between users and BMS is crucial for system acceptance. That is why the application-oriented interaction model and simple intuitive user interfaces for control and information panels are a must. The users are expected to interact implicitly through their behavior and explicitly through the dedicated user interfaces. For implicit individual sensor input and monitoring there should be a possibility to measure the current comfort parameters like light level, temperature and air quality exactly on user's physical position from indoor localization in the building. In order to address the user acceptance issues like in [16] I am developing the methods to orchestrate the available building automation technologies in a way that:

1. The user is provided with individual feedback about user actions, like visualizing the energy consumption level by actual user behavior / settings
2. Individual needs and conflicts between user preferences are recognized
3. Users have clear information and intuitive control on system decisions
4. The system is able to learn from the long-term user behavior changes
5. User satisfaction level is constantly but transparently measured

5   A Sketch of the Applied Research Methodology

The approach of classic user centered design [17] is used as research methodology:

- Analysis of user needs, environment and user context
- Development of the basic prototype and typical users
- Development of simple usage scenarios
- Design of interaction model and functional prototypes including user interfaces for control, information panels, and also mobile devices
- Usability-tests of scenarios and prototypes in the iHomeLab Living Lab
- Design iteration development update based on the usability-tests
- Field usability-tests
- Design iteration development update based on the usability-tests

The usability-tests will be done according to the well-defined usability criteria [18, 19]. User satisfaction can be measured using the online questionnaire with questions from the relevant study on user satisfaction in office buildings [16].

6   Ph.D. Project's Contribution to the Problem Solution

Through the contributions of this Ph.D. project, the properties of adaptability, user interaction, and self-managing behavior will appear in the next generations of BMS.

The adaptability will be achieved through a combination of flexible Semantic Building architecture with Artificial Intelligence based information retrieval mechanisms and simulated / real involvement of the user behavior. The unique combination of the user and context / situation recognition based on the flexibility of Service Oriented Architecture and ability for self-learning will create a new level of the transparence in the HBI's user feedback as well. Self-managing issues including the feedback from the user will be addressed through combinatorial methods to secure the optimal BMS composition, operation and evolution. The user-centered design research methodology for BMS development shall ensure the involvement of end-users from the very early stage of analysis to the later stages of development, validation, and testing of use scenarios that will be reflected by positive user experiences during the operation of future BMS.

As a result of all measures, the future BMS will reduce the energy consumption of buildings while enhancing the comfort, security and safety in a user-friendly way.

7   A Discussion of How the Suggested Solution is Different, New, or Better as Compared to Existing Approaches to the Problem

Based on the input from user identification and indoor localization subsystems, the adaptive BMS is able to automatically learn about different user situations / contexts with the goal to forecast the trends and adapt the BAS parameters accordingly. The adaptive BMS automatically chooses between different strategies, algorithms and approaches to make the optimal control decisions. The proposed architectures for adaptive BMS are also specially tackled to the conflict resolution between multiple building users. Adaptive transparent HBI also contributes to increased user acceptance and leads to sustainable energy- and safety-aware behavior of the user.

The existing BMSes generally do not consider users in their run-time. The proposed user-centric solution with self-learning abilities moves to recognize and predict the context, intentions and wishes of the user. While still preserving the existing level of energy efficiency, safety and security, the self-adaptive architecture of BMS will firstly care about user satisfaction.

References

1. Baldlauf, M., Schahram, D., Rosenberg, F.: A survey on context-aware systems. Journal of Ad Hoc and Ubiquitous Computing 2(4) (June 2007)
2. Cook, D., Augusto, J., Jakkula, V.: Ambient intelligence: Technologies, applications, and opportunities. Pervasive and Mobile Computing 5(4), 277–298 (2009)
3. Aztina, A., Izaguirre, A., Augusto, J.C.: Learning Patterns in Ambient Intelligence Environments: a Survey. Artificial Intelligence Review 34(1), 35–51 (2010)
4. Huebscher, M.C., McCann, J.A.: A Survey of Autonomic Computing—Degrees, Models, and Applications. ACM Computing Survey 40(3), Article 7 (2008)
5. Cook, D.: Multi-agent smart environments. Journal of Ambient Intelligence and Smart Environments 1(1), 51–55 (2009)
6. Tazari, M.-R.: An Open Distributed Framework for Adaptive User Interaction in Ambient Intelligence. In: de Ruyter, B., Wichert, R., Keyson, D.V., Markopoulos, P., Streitz, N., Divitini, M., Georgantas, N., Mana Gomez, A. (eds.) AmI 2010. LNCS, vol. 6439, pp. 227–238. Springer, Heidelberg (2010)
7. Hewitt, D., Higgins, C., Heatherly, P., Turner, C.: A Market-Friendly Post-Occupancy Evaluation: Building Performance Report. In: C 10091, New Buildings Institute (2005)
8. Eckholm, A., Fridquist, S.: A concept of space for building classification, product modeling, and design. Automation and Construction 9, 315–328 (2000)
9. Tabak, V.: User Simulation of Space Utilisation: System for Office Building Usage Simulation. Dissertation, TU Eindhoven (2009)
10. Zimmermann, G.: Modeling and simulation of individual user behavior for building performance predictions. In: Proc. of SCSC, San Diego, CA, USA, pp. 913–920 (2007)
11. Andrushevich, A., Staub, M., Kistler, R., Klapproth, A.: Towards semantic buildings: Goal-driven approach for building automation service allocation and control. In: Proceedings of IEEE Conference on Emerging Technologies and Factory Automation, pp. 1–6 (September 2010)

12. Andrushevich, A., Fercu, M., Hopf, J., Portmann, E., Klapproth, A.: Prometheus Framework for Fuzzy Information Retrieval in Semantic Spaces. In: Hippe, Z.S., Kulikowski, J.L., Mroczek, T. (eds.) Human – Computer Systems Interaction, Part I. AISC, vol. 98, pp. 183–199. Springer, Heidelberg (2012)
13. Andrushevich, A., Tomek, S., Klapproth, A.: The Autonomic Computing Paradigm in Adaptive Building / Ambient Intelligence Systems. In: Keyson, D.V., Maher, M.L., Streitz, N., Cheok, A., Augusto, J.C., Wichert, R., Englebienne, G., Aghajan, H., Kröse, B.J.A. (eds.) AmI 2011. LNCS, vol. 7040, pp. 98–104. Springer, Heidelberg (2011)
14. Levin, M., Andrushevich, A., Klapproth, A.: Composition of management system for smart homes. Journal for Information Processes 10(1), 78–86 (2010)
15. Levin, M., Andrushevich, A., Klapproth, A.: Improvement of Building Automation System. In: Mehrotra, K.G., Mohan, C.K., Oh, J.C., Varshney, P.K., Ali, M. (eds.) IEA/AIE 2011, Part II. LNCS, vol. 6704, pp. 459–468. Springer, Heidelberg (2011)
16. Gossauer, E.: Nutzerzufriedenheit in Bürogebäuden. Dissertation, TH Karlsruhe (2008)
17. Nielsen, J.: Usability Engineering. Morgan Kaufmann Publishers, San Francisco (1993)
18. ISO 9241-11:1998 Ergonomic requirements for office work with visual display terminals (VDTs) – Part 11: Guidance on usability
19. ISO/IEC 18021:2002 Information technology – User interfaces for mobile tools for management of database communications in a client-server model

A Pattern Language of Firefighting Frontline Practice to Inform the Design of Ubiquitous Computing

Sebastian Denef[1, 2]

[1]Fraunhofer FIT, Germany
sebastian.denef@fit.fraunhofer.de
[2]TU Delft, Netherlands

Abstract. This research studies firefighting frontline practice and the effects on this practiceposed by the introduction of computing systems.As the central result, a pattern languagedescribes the practice as an overall configuration. The languageallows for discussing changes and potential impactswhen designing computing systems for frontline firefighters.

Keywords: Ethnography, Ubiquitous Computing, Firefighting.

1   Research Problem

Ubiquitous computing solutions have the potential to provide viable support to firefighters working on the frontline. As of today, little information technology (IT) support exists for such hazardous environments.

The work context on the frontline of an intervention poses a complex set of requirements for the design of IT systems. Fighting fire is a multi-faceted task in a hazardous environment that changes dynamically during an intervention. The work on the frontline requires a set of very specific skills and tools. It is often conducted in buildings full of smoke, which can only be accessed by crawling on the floor due to the heat distribution.

While current IT research targeting the firefighting domain proposes systems to support navigation, health monitoring or communication (e.g. [13, 17]), designing meaningful support to firefighters working on the frontline remains an open challenge.Some researchers avoid the constraints of the frontline by focusing on the part of the firefighting that takes place in relatively safe and less restrictive environments [12].Other research projects target the frontlinebut use firefighting scenarios only as a motivation or explanation for the need of a certain technological development [10, 18]. The little work that specifically focuses on technology for the frontlinetakes outcertain aspects but does not consider overall firefighting practice such as the collaborative nature of the job[15].Firefighting practice is, however, very likely to be negatively affected by systems that do not take into account the full complexity of the task and the challenges posed by the work environment.As a result and despite promising visions and the ongoing research efforts, firefighting on the frontline, to this day,remains an activity with almost no IT support.

Supervisor: David V. Keyson[2], ReinhardOppermann[1].

R. Wichert, K. Van Laerhoven, J. Gelissen (Eds.): AmI 2011 Workshops, CCIS 277, pp. 308–312, 2012.

While introducing technology into this life-threatening work contextshows not to be an easy task, firefighters themselves are experts on how to deal with the challenging environment. Current practices are the results of long time experiences, with firefighting as a profession dating back to ancient Rome [11].Leveraging this experience when designing tools has the potential to be highly beneficial.It is, however, not trivial to grasp and communicate experience embedded in work practice and to understand the relation and relevance for the design of ubiquitous computing technology. On the one hand, firefighters know how to successfully accomplish their missions using existing tools but they may not be able to explain the intrinsic principles of their work and lack experience with the design of novel tools.On the other hand, technology designers know little about a work context fairly different from their daily experiences and yet are confronted with the challenge to provide meaningful tools.This gap leaves the design spacefor ubiquitous computing support on the frontlineyet to be discovered.

The aim of this thesis is therefore tobuild a theoretical foundation to understand existing firefighting frontline practice and the reaction of this social configuration to technological changesposed by ubiquitous computing systems. Thisthesis addresses the questions:*How do frontline firefighters successfully cope with the hazardous work environment that they are confronted with? How is this existing practice being influenced by ubiquitous computing technologies? What can we learn from the interaction between new technologies and existing practice for the design of future ubiquitous computing systems?*

2   Methods

This research is guided by the works of Erickson [9] and Crabtree et al.[4] intheir interpretation of Alexander's work [1, 2] to understand the configuration of environments and to guide, inspire and reflect design by means of patterns of events derived from ethnographic data.

For Alexander, any environment, any system can be describes as a configuration of interacting patterns. In this original interpretation, patterns are not primarily distinct rules or best practices as they have been introduced to the field of software engineering; instead they are a means to learn about the configuration of a working whole.

Referring to Alexander, Erickson suggests patterns for Human-Computer Interaction Research (HCI) as the building blocks of a lingua franca in interaction design and presents exemplary patterns of collaborative office work [9]. Rooted in ethnographic research, patterns form a bridge between designers and users and inform change processes posed by ICT. A pattern language can be used "for discussing changes and reflecting on their possible impacts, both in terms of the activities of the organization, and in terms of the qualities of work life which its members value." [9]

In the same spirit, Crabtree et al. point to patterns of social action as a means "for structuring and presenting ethnographic fieldwork" [4 p265] that can make "unsupported use practices available to the design of future technological arrangements in place." [4 p269]

To solidify the methodology of pattern research, *grounded theory*, as a qualitative method to identify patterns in empirical data, and *action research*[3], as a concept that allows studying the interaction between new technologies and existing practice, are applied to conduct and analyze workshops with French and German firefighters at professional training facilities and fire stations.The workshops comprise *ethnographic studies* to understand firefighting from an observer's perspective, *empathic exercises* [19]to gain a hands-on experience of firefighting practice andthe introduction of *triggering artifacts*[14]to learn from changes posed by the new technology. Video and audio recordings and notes from the workshops form the empirical base and feed intoan open coding process that leads to the formation of the pattern language offirefighting frontline practice.

The reflective analysis of the participatory design process of a navigation support system for frontline firefighters and the discussion of other novel system proposals for frontline firefighters with developers helps to understand the value of the pattern language for informing the design processes.

3   Expected Contributions

The result of this research should support both technology designers and practitioners in jointly designing novel, meaningful computing systems. The thesis serves technology designers as an insight into existing practice, a starting point for envisioning systems, an analytical lens when deciding on what to design or when evaluating improving existing system. Practitioners gain a formalized description of their work practice that they can use to reflect on introducing new technology and changing practice. Also, the results can serve as a means to facilitate communication between the two parties.

The central outcome of the research is a language of patterns that describe qualities inherent in frontline firefighting as a guide and inspiration for the design of ubiquitous computing systems.

Apart from the firefighting context, the research provides an example of how to approach a complex work practice and connect ethnographic studies with a design process.

4   Achieved Results

Over a period of three years, I have collected data in 21 workshops with firefighters with the firefighters in Paris, France at their training center and fire station in St. Denis and with the firefighters of Cologne, Germany.In Germany studies were conducted at a local fire stationin Cologne that includes a heat training facility and at Europe's most advanced firefighting training facility, the firefighting school of the state of North-Rhine-Westphalia in Münster, Germany. The facility allows simulating entire interventions close to real world conditions. Additionally, I joined exercises with firefighters in a subway tunnel, at a chemical plant and at a container port terminal.

As part of the workplace studies, I learned aboutthe work practice in search and rescue missions[7] and analyzed the equipment and tools used by firefighters to extract the qualities that make these tools fit the challenging environment [6]. Results of the empathy-building approach, including the role-playing of an entire intervention and trainings in hazardous conditions with real fire can be found in [7] and [8].

Change-oriented studies included the introduction of a wizard-of-oz based navigation and command system. A firefighting commander received a visualization of all the exact positions of each of his troops during a simulated mission in a firefighting training facility. A description of the studyand its results can be found in [7]. Also, I tested a novel commercial system that allows firefighters to find comrades in cases of emergency in a scenario for search and rescue missions. An experience prototype for visual feedback inside the SCBA mask has beenconstructedand evaluated with firefighters.

Using the constant comparative method, I have analyzed the data and described initial patterns that describe how firefighters organize their work. The recently completed pattern language comprises 16 patterns, some of which have been presented in [5]. The languagedetails how firefighters organize the division of tasks and roles, how they deal with information in a dynamic environment, how they form a social binding and how they improvise, provide safety and prepare their work.

The language has been evaluated in two ways. First, the understanding of the practice that has been captured in interacting patterns directly impacted a participatory design process with firefighters constructing a navigation support system. In collaboration with firefighters initial concepts were revised and the current prototype described in [16] linksclosely tothe existingnavigation practice. Second, the pattern languagehas been used as a communicative means to reviewnovel technology concepts for frontline firefighters with developers who had no prior knowledge of the practice.

Answering the research questions, the pattern language shows how firefighters combine an *order of stiff hierarchies and procedures* that enable them to act promptly with *fluid elements of situated innovation* that allow them to flexibly adapt to changes in the environment. This *fluid order* is a crucial element of the practice but easily to be disturbed with new computing systems. Better monitoring capabilities, for instance, can lead to a decreased independence of the engaging teams. Computing systems to support frontline firefighting, therefore, need to be support the existing*fluid order* to provide meaningful support.

References

[1] Alexander, C.: The timeless way of building, p. 552. Oxford University Press, New York (1979)
[2] Alexander, C.: The Nature of Order, Book 1: The Phenomenon of Life. Center for Environmental Structure, Berkeley (2002)
[3] Baskerville, R., Pries-Heje, J.: Grounded action research: a method for understanding IT in practice. Accounting, Management and Information Technologies 9(1), 1–23 (1999)

[4] Crabtree, A., Hemmings, T., Rodden, T.: Pattern-based support for interactive design in domestic settings. In: Proc. DIS 2002: Processes, Practices, Methods, and Techniques, pp. 265–276. ACM, London (2002)

[5] Denef, S., Keyson, D.V., Oppermann, R.: Rigid Structures, Independent Units, Monitoring: Organizing Patterns of Frontline Firefighting to Inform the Design of Ubiquitous Computing. In: Proc. CHI 2011, pp. 1949–1958. ACM, NYC (2011)

[6] Denef, S., Ramirez, L., Dyrks, T.: Letting Tools Talk: Interactive Technology for Firefighting. In: Ext. Abstr. of CHI 2009, pp. 444–447. ACM, NYC (2009)

[7] Denef, S., Ramirez, L., Dyrks, T., Stevens, G.: Handy navigation in ever-changings Spaces: an ethnographic study of firefighting practices. In: Proc. DIS 2008, pp. 184–192. ACM, Cape Town (2008)

[8] Dyrks, T., Ramirez, L., Denef, S.: Designing for Firefighters—Building Empathy through Live Action Role-Playing. In: Abstracts ISCRAM 2009, Gothenburg, Sweden, May 10-13 (2009)

[9] Erickson, T.: Lingua Francas for design: sacred places and pattern languages. In: Proc. DIS 2000. ACM Press (2000)

[10] Jiang, X., Chen, N.Y., Hong, J.I., Wang, K., Takayama, L., Landay, J.A.: Siren: Context-aware Computing for Firefighting. In: Ferscha, A., Mattern, F. (eds.) PERVASIVE 2004. LNCS, vol. 3001, pp. 87–105. Springer, Heidelberg (2004)

[11] Kenlon, J.: Fires And Fire-Fighters; A History Of Modern Fire-Fighting With A Review Of Its Development From Earliest Times. Young Press (2008)

[12] Landgren, J., Nulden, U.: A study of emergency response work: patterns of mobile phone interaction. In: Proceedings of the SIGCHI Conference on Human Factors in Computing Systems, pp. 1323–1332. ACM, NYC (2007)

[13] Landmarke. landmarke project (2008), http://landmarke-projekt.de (cited August 17, 2010)

[14] Mogensen, P., Robinson, M.: Triggering Artefacts. AI & Society 9, 373–388 (1995)

[15] Naghsh, A.M., Roast, C.R.: Designing user interaction with robots swarms in emergency settings. In: Proc. NordiCHI 2008, pp. 519–522. ACM (2008)

[16] Ramirez, L., Denef, S., Dyrks, T.: Towards Human-Centered Support for Indoor Navigation. In: Proc. CHI 2009, pp. 1279–1282. ACM, Boston (2009)

[17] U2010. Ubiquitous, I.P.: Centric Government & Enterprise Next Generation Networks (2008), http://www.efipsans.eu/ (cited August 17, 2010)

[18] Wilson, J., Bhargava, V., Redfern, A., Wright, P.: A Wireless Sensor Network and Incident Command Interface for Urban Firefighting. In: Mobile and Ubiquitous Systems: Networking & Services, MobiQuitous 2007. IEEE Computer Society (2007)

[19] Wright, P., McCarthy, J.: Empathy and experience in HCI. In: Proc. CHI 2008, pp. 637–646. ACM, Florence (2008)

Understanding Total Hip Replacement Recovery towards the Design of a Context-Aware System

Juan Jimenez Garcia

Delft University of Technology, Department of Industrial Design Engineering,
ID-StudioLab, Landberstraat 15 2628 CE Delft, The Netherlands
j.c.jimenezgarcia@tudelft.nl

Abstract. Total Hip Replacement (THR) is a common procedure to improve the mobility of elderly with osteoarthritis. Presently information about the recovery process after discharge is unclear. As consequence patients and physiotherapists face uncertainties to follow an adequate trajectory for recovery. Current methods for measuring recovery outcomes do not assess individual experiences over time. This research aims to design, implement and evaluate a context-aware system supporting patients undergoing recovery at home. In order to define the functional requirements of the system, a research tool was developed to gain an understanding of patients' experiences during the recovery process. The findings gathered thus far suggest that the next step involves the design of a richer communicational tool between the THR patient and the physiotherapist.

Keywords: Total Hip Replacement, recovery, context-aware systems, Experience Sampling Method.

1 Introduction

The Total Hip Replacement (THR) is a common surgery for osteoarthritis (OA) [1]. It reduces pain and stiffness of the hip providing the patient with the ability to lead physically comfortable and independent living. The new advances in surgery and the increase of in-patient care costs tend to lead to shorter hospitalization period. This paradigm shift in healthcare has its consequences, one of them being unclear information around the patient's recovery experience during rehabilitation at home [2]. In this context, physiotherapists find it difficult to prioritize care-related needs of individual patients sending them home without adequate educational preparation to self-manage their recovery and at the same time making them responsible for achieving the expected results [3]. The recovery outcomes are measured using standardized questionnaires and observed performance-related tests [4]. These methods have been reported with strong validity, however, their limitations have been also documented. First, these methods only reflect cross-population health outcomes in a particular time, overlooking individual daily life experiences [4,5]. THR, as many other conditions, are strongly related to the personal and emotional experience during recovery. Also, these methods capture snapshots situations prior and post surgery,

R. Wichert, K. Van Laerhoven, J. Gelissen (Eds.): AmI 2011 Workshops, CCIS 277, pp. 313–317, 2012.
© Springer-Verlag Berlin Heidelberg 2012

overlooking meaningful changes overtime. Finally, these methods rely on patients' ability to recall past situations increasing the possibility to report inaccurate information [6].

The goals of this PhD project include research, development and implementation of a context-aware system to support physical and psychological conditions of patients undergoing recovery at home. This system measures physical activity in free-living conditions of THR patients. It not only captures motion parameters of the user, but also self-organizes and processes data into an in-situ wireless network to extract relevant features, applies distributed inference to assess the physical activity and condition of the user, and eventually provides real-time feedback. The success to implement this system requires to first understand and maximize information regarding patients' functional, psychological, social and emotional situation during their recovery. The premise of the current research is construed upon an observation that the methods used by clinicians are inadequate for helping researchers and physiotherapists to understand patients' experiences during the recovery.

Therefore, the presented work describes ESTHER, a tool based on Experience Sampling Method (ESM) [7] that is able to describe the situation of the patient, the changes of factors throughout the recovery period, and the influences of issues related to patient's emotional transition. The results should then become a basis for the design and development of a context-aware tool supporting and coaching the patient during the recovery process, facilitating the communication patient-physiotherapist, and helping to grasp richer information for their daily life and practice.

2   Research Approach

The design of the envisioned system is challenging both from the technological and design perspective in terms of identifying user needs. A user-centred approach steered by Design Inclusive Research paradigm [8] is taken to address this challenge. The project outline is built upon an incremental and iterative approach towards the design and contextual evaluation of the proposed solutions with patients (see: Fig. 1).

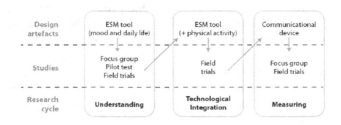

Fig. 1. The outline of the design process including three research cycles, in which the designed artifacts are iteratively tested in the field

The goal of the present research cycle is to reach an understanding regarding patients' recovery process. To achieve this goal, the following research questions need to be addressed: a)how can we capture the qualitative indicators from patients' everyday experiences and emotions when undergoing recovery at home?, and b) how can we fill in the current gap regarding the process of identifying patient's recovery patterns? To answer these questions we propose to build ESTHER (Experience Sampling for Total Hip Replacement). This first design iteration is based on ESM, exploring in-situ and in the field the context of THR. It enables patients to capture their experiences such as daily events, moods and needs in relation to their hip recovery and regarding a particular moment in time or event.

ESM is seen as reliable method and relatively highly accepted in health care [9]. Using portable and context-aware technologies this method offers a number of advantages: it allows the researcher to approach the patient at opportune moments by triggering questions at specific events and to provide feedback only when needed. Such a communication can be executed using portable computing devices, using scheduled self-report entries and keeping as low level of user's demand of input as possible. Body sensors can be implemented to complement this data loop being more aware about patients' current status and activities.

2.1   Development of a Design-Research Tool

ESTHER samples automatically data on a fixed interval schedule. Four prompts are equally spread over the day every 4 hours based on 4 recognizable daily life moments: 1) at waking up, 2) before/after lunch, 3) tea time, and 4) before to go to bed. A prompt is composed by an open question: "how are you doing?"following by an open/close question that uses a pictorial-avatar mood diagram (PMRI)[10], asking participants to position themselves in the diagram, and to explain their choice. These prompts were built as a step-by-step interactive application embedded in a touch-screen device (tablet). These devices have shown interesting results in ubiquitous and pervasive technologies [11,12]. For this tool, it enables simple data collection, and providing a more intuitive way to interact with the questions.

The novelty of this approach is three-fold: It is sensitive enough to capture individual experiences of patients; it explores the recovery as a continuous process when collecting patients' experiences over time; and it depicts small changes in daily based experiences. These qualities are something that has not being investigated by traditional methods.

2.2   Evaluation of the Tool

Three different test settings were arranged to evaluate the understanding, technical reliability, and use potential of the tool. First, a focus group was organized with 6 elderly with the main goal to test the understanding and improve usability issues of the tool. Next, a pilot study was set with 1 THR patient with the purpose of testing the technical improvements. Finally, a case study was conducted with two volunteer elderly patients (1 male, 1 female) for two weeks immediately after the discharge with the purpose of collecting material from realistic scenarios, and thus, analyse the sensitivity ability of the tool. For this case study, three types of data collection techniques were used: patients' reports on the application, semi-structured interviews, and informal feedback such as researcher visits and phone calls. The patients' inputs were qualitatively analysed (response rate, average lengths of the reports, time between the prompts and responses) and quantitatively analysed by means of a coding analysis (Grounded Theory technique) [13]. The coding scheme defined dimensions of recovery: *hip function* (pain, mobility, rest), *psychological* (ways of coping, resources, recovery, dependence), *social* (social life, social roles), *context* (atmosphere) and *general health* (Body) were identified throughout every patient response. Each code was also qualified as positive or negative to identify the effect on the recovery. This coding scheme was defined by two researchers in a number of iterations, and then triangulated by a third researcher. This analysis aims to provide evidence of ESTHER to inform relevant information for patients and physiotherapists over the recovery process.

3   Findings and Future Work

The results to date provide evidence of ESTHER is a sensible tool to capture several factors that affect the recovery process; their level of intensity over time, as well as high granularity to inform about individual experiences. It was identified that three dimensions (*functional, psychological and social*) are aligned to qualitative studies about the determinants of THR [14,15] Data analysis uncovered two additional dimensions that are not considered by standardized scores describing situations related to the context and external factors that also affect the recovery and trigger emotional states: *context*, such as home feeling; and *general health*, such as bruises or fever. It was observed that mood reports highlights over the patients' inputs. When a high arousal mood was observed, it reflected important events during recovery. On the other hand, when the recovery is going normal moods reports remain at medium arousal level. The results also showed nuances between the patients. For instance, personal and medical background influenced the provided reports. The analysis of interviews and informal feedback offered initial insights regarding motivation strategies that could be applied during communication between the physiotherapist and the elderly patients. The intrinsic motivation patients have for using the application on regular basis is that they look for ways to share knowledge and communicate issues regarding their recovery to others. The interviews disclosed that patients feel motivated to help others to achieve their goals.

We acknowledge that larger cases studies are needed to generalize these findings. However, the tool and the data it collects appear to be a source of rich information with the potential to help patients and physiotherapists during recovery process. The dynamic ability of ESTHER in collecting sensitive data can be used to systematically inform and notify the patient and the physiotherapist about the on-going process of recovery, and to raise flags critical situations.

Future research cycles will focus on an incremental capability of ESTHER in collecting and informing recovery process to both the patient and the physiotherapist. The use of this source of data over the five recovery dimensions pursue the design of a system that offers assistive mechanisms to guide and support the daily life of patients' recovery and optimize physiotherapists' practice. On-body sensors (inertial and pressure sensors on the shoe sole) aim to complement the subjective data that ESTHER is being captured. This integration contemplates the challenge of creating a communication and motivational tool for the patient. Therefore, motivational strategies should be integrated in the feedback for the following iterations. A second challenge is to better define the prompts to generate a tool than can automatically infer/indicate the route of recovery of the patient.

Acknowledgments. I would like to thank Hester Anderiesen and Natalia Romero for their contribution as researchers in the analysis of the collected data, and SENIOR consortium.

References

1. Wong, J., Wong, S., Brooks, E., Yabsley, R.H.: Home readiness and recovery pattern after total hip replacement. Journal of Orthopaedic Nursing 3(4), 210–219 (1999)
2. Stevens, M., Spriensma, A., Boss, A., Diercks, R.: The Groningen Orthopedic Exit Strategy (GOES): a home-based support program for total knee arthroplasty patients after shortened hospital stay. Patient Education Counseling 54, 95 (2004)
3. Fielden, J.M., Scott, S., Horne, J.G.: An Investigation of Patient Satisfaction Following Discharge After Total Hip Replacement Surgery. Orthopedic Nursing 22, 429–436 (2003)
4. Parent, E., Moffet, H.: Comparative responsiveness of locomotor tests and questionnaires used to follow early recovery after total knee arthroplasty. Archives of Physical Medicine and Rehabilitation 83(1), 70–80 (2002)
5. Stratford, P.W., Kennedy, D., Pagura, S.M., Gollish, J.D.: The Relationship Between Self-Report and Performance-Related Measures: Questioning the Content Validity of Timed Tests. Arthritis Care and Research: the Official Journal of the Arthritis Health Professions Association 49(4), 535–540 (2003)
6. Cole, B., Finch, E., Gowland, C., Mayo, N.: Physical Rehabilitation Outcome Measures. Canadian Physiotherapy Association, Toronto (1994)
7. Hektner, J.M., Schmidt, J.A., Csikszentmihalyi, M.: Experience Sampling Method: Measuring the Quality of Everyday Life. Sage Publications, London (2007)
8. Horváth, I.: Comparison of three methodological approaches of design research. In: International Conference on Engineering Design, ICED 2007, pp. 28–31 (2007)
9. Csikszentmihalyi, M., Larson, R.: Validity and reliability of the Experience Sampling Method. The Journal of Nervous and Mental Disease 175, 526–536 (1987)
10. Vastenburg, M.H., Romero, N.: PMRI: Development of a Pictorial Mood Reporting Instrument. Work in Progress. CHI 2011 Extended Abstracts Proceedings, Presented at the CHI (2011)
11. Greenstein, J.S., Arnaut, L.Y.: Input Devices. In: Helander, M. (ed.) Handbook of Human-Computer Interaction. North Holland, Amsterdam (1988)
12. Basdogan, C., Srinivasan, M.A.: Haptic rendering in virtual environments. In: Stanney, K. (ed.) Handbook of Virtual Environments. Lawrence Erlbaum, Inc., London (2002)
13. Corbin, J., Strauss, A.: Grounded theory research: Procedures, canons, and evaluative criteria. Qualitative Sociology 13, 3–21 (1990)
14. Grant, S., St John, W., Patterson, E.: Recovery From Total Hip Replacement Surgery: "It's Not Just Physical". Qualitative Health Research 19, 1612–1620 (2009)
15. Montin, L., Suominen, T., Leino-Kilpi, H.: The experiences of patients undergoing total hip replacement. Journal of Orthopaedic Nursing 6(1), 23–29 (2002)

Model-Based Evaluation of Adaptive User Interfaces

Michael Quade

DAI-Labor, Technische Universität Berlin
Ernst-Reuter-Platz 7, 10587 Berlin, Germany
michael.quade@dai-labor.de

Abstract. This thesis presents an approach for the automated usability evaluation of model-based adaptive user interfaces. The described approach is supposed to be used complementary to custom evaluations at development time. By combining a user model with user interface models from a model-based development framework, providing different adaptation alternatives, interaction can be simulated and evaluated accordingly. This way, no additional descriptions of the application need to be created for the evaluation. As a result the complexity and costs for applying an automated usability evaluation can be reduced significantly.

Keywords: Automated Usability Evaluation, Model-based Adaptive User Interfaces.

1 Problem Description

With the constant increase of computation power, software applications and their potential usage for a vast amount of different activities tend to become more complex. In the past years, former stand-alone computer systems have been evolving into everyday appliances and are becoming parts of our daily lives [17,1]. Such ubiquitous spaces are commonly described as smart environments and are characterized by different physical interaction devices and multiple networked applications. Poorly designed user interfaces (UI) of such interactive applications might frustrate and irritate their users. As a result certain parts of the applications might not be used at all. Consequently, all applications that make up a smart environment need to present required information properly and tailored to the current users' needs and their abilities [13]. The majority of these newly arising demands are currently approached by the development of adaptive applications which aim at providing UIs that are able to adapt to users instead of requiring users to adapt to the UI. However, this also poses new demands on the evaluation of these adaptive applications.

In general, adaptive applications are described as being able to adapt to the current context-of-use in order to cope with the increasing complexity and diversity gathered by sensor mechanisms and via knowledge about their users. Nevertheless, detailed information about end users and their influence on the interaction, e.g. vision, hearing and motor capabilities, are hard to foresee by

R. Wichert, K. Van Laerhoven, J. Gelissen (Eds.): AmI 2011 Workshops, CCIS 277, pp. 318–322, 2012.
© Springer-Verlag Berlin Heidelberg 2012

the designer. Especially the high complexity within the context-of-use leads to problems with fully evaluating adaptive applications with common approaches like *user tests*, *heuristic evaluation* or *cognitive walkthrough*. Expensiveness, time consumption and the availability of appropriate participants are the main drawbacks of user tests. In difference to this, approaches based on expert evaluations require evaluators who have deep insight knowledge of the domain and the applied methodology. In general, usability evaluations are based on iterative cycles of implementation and evaluation. Therefore, they usually require a lot of time to be applied conveniently on adaptive UIs when being carried out separately.

As a result from this trend towards adaptive applications, there is an emerging need for automated usability evaluation (AUE). In difference to custom usability evaluations, AUE can be used to uncover various types of errors more consistently than different experts would do and the coverage of features to be evaluated can also be increased [8]. This becomes especially true when the multitude of different combinations of parameters needs to be considered, e.g. users, task and UI. While there are also AUE methods which assist in capturing real user interaction, most promising approaches are based on predictive analytical modeling and predictive simulation [8]. Currently, there are two general streams: GOMS-based methods and cognitive architectures. The main goal of GOMS is the automated prediction of interaction time and learning time for expert interaction [11]. GOMS-based methods require a human expert to manually configure and conduct the evaluation. Using these methods, expert evaluators are able to predict parameters like interaction time depending on influencing factors such as UI layout and tasks. In order to do so, GOMS requires a set of formal descriptions covering potential configurations for each of these parameters. Yet another approach deploys cognitive architectures in the domain of AUE, e.g. ACT-R [2]. Cognitive architectures give detailed insights on how human users are processing information. Similar to GOMS, specific models of the user, the task and the UI are required, which the expert evaluator is expected to create and maintain.

While existing AUE approaches have been proven to correctly predict quantitative measures for expert interaction, some major challenges remain. A non-exhaustive list of costs for applying AUE is provided in [9]. More specifically, the main barriers of AUE adoption by interaction design industry are:

Costly and time-consuming modeling process. Current AUE approaches require additional specific descriptions of the UI and the task. In most cases, such descriptions of the UI and tasks do not exist or cannot be automatically derived from the UI by automatic routines or the (potentially unavailable) source code. Therefore, such models need to be provided by the evaluators themselves, which is a time-consuming and complex task.

Complexity of modeling process. Although the ACT-R method is powerful for specific evaluation purposes (e.g. repetitive tasks), it is hard to apply to complex tasks and general evaluations of the UI. Similar to GOMS methods, cognitive architectures are not widespread out of the laboratory due to their high effort in creating the required models and rules for cognitive processes. In fact, this is a very complex task and requires highly skilled evaluators.

A well-established approach for engineering UIs is model-based development, e.g. as proposed in [12,3,5]. Here, the core idea is to create final UIs based on abstract models of interaction means, target users and tasks. One way to address the described barriers would be to use these already existing models for the purpose of AUE. By directly using these models, my approach will bypass manually creating additional models. Manual creation of models required by AUE methods would be a tedious task and is usually not practicable for dynamic adaptive applications. Thus, within this research, I intend to explore to which extent model-based UIs can be utilized for automatic acquisition of information required for an AUE, e.g. UI layout, user tasks and interaction possibilities.

The expected contributions of my proposed thesis are as following:

- A method for interaction simulation and evaluation based on abstract UI models that are used for both UI generation and evaluation.
- Modeling, development and evaluation of an environment for AUE.
- A quantitative validation of the proposed AUE concept.

2   Related Work

CogTool [10] is used for analytical modeling with the goal of predicting execution times for specific tasks. It eases the complexity for creating required ACT-R models by manually demonstrating expert interaction on a storyboard of the UI. Therefore, different screen shots can be imported and the designer needs to manually add UI elements and task logic which still poses a complex task. These issues can be approached by using converter code in combination with mock-ups as has been demonstrated in [7]. This reduces the need to create additional models of the UI layout, but the need to demonstrate user tasks and interaction logic remains the same. In [4] an approach is described which allows predictive simulation of interaction for able-bodied and disabled users with a focus on easily applying the evaluation process for UI designers. However, creating the models still puts a crucial challenge especially in the domain of adaptive UIs. AIDE [16] is a tool which allows analyzing efficiency by integrating task information and thus comparing different design alternatives. Finally, an overview of current approaches with a focus on the inspection of underlying task models and their usage in the design process is described in [15]. While some approaches allow simulating the application's behavior and manually inspecting the interaction logic, none of them covers an integrated approach for AUE.

3   Approach

My approach for AUE will be based on a framework which utilizes models for reflecting the internal state of an adaptive application and for changing its underlying configuration at runtime [5]. Thus, as shown in Fig. 1, no additional specific models of the application's tasks *(I)* and its UI *(II-IV)* need to be created additionally as they already stem from the development process. Further, my approach employs a user model *(V-VIII)* that performs simulated interaction on specified user tasks *(VIII)* with models of interactive applications. General feasibility of the approach has been demonstrated in [6]. The user model will include a process for perception, processing and interaction *(VI)* with the UI models. During interaction, the user model performs a goal-oriented process following the *maximum rationality hypothesis* [14] by selecting goals for the simulation run which influence the actions to be performed. By using the application's task models *(I)* all required (sub-)tasks needed to fulfill the goals of interaction can be accessed directly and therefore reduce the need to provide them by hand. I am planning to further evaluate a rule-based approach *(V)*, which sets user attributes *(VII)* in relation to information from the UI and task. This way, difficulties certain users might have, e.g. due to bad vision or tremor, are formalized as rules which have an impact on the interaction process. Consequences of these rules are variations of probabilities for choosing and performing an interaction as explained in [6]. By doing so, non-expert interactions can be evaluated and reasons for interaction problems can be revealed. Finally, an interaction time prediction based on GOMS will be provided.

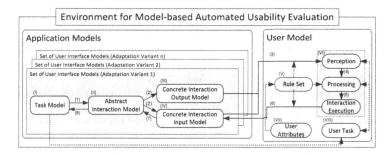

Fig. 1. Proposed components (I-VIII) of the model-based AUE environment. The chain of actions is labeled with (1-8), while dotted lines display influences between the models.

4   Future Work and Evaluation

The next steps are analyzing the required models and validating the described features. In order to enhance the rule-based approach, criteria from general guidelines, cognitive walkthrough, heuristic evaluation and user tests are considered to be integrated.

I am planning to evaluate the applicability of my approach with the help of a group of 7-10 randomly chosen UI designers, preferentially practitioners of UI development. The practitioners will have to model and evaluate specific tasks and adaptation sets for a given UI. Afterwards, subjective questionnaires have to be answered in order to collect qualitative information, e.g. the effort involved in creating the models and the time spent. Additionally, uncovered usability problems will be validated and compared to existing AUE methods. As a basis for comparison, custom usability evaluation methods, e.g. heuristic evaluation and cognitive walkthrough could be applied again.

References

1. Aarts, E., Encarnao, J.: True Visions: The Emergence of Ambient Intelligence. Springer Publishing Company, Incorporated (2008)
2. Anderson, J.R., Bothell, D., Byrne, M.D., Douglass, S., Lebiere, C., Qin, Y.: An integrated theory of the mind. Psychological Review 111(4), 1036–1060 (2004), http://dx.doi.org/10.1037/0033-295X.111.4.1036
3. Balme, L., Demeure, A., Barralon, N., Calvary, G.: CAMELEON-RT: A Software Architecture Reference Model for Distributed, Migratable, and Plastic User Interfaces. In: Markopoulos, P., Eggen, B., Aarts, E., Crowley, J.L. (eds.) EUSAI 2004. LNCS, vol. 3295, pp. 291–302. Springer, Heidelberg (2004)
4. Biswas, P., Robinson, P.: Automatic evaluation of assistive interfaces. In: Proceedings of the 13th International Conference on Intelligent user Interfaces, IUI 2008, pp. 247–256. ACM, New York (2008), http://doi.acm.org/10.1145/1378773.1378806
5. Blumendorf, M., Albayrak, S.: Towards a Framework for the Development of Adaptive Multimodal User Interfaces for Ambient Assisted Living Environments. In: Stephanidis, C. (ed.) UAHCI 2009. LNCS, vol. 5615, pp. 150–159. Springer, Heidelberg (2009)
6. Engelbrecht, K.P., Quade, M., Möller, S.: Analysis of a new simulation approach to dialog system evaluation. Speech Commun. 51(12), 1234–1252 (2009)
7. Harris, B.N., John, B.E., Brezin, J.: Human performance modeling for all: importing ui prototypes into cogtool. In: Proceedings of the 28th of the International Conference Extended Abstracts on Human Factors in Computing Systems, CHI EA 2010, pp. 3481–3486. ACM, New York (2010)
8. Ivory, M.Y., Hearst, M.A.: The state of the art in automating usability evaluation of user interfaces. ACM Comput. Surv. 33(4), 470–516 (2001)
9. John, B.E., Jastrzembski, T.: Exploration of costs and benefits of predictive human performance modeling for design. In: Proceedings of International Conference on Cognitive Modeling 2010 (2010)
10. John, B.E., Prevas, K., Salvucci, D.D., Koedinger, K.: Predictive human performance modeling made easy. In: CHI 2004: Proceedings of the SIGCHI Conference on Human Factors in Computing Systems, pp. 455–462. ACM Press, New York (2004)
11. Kieras, D.: Guide to GOMS model usability evaluation using NGOMSL. In: Helander, P., Prabhu, M. (eds.) Handbook of Human-Computer Interaction. Elsevier Science B.V. (1997)
12. Myers, B., Hudson, S.E., Pausch, R.: Past, present, and future of user interface software tools. ACM Trans. Comput.-Hum. Interact. 7(1), 3–28 (2000)
13. Nazari Shirehjini, A.A.: A Multidimensional Classification Model for the Interaction in Reactive Media Rooms. In: Jacko, J. (ed.) HCI 2007, Part III. LNCS, vol. 4552, pp. 431–439. Springer, Heidelberg (2007)
14. Newell, A.: Unified theories of cognition. Harvard University Press, Cambridge (1990)
15. Paternò, F.: Model-based tools for pervasive usability. Interacting with Computers 17(3), 291–315 (2005), http://dx.doi.org/10.1016/j.intcom.2004.06.017
16. Sears, A.: Aide: a step toward metric-based interface development tools. In: UIST 1995: Proceedings of the 8th Annual ACM Symposium on User Interface and Software Technology, pp. 101–110. ACM Press, New York (1995)
17. Weiser, M.: The computer for the 21st century. Scientific American 265(3), 66–75 (1991)

Supporting Behavior Change in Cooperative Driving

Qonita Shahab

Department of Industrial Design, Eindhoven University of Technology, P.O. Box 513,
5600MB Eindhoven, The Netherlands
q.m.shahab@tue.nl

Abstract. Cooperation among vehicles is aimed to create a smooth traffic flow
and minimize shockwaves and traffic jams. Before the technology gets mature,
cooperative driving may already be made possible by involving the drivers.
This paper reports a literature survey on two issues: 1) cooperation in traffic and
motivations in driving; 2) persuasive technology and applications of extrinsic
feedback. Informed by the literature survey, we propose concepts for supporting
driver's behavior change for the purpose of cooperative driving.

Keywords: persuasive technology, driving assistance, user-centered design.

1 Introduction

Enabling cooperation is one of the biggest challenges in traffic. If all vehicles on the
highway drive at the appropriate acceleration and distance, the traffic flow is smooth
and shockwaves are minimized reducing the probability of traffic jams. Installing
Cooperative Adaptive Cruise Control would make all vehicles behave the same, but
the technology will take some time to mature to be dispersed sufficiently to be
effective. To develop cooperation among existing vehicles today, the drivers need to
be put in the loop. The goal of the Cooperative Speed Assistance (CSA) system is to
determine, and advise drivers about, the appropriate acceleration/speed/distance of the
vehicle so that the vehicle can be part of a platoon of cooperative vehicles.

For applying proper acceleration/speed/distance, we hypothesized that drivers need
to have the ability, the opportunity and the motivation to do so. An example of
lacking one or more of these three factors is the fact that drivers tend to neglect the
dynamic speed advice displayed on signs above highways. Often they do not see the
need of complying with advisory speeds and the benefits of doing so. This
phenomenon portrays the limited awareness of drivers of the social nature of driving.
One option is to use Persuasive Technology to establish the desired behavior change
by supporting the driver's ability, informing the driver about opportunities, and
increasing the driver's motivation.

The main research question in this work is to find the What-When-How of
messages to be presented to drivers, analyzed both from cognitive and social
perspectives. In our previous research, the cognitive part of What-When-How has
been solved by using peripheral visual information and designed auditory tones. The
social part of this research has been partially tackled through speed messages and

R. Wichert, K. Van Laerhoven, J. Gelissen (Eds.): AmI 2011 Workshops, CCIS 277, pp. 323–327, 2012.
© Springer-Verlag Berlin Heidelberg 2012

explanatory messages, but these mainly address the driver's ability. The support for opportunity and motivation is yet to be investigated and integrated into a design concept.

This paper is constructed as follows: Section 2 identifies social issues typical for the driving context and to be addressed by CSA; Section 3 gives an overview of persuasion literature relevant for our decision on the CSA concept; and Section 4 summarizes the proposed concepts and discusses the issues to be refined into a clear direction.

2   Driving Context

Driving is considered by drivers as an individual activity. It is associated with freedom compared to using public transport. Conversely, driving is actually a social activity, because cooperation between road users is needed. The lack of cooperation is one of the causes of traffic jam, as proven by the phantom traffic jam phenomenon [1]. How to make drivers cooperate on the road? A motivational source for inducing cooperative behavior is the strong reciprocity of people [2]. This behavior theory explains that people have a tendency to reward cooperators and punish non-cooperators. The existing fine system in the traffic law mainly focuses on punishing non-cooperators. Instead, we would like to introduce rewards for the purpose of motivation support.

While people are not aware of the fact that lack of cooperation causes traffic jams, people also seem to be fooled by traffic jams in terms of perception of time and social justice. The motivation for constant/needless lane changes is because the other lane seems faster [3]. Our preliminary user study on Cooperative Driving by conducting focus group discussions also identified this issue. Therefore, opportunity information might help people in overcoming the illusion of gaining time and faster lanes.

A study on speed choice [4] indicates that speed choice is influenced by three factors. The first factor is 'How fast can I go?', which depends on the driver's (and the car's) ability to reach a certain speed and on the road conditions. The second factor is 'How fast do I need to go?', which is the obligation by time or route, so that the driver needs to recognize opportunities of applying a certain speed. The third factor is 'How fast do I want to go?', which refers to driver's motivation on making a speed choice. This study supports our hypothesis that the means of influencing speed choice may support the driver's ability of maintaining the advised speed, inform the driver about the opportunity of getting to the destination with the advised speed, and increase the driver's motivation of maintaining the advised speed.

Our hypothesis about the different supports needed by drivers in order to perform cooperative driving was addressed in our previous driving experiments with only ability support. Test participants expressed their wishes for opportunity information to support participation in cooperative driving. Some of them also expressed a lack of motivation towards cooperative driving. This indicates that some people may already have the ability thus prefer opportunity support or motivation support, while others may already have the motivation thus only need ability support or opportunity support.

3   Persuasion

The Motivation-Ability-Opportunity (MAO) model [5] is an established behavioral model. This model can directly address the motivation, ability, and opportunity of driving (as explained in Section 2) for the purpose of changing behavior toward cooperative driving. In addition, the Captology concept [6] provides a suitable implementation of the MAO model within the Human-Computer Interaction domain. Captology conceives computers as Actors, Tools, and Media. Computers as Actors can motivate people; computers as Tools can support people's ability; computers as Media can provide simulated experience for informing opportunity.

While ability support and opportunity support are quite straightforward, we need to refine the motivation support. Do we motivate drivers intrinsically or extrinsically? Does the system give immediate feedback or delayed feedback? Do we design the system as one fits all or adaptive depending on driver's need?

In motivation theories, it has been said that people can have either intrinsic or extrinsic motivation to perform a task. Intrinsic motivation concerns the joy or satisfaction in doing a task, while extrinsic motivation is expecting rewards upon the completion of a task. Previous studies found that extrinsic financial feedback undermines intrinsic motivation [7][8][9]. Financial/material feedbacks can be useful for increasing performance of algorithmic behavior (dull task), but not of heuristic behavior (interesting task) [10]. We categorize the accelerate/decelerate actions of driving as algorithmic behavior, so that we opt for extrinsic motivation.

Immediate feedback has been proven useful for forming energy saving behavior [11][12]. Immediate negative feedback does not work for a positive long term goal [13], which is explained as the problem of delayed gratification. This implies that for long term goals such as the achievement of smooth traffic, immediate positive feedback would have more persuasion power.

Kaptein et al proposed the Persuasion Profile, which characterizes a user as to the type of persuasion he/she is most susceptible to in system usage [22]. This approach works on the motivational part of system's messages, or Actor's role as in Captology. However, since our hypothesis stated that drivers need different supports from among motivation, ability, and opportunity, we would apply persuasion profiles based on user's susceptibility to Actors, Tools, and Media. By applying persuasion profiles, we can avoid undermining the intrinsic motivation of drivers who already have the motivation to perform cooperative driving.

Selecting the most suitable persuasion means is important. Involving people in the selection of persuasion means may increase compliance [14]. Similarly, people tend to comply more with systems having the same goals as they have [15]. Therefore, we would like to let drivers choose to use the system with their preferred persuasion means.

4   Concept and Discussion

We sketched four different concepts and invited two designers to evaluate them. The first concept is Ability Support where CSA informs the driver about current and target speed/acceleration. The second concept is Opportunity Support where CSA informs the driver about the length (in time) of a traffic jam. The traffic jam's growth/shrinkage is simulated graphically. The third concept is Motivation Support where CSA shows the "happiness" of the system with a smiley. The fourth concept is Extrinsic Feedback where the driver can: 1) Earn credits depending on the frequency of compliance; 2) Achieve a score reflecting the driver's positive influence on the traffic jam. Both the credits and score are exchangeable with material rewards outside the traffic system.

This evaluation with designers served as a way to fine tune the design. Concept 1 was evaluated as useful and reasonable. Concept 2 was evaluated as providing better opportunity support compared to the existing traffic information system. Concept 3 was evaluated as having low motivational force. Concept 4 was evaluated as promising, because material rewards can be suited to different types of driver's personal needs.

The next step is to evaluate the concepts in tests with a medium-fidelity driving simulator. A challenge here is that participants may bring a high motivation already to the use of the system by coming to the experiment sessions. How to overcome this potential bias towards intrinsic motivation needs further discussion.

As part of evaluating the concepts in an experiment, we need to find the relation between driving traits and the susceptibility to Actors, Tools, Media persuasion. Another question is whether stronger persuasion is caused by the freedom to choose a persuasion means or by the appropriate design, i.e. using driving traits for selecting the appropriate persuasion means.

References

1. Sugiyama, Y., Fukui, M., Kikuchi, M., Hasebe, K., Nakayama, A., Nishinari, K., Tadaki, S., Yukawa, S.: Traffic jams without bottlenecks—experimental evidence for the physical mechanism of the formation of a jam. New Journal of Physics 10, 033001 (2008)
2. Fehr, E., Fischbacher, U., Gächter, S.: Strong reciprocity, human cooperation, and the enforcement of social norms. Human Nature 13, 1–25 (2002)
3. Vanderbilt, T.: Traffic: Why We Drive the Way We Do. Penguin Books (2008)
4. Stradling, S.G.: Car driver speed choice in Scotland. Ergonomics 50, 1196–1208 (2007)
5. Olander, F., Thogersen, J.: Understanding of consumer behaviour as a prerequisite for environmental protection. Journal of Consumer Policy, 345–385 (1995)
6. Fogg, B.J.: Persuasive Technology: Using Computers to Change What We Think and Do. Morgan Kaufmann (2002)
7. Deci, E.: Effects of externally mediated rewards on intrinsic motivation. Journal of Personality and Social Psychology 18, 105–115 (1971)
8. Lepper, M.R., Greene, D., Nisbett, R.E.: Undermining children's intrinsic interest with extrinsic reward: A test of the "overjustification" hypothesis. Journal of Personality and Social Psychology 28, 129–137 (1973)
9. Frey, B., Jegen, R.: Motivation crowding theory. Journal of Economic Surveys 15, 589–611 (2001)
10. Deci, E.L., Koestner, R., Ryan, R.M.: Extrinsic Rewards and Intrinsic Motivation in Education: Reconsidered Once Again. Review of Educational Research 71, 1–27 (2001)

11. Arroyo, E., Bonanni, L., Selker, T.: Waterbot: Exploring feedback and persuasive techniques at the sink. In: Proceedings of the ACM SIGCHI Conference on Human Factors in Computing Systems (2005)
12. Davis, J.: Early Experiences with Participatory Design of Ambient Persuasive Technology. In: Proceedings of ACM SIGCHI Conference on Human Factors in Computing Systems (2009)
13. Ariely, D.: Predictably Irrational: The Hidden Forces that Shape Our Decisions. HarperCollins (2009)
14. Kaptein, M., Duplinsky, S., Markopoulos, P.: Means Based Adaptive Persuasive Systems. In: Proceedings of the ACM SIGCHI Conference Extended Abstracts on Human Factors in Computing Systems (2011)
15. Verberne, F., Ham, J., Midden, C.: Persuading to Rely on Technology: The Influence of Sharing User Goals and Information on Trust in and Acceptance of Smart Systems in Cars. In: Persuasive 2011 (2011)

Author Index

Alessandrini, Andrea   29
Aliakseyeu, Dzmitry   25, 29, 45
Amirat, Yacine   296
Andersen, Hans J.   128
Andrushevich, Aliaksei   302
Arif, Taslim   152
Arroyo, Ernesto   229

Badii, Atta   206
Beck, Elke   274
Bekker, Tilde   233, 238
Bertolo, Maresa   218
Blat, Josep   229
Blom, M.   146
Boll, Susanne   35
Borcea-Pfitzmann, Katrin   280
Braun, Andreas   162, 184

Carincotte, Cyril   110
Carreira, Paulo   29
Chibani, Abdelghani   296
Correia, Nuno   224
Cristani, Marco   72
Crocco, Marco   72

David, Klaus   101
de Boer, M.E.   146
de Graaf, Mark   238
De Luca, Vanessa   218
Denef, Sebastian   308
de Ruyter, Boris   49
Descamps, Adrien   110
de Valk, Linda   238
de Witte, L.   146
Dröes, R.M.   146

Eby, Chad   29
Eggen, Berry   57, 238
Eisenbarth, Michael   152

Feilner, Sven   196
Ferring, Dieter   162, 166
Fritsch, Lothar   267
Fugard, Andrew J.B.   274
Furfari, Francesco   206

Gade, Rikke   128
Garcia, Juan Jimenez   313
Gärtner, Magdalena   274
Gavrila, Dariu   68
Gehring, Sven   63
Gosselin, Bernard   110
Groven, Arne-Kristian   267
Gudymenko, Ivan   280

Harjumaa, Marja   170
Heuten, Wilko   35
Heynderickx, Ingrid   49
Hochleitner, Christina   264
Hoepman, Jaap-Henk   287
Hoffmeyer, Andre   137
Hung, Hayley   68

Immonen, Milla   162, 201

Jensen, Ole B.   128

Kaartinen, Jouni   201
Kamieth, Felix   157
Karamouzi, Aimilia   41
Karkowski, I.   146
Kasugai, Kai   1, 12
Kemal Koc, Alper   91
Khan, Vassilis-Javed   45
Kiriyama, Takashi   1, 5
Kirste, Thomas   137
Klapproth, Alexander   302
Klauß, Kerstin   192
Klein, Bernd Niklas   101
Klein, Peter   192
Kokko, Jaana   170
Konttila, Antti   201
Koolwaaij, Johan   81
Kudo, Mineichi   119
Kuijsters, Andre   49
Kung, Antonio   206

Leist, Anja   166
Lepri, Bruno   249, 252

Mabrouki, Olfa   296
Majewski, Martin   157

Mason, Jon   25, 29, 45
Meerbeek, Bernt   25, 29
Meiland, F.J.M.   146
Moeslund, Thomas B.   128
Muhammad, Syed Agha   101
Mulvenna, M.D.   146
Murino, Vittorio   72
Muuraiskangas, Salla   170

Neves Madeira, Rui   224
Nonaka, Hidetoshi   119

Odobez, Jean-Marc   68
Offermans, Serge   25, 29, 57
Oksman, Virpi   1

Papalexopoulos, Dimitris   41
Peddemors, Arjan   81
Pentland, Alex Sandy   252
Pesarin, Anna   72
Pianesi, Fabio   252
Plewe, Daniela Alina   1, 19
Popa, Mirela   91
Postolache, Octavian   224
Poulsen, Esben S.   128
Putz, Wolfgang   152

Quade, Michael   318

Redi, Judith   49
Rijnbout, Pepijn   238
Röcker, Carsten   1, 12
Roelofsma, Peter H.M.P.   162, 175,
    181, 189
Rosales, Andrea   229
Rothkrantz, Leon J.M.   91

Sachinopoulou, Anna   201
Salah, Albert Ali   249, 252
Salomon, Ralf   302
Sanesi, Valentina   29
Sato, Masahiko   5
Schlehuber, Christian   157
Schmitt, Mario   152

Schouten, Ben   213, 233, 238
Schrammel, Johann   264
Schulz, Trenton   267
Shahab, Qonita   323
Shan, Caifeng   91
Storf, Holger   152
Struck, Matthias   196
Sturm, Janienke   213, 233

Tamanini, Christian   157
Tantinger, Daniel   196
Tao, Shuai   119
Tazari, Mohammad-Reza   206
Teeuw, Wouter B.   81
Teipel, Stefan   137
Tieben, Rob   233
Tietze, Katja   280
Toyama, Jun   119
Tscheligi, Manfred   264
Turkama, Petra   206

Ünalan, Özgür   152

van der Leeuw, J.   146
van Essen, Harm   25, 29, 57
van Hoof, J.   146
Van Laerhoven, Kristof   101
Varoudis, Tasos   41
Vatavu, Radu-Daniel   245
Versteeg, Leo   181, 189
Vinciarelli, Alessandro   72

Walker, Martin   45
Weigand, Christian   196
Wichert, Reiner   184
Wieland, Andreas   157
Wiethoff, Alexander   63
Wiggers, Pascal   91

Yordanova, Kristina   137

Zaiţi, Ionuţ-Alexandru   245
Zannoni, Michele   218